ETL with Azure Cookbook

Practical recipes for building modern ETL solutions
to load and transform data from any source

Christian Cote

Matija Lah

Madina Saitakhmetova

Packt>

BIRMINGHAM—MUMBAI

ETL with Azure Cookbook

Copyright © 2020 Packt Publishing

Commissioning Editor: Sunith Shetty

Acquisition Editor: Ali Abidi

Senior Editor: David Sugarman

Content Development Editor: Nathanya Dias

Technical Editor: Manikandan Kurup

Copy Editor: Safis Editing

Project Coordinator: Aishwarya Mohan

Proofreader: Safis Editing

Indexer: Pratik Shirodkar

Production Designer: Vijay Kamble

First published: September 2020

Production reference: 1290920

Published by Packt Publishing Ltd.
Livery Place
35 Livery Street
Birmingham
B3 2PB, UK.

ISBN 978-1-80020-331-0

www.packt.com

Packt>

Packt.com

Subscribe to our online digital library for full access to over 7,000 books and videos, as well as industry leading tools to help you plan your personal development and advance your career. For more information, please visit our website.

Why subscribe?

- Spend less time learning and more time coding with practical eBooks and Videos from over 4,000 industry professionals

- Improve your learning with Skill Plans built especially for you

- Get a free eBook or video every month

- Fully searchable for easy access to vital information

- Copy and paste, print, and bookmark content

Did you know that Packt offers eBook versions of every book published, with PDF and ePub files available? You can upgrade to the eBook version at packt.com and as a print book customer, you are entitled to a discount on the eBook copy. Get in touch with us at customercare@packtpub.com for more details.

At www.packt.com, you can also read a collection of free technical articles, sign up for a range of free newsletters, and receive exclusive discounts and offers on Packt books and eBooks.

Contributors

About the authors

Christian Cote is an IT professional with more than 15 years of experience working on data warehouse, big data, and business intelligence projects. Christian has developed expertise in data warehousing and data lakes over the years and has designed many ETL/BI processes using a range of tools on multiple platforms. He's presented at several conferences and code camps. He currently co-leads the SQL Server PASS chapter. He is also a Microsoft Data Platform Most Valuable Professional (MVP).

Matija Lah has more than 18 years of experience working with Microsoft SQL Server, mostly from architecting data-centric solutions in the legal domain. His contributions to the SQL Server community have led to him being awarded the MVP Professional award (Data Platform) between 2007 and 2017/2018. He spends most of his time on projects involving advanced information management and natural language processing, but often finds time to speak at events related to Microsoft SQL Server where he loves to share his experience with the SQL Server platform.

Madina Saitakhmetova is a developer specializing in BI. She has been in IT for 15 years, working with Microsoft SQL, .NET, Microsoft BI, Azure, and building BI solutions for medical, educational, and engineering companies. Her adventure with Microsoft BI began with Analysis Services and SSIS, and in later years she has been building her expertise in ETL/ELT, both on-premises and in the cloud. Finding patterns, automating processes, and making BI teams work more efficiently are challenges that drive her. During the past few years, BIML has become an important part of her work, increasing its efficiency and quality.

About the reviewers

Steph Martin is a senior customer engineer in the FastTrack for Azure team at Microsoft. She has a background in SQL Server database design and development and extensive knowledge of SSIS and ETL patterns and practices. Steph helps customers to achieve success with their projects, providing architecture design reviews, best practice guidance, and in-depth knowledge sharing across the platform, covering migration to Azure as well as cloud-first deployments. She has wide-ranging experience of Azure data services, specializing in Azure SQL Database and Managed Instance, and Azure Data Factory. Steph is an active member of the data platform community, running a PASS affiliated meetup in the UK and helping to co-ordinate the volunteer team at SQLBits.

Aaditya Pokkunuri is an experienced Senior Database Engineer with a demonstrated history of working in information technology and services industry. He is skilled in performance tuning, SQL Database, requirements analysis, databases, and servers, SSIS, and SSRS. He possesses strong knowledge on Clustering, SQL server high-availability options, and ITIL of processes. Aaditya's expertise lies in Windows administration tasks, active directory, and Microsoft Azure technologies. He is a strong information technology professional with a Bachelor of Technology degree, specializing in computer science and engineering from SASTRA University, Tamil Nadu.

Packt is searching for authors like you

If you're interested in becoming an author for Packt, please visit `authors. packtpub.com` and apply today. We have worked with thousands of developers and tech professionals, just like you, to help them share their insight with the global tech community. You can make a general application, apply for a specific hot topic that we are recruiting an author for, or submit your own idea.

Table of Contents

3

Creating and Using SQL Server 2019 Big Data Clusters

4

Azure Data Integration

5

Extending SSIS with Custom Tasks and Transformations

6

Azure Data Factory

7

Azure Databricks

8

SSIS Migration Strategies

9

Profiling data in Azure

10
Manage SSIS and Azure Data Factory with Biml

Other Books You May Enjoy

Index

Preface

Extract, Transform, Load (ETL) is one of the most common and tedious procedures for moving and processing data from one database to another. With the help of this book, you will be able to speed up the process by designing efficient ETL solutions using the Azure services available for handling and transforming any data to suit your requirements.

With this cookbook, you will become well versed in all the features of **SQL Server Integration Services** (**SSIS**) to perform data migration and ETL tasks that integrate with Azure. You will learn how to transform data in Azure and understand how legacy systems perform ETL on-premises using SSIS. Later chapters will get you up to speed with connecting and retrieving data from SQL Server 2019 Big Data Clusters, and even show you how to extend and customize the SSIS toolbox using custom-developed tasks and transformations. This ETL book also contains practical recipes for moving and transforming data with Azure services, such as Data Factory and Azure Databricks, and lets you explore various options for migrating SSIS packages to Azure. Toward the end, you will find out how to profile data in the cloud and automate package development with **Business Intelligence Markup Language** (**BIML**).

By the end of this book, you will have developed the skills you need to create and automate ETL solutions on-premises as well as in Azure.

Who this book is for

This book is for data warehouse architects, ETL developers, or anyone else who wants to build scalable ETL applications in Azure. Those looking to extend their existing on-premises ETL applications to use big data and a variety of Azure services, or others interested in migrating existing on-premises solutions to the Azure cloud platform, will also find the book useful. Familiarity with SQL Server services is necessary to get the most out of this book.

What this book covers

Chapter 1, Getting Started with Azure and SSIS 2019, describes, in step-by-step fashion, how to set up SQL Server 2019 to deploy the features that are used throughout the book. It also covers how to set up an Azure subscription.

Chapter 2, Introducing ETL, explains why ETL is needed, where it comes from, and the differences between ETL and ELT.

Chapter 3, Creating and Using SQL Server 2019 Big Data Clusters, discusses how to create, deploy, connect to, and retrieve data from SQL Server 2019 Big Data Clusters.

Chapter 4, Azure Data Integration, talks about the Azure Feature Pack, which allows SSIS to integrate Azure data from blob storage and HDInsight clusters.

Chapter 5, Extending SSIS with Custom Tasks and Transformations, talks about extending and customizing the built-in toolset with custom-developed control flow tasks and data flow transformations.

Chapter 6, Azure Data Factory, talks about using Azure Data Factory to move and transform data in the cloud.

Chapter 7, Azure Databricks, talks about using Azure Databricks to transform data in the cloud.

Chapter 8, SSIS cloud Migration Strategies, talks about scaling out SSIS packages to Azure.

Chapter 9, Profiling data in Azure, contains various recipes that show you how to perform data profiling in Azure Databricks.

Chapter 10, Manage SSIS and Azure Data Factory with BIML, contains various recipes that demonstrate how to manage SSIS and Azure Data Factory with **BIML** using metadata.

To get the most out of this book

Basic or working knowledge of SQL Server, SSIS, and Azure is needed, as is basic knowledge of ETL techniques and Azure SQL Server databases. You also need a personal computer running Microsoft Windows 10.

Software/Hardware covered in the book	OS Requirements
SQL Server 2019	Windows 10
Azure Data Explorer	
SQL Server Management Studio	
Visual Studio 2019	

Some of the recipes in this cookbook contain partial, incomplete solutions that you will complete by following the instructions in the recipe. If, for some reason, you get stuck and are unable to complete the tasks successfully, the complete copies of the solutions are available in the Solution folder of the corresponding chapter. Please, use these files as a reference when working on the recipes; they are there to assist you, not to prevent you from learning by performing the work yourself.

If you are using the digital version of this book, we advise you to type the code yourself or access the code via the GitHub repository (link available in the next section). Doing so will help you avoid any potential errors related to the copying and pasting of code.

Download the example code files

You can download the example code files for this book from your account at www. packt.com. If you purchased this book elsewhere, you can visit www.packtpub.com/ support and register to have the files emailed directly to you.

You can download the code files by following these steps:

1. Log in or register at www.packt.com.
2. Select the **Support** tab.
3. Click on **Code Downloads**.
4. Enter the name of the book in the **Search** box and follow the onscreen instructions.

Once the file is downloaded, please make sure that you unzip or extract the folder using the latest version of:

1. WinRAR/7-Zip for Windows
2. Zipeg/iZip/UnRarX for Mac
3. 7-Zip/PeaZip for Linux

The code bundle for the book is also hosted on GitHub at `https://github.com/PacktPublishing/ETL-with-Azure-Cookbook` In case there's an update to the code, it will be updated on the existing GitHub repository.

We also have other code bundles from our rich catalog of books and videos available at `https://github.com/PacktPublishing/`. Check them out!

Download the color images

We also provide a PDF file that has color images of the screenshots/diagrams used in this book. You can download it here: `https://static.packt-cdn.com/downloads/9781800203310_ColorImages.pdf`.

Conventions used

There are a number of text conventions used throughout this book.

`Code in text`: Indicates code words in text, database table names, folder names, filenames, file extensions, pathnames, dummy URLs, user input, and Twitter handles. Here is an example: "For the location, use `hivesource` as the folder path and `sales.dat` as the filename."

A block of code is set as follows:

```
INSERT OVERWRITE TABLE ETLInAzure.SalesAgg
SELECT storename , zipcode , SUM(unitcost) AS unitcost,
AVG(unitprice) AS unitprice, SUM(salesamount) AS salesamount,
SUM(salesquantity) AS salesquantity, CalendarMonth
FROM etlinazure.salesource
GROUP BY storename, zipcode, CalendarMonth;
```

Any command-line input or output is written as follows:

```
USE master;
GO


CREATE DATABASE Staging;
GO
```

Bold: Indicates a new term, an important word, or words that you see onscreen. For example, words in menus or dialog boxes appear in the text like this. Here is an example: "Click on the list beside the **Enumerator** property and select **Foreach Azure Blob Enumerator**."

> **Tips or important notes**
> Appear like this.

Sections

In this book, you will find several headings that appear frequently (*Getting ready*, *How to do it...*, *How it works...*, *There's more...*, and *See also*).

To give clear instructions on how to complete a recipe, use these sections as follows:

Getting ready

This section tells you what to expect in the recipe and describes how to set up any software or any preliminary settings required for the recipe.

How to do it...

This section contains the steps required to follow the recipe.

How it works...

This section usually consists of a detailed explanation of what happened in the previous section.

There's more...

This section consists of additional information about the recipe in order to make you more knowledgeable about the recipe.

See also

This section provides helpful links to other useful information for the recipe.

Get in touch

Feedback from our readers is always welcome.

General feedback: If you have questions about any aspect of this book, mention the book title in the subject of your message and email us at customercare@packtpub.com.

Errata: Although we have taken every care to ensure the accuracy of our content, mistakes do happen. If you have found a mistake in this book, we would be grateful if you would report this to us. Please visit www.packtpub.com/support/errata, selecting your book, clicking on the Errata Submission Form link, and entering the details.

Piracy: If you come across any illegal copies of our works in any form on the Internet, we would be grateful if you would provide us with the location address or website name. Please contact us at copyright@packt.com with a link to the material.

If you are interested in becoming an author: If there is a topic that you have expertise in and you are interested in either writing or contributing to a book, please visit authors.packtpub.com.

Reviews

Please leave a review. Once you have read and used this book, why not leave a review on the site that you purchased it from? Potential readers can then see and use your unbiased opinion to make purchase decisions, we at Packt can understand what you think about our products, and our authors can see your feedback on their book. Thank you!

For more information about Packt, please visit packt.com.

1

Getting Started with Azure and SSIS 2019

In this cookbook, we are going to cover **Extract, Transform, Load** (ETL) development with **Microsoft Azure**. We will start with Microsoft **SQL Server 2019 Integration Services (SSIS)** and then gradually move on to data management capabilities in Azure. Throughout this cookbook we will use hands-on examples, which will not only provide you with genuine first-hand experience in SSIS development but also demonstrate how to design a working ETL solution or a module that could be built into an ETL solution.

Let's start by establishing your development environment. We are going to guide you through the installation of a new SQL Server instance, including all the components needed for on-premises as well as cloud-based SSIS solution development. You are also going to install the tools used in administering and maintaining SQL Server instances – either on-premises or in the cloud. You are also going to install the tools used in developing, testing, and deploying your SSIS solutions. You will finish this chapter by creating an Azure subscription, which will allow your on-premises development environment to extend into the cloud.

This chapter covers the following recipes that will help you get started with SSIS development on-premises as well as in the cloud:

- Installing Microsoft SQL Server 2019 Integration Services
- Installing SQL Server Management Studio

- Installing SQL Server Data Tools
- Installing Azure Data Studio
- Creating an Azure subscription

Technical requirements

In order to install the necessary components, you will need a workstation – either a **physical** personal computer or a **virtual** one – running a compatible Microsoft Windows operating system. SQL Server 2019 can be installed on any edition of the Microsoft Windows Server operating system, starting with Windows Server 2016, or even on its desktop edition, Windows 10, starting with version TH1, build 1507.

Depending on the features installed, SQL Server is going to require between 6 and roughly 8 GB of free space on the hard drive, and at least 1 GB of available system memory, though around 4 GB is the recommended minimum. Practically any 64-bit CPU is supported.

> **Important note**
>
> You can find more detailed information about SQL Server 2019 hardware and software requirements in the online vendor documentation (SQL docs) article entitled *SQL Server 2019: Hardware and software requirements*, at `https://docs.microsoft.com/en-us/sql/sql-server/install/hardware-and-software-requirements-for-installing-sql-server-ver15`.

Speaking of online documentation, your workstation is going to need internet access – even to perform the installations.

Installing Microsoft SQL Server 2019 Integration Services

You are going to install a new instance of SQL Server on your workstation; if you prefer, you can also upgrade an existing SQL Server instance, as noted in the recipe. The installation will include all the features necessary to design SSIS solutions generally, not just to perform the work presented in this book.

The Client Tools **Software Development Kit (SDK)**, an otherwise optional SQL Server component, must be installed on the workstation used in SSIS development. It contains the .NET managed assemblies with design-time access to the SSIS runtime, without which SSIS development simply cannot take place.

The installation of the **SQL Client Connectivity SDK**, another optional component, is recommended, though not necessary. It contains SQL Server Native Client connectivity resources that you might need in database application development.

> **Important note**
>
> None of the SDKs mentioned would ever need to be installed on a server used for hosting data, as such a server would normally not be used for SSIS development.

Getting ready

You need access to the SQL Server 2019 installation media. Since this is going to be a typical development workstation installation, you can use the free, specialized **SQL Server 2019 Developer Edition**, available for download at `https://www.microsoft.com/en-us/sql-server/sql-server-downloads`. Alternatively, you can also use a free trial edition of **SQL Server 2019 Standard**, or the **Data Center** editions, but please note that their use is limited to 180 days.

> **Important note**
>
> The Developer edition of SQL Server 2019 is a full-featured **free** edition, licensed for use as a development and test database in a non-production environment.

Either download the installation media from the website or use the installation media provided by the administrator in your organization. If you decide to use the Developer edition of SQL Server 2019, download the executable from the website, and save it to the local drive on the workstation that you will be using for the recipes in this book. If you prefer to use the Evaluation edition of SQL Server 2019, you will have to sign up on the website by providing some of your personal information before being able to access the installation media.

How to do it...

Start your workstation and log in with an account with administrative operating system privileges. Make sure the workstation has access to the SQL Server 2019 installation media – for instance, make sure that the Developer edition executable file is available on the local drive:

1. Locate the installation media, and double-click the installation executable (for instance, `SQL2019-SSEI-Dev.exe` for SQL Server 2019 Developer Edition) to start the installation.

    When prompted by the operating system, which will ask whether you want to allow the application to make changes to your device, as shown in the following screenshot, click **Yes** to continue:

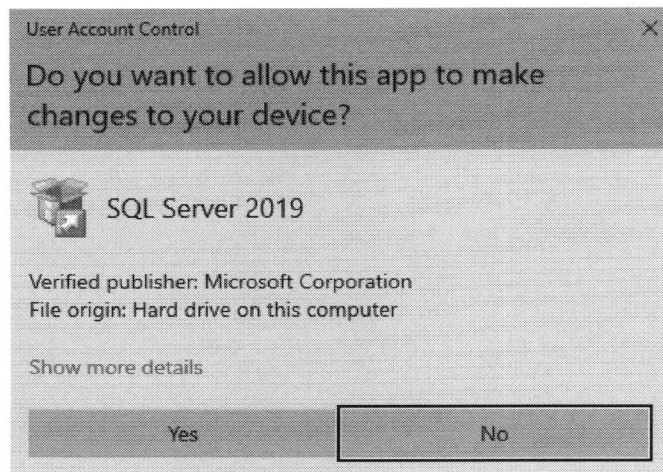

Figure 1.1 – The SQL Server installation User Account Control dialog

2. At the beginning of the installation, you are asked whether you would like to use the basic settings, customize them, or simply download the rest of the installation media.

    > **Tip**
    > Generally, you will only download the installation media if you plan to install SQL Server on additional devices. On the other hand, a very good reason for having the media available locally would be in case you need to repair the installation later.

    Select **Custom** to continue.

3. You now have to select the location of the installation files. Use the **Default** folder unless you prefer to use an alternative location.

When ready, click **Install** to continue. Depending on your internet connection, it should take just a few minutes to download and extract the files.

4. After the installation files have been prepared, the **SQL Server Installation Center** window will open, as shown in the following screenshot:

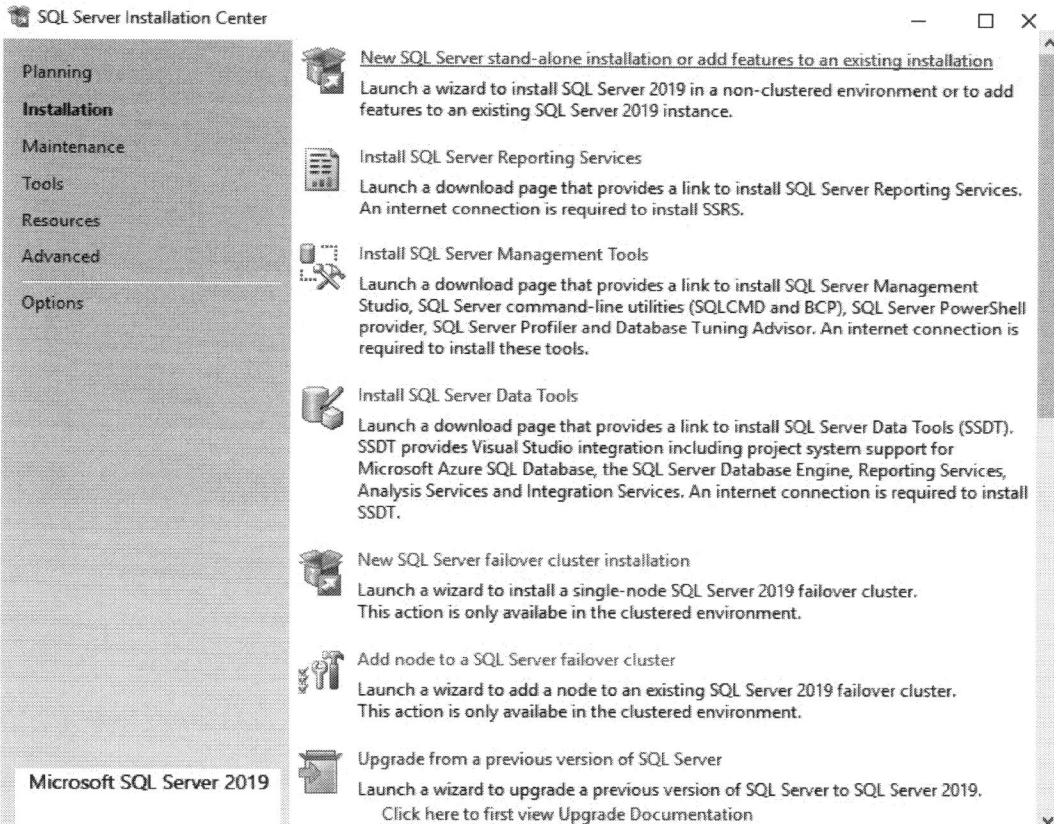

Figure 1.2 – SQL Server Installation Center

On the **Installation** page, select the **New SQL Server stand-alone installation or add features to an existing installation** option to start the setup wizard.

5.   On the **Product Key** page, either specify your free edition (Developer or Evaluation) or provide the product key of a licensed edition that you are allowed to install.

> **Important note**
> Do not install the Express edition of SQL Server 2019, as it does not include SSIS, nor does it come with many of the other features that you will need for the recipes in this cookbook.

6.   Specify the appropriate edition, as shown in the following screenshot:

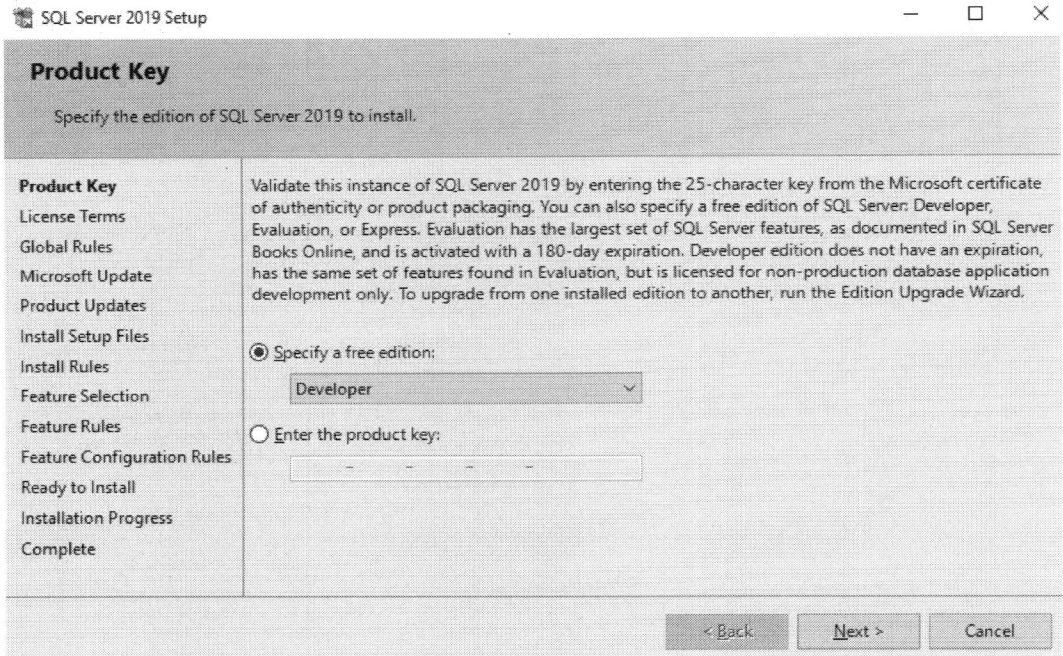

Figure 1.3 – Specifying the SQL Server edition

Click **Next** to continue.

7.   On the **License Terms** page, read and accept the license terms, and then click **Next** to continue.

8. On the **Microsoft Update** page, shown in the following screenshot, check **Use Microsoft Update to check for updates** to include the latest updates for the product, unless you prefer to install them later:

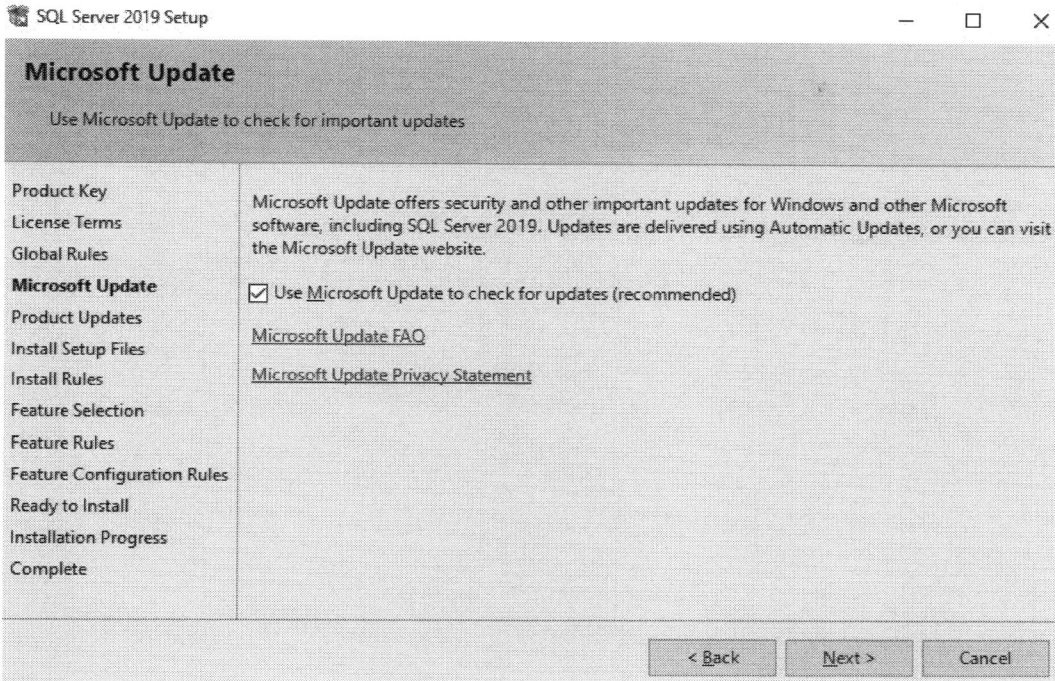

Figure 1.4 – Adding available updates to the installation

Click **Next** to continue.

The setup program should now perform a few checks of your system to verify whether the installation can proceed.

9. On the **Install Rules** page, you should see the system validation results.

    If there are **errors**, click on the link in the **Status** column to access each error message. Depending on the error, the installation might not proceed until you correct the cause or might even have to be aborted and restarted after the problem has been resolved.

If there are **warnings**, the installation should allow you to continue; however, you should inspect the warning messages anyway, as shown in the following screenshot, as additional activities might be needed during or after the installation in order for the SQL Server instance or one or more of the shared features to work as expected:

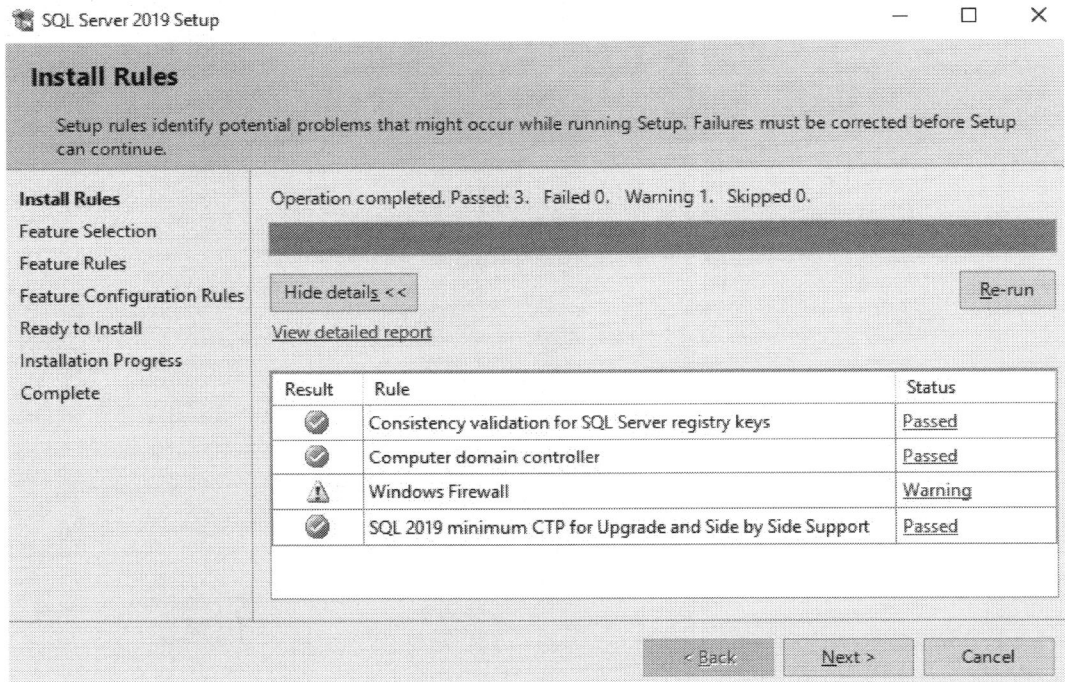

Figure 1.5 – Install Rules

> **Tip**
> If SQL Server has not been installed on this workstation before or has not yet been configured for external access, you might see the **Windows Firewall** warning, as shown in the screenshot. In this particular case, the warning points to information on configuring the Windows firewall in order to allow external access to the SQL Server instance.

You do not have to make any changes to your workstation's firewall at this time.

When ready, click **Next** to continue.

If the installation detects an existing SQL Server instance, an additional step is added, shown in the following screenshot, asking you to either create a new SQL Server instance or add features to an existing one:

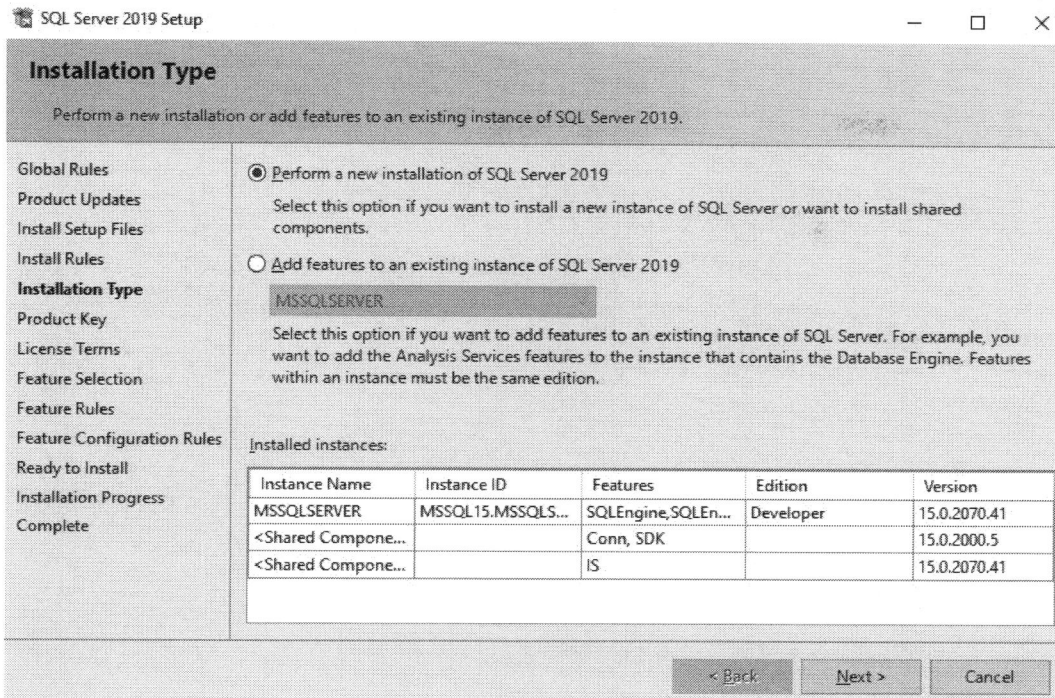

Figure 1.6 – Installation Type

This cookbook assumes that you will be using a workstation where SQL Server has not been installed before, but you can also use an existing SQL Server instance if you prefer.

10. On the **Feature Selection** page, select the following features to be installed:

a) **Database Engine Services**

b) **PolyBase Query Service for External Data**

c) **Java connector for HDFS data sources**

d) **Client Tools Connectivity**

e) **Integration Services**

f) **Client Tools SDK**

g) **SQL Client Connectivity SDK**

You can see part of the selection in the following screenshot:

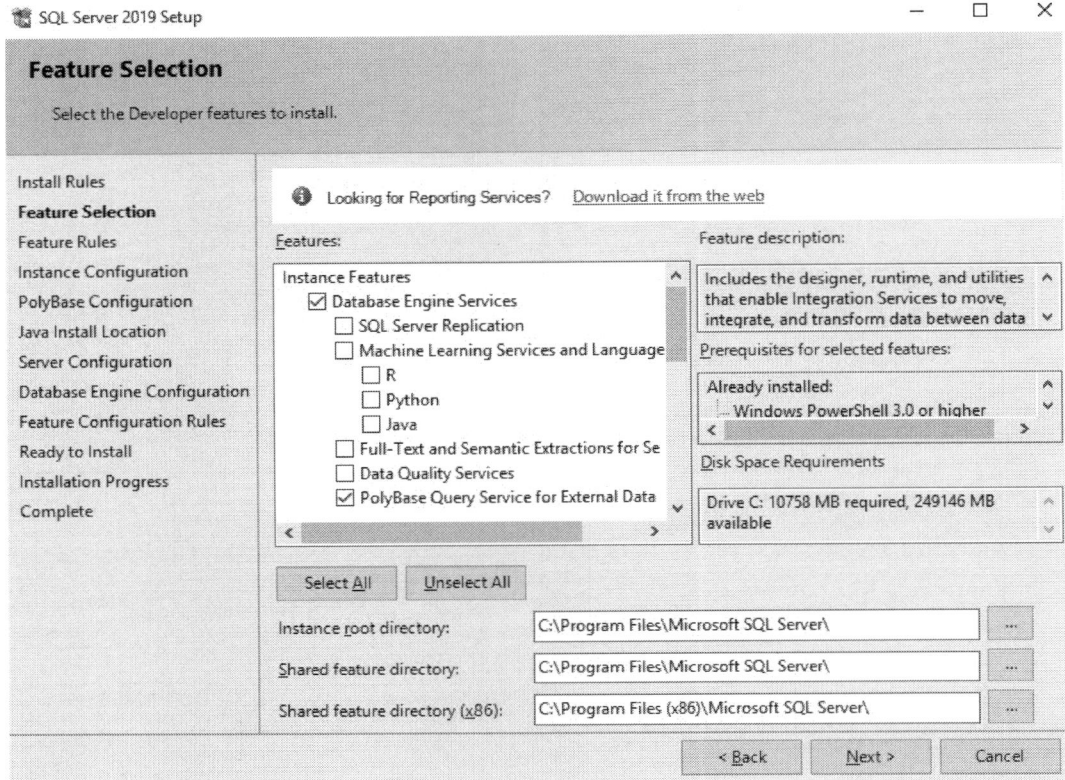

Figure 1.7 – SQL Server 2019 Feature Selection

When ready, click **Next** to continue.

11. If you are installing this SQL Server instance on a workstation where SQL Server has not been installed before, you can create either a new **default** instance or a **named** instance. Otherwise, your options will depend on what parts of SQL Server are already installed on the system:

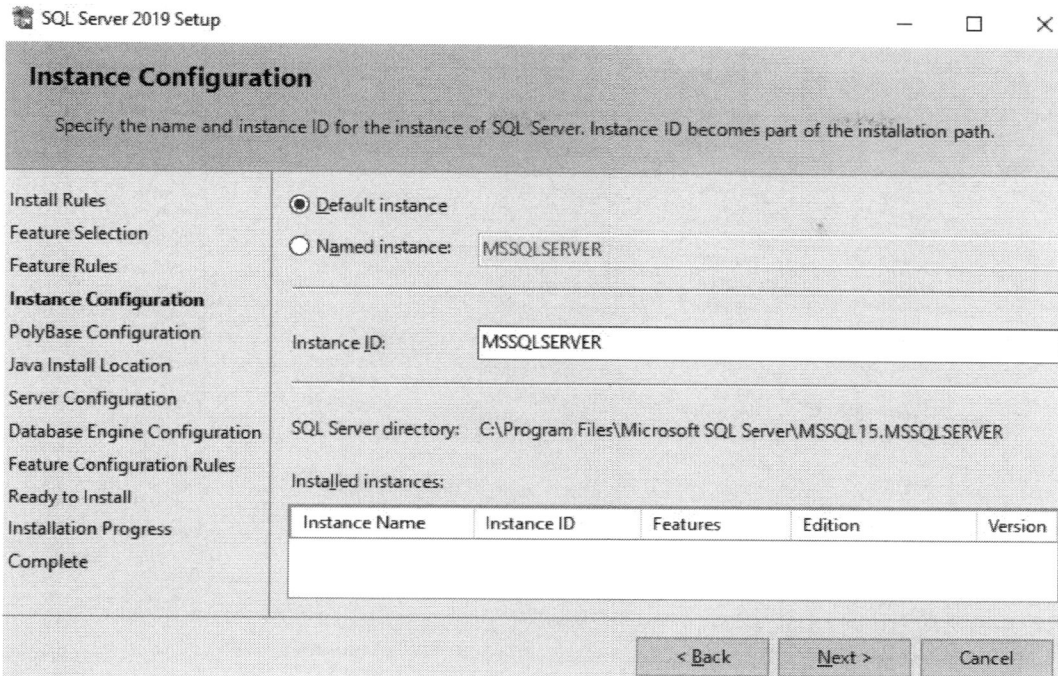

Figure 1.8 – SQL Server 2019 Instance Configuration

If possible, use the **default** instance, as the preceding screenshot shows; however, if you decide on using a named instance instead, we recommend that you use **MSSQL2019** as its name. Throughout this book, we will refer to this SQL Server instance either as **localhost** (the **default** instance) or **MSSQL2019** – in both cases, this will mean the same SQL Server instance.

When ready, click **Next** to continue.

12. On the **PolyBase Configuration** page, leave the default settings unchanged, as shown in the following screenshot, and click **Next** to continue:

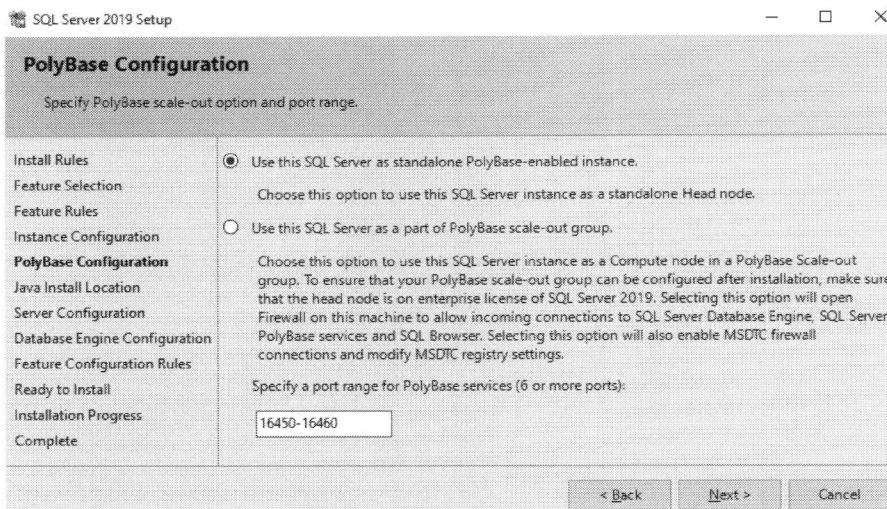

Figure 1.9 – PolyBase Configuration

13. On the **Java Install Location** page, leave the default option selected to install the version of the Java runtime environment included in the installation, as shown in the following screenshot, unless you are installing to an environment where a different version is required by your administrators:

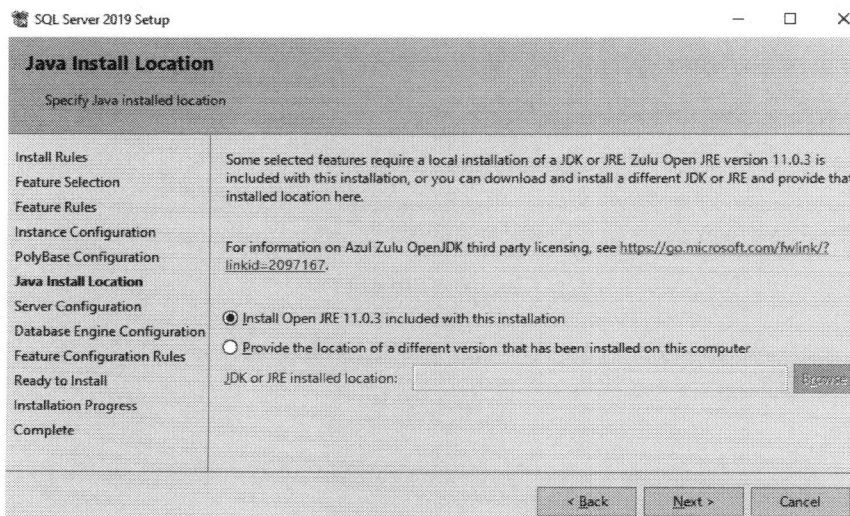

Figure 1.10 – Java Install Location

If you have to install a different version, select the second option, and use **Browse** to locate the installation files.

When ready, click **Next** to continue.

14. On the **Server Configuration** page, on the **Service Accounts** tab, change the **Startup Type** setting of the **SQL Server Agent** feature to **Automatic**.

Leave all other settings on this tab unchanged, as displayed in the screenshot that follows:

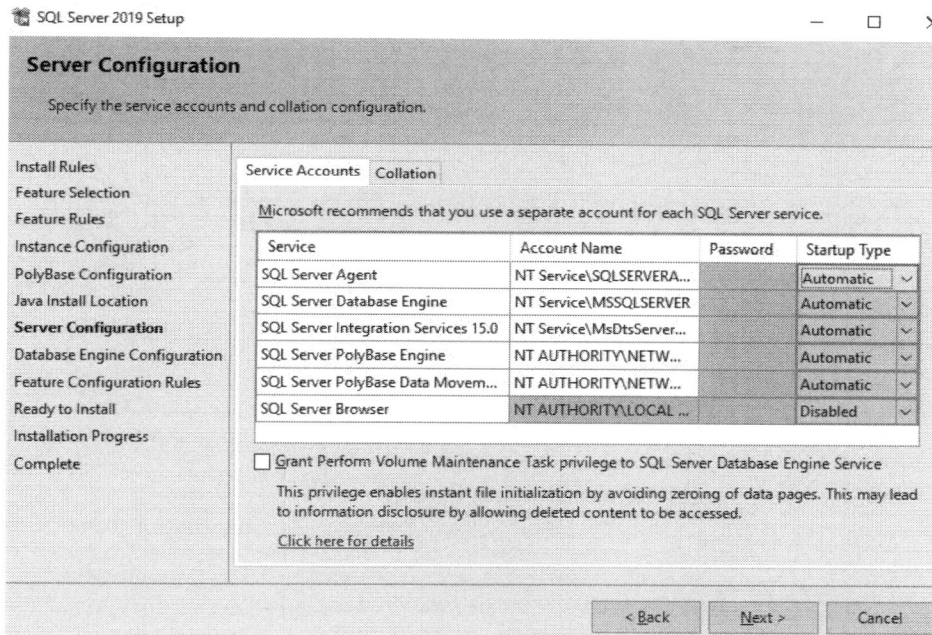

Figure 1.11 – SQL Server service accounts

15. On the **Collation** tab of the same page, you can leave the default collation for the database engine; however, it is recommended to use a Windows collation instead.

To change the collation, click **Customize** next to the **Database Engine Collation** setting, and then in the **Customize the SQL Server 2019 Database Engine Collation** dialog, select the **Windows collation designator and sort order** option with the following settings:

a) **Collation designator: Latin1_General_100**

b) **Accent-sensitive:** Checked

c) **Char/Varchar Storage Options: UTF-8**

The recommended settings are shown in the following screenshot:

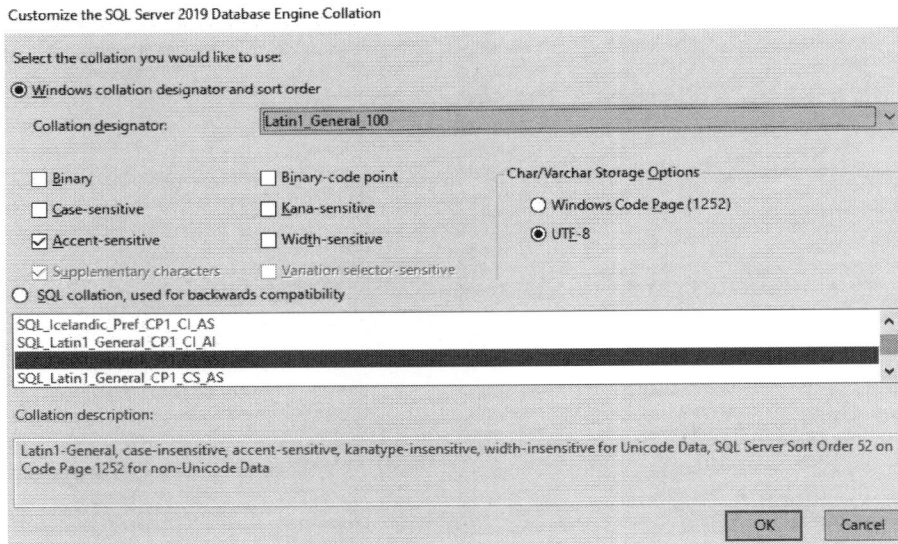

Figure 1.12 – Setting the default collation for the SQL Server instance

Click **OK** to confirm the settings.

Review the settings on the **Collation** tab; the full name of the collation should be **Latin1_General_100_CI_AS_SC_UTF8**, as shown in the following screenshot:

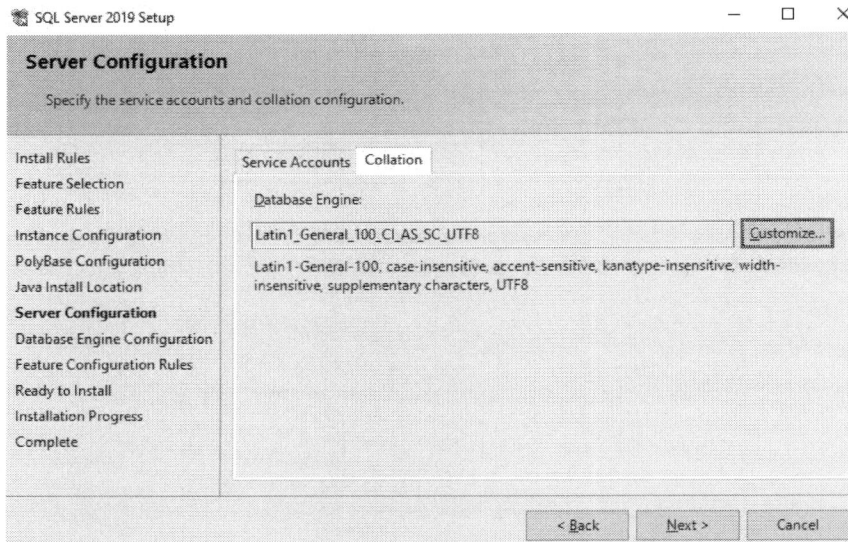

Figure 1.13 – The default SQL Server collation

When ready, click **Next** to continue.

16. On the **Database Engine Configuration** page, on the **Server Configuration** tab, shown in the following screenshot, leave **Windows authentication mode** selected for **Authentication Mode**:

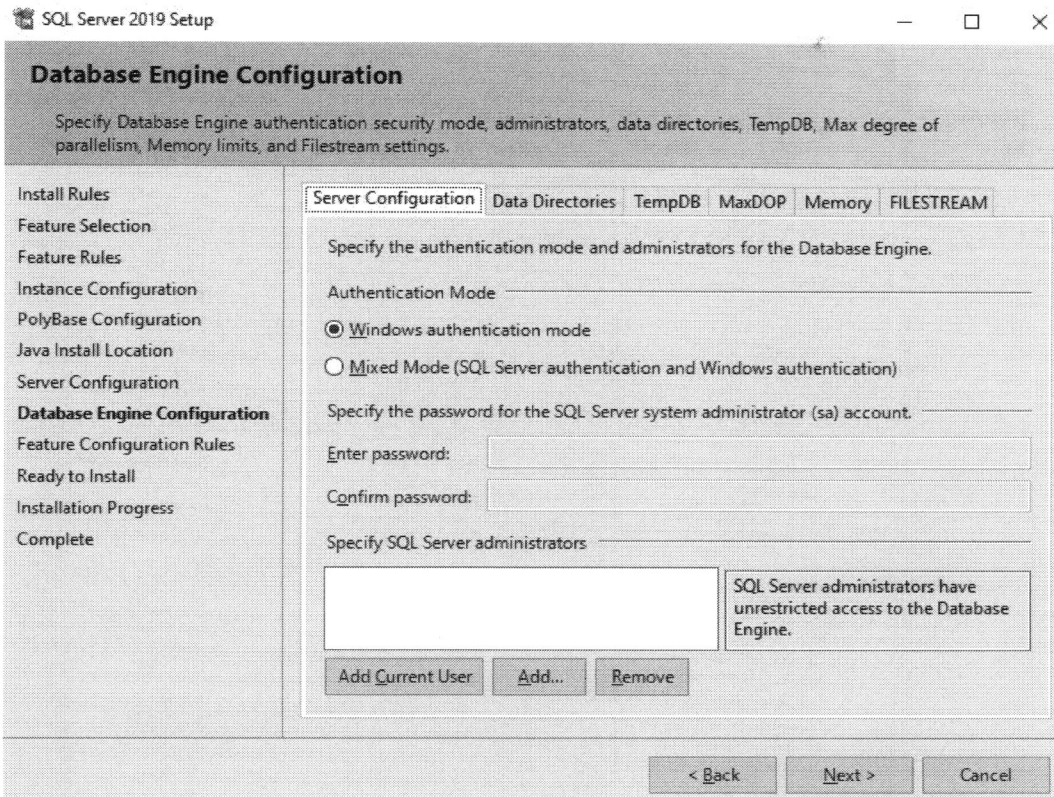

Figure 1.14 – Database Engine Configuration

Add the account you are currently using to the **SQL Server administrators** role by clicking the **Add Current User** button.

After a few moments, your username should appear in the SQL Server administrators list box.

You do not have to make any changes to the rest of the settings on this page unless you want to change the location of the database files, which you can do on the **Data Directories** tab.

> **Important note**
>
> For the purposes of this cookbook, you can use the default locations on the
> C: drive for the database files; however, in a real-life environment – even if
> solely for testing purposes – it is recommended to host the database files on a
> different drive, not the one used for the operating system and other installed
> features files.

When ready, click **Next** to continue.

17. On the **Ready to Install** page, review the installation options listed in *Steps 5* through *16*.

    When you are sure that everything has been configured in accordance with the instructions in this recipe, click **Install** to start the automated part of the installation. On modern hardware, the installation should complete within a few minutes.

18. Once the installation has completed, inspect the installation status of each installed feature. If any errors are encountered during the installation, they will be marked with a **Failed** installation status. When you select each feature reported as failed, additional information about the failure should be displayed in the **Details** section:

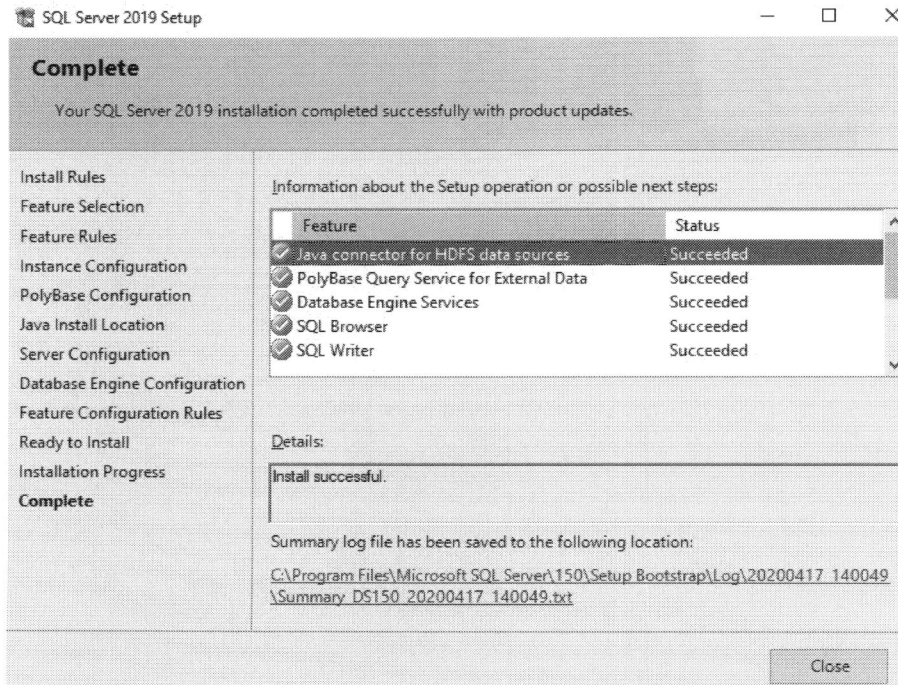

Figure 1.15 – The final step of the SQL Server 2019 installation

Inspect any error messages and address the cause of each problem based on the information provided. You can repeat the installation after you have resolved the problems.

Click **Close** to complete the installation.

One more task awaits you, and then the installation can be considered finished (for the time being, at least). In order to allow the PolyBase services access to the SQL Server instance, you must allow connections to the instance through the TCP/IP protocol.

19. In the Windows Start menu, in the `Microsoft SQL Server 2019` folder, locate **SQL Server 2019 Configuration Manager** and start it:

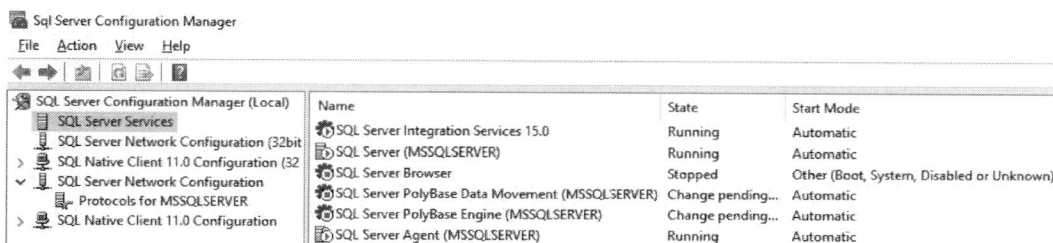

Figure 1.16 – SQL Server Configuration Manager

In **Configuration Manager**, shown in the preceding screenshot, under **SQL Server Services**, you should see that the SQL Server instance that you just installed is running; however, both SQL Server PolyBase services will either be **Stopped** or in the **Change pending…** state.

The reason for this is that the services are unable to connect to the SQL Server instance. They use TCP/IP to connect, and on a newly installed SQL Server instance, this protocol is not enabled.

20. Under **SQL Server Network Configuration | Protocols for MSSQLSERVER**, shown in the following screenshot, right-click the disabled **TCP/IP** protocol, and select **Enable** from the shortcut menu:

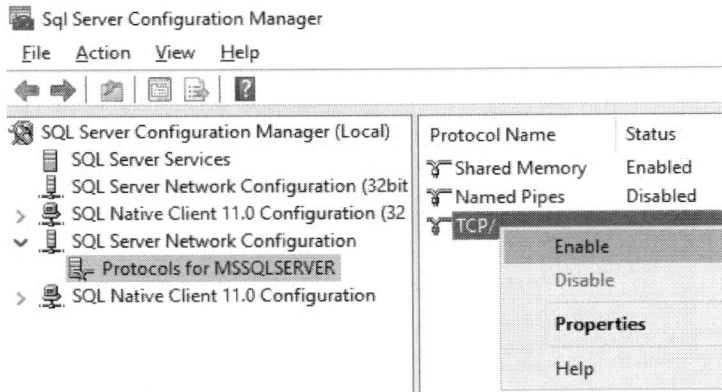

Figure 1.17 – Enabling the TCP/IP protocol

A warning is displayed, telling you that in order for the changes to take effect, the affected service must be restarted. Click **OK** to close the warning.

21. Back under **SQL Server Services**, right-click the **SQL Server (MSSQLSERVER)** service, and select **Restart** from the shortcut menu:

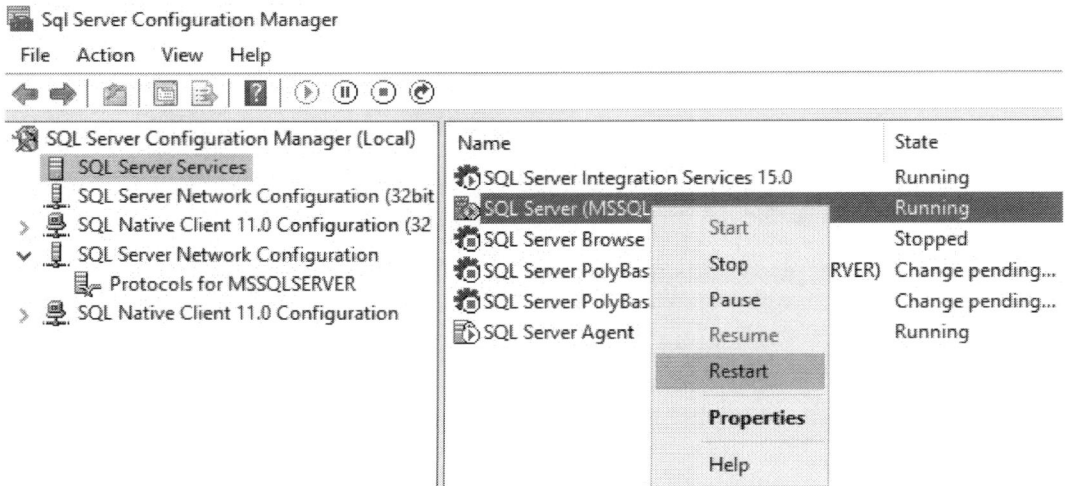

Figure 1.18 – Restarting the SQL Server instance

22. Wait for the service to restart. When prompted to stop or restart any other dependent service, confirm those as well. After the SQL Server instance has restarted, the PolyBase services should start as well. However, if they stay in the **Change Pending…** state for an extended period of time, try starting them manually. If even that fails, you might have to restart the workstation.

Close **SQL Server 2019 Configuration Manager**.

How it works...

You have just successfully installed a new SQL Server instance. You will use it to complete the rest of the recipes in this cookbook; of course, it can also be used for other development work involving the SQL Server platform. If you later determine that you need additional features, you can add them by starting the installation again from **SQL Server Installation Center**.

> **Important note**
>
> If you have installed the Developer edition of the product, please remember that it has not been licensed for production use. You are only allowed to use it for application development and testing.
>
> If you have installed an Evaluation edition of the product, remember that the license expires 180 days after the installation.

Installing SQL Server Management Studio

SQL Server Management Studio (or **SSMS**, for short) is the principal tool used in SQL Server administration, maintenance, and development. It can be used to administer relational databases hosted on the Database Engine, or analytical databases and solutions hosted in Analysis Services. It can be used to administer the **SQL Server Integration Services and Database (SSISDB)** catalog, used for SSIS project deployments. You can even use it to administer the legacy SSIS service, used for legacy SSIS package deployments.

> **Important note**
>
> While most SSIS development activities will take place in **SQL Server Data Tools (SSDT)**, you should still install SSMS on the workstation. Its programming capabilities complement SSDT, whereas its administrative and maintenance capabilities far exceed those available in SSDT.

Of course, SSMS supports numerous programming languages and data management standards typically associated with data management: **Transact-SQL** (**T-SQL**, for short) to manipulate data in relational databases, **Multidimensional Expressions** (**MDX**) and **Data Mining Extensions** (**DMX**) for data analysis and knowledge extraction, and **XML for Analysis** (**XMLA**) to administer **SQL Server's Analysis Services** (**SSAS**) databases. You can even use SSMS to create and edit XML documents.

Getting ready

For several years now, SSMS has been delivered as a standalone tool, no longer closely associated with a particular version of SQL Server. This decision allows Microsoft to develop the tool in its own development cycle, pretty much completely independently of the development cycle they use for the SQL Server platform. It also grants the development team behind the tool more flexibility in terms of the features being deployed or upgraded in each version.

SSMS is, therefore, no longer included as part of the SQL Server installation, as it used to be in the past, and must be installed separately. It is available for download at `https://docs.microsoft.com/en-us/sql/ssms/download-sql-server-management-studio-ssms`.

The download site can also be accessed from **SQL Server Installation Center**.

> **Tip**
> It is recommended to always use the latest version of SSMS, as it typically contains the latest security, stability, and user-experience fixes. The latest features and capabilities are, naturally, also only available in the most recent version of SSMS.
>
> In fact, this is true for every tool that you will be installing in this and later chapters.

How to do it...

Use your favorite internet browser to navigate to the SSMS download site listed previously, or start **SQL Server Installation Center** – it is located in the Start menu, in the `Microsoft SQL Server 2019` folder – and then, on the **Installation** page, select the **Install SQL Server Management Tools** option.

You will start this recipe by installing SSMS and complete it by downloading a sample database from GitHub and deploying it to the SQL Server instance you installed in the previous recipe, *Installing Microsoft SQL Server 2019 Integration Services*:

1. In the **Microsoft docs** article entitled *Download SQL Server Management Studio (SSMS)*, inspect the latest information about the download. Pay close attention to any warnings or considerations that the vendor might have provided.

   When ready, click the **Download SQL Server Management Studio (SSMS)** HTML link to initiate the download.

2. If prompted to save the executable to your drive, click **Save**, wait for the download to complete, and then click **Run** to start the installation.

   If the download is performed in the background, use Windows Explorer to locate the file in your downloads folder, and start the execution from there – for instance, by executing the SSMS-Setup-ENU.exe file.

3. On the first screen of the installation dialog, leave the default location unchanged, and click **Install** to continue.

4. The installation should complete within a few minutes.

   If the installation is interrupted by an error, investigate the cause based on the information provided in the installation dialog. Otherwise, click **Close** to finish the installation.

5. In the Windows Start menu, locate the Microsoft SQL Server Tools 18 folder, and in it the *Microsoft SQL Server Management Studio 18* shortcut. Open it.

6. In the **Connect to Server** dialog, select the SQL Server instance you created in the previous recipe, *Installing Microsoft SQL Server 2019 Integration Services*.

   The instance should now be displayed in the SSMS **Object Explorer**.

7. Open **SQL Server Installation Center**, and on the **Resources** page, locate the *SQL Samples Web Site* link. Follow the link to navigate to the Microsoft SQL Server Samples site.

   In your internet browser, scroll down to the *SQL Server Samples Repository* section, and click on the link to the **Wide World Importers sample database** web page.

8. On the new page, locate the WideWorldImporters-Full.bak file and click the link to start the download.

   Depending on your internet connection, the download should complete within a few minutes.

9. In SSMS, in **Object Explorer**, right-click the **Databases** node, and then select **Restore database…** from the shortcut menu, as shown in the following screenshot:

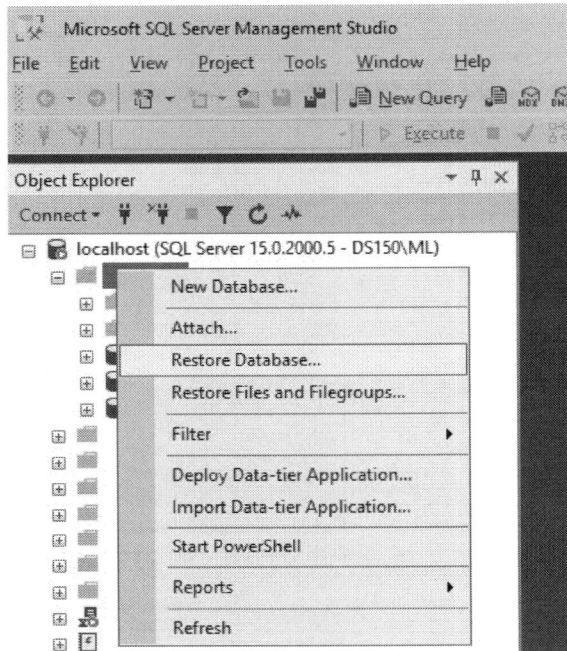

Figure 1.19 – Restoring a SQL Server database

10. In the **Restore Database** dialog, on the **General** page, select **Device** as the source, and open the **Select backup devices** dialog by clicking the ellipsis icon to the right of the **Device** text box, as shown in the following screenshot:

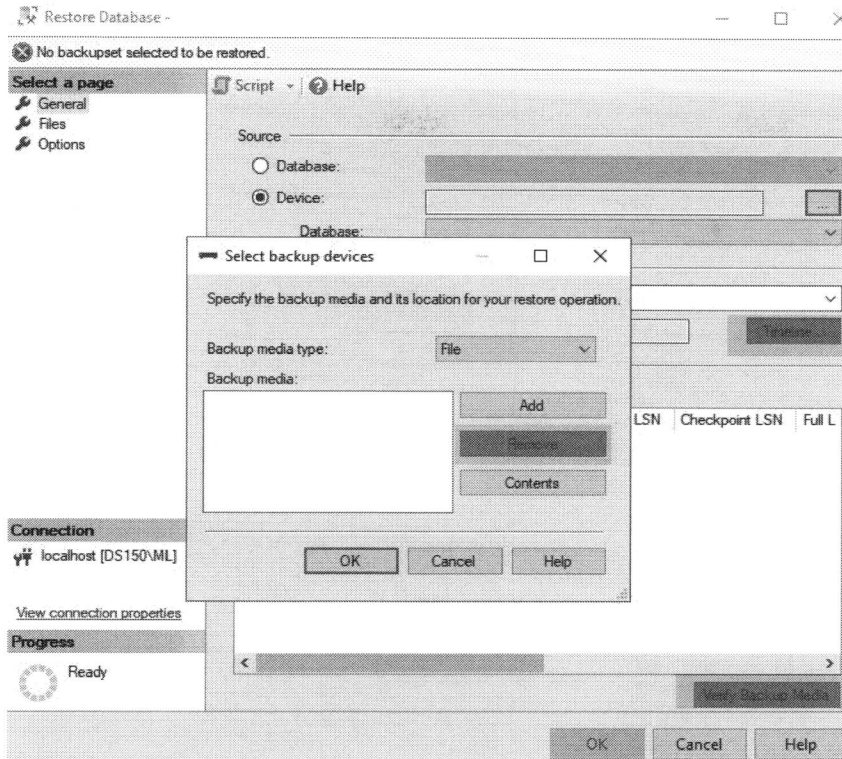

Figure 1.20 – Selecting the backup device

11. In the **Select backup devices** dialog, click **Add** to open the **Locate Backup File** dialog, and then navigate the filesystem on the left to locate the file you downloaded in *Step 8*.

    Select the file and click **OK** to confirm the selection.

12. In the **Select backup devices** dialog, click **OK** to confirm the selection.

13. In the **Restore Database** dialog, click **OK** again to start the restore operation.

    It should take about a minute to restore the sample database.

    Once the message box opens with the **Database 'WideWorldImporters' restored successfully** message, the database should be available on the selected instance.

    If there are any errors, inspect the error messages, make the necessary corrections, and repeat the process accordingly.

14. After the database has been restored successfully, click **OK** to close the message box, which also closes the **Restore Database** dialog.

Now that you have your first tool installed, you can change two more settings that you might need later.

15. In SSMS, open a new query window, connect to the **master** database, and then use the following T-SQL command to inspect the **Hadoop** connectivity instance settings:

```
EXEC sp_configure
    @configname = 'hadoop connectivity';
```

In the execution result, observe the run_value column; if its value is 0, change it to 7 by executing the following T-SQL commands:

```
EXEC sp_configure
    @configname = 'hadoop connectivity',
    @configvalue = 7;
reconfigure;
```

By turning this configuration setting on, you allow your SQL Server instance to connect to remote Hadoop or Azure Blob storage locations. By using the configuration value of 7, you allow connections to all versions and both editions of Hortonworks, as well as to the Azure Blob storage.

> **Tip**
>
> More information about this setting is available in the vendor documentation, at https://docs.microsoft.com/en-us/sql/database-engine/configure-windows/polybase-connectivity-configuration-transact-sql. You should be familiar with the setting and its possible values before using the feature in a production environment.

16. Use the following T-SQL command to check whether the **PolyBase** service is enabled on your SQL Server instance:

```
EXEC sp_configure
    @configname = 'polybase enabled';
```

If the value of the `run_value` column is 0, that means that PolyBase is not enabled; enable it by changing the configuration value to 1 by executing the following T-SQL commands:

```
EXEC sp_configure
    @configname = 'polybase enabled',
    @configvalue = 1;
RECONFIGURE;
```

> **Tip**
>
> More information about this setting, and the PolyBase services in general, is available in the vendor documentation, at `https://docs.microsoft.com/en-us/sql/relational-databases/polybase/polybase-installation`. You should be familiar with the setting and its possible states before using the feature in a production environment.

17. If all the commands complete successfully, close **SSMS**. This time, you do not have to save the script or the solution.

18. Open **SQL Server 2019 Configuration Manager**, and restart the **MSSQLSERVER** instance, as you did in *Step 20* of the previous recipe, *Installing Microsoft SQL Server 2019 Integration Services*.

> **Important note**
>
> The SQL Server instance must be restarted in order for these two configuration settings to take effect, as they affect the dependent PolyBase services. Also, you cannot restart a SQL Server instance running PolyBase from within SSMS when **Object Explorer** is connected to the service and prevents the service from being stopped.

After the instance is restarted, you can close **Configuration Manager**.

How it works...

You have installed the principal development and administration tool for SQL Server. You will be using SSMS throughout this cookbook. Of course, if you have worked with SQL Server before, you should already be familiar with SSMS and its capabilities. If this is the first time you have used SSMS, do not worry – every feature used in the recipes in this book will be explained when needed.

You finished the recipe by deploying a sample database to the newly installed SQL Server instance. You will use this database in other recipes of this cookbook, and you are free to use it whenever you are exploring SQL Server and its capabilities.

Installing SQL Server Data Tools

SSDT is a specialized edition of the **Microsoft Visual Studio integrated development environment (IDE)**. It can be used to develop a variety of projects related to SQL Server, such as relational and Azure databases, Analysis Services data models, Reporting Services reports, or Integration Services projects, to name just a few.

In the past, SSDT used to be a standalone tool, requiring only a subset of Visual Studio features to be installed. However, starting with Visual Studio 2019 (or SQL Server 2019), SSDT represents an extension (or better: a set of extensions) of the principal Visual Studio IDE.

To use the 2019 version of SSDT, you first need to install Visual Studio 2019, and then add the SSDT extensions, followed by the extensions needed to develop Analysis Services, Integration Services, and/or Reporting Services projects. This does increase the complexity of the installation procedure, but it also more closely follows the standard approach of adding features to the core Visual Studio installation.

Getting ready

If you do not have a valid **Visual Studio 2019 Professional** or **Enterprise** license at your disposal, you can also use the free **Community** edition of Visual Studio 2019. All editions are available to download at `https://docs.microsoft.com/en-us/sql/ssdt/download-sql-server-data-tools-ssdt`. This location can also be accessed from **SQL Server Installation Center**.

How to do it...

Use your favorite internet browser to navigate to the Visual Studio 2019 download site listed previously, or start **SQL Server Installation Center**, and then on the **Installation** page, select the **Install SQL Server Data Tools** option.

This recipe assumes that Visual Studio 2019 has not yet been installed on the workstation, and the instructions will show you how to install **Visual Studio 2019 Community Edition**:

1. On the **Download SQL Server Data Tools (SSDT) for Visual Studio** web page, in the **Install SSDT with Visual Studio 2019** section, locate the link to **Visual Studio 2019 Community**, and follow that link to the Visual Studio 2019 **Downloads** page. Click **FREE DOWNLOAD** in the **Community** column to start the download operation and save the file to the local drive on your workstation.

2. When prompted, click **Run** to start the installation; otherwise, use Windows Explorer to navigate to your folder, and start the installation by opening the vs_Community.exe file.

3. The installation begins with the setup of a few prerequisites. You can take this moment to inspect the **Microsoft Privacy Statement** and the **Microsoft Software License Terms** by following the links provided in the message box:

Figure 1.21 – Visual Studio Installer

When ready, click **Continue**.

The installation now downloads and extracts the files, after which the **Installing — Visual Studio 2019 Community** dialog should open.

4. On the **Workloads** page, in the **Desktop & Mobile** section, check **.NET desktop development**, and in the **Other Toolsets** section, check **Data storage and processing**:

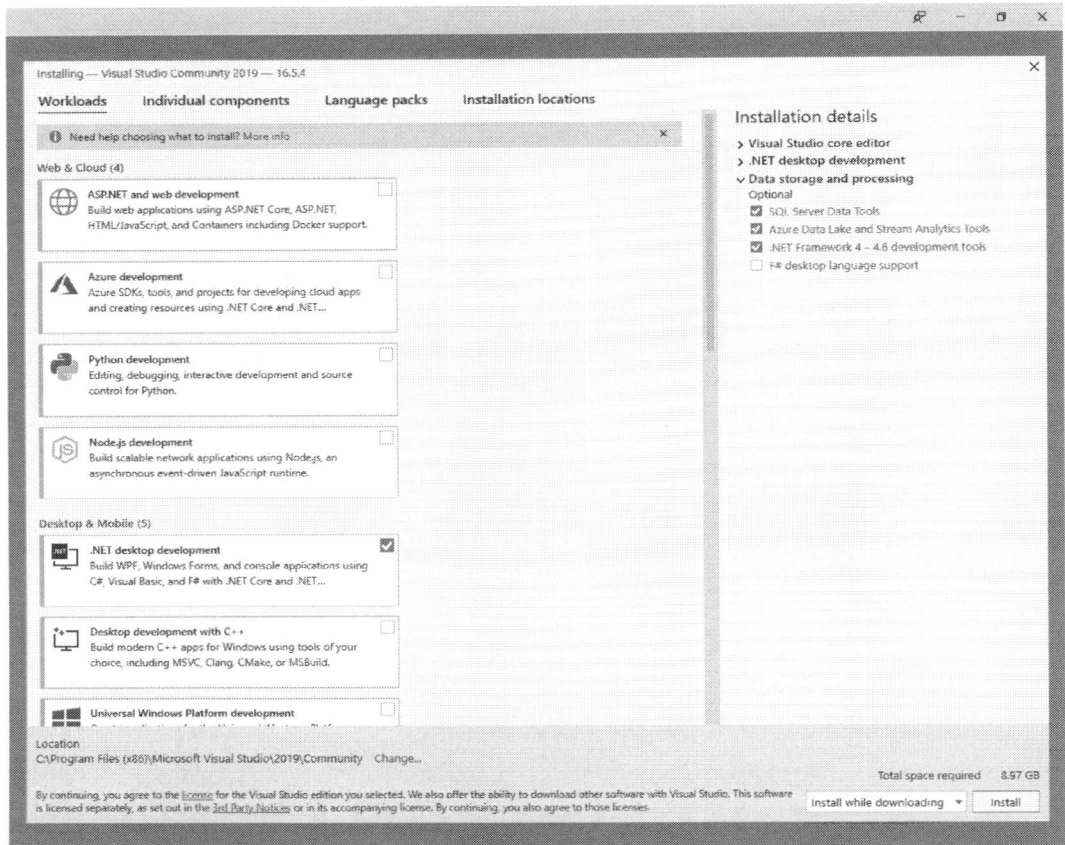

Figure 1.22 – The Visual Studio 2019 installation details

Check the list of items in the right column – the same items should be listed as the ones shown in the screenshot.

5. Leave the **Install while downloading** option selected in the combo box next to the **Install** button.

When ready, click **Install** to continue.

The installation should take a few minutes, depending on your internet connection, after which the Visual Studio will greet you with the **Sign in** screen.

6. Click **Not now, maybe later** to skip the sign-in process for the time being.

7. In the next dialog, select your development settings and your color theme, and click **Start Visual Studio**.

   Of course, you can also change these settings in **SSDT** later.

8. After a few minutes, **Visual Studio 2019** should open, with the **Open recent/Get Started** dialog.

   At this time, you only need to access the **Visual Studio 2019 IDE** to install additional SQL Server extensions.

   Click **Continue without code**.

9. **Visual Studio** opens without any solutions or projects loaded.

   In the **Extensions** menu, select the **Manage Extensions** command.

10. In the **Manage Extensions** dialog, on the **Online | Visual Studio Marketplace** page, use the search text box located at the top right to search for `integration services`, as shown in the following screenshot:

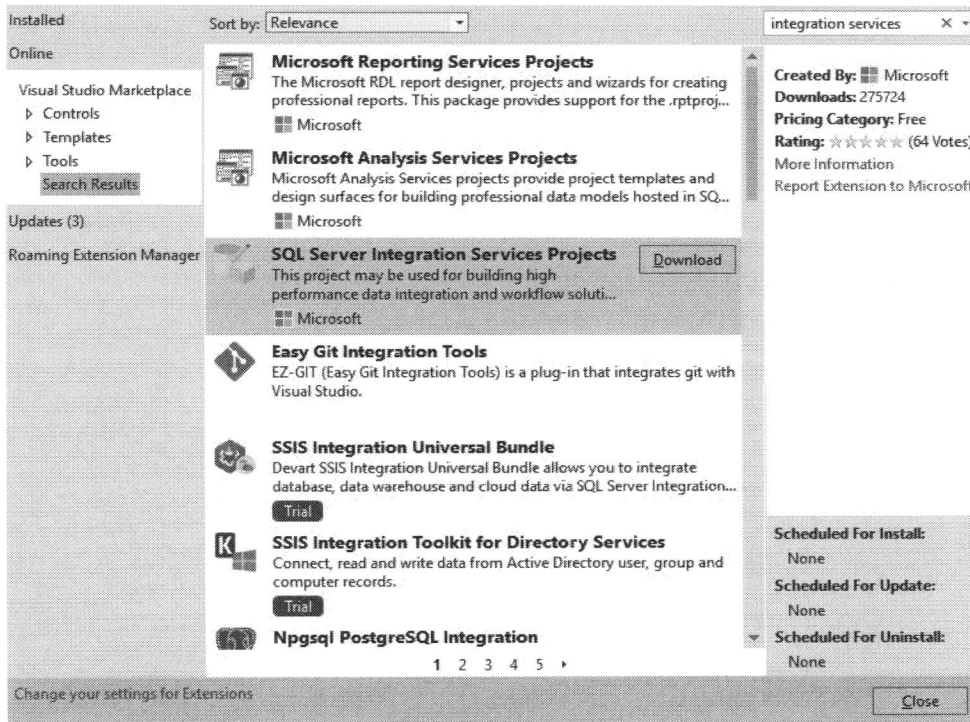

Figure 1.23 – The Visual Studio 2019 extensions

In the search result list, locate **SQL Server Integration Services Projects** and click **Download**.

11. An internet browser window should open, prompting you to save the file to your local drive. Save the file to the local drive on your workstation.

12. If prompted by the browser to run the file, click **Run** to start the installation; otherwise, use Windows Explorer to navigate to your `downloads` folder, and open the `Microsoft.DataTools.IntegrationServices.exe` file to start the installation.

13. In the first dialog, select the language to be used during the installation. You can use any of the supported languages; however, note that these instructions assume that you selected the English language. When ready, click **OK** to continue.

14. In the next dialog, simply click **Next** to continue.

15. In the next dialog, make sure that your edition of Visual Studio 2019 is selected as the installation target, but do not click **Install** yet.

16. Switch to Visual Studio 2019, close the **Manage Extensions** dialog, and then close Visual Studio as well.

> **Important note**
> During the installation of a Visual Studio extension, changes might have to be made to Visual Studio files, which cannot be done if these files are open. Therefore, this is the perfect moment during the installation to close Visual Studio. If files are open, an error message might be displayed, prompting you to close them before being able to continue.

17. Switch back to the Visual Studio extensions installer, and now do click **Install** to continue.

18. If prompted by the operating system whether to allow SQL Server Integration Services Projects to make changes to your device, click **Yes** to continue. The installation should complete within a few minutes.

19. In the final dialog, click **Close** to finish the installation.

Close the internet browser window that was used to download the SQL Server Integration Services Projects installer, and **Visual Studio Installer**, if they are still open.

How it works...

You have installed Visual Studio 2019 with the features needed to complete the rest of the recipes in this book. These recipes will cover typical SSIS development, but also control flow and data flow customization.

You can use the same setup to complete many other development tasks, and if needed, you can install any additional features at any time, by running **Visual Studio Installer** – available from the Windows Start menu.

> **Important note**
>
> In order to continue using the Community edition of Visual Studio 2019 beyond the 30-day evaluation period, you will have to sign in with a Microsoft Live account. You can use the same account that you will be using later in this chapter to create the Azure subscription.
>
> A few days before the evaluation period expires, if you try to open SSDT, you will be prompted to sign in, but you can also sign in at any time.

Installing Azure Data Studio

Azure Data Studio (**ADS**) represents a new database administration, maintenance, and development tool to be used with Microsoft data platforms on-premises or in the cloud. In contrast to SSMS, not only can ADS be installed on Windows, but also on macOS or Linux.

ADS offers a new approach to development with a visually and functionally rich T-SQL editor, IntelliSense, and code snippets. It visually integrates execution results with the T-SQL queries that were executed to generate them and allows you to export query results in several standard formats.

The aim of ADS is not to completely replace SSMS as the principal data administration, maintenance, and development tool, but rather to complement it, especially as a cross-platform tool.

If you are new to ADS, or need help in determining how to balance your work between ADS and SSMS, we recommend the *What is Azure Data Studio?* introductory article, available online at https://docs.microsoft.com/en-us/sql/azure-data-studio/what-is.

Getting ready

The ADS installation is available online, at https://docs.microsoft.com/en-us/sql/azure-data-studio/download-azure-data-studio.

How to do it...

Use your favorite internet browser to navigate to the ADS download site listed previously:

1. On the **Download and install Azure Data Studio** web page, locate the recommended **User Installer** link, and follow it to start the download. When prompted, save the file to the local drive on your workstation.

    Depending on your internet connection, the download should complete within a minute.

2. When prompted by the browser, click **Run** to start the installation; otherwise, use Windows Explorer to navigate to your downloads folder, and initiate the installation there.

3. Review the license agreement, and then click **Next** to continue.

4. On the **Select Destination Location** page, leave the default folder selected, and click **Next** to continue.

5. On the **Select Start Menu Folder** page, leave the default folder name, and click **Next** to continue.

6. On the **Select Additional Tasks** page, you can check the **Create a desktop icon** option if you want to place the ADS shortcut on the desktop. You can also check the **Register Azure Data Studio as an editor for supported file types** option if you want all files normally associated with SSMS to be opened in ADS by default:

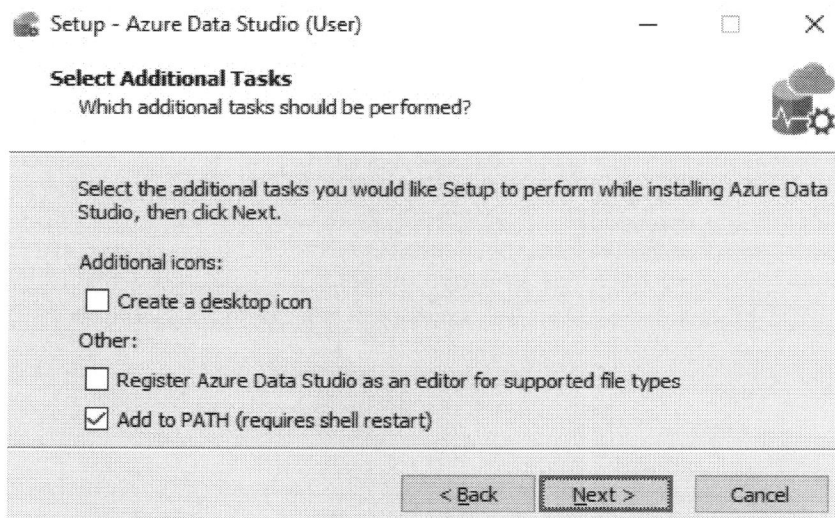

Figure 1.24 – Selecting additional tasks in the ADS setup

If you are not planning to replace SSMS with ADS at this time, leave the default settings unchanged, as shown in the screenshot.

When ready, click **Next** to continue.

7. On the **Ready to Install** page, review the setup options. When ready, click **Next** to start the automated part of the installation. The installation should complete within a few minutes.

8. On the final page, uncheck the **Launch Azure Data Studio** option, and click **Finish** to close the installer.

You do not have to start ADS at this time.

How it works...

You have now installed ADS, the newest addition to the Microsoft data platform development and administration toolset. Some of the recipes in this cookbook will require the use of features that are available in ADS, but not in SSMS.

Creating an Azure subscription

One of the objectives of this cookbook is to show you how to integrate your on-premises data warehousing solutions with cloud-based data storage, maintenance, and consumption capabilities of the Microsoft data platform. One of the prerequisites needed to follow this objective is an active Azure subscription.

Azure provides a variety of services and features that you can use to host your data off-premises, extend your own on-premises and cloud-based data management solutions with cloud-based services provided by Microsoft and Microsoft Partner Network, and even host your own solutions as cloud-based services to be used by your clients.

If you already have access to a valid Azure subscription, you are welcome to use it for all the relevant recipes in this book; otherwise, you can use this recipe to create a new one.

An Azure free subscription will provide you with access to the services for 12 months – free of charge. A number of services are even provided at no cost independently of the subscription period.

The free subscription includes a credit of 200 USD to be used for paid services for a period of 30 days from the subscription activation. This period should be enough for you to run all of the cloud-oriented recipes provided in this cookbook.

> **Important note**
>
> Certain paid services in Azure incur costs while online, even if they are not actually being used. This will be pointed out in each recipe dealing with such services, and the instructions on how to either turn a feature off or remove it completely will be provided.
>
> However, by using Azure, you take full responsibility for all the costs involved in using the services provided therein.

Getting ready

Azure is an online service, located at `https://portal.azure.com/`. Generally, you would use an internet browser to access it; however, on the latest versions of the Windows operating system, you can also use the Azure portal application. The instructions in this cookbook use an internet browser to access the Azure portal.

How to do it...

Use your favorite internet browser and navigate to the Azure portal website:

1. On the **Azure Portal app** landing page, click **Continue to Azure Portal website**.

2. On the **Sign in** page, do not sign in with your existing Microsoft Azure credentials, but instead, click **Create one!** to create a new account.

   On the next screen, provide a valid email address for the account. Use the address of an existing email account that you have access to and is not currently associated with an existing Azure subscription.

   Alternatively, you can use a phone number instead of an email. If you prefer to use a phone number, click **Use a phone number instead**, and the form will allow you to enter it. Again, use an existing phone number of a smart device that you have access to and that is not currently associated with an Azure account.

You can even create a new email account. If you prefer to use a new email account, click **Get a new email address**, and the form will allow you to create a new outlook.com or hotmail.com email account. When ready, click **Next** to continue.

3. On the next screen, create a password for the account. It is recommended that you follow the standard recommendations on how to create a safe password.

4. On the next screen, provide your country/region information and the date of your birth. When ready, click **Next** to continue.

    An automated confirmation email will be sent to the email address you used earlier, or a message will be sent to your phone if you used a phone number.

5. Copy the code you were sent in the message from the Microsoft account team into the text box of the **Verify email** form. When ready, click **Next** to continue.

6. On the next screen, you will be required to prove that you are a real person by entering the characters you recognize in the screenshot.

    If the characters are difficult to read, click **New** for a new image, or click **Audio** for the images to be read out through your audio device.

    When you have entered the correct characters, click **Next** to continue.

7. After the account has been created, the **Welcome to Azure** web page will open, prompting you to start the tour. Click **Maybe later** to close the dialog.

    In a new free Azure account, none of the paid services can be accessed until the trial is activated. You do not have to activate it at this time; this can be done when you go through the recipes in the following chapters in which paid Azure services are required.

    You can close the internet browser. However, if you do want to activate the trial, continue on to *Step 8*.

8. To start the free trial, click **Start**:

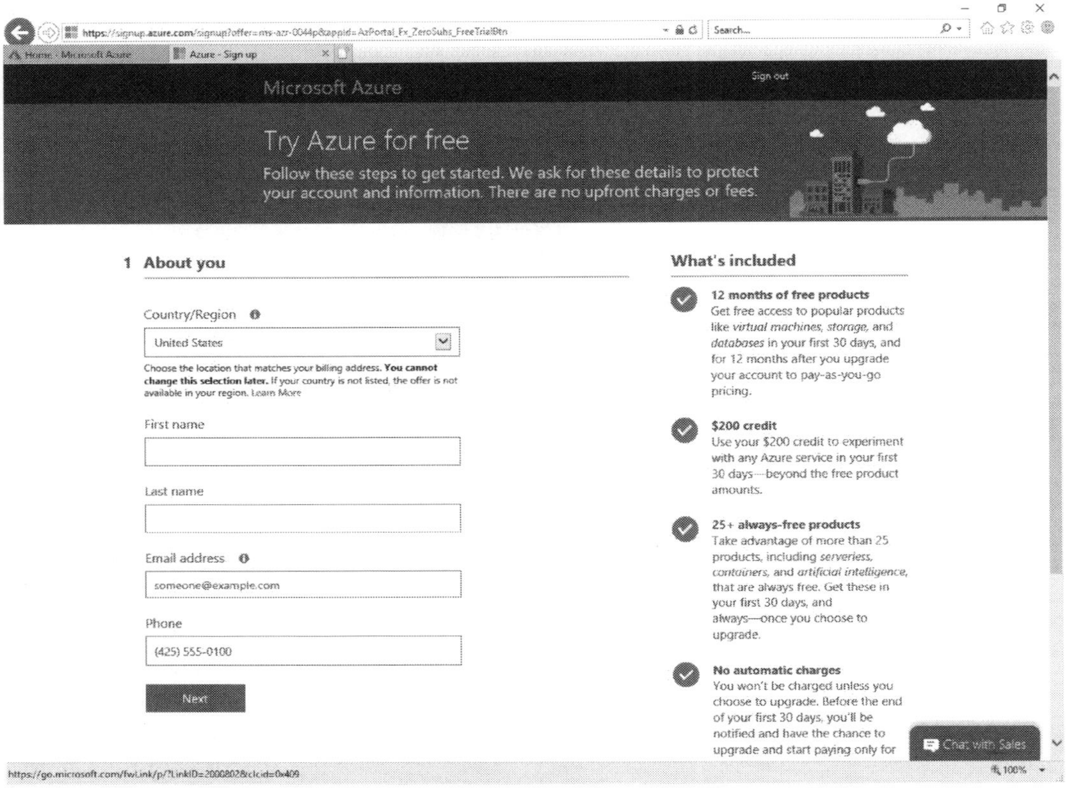

Figure 1.25 – Activating the Microsoft Azure Free Trial

9. Follow the instructions on the web page. You will have to provide some of your personal information, including an email address and a valid phone number.

Important note

If Azure is not available in your region, please contact Microsoft, and they will be able to assist you further.

To complete the activation, your identity will be verified by phone using the method you select – via a text message or through a call from the service center.

As part of the identity verification, you will also have to provide valid credit card details.

> **Important note**
>
> Credit card information will not be used unless you upgrade your free subscription to a pay-as-you-go subscription.

Before you can complete the activation procedure, you also have to read and accept the subscription agreement.

> **Important note**
>
> We recommend that you familiarize yourself with the subscription agreement, the details of the offer, and the privacy statement before continuing.

10. When ready, click **Sign up** to activate your Azure free trial.

The activation should complete within a few minutes.

How it works...

You have just created a free Azure subscription; it will not only allow you to complete most of the recipes in this cookbook but will also allow you to explore additional services that you can use for your personal or professional needs.

> **Important note**
>
> One of the purposes of this cookbook is to introduce SSIS development in the cloud, using more than just the basic features of SQL Server or Azure. Unfortunately, the free Azure subscription does not provide access to more advanced features (such as the Azure Kubernetes Service or Azure Databricks); therefore, in order to complete specific recipes, you will have to upgrade your account.
>
> Each of those recipes will contain a special warning and provide the appropriate instructions on how to proceed.

There's more...

If you decide on using Azure for more than just learning about SSIS development, you will eventually have to upgrade your account. If you design applications or provide services that can also be hosted in Azure, you might even consider joining the Microsoft Partner Network yourself.

2
Introducing ETL

When I first started in the data warehousing business, something like 20 years ago, I was asked in an interview to define ETL. Being at my first job interview, I had no clue what the interviewer meant by ETL. Luckily, the interviewer kind of liked me and hired me anyway. He told me that I would know all about ETL quite soon. Being in data warehouse businesses for many years, and more recently a data engineer, ETL is what has kept me busy most of the time since then.

ETL stands for **Extract, Transform, and Load**. ETL is a data moving technique that has been used in various forms since the first enterprise data warehouses' inceptions.

Microsoft formalized the ETL concept near the end of the 1990s with a tool called DTS: Data Transformation Service. This ETL tool, aimed at helping database administrators load data into and from SQL Server, used SQL and ActiveX to move and transform data on-premises.

Microsoft brought its ETL tool to the cloud with the introduction of **Azure Data Factory (ADF)**. In 2018, Microsoft extensively overhauled ADF to create **Azure Data Factory v2**, which allowed the user to complete many tasks within ADF that had previously required the use of more software.

Another commonly used Azure ETL tool is **Databricks**. This tool uses Apache Spark as a compute service, allowing developers to use many languages to develop their transformations: Python, Scala, R, and SQL. Java can also be used to develop shared components to be used by many ETL pipelines.

Doing ETL is a necessary step for any data warehouse or data science project. It is used in various forms and shapes in IT for tasks such as the following:

- Storing procedures or script used in reports: Data is extracted from a data source first and transformed every time a column is created; a calculation is done for various reports' sections.

- BI tools such as **Power BI**: This kind of tool has a model in which we can add measures or columns that fill some missing attributes in the data source.

- Data warehouse and science projects: Every time a program or script cleans up data or transforms it for specific consumption purposes, we are doing ETL.

In the next chapters, we will explore all these tools and give you access to recipes that will show you how to do ETL in Azure.

In this chapter, we will cover the following recipes:

- Creating a SQL Azure database
- Connecting SQL Server Management Studio
- Creating a simple ETL package
- Loading data before its transformation

Creating a SQL Azure database

To do ETL, we need to have a source to query data and a target (often called a **sink**) to land the transformed data. Our first recipe will create a simple SQL Azure database that will be used as both the source and sink in all recipes of this chapter.

Getting ready

In *Chapter 1, Getting Started with Azure and SSIS 2019*, you were shown how to install SQL Server on-premises, **SQL Server Management Studio (SSMS)**, and Visual Studio 2019 with the SSIS extension. This chapter will show you how to set up SQL Server in Azure and the recipes will use this version of SQL Server.

How to do it...

In a browser, go to the Microsoft Azure portal using the following URL: `https://portal.azure.com/#home`.

On the main portal page, we'll create a resource group to group all Azure services together. It's much easier to find and manage them later.:

1. From the main portal page, click on the + sign to create a new resource, as shown in the following screenshot:

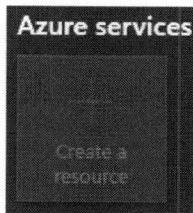

Figure 2.1 – Create a resource in Azure

2. In the search box, type `resource`. Click on the search result **Resource group** that appears, as in the following screenshot:

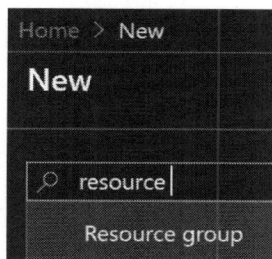

Figure 2.2 – Choose Resource group from the search list

3. In the **Resource group** blade, click **Create** to create a new resource group, as shown in the following screenshot:

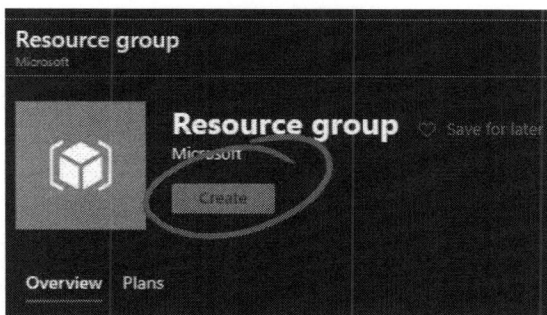

Figure 2.3 – Create a resource group after selection

4. Select the subscription, give the resource group a name, and choose the region, as shown in the following screenshot:

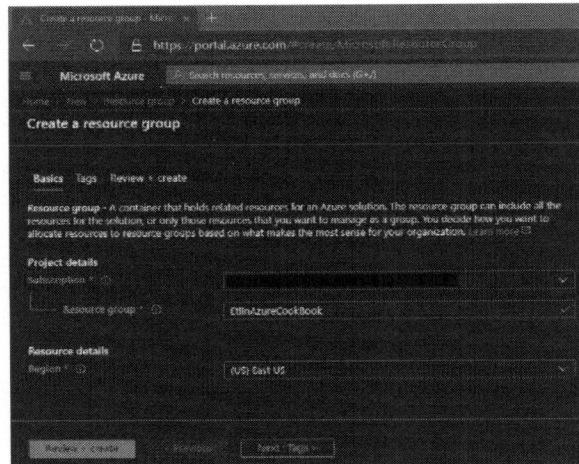

Figure 2.4 – New resource group properties

The region you select here will be the default for all the resources you create in the resource group in the future. Ideally, you should choose a location not too far from where you live. We can always override this setting in each resource we create in the future.

Click on **Review + create** at the bottom left of the blade to validate the entries we made. Once validated, click **Create** to create the resource group.

5. Once the resource group is created, click **Go to resource group** from the activity log message that is displayed. Or you can click on **Home** on the left-hand menu and click on your resource group in the **Recent resource** list. Once in the resource group, click on **Create resources** as shown in the following screenshot:

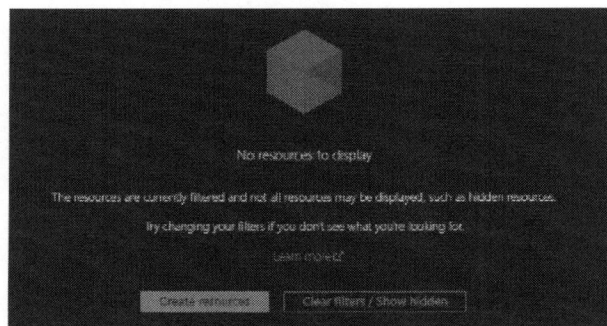

Figure 2.5 – Add a resource to a resource group

6. From the blade that appears, select **Databases** on the left and click on **SQL Database** as shown in the following screenshot:

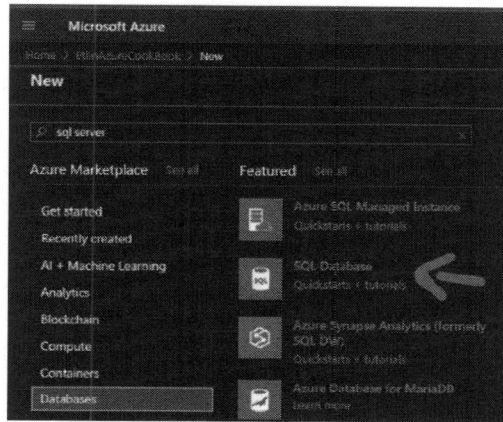

Figure 2.6 – Select SQL Database

7. The **Create SQL Database** blade opens. Set the properties as shown in the following screenshot:

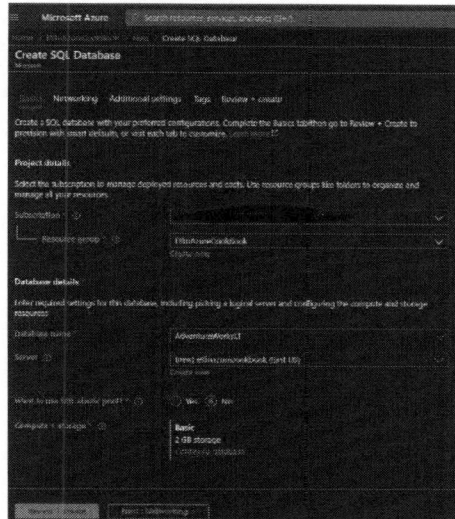

Figure 2.7 – Database properties

Let's look at the database properties:

a) **Subscription**: Your subscription.

b) **Resource group**: **EtLInAzureCookBook** or the resource group created before.

c) **Database name**: We're going to restore a sample database that will be used in future recipes. We'll name it **AdventureWorksLT**.

d) **Server**: Click on **Create new** below the combo list. The **New server** blade appears:

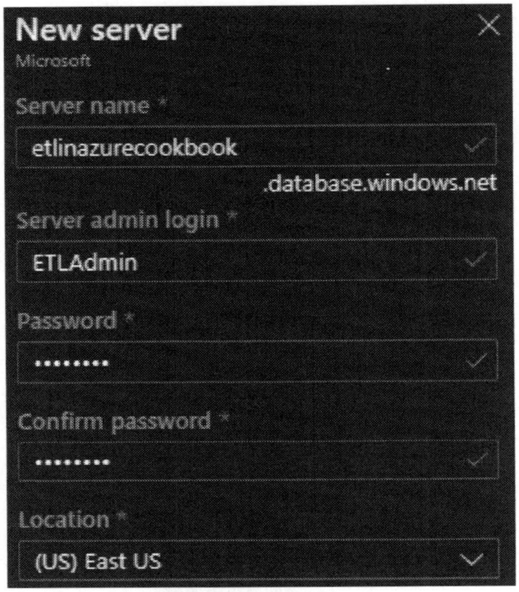

Figure 2.8 – New server properties

Let's look at the server properties:

a) **Server name**: You should use something like `<yourname>`
   `etlinazurecookbook` all in lower case. Here's the reference from Microsoft for SQL Server naming: `https://docs.microsoft.com/en-us/azure/azure-resource-manager/management/resource-name-rules#microsoftsql`.

b) **Server admin login**: **ETLAdmin**.

c) **Password**: Create a password.

d) **Confirm password**: Confirm the password created.

e) **Location**: Select an Azure location. You should use the same region as the resource group created before.

f) Click on **OK** to create the server.

g) Back in the database creation blade, set the **SQL elastic pool** option to **No**.

h) **Compute + Storage**: Click on the **Configure database** link. We'll select the **Basic** configuration for now.

i) From the **Configure** blade, click on the **Looking for basic, standard, premium?** link as shown in the following screenshot:

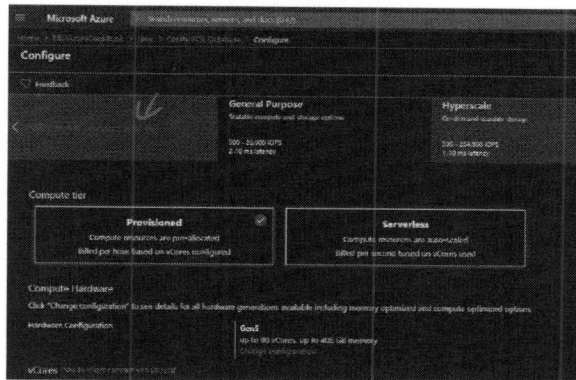

Figure 2.9 – Change server capacity

- Select **Basic**.

- On the **Create SQL Database** blade, click on **Networking**. The **Networking** blade appears as shown in the following screenshot:

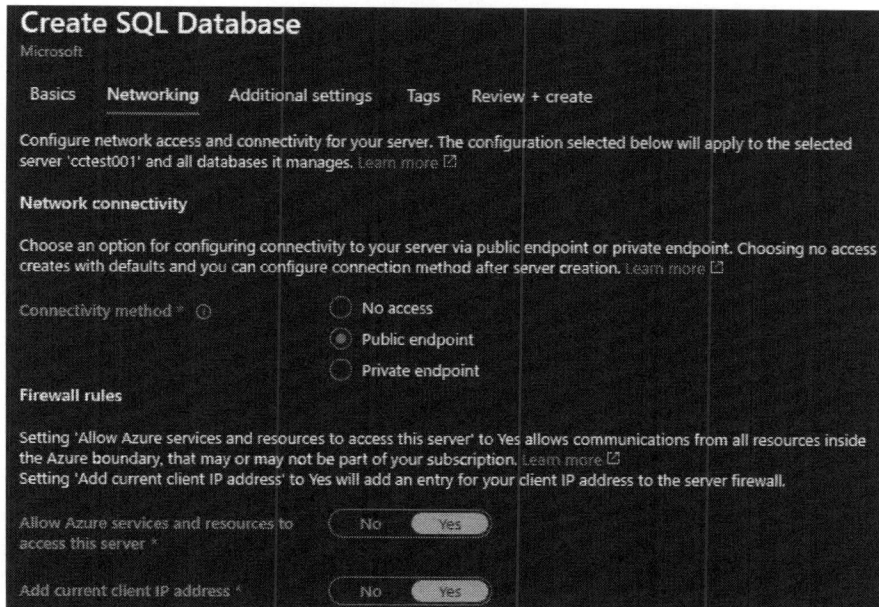

Figure 2.10 – Server Networking blade

- Set **Connectivity method** to **Public endpoint**.

- In the **Firewall rules** section, set **Allow Azure services and resources to access this server** to **Yes**. This will be needed in later chapters when we use Azure services such as Azure Data Factory.

- Also, set **Add current client IP address** to **Yes**. This will whitelist your current PC IP address and therefore allow you to connect to the database using **SQL Server Management Studio (SSMS)** and **SQL Server Integration Services (SSIS)**.

- Click on **Additional settings**.

- The **Additional settings** blade appears. In the **Use existing data** setting, click on **Sample** as shown in the following screenshot:

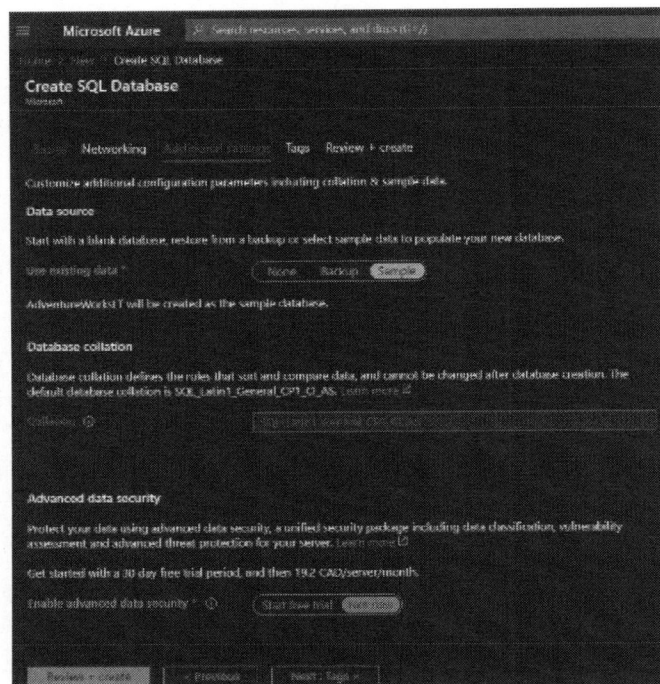

Figure 2.11 – Server Additional settings

- Click on **Review + create** and then **Create** to create the database.

8. Now, we'll check whether the sample database has been created correctly. Go into the resource group and click on the **AdventureWorksLT (etlinazurecookbook/ AdventureWorksLT)** resource. The database blade opens. As shown in the following screenshot, click on **Query editor (preview)**:

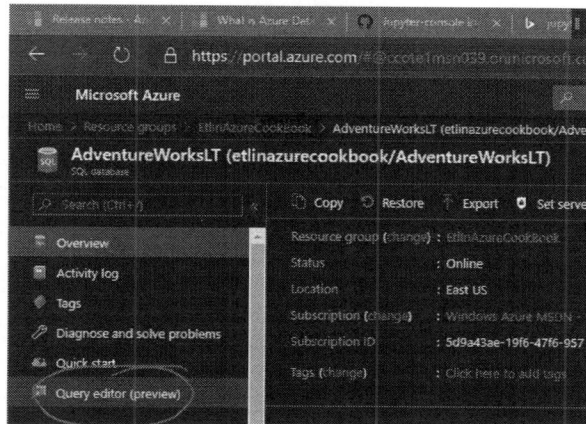

Figure 2.12 – Database query editor

Enter the login and password. The query editor opens. Expand the **Tables** folder, right-click on any table, and click **Select Top 1000 Rows** from the submenu that appears, as shown in the following screenshot:

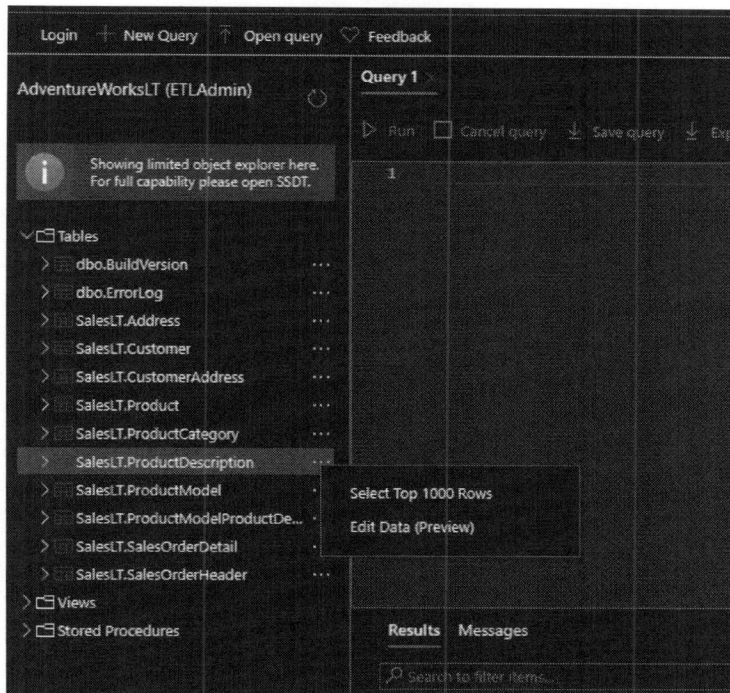

Figure 2.13 – Database Select Top 1000 Rows

9.   Click the **Run** button to execute the query.

Let's move on to the next section!

How it works...

We created a SQL server in Azure and we stored a sample database on it: **AdventureWorksLT**. Everything was done using a web browser, with no need to install anything on a PC. The next recipes will show how to use that database with on-premises software.

Connecting SQL Management Studio to Azure SQL

This recipe will show you how to connect to our Azure SQL database from your computer.

Getting ready

This recipe assumes that you have installed SSMS.

How to do it...

This is a very short and simple recipe! Let's begin by opening SSMS:

1. We're going to connect to the Azure database that we created in the previous recipe, *Creating a SQL Azure database*. Log into your Azure subscription and navigate to the **ETLInAzureCookBook** resource group.

2. Click on the **AdventureWorksLT** SQL database to open its blade. Copy the server name found at the top right as shown in the following screenshot:

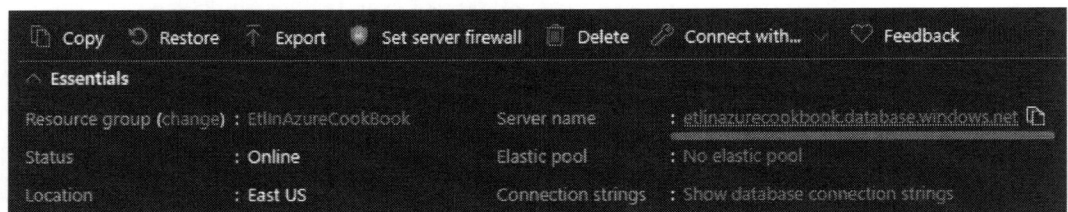

Figure 2.14 – Get the server name from the Azure subscription

3. Using SSMS, log into the server using the username and password that we used in *Step 7* of the previous recipe: *Creating a SQL Azure database*. Once connected, the Object Explorer shows the database and its related objects. Expanding the **Tables** folder lists all the tables, as shown in the following screenshot:

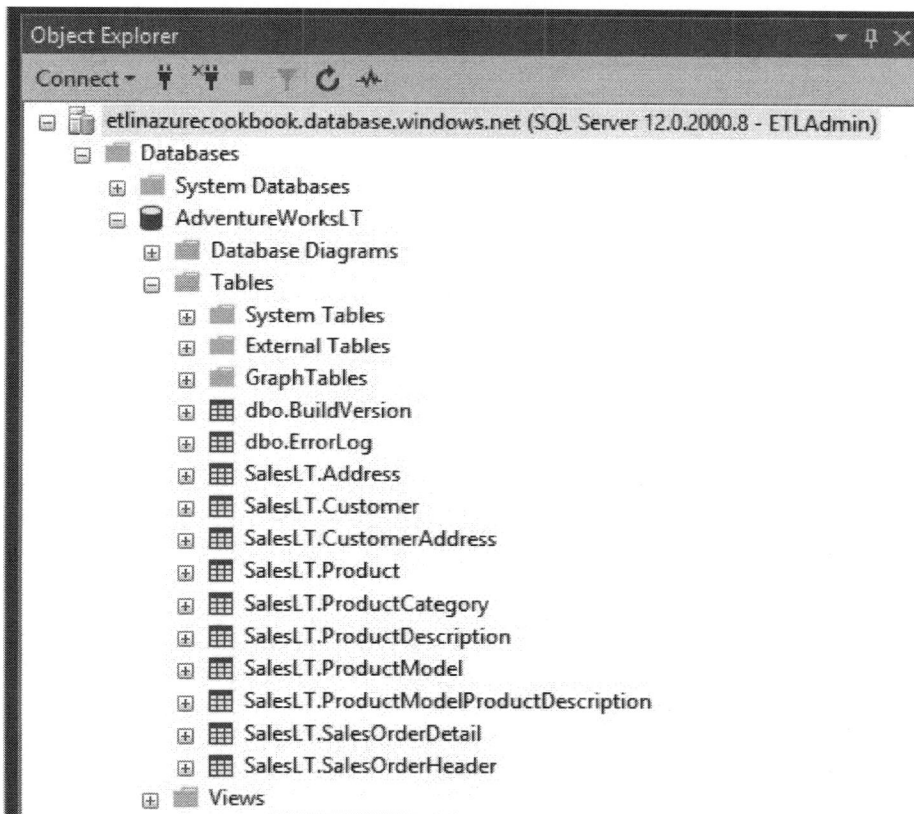

Figure 2.15 – Azure SQL SSMS Object Explorer

That's it! We have connected to our Azure SQL server from an on-premises program.

How it works...

Connecting to a SQL Azure database is not as simple as a regular on-premises database. We must open firewall rules to access the database on-premises. This is done by design to prevent any malicious data from accessing our data in Azure. But, once we are connected, we can query the data as simply as if it was a regular SQL Server database on-premises.

Creating a simple ETL package

This recipe will show you how to build a simple ETL package that does the following:

- Extract data from the **AdventureWorksLT SalesLT.Customer** table.
- Transform data: Concatenating all customer-name-related information into a single column called **FullName**.
- Load the data into a new table called **SalesLT.CustomerFullName**.

The table we create will be used in the final recipe in this chapter, *Loading data before its transformation*, to explain ELT.

Getting ready

This recipe assumes that you have installed SSMS, Visual Studio 2019, and SSIS.

How to do it...

Let's begin by opening Visual Studio 2019:

1. Select **Create a new project** from the main screen.
2. Select **Integration Services Project** from the screen that appears, as shown in the following screenshot:

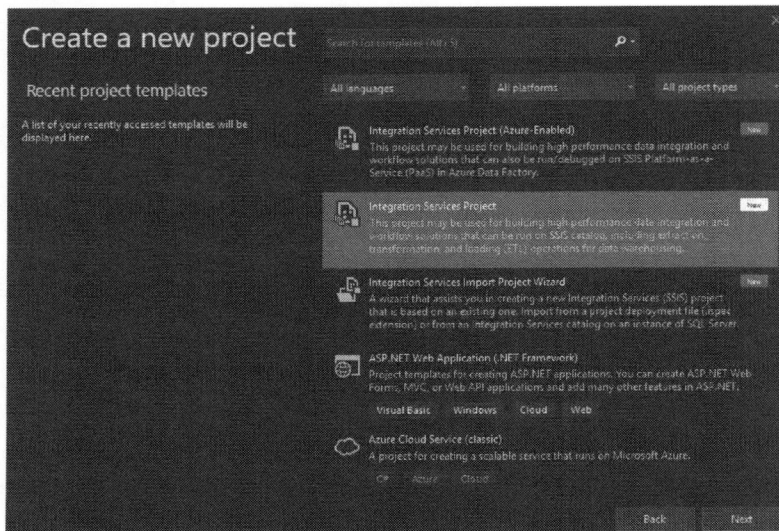

Figure 2.16 – Visual Studio – creating a new Integration Services Project

3. As shown in the following screenshot, name the project **AdventureWorksETL** and select a folder for it. Click **Create** to complete the project creation:

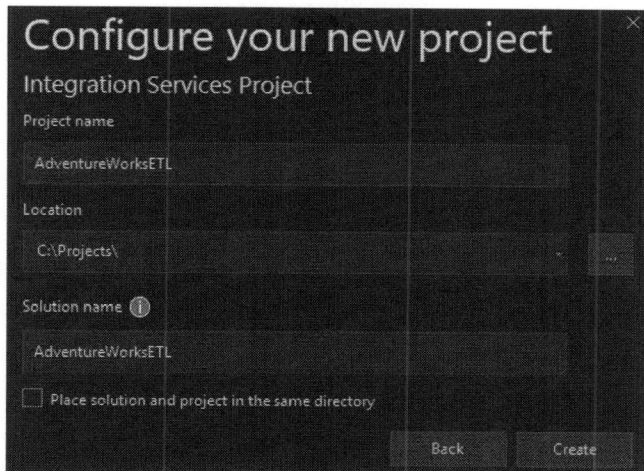

Figure 2.17 – SSIS project configuration

4. The project is created and opened, along with a package named **Package.dtsx**. Right-click in the **Connection Managers** section at the bottom of the package and select **New OLE DB Connection...** as shown in the following screenshot:

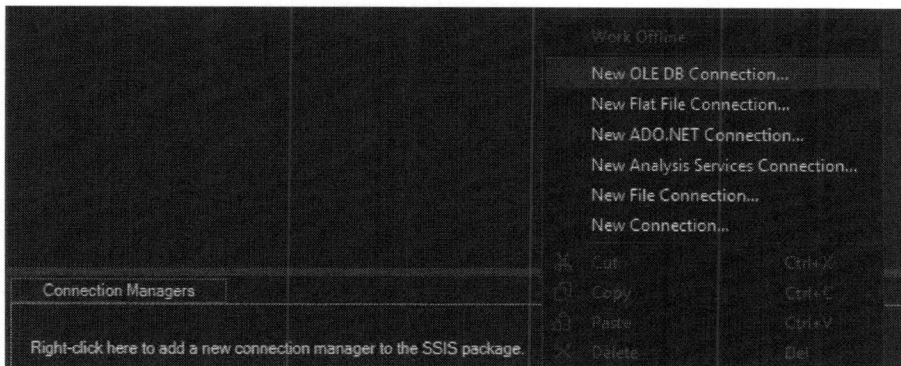

Figure 2.18 – Add a New OLE DB Connection

5. Click on **New....** Enter the database name, select **SQL Server Authentication**, and type the username and password. Select **AdventureWorksLT** as the database name and click on **OK**, as shown in the following screenshot:

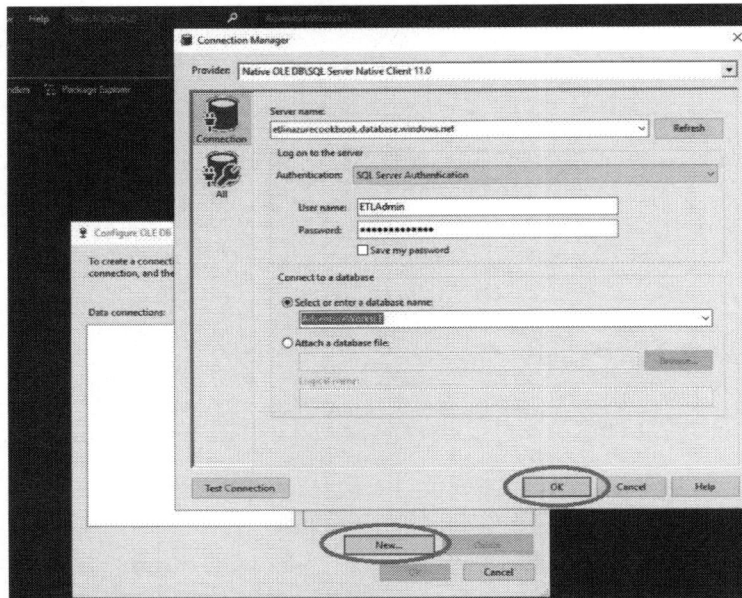

Figure 2.19 – New OLE DB connection configuration

6. Back on the connection manager configuration window, click on **OK** to complete the connection manager creation, as shown in the following screenshot:

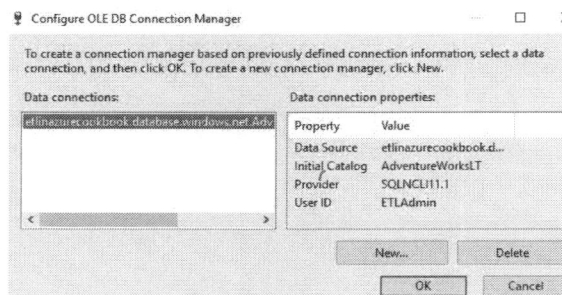

Figure 2.20 – New OLE DB connection

7. Click on the *F2* function key on your keyboard to rename the connection manager to **cmgr_etlinazurecookbook.database.windows.net.AdventureWorksLT. ETLAdmin**. We simply prefix the name with **cmgr_**. This is a standard naming convention in SSIS that allows package creation standards.

8. Right-click on the connection manager and select **Convert to Project Connection** from the contextual menu, as shown in the following screenshot:

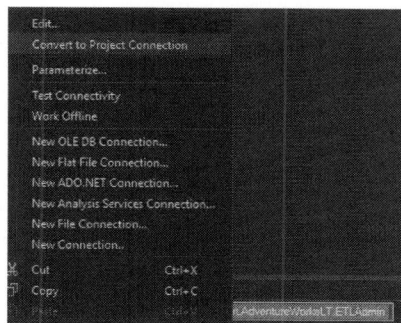

Figure 2.21 – Convert to Project Connection manager

Having a project connection manager makes the connection available on every package we create from now on. The connection manager will simply be present on all the packages in the project so we will not need to add a new connection, repeating the preceding steps, every time we add a new package to the project.

9. From the SSIS toolbox on the left, drag and drop a Data Flow Task onto the package surface. Name it **DFT_SalesLT_CustomerFullName**. This is a naming convention that indicates this dataflow is processing data for **SalesLT.CustomerFullName**.

10. Double-click on the Data Flow Task and add an **OleDB** data source from the **Other sources** section of the SSIS toolbox. Call it **OLEDBSRC_SalesLT_Customer**. This indicates that the source we are using is an OLEDB source, and extracts data from the **SalesLT.Customer** table.

11. Double-click on the OLEDB connection manager and set it to the one we created before. Set **Data access mode** to **SQL Command**. Then type the following SQL statement inside the **SQL command** textbox:

```
SELECT [CustomerID]
      ,[NameStyle]
      ,[Title]
      ,[FirstName]
      ,[MiddleName]
      ,[LastName]
      ,[Suffix]
  FROM [SalesLT].[Customer]
```

Click on **Preview** to ensure that the query works correctly. Click on **OK** to close the OLE DB source component.

12. Drag and drop a **Derived Column** transform onto the Data Flow and attach it to the OLE DB source created earlier. Rename it **DER_FullName**, indicating that this is adding a new column called **FullName** to the pipeline.

13. Double-click on it to open it. In the **Derived column name** field, type **FullName**. In the **Expression** field, type the following expression and click **OK**:

```
TRIM(REPLACENULL(Title,"") + " " +
REPLACENULL(FirstName,"") + " " +
TRIM(REPLACENULL(MiddleName,"") + " ") +
REPLACENULL(LastName,"") + " " + REPLACENULL(Suffix,""))
```

14. From **Other Destinations** in the SSIS toolbox, add an OLE DB destination to the Data Flow and attach it to the **DER_FullName** derived column transform created in *Step 13* of this recipe. Rename it **OLEDBDST_SalesLT_CustomerFullName** to indicate that we're loading data into the **SalesLT.CustomerFullName** table.

15. Double-click on it to open it. Make sure the **OLEDB connection manager** is set to the one we created before and **Table access mode** is set to **Table or view – fast load**.

16. Click on the **New...** button beside **Name of the table or the view** and set the properties as shown in the following screenshot:

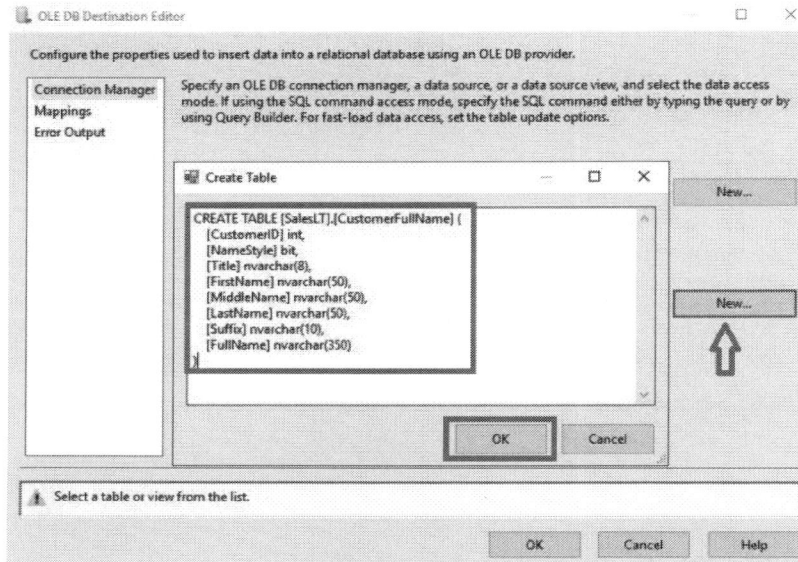

Figure 2.22 – Create a table in OLE DB Destination Editor

17. Make sure to use the table name [SalesLT].[CustomerFullName]. Failure to do so will fail other steps of the recipe. The SQL DDL script to create the table is the following:

```
CREATE TABLE [SalesLT].[CustomerFullName] (
    [CustomerID] int,
    [NameStyle] bit,
    [Title] nvarchar(8),
    [FirstName] nvarchar(50),
    [MiddleName] nvarchar(50),
    [LastName] nvarchar(50),
    [Suffix] nvarchar(10),
    [FullName] nvarchar(350)
)
```

18. Click on **OK** to close the **Create Table** window and return to the previous screen. Click on **Mappings** on the left of **OLE DB Destination Editor**. Your screen should look like the following screenshot. Click on **OK** to close the editor and return to the Data Flow Task:

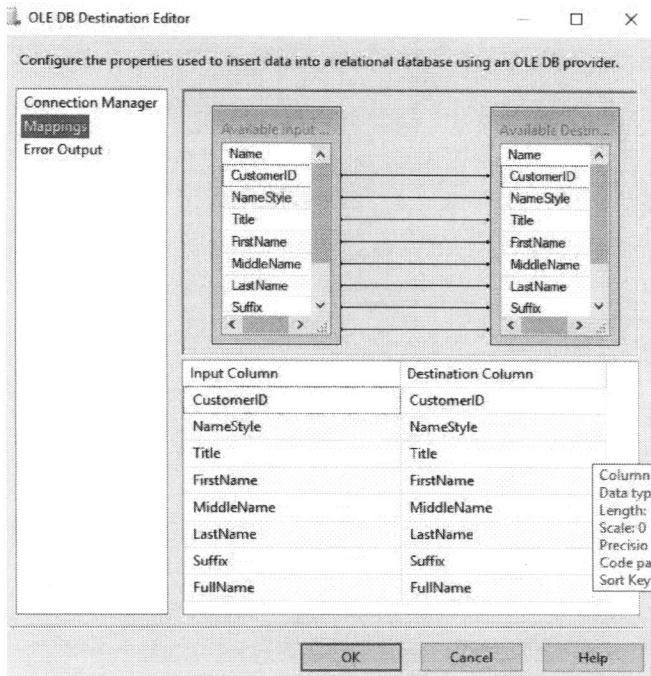

Figure 2.23 – Destination OLE DB Destination Editor Mapping tab

19. To correctly align the Data Flow content, right-click on the taskbar and select **Layout** from the submenu as shown in the following screenshot:

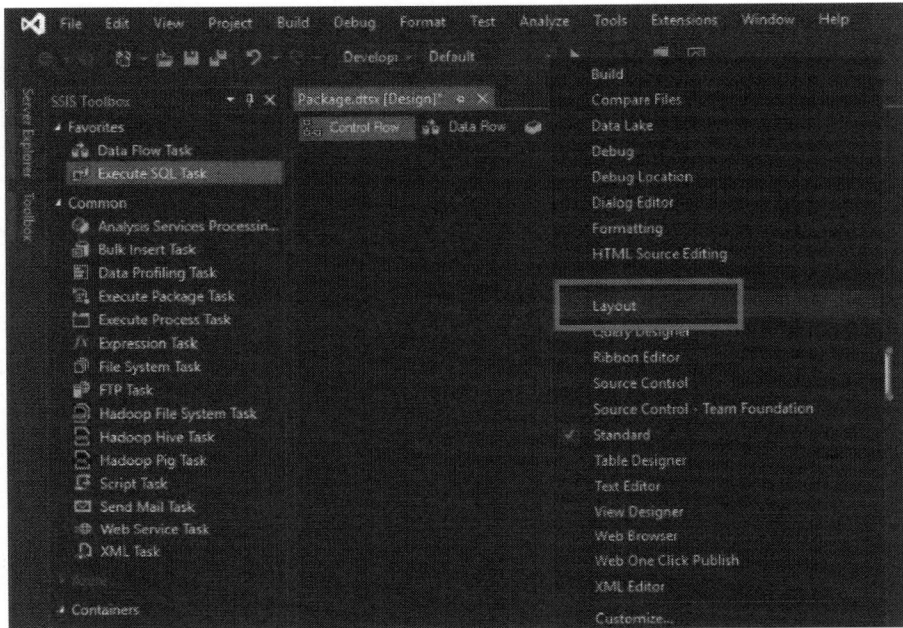

Figure 2.24 – Add a Layout button on the toolbar

20. Now, select all items in the Data Flow task (*Ctrl + A*) and click on the **Make same width** icon on the **Layout** toolbar.

21. For the final finishing touch, we'll auto-align all transforms on the Data Flow. From the **Format** menu, select **Auto Layout** and **Diagram** as shown in the following screenshot:

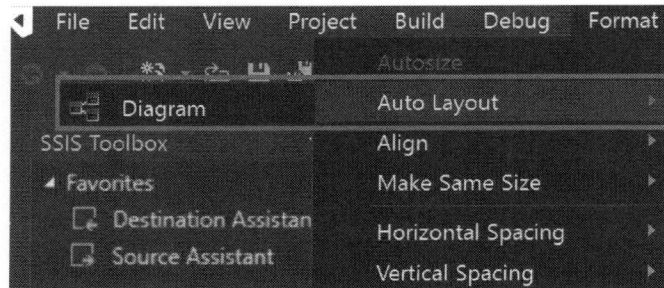

Figure 2.25 – Auto Layout Diagram menu selection

The Data Flow should now look like the following screenshot:

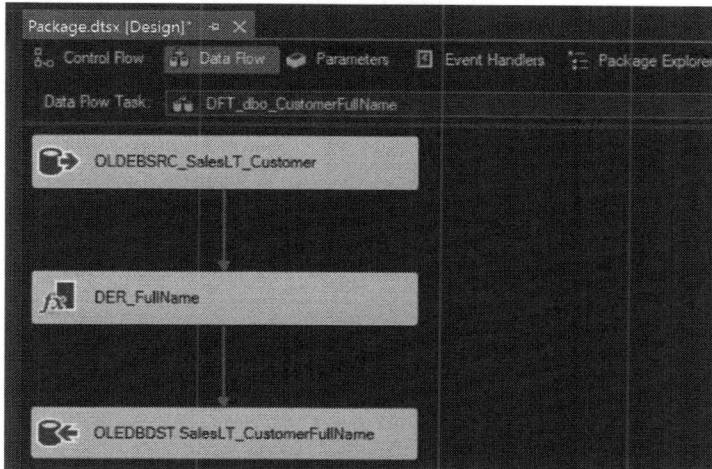

Figure 2.26 – Dataflow layout

22. Right-click on the arrow (path) between the **DER_FullName** transform and
OLEDBDST and select **Enable Data Viewer** as shown in the following screenshot:

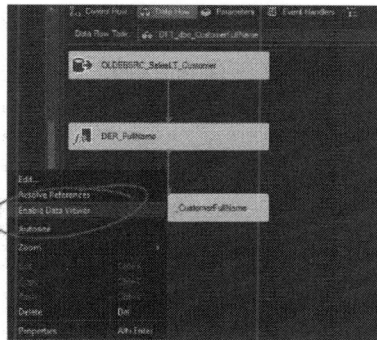

Figure 2.27 – Data Flow Enable Data Viewer

23. Close the **Data Viewer**. Now, right-click anywhere on the Data Flow task background and select **Execute Task** as shown in the following screenshot:

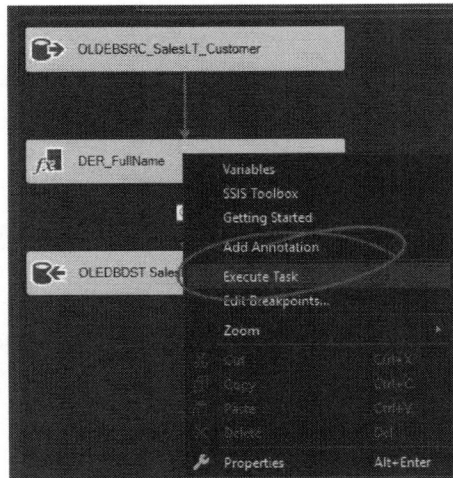

Figure 2.28 – Execute the dataflow

The Data Flow Task should execute successfully, and you should see the Data Viewer with the new column added as shown in the following screenshot:

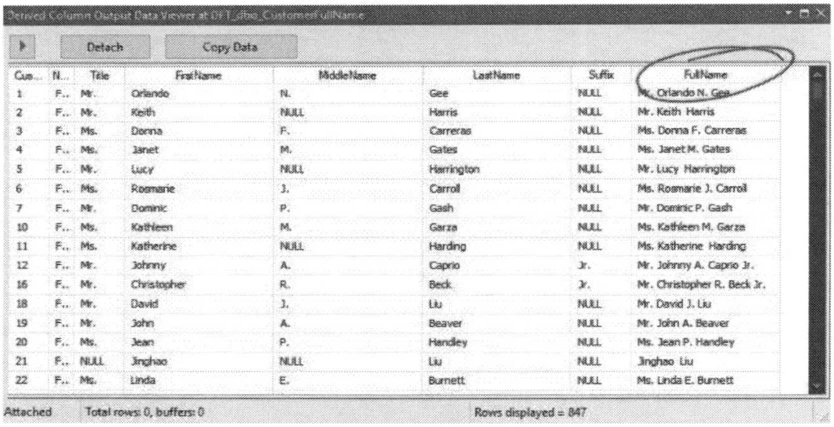

Figure 2.29 – Data Viewer during dataflow execution

24. Now, right-click on the path between the derived column and destination again to **Disable Data Viewer** as we don't need it anymore. Stop the execution of the Data Flow by clicking the **Stop** button.

25. As a final step, we'll make our package **idempotent**, that is, making sure that anytime we execute it, the destination data will be the same.

Go back to the package's control flow and add an **Execute T-SQL** task from the **Favorite Tasks** section of the SSIS toolbox. Double-click on it to open it. Set the properties as follows:

a) **Name: SQL_Truncate_SalesLT_CustomerFullName**

b) **Connection: the connection manager of the package**

c) **SQLSourceType: Direct Input**

d) **SQL Statement: TRUNCATE TABLE SalesLT.CustomerFullName**

Click on **OK** to close **Execute SQL Task Editor**. Back on the control flow, attach the Data Flow task to the **Execute SQL Task** just created.

26. Like we did for the Dataflow items, select both tasks and, from the **Layout** toolbar, click on **Make same width**. From the **Format** menu, select, **Format > Auto Layout > Diagram**. Your package should look like the following screenshot:

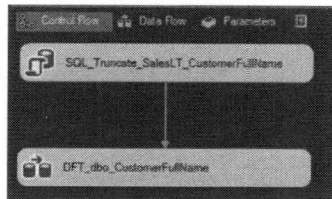

Figure 2.30 – Control flow after autolayout

27. Save the package, right-click on the package in the Solution Explorer (at the right of Visual Studio), and select **Rename** from the submenu. Rename the package to **SalesLT.CustomerFullName.dtsx**.

28. Finally, execute the package. Again, right-click on it and select **Execute package** from the submenu that appears. The package will execute, and your screen should look like the following screenshot:

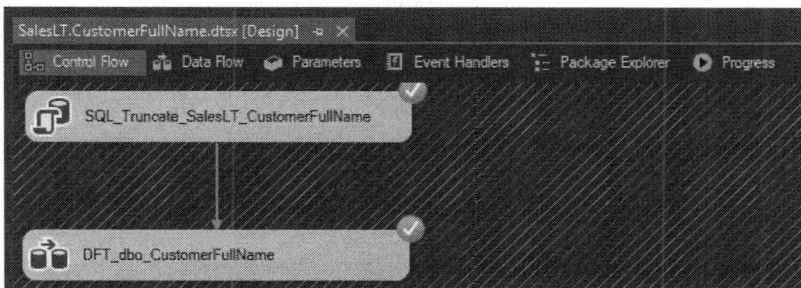

Figure 2.31 – Control flow after successful execution

How it works...

This recipe showed a simple ETL design pattern. Most ETL packages are more complex but they usually follow the same pattern: **Source > Transformation > Load** into a destination. The transformation phase is quite simple: it uses an expression to concatenate the name-related columns, taking care of the fact that the column may be NULL. The outer TRIM command takes care of the space at the front and end of the column because the **Title** and **Suffix** columns might be NULL. It is the same for the inner TRIM column that is taking care of the **NULL MiddleName** column.

Loading data before its transformation

ELT is very similar to ETL, but with a crucial difference: the order of the transform and load steps are inverted. This is very useful with big data in the cloud or when we do not have an ETL tool on-premises. This recipe will be much simpler than the previous one, as we'll implement ELT using a database, so no tools are involved here except for calling the ELT task.

It also relies on the previous recipe, *Creating a simple ETL package*, since we're going to use the **SalesLT.CustomerFullName** table data to implement the ELT pattern.

There are essentially two parts to this recipe:

1. Extract and load data into our data lake. Here, we don't have a real data lake; we're using **AdventureWorksLT** on Azure to mimic the data lake concept.

2. Transform the data inside the database using a simple SQL script. We're going to add the **FullName** column to the **SalesLT.Customer** table and update it using this script.

Getting ready

This recipe assumes that you have installed SSMS, Visual Studio 2019, and SSIS.

How to do it...

Let's dig into the recipe:

1. In the SSIS solution, right-click on the **SSIS packages** folder and select **New SSIS package**. Rename the package from **Package1** to **SalesLT.Customer**.

2. Drag and drop **Execute SQL Task** from the **Favorites** section of the SSIS toolbox onto the control flow and name it **SQL_ELT_SalesLT_Customer**.

3. We're going to add the **FullName** column to **SalesLT.Customer**. Open SSMS and connect it to our Azure database. Make sure that the context is set to the **AdventureWorksLT** database as shown in the following screenshot:

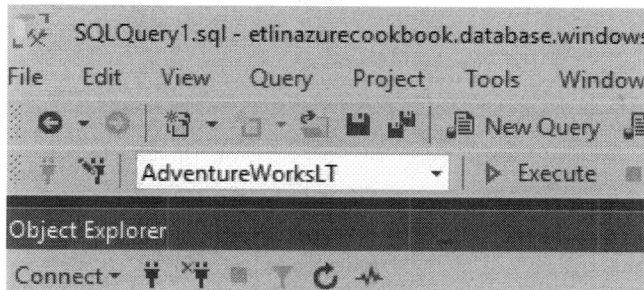

Figure 2.32 – SSMS AdventureWorksLT database context

4. In the query window, type the following DDL statement:

```
ALTER TABLE SalesLT.Customer ADD FullName NVARCHAR(350)
```

5. Execute the command and verify that the **FullName** column has been successfully added in the Object Explorer as shown in the following screenshot:

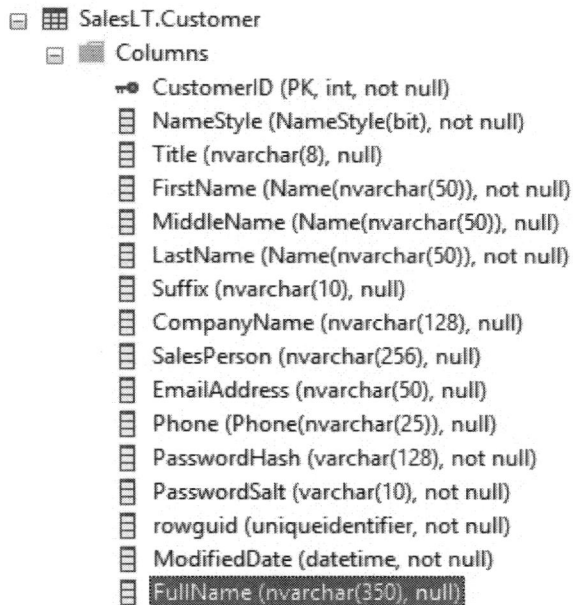

Figure 2.33 – SSMS Object Explorer FullName column

6. Go back to the SSIS package. Double-click on the **SQL_ELT_SalesLT_Customer** task to open **Execute SQL Task Editor**. Set the properties as follows:

a) **Connection**: **cmgr_etlinazurecookbook.database.windows.net. AdventureWorksLT.ETLAdmin**

b) **SQL SourceType**: **Direct input**

c) **SQL Statement**:

```
UPDATE c
SET FullName = cfn.FullName
FROM SalesLT.Customer AS c
INNER JOIN SalesLT.CustomerFullName as cfn
ON c.CustomerID = cfn.CustomerID;
```

Click on **OK** to close the editor and go back to the control flow.

7. Execute the package.

8. Go back into SSMS, create a new query, and type the following SQL statement:

```
SELECT [CustomerID]
      , [FullName]
      , [NameStyle]
      , [Title]
      , [FirstName]
      , [MiddleName]
      , [LastName]
      , [Suffix]
      , [CompanyName]
      , [SalesPerson]
      , [EmailAddress]
      , [Phone]
  FROM [SalesLT].[Customer]
```

The result should look like the following screenshot:

	CustomerID	FullName	NameStyle	Title	FirstName	MiddleName	LastName	Suffix	CompanyName	SalesPerson	EmailAddress	Phone
1	1	Mr. Orlando N.Gee	0	Mr.	Orlando	N.	Gee	NULL	A Bike Store	adventure-works\pamela0	orlando0@adventure-works.com	245-555-0173
2	2	Mr. Keith Harris	0	Mr.	Keith	NULL	Harris	NULL	Progressive Sports	adventure-works\david8	keith0@adventure-works.com	170-555-0127
3	3	Ms. Donna F Carreras	0	Ms.	Donna	F.	Carreras	NULL	Advanced Bike Components	adventure-works\jillian0	donna0@adventure-works.com	279-555-0130
4	4	Ms. Janet M.Gates	0	Ms	Janet	M.	Gates	NULL	Modular Cycle Systems	adventure-works\jillian0	janet1@adventure-works.com	710-555-0173
5	5	Mr. Lucy Harrington	0	Mr	Lucy	NULL	Harrington	NULL	Metropolitan Sports Supply	adventure-works\shu0	lucy0@adventure-works.com	828-555-0186
6	6	Ms. Rosmarie J.Carroll	0	Ms	Rosmarie	J.	Carroll	NULL	Aerobic Exercise Company	adventure-works\linda3	rosmarie0@adventure-works.com	244-555-0112
7	7	Mr. Dominic P.Gash	0	Mr	Dominic	P.	Gash	NULL	Associated Bikes	adventure-works\shu0	dominic0@adventure-works.com	192-555-0173
8	10	Ms. Kathleen M Garza	0	Ms	Kathleen	M.	Garza	NULL	Rural Cycle Emporium	adventure-works\jose1	kathleen0@adventure-works.com	150-555-0127
9	11	Ms. Katherine Harding	0	Ms	Katherine	NULL	Harding	NULL	Sharp Bikes	adventure-works\jose1	katherine0@adventure-works.com	926-555-0159
10	12	Mr. Johnny A.Caprio Jr.	0	Mr.	Johnny	A.	Caprio	Jr.	Bikes and Motorbikes	adventure-works\garrett1	johnny0@adventure-works.com	112-555-0191
11	16	Mr. Christopher R.Beck Jr.	0	Mr.	Christopher	R.	Beck	Jr.	Bulk Discount Store	adventure-works\jae0	christopher1@adventure-works.com	1 (11) 500 555-0132
12	18	Mr. David J.Liu	0	Mr.	David	J.	Liu	NULL	Catalog Store	adventure-works\michael9	david20@adventure-works.com	440-555-0132
13	19	Mr. John A.Beaver	0	Mr.	John	A.	Beaver	NULL	Center Cycle Shop	adventure-works\pamela0	john8@adventure-works.com	521-555-0195
14	20	Ms. Jean P.Handley	0	Ms.	Jean	P.	Handley	NULL	Central Discount Store	adventure-works\david8	jean1@adventure-works.com	582-555-0113
15	21	Jinghao Liu	0	N...	Jinghao	NULL	Liu	NULL	Chic Department Stores	adventure-works\jillian0	jinghao1@adventure-works.com	928-555-0116
16	22	Ms. Linda E.Burnett	0	Ms.	Linda	E.	Burnett	NULL	Travel Systems	adventure-works\jillian0	linda4@adventure-works.com	121-555-0121
17	23	Mr. Kerim Hanif	0	Mr.	Kerim	NULL	Hanif	NULL	Bike World	adventure-works\shu0	kerim0@adventure-works.com	216-555-0122
18	24	Mr. Kevin Liu	0	Mr.	Kevin	NULL	Liu	NULL	Eastside Department Store	adventure-works\linda3	kevin5@adventure-works.com	926-555-0164
19	25	Mr. Donald L.Blanton	0	Mr.	Donald	L.	Blanton	NULL	Coalition Bike Company	adventure-works\shu0	donald0@adventure-works.com	357-555-0161

Figure 2.34 – SSMS Query Editor result

How it works...

This recipe showed you the pattern of ELT. Data was **extracted** from the source first, then **loaded** into the database (as we saw in the previous recipe, *Creating a simple ETL package*). We then **transformed** the **SalesLT.Customer** data by using already loaded data.

3
Creating and Using SQL Server 2019 Big Data Clusters

In this chapter, you will learn how to prepare and deploy a **SQL Server 2019 Big Data Cluster**. You will learn how Big Data Clusters can be used in data management operations, implemented as **SQL Server Integration Services (SSIS)** solutions. We will show you how to use SSIS to load data into a Big Data Cluster **Hadoop Distributed File System (HDFS)** file store and how to perform basic data processing operations on the Spark platform, and we will finish the chapter by demonstrating how to retrieve data from a Big Data Cluster, to be used in a database hosted locally.

After you have created and deployed your new Big Data Cluster instance in Azure, we are also going to show you how to efficiently maintain your development environment by suspending specific Azure resources when they are not used, which will allow you to reduce the cost of your Azure subscription.

This chapter covers the following recipes that will get you started with Big Data Clusters:

- Creating a SQL Server 2019 Big Data Cluster
- Stopping and starting Azure resources

- Setting up a Big Data Cluster
- Loading data into a Big Data Cluster
- Extracting data from a Big Data Cluster

Technical requirements

The recipes in this chapter assume that you already have an appropriate development environment in place on your workstation, including a SQL Server 2019 instance, with the administration and development tools installed and access to a valid Azure subscription. All these prerequisites are covered in *Chapter 1* of this cookbook, entitled *Getting Started with Azure and SSIS 2019*.

> **Important note**
>
> The resources required by the Big Data Clusters service in Azure exceed the terms and restrictions of the **free** Azure subscription; therefore, you are going to need a **Pay-As-You-Go** Azure subscription in order to complete the recipes in this chapter. Make sure to remove the resources after you have completed all the recipes to reduce the cost of your subscription.

Instructions on how to upgrade your free Azure subscription are provided in the *Getting ready* section of this chapter's first recipe.

Creating a SQL Server 2019 Big Data Cluster

SQL Server 2019 Big Data Clusters represents a new feature of the SQL Server platform, combining specific services and resources used in efficiently managing and analyzing very large sets of mostly non-relational data, and allowing it to be used alongside relational data hosted in SQL Server databases. To achieve these principal objectives, Big Data Clusters implement a **highly scalable big-data storage** (**HDFS**) system, highly versatile querying capabilities (**Spark**), the power of distributed computing (**Kubernetes**), and a data virtualization infrastructure (**PolyBase**).

To deploy all the required features that represent a single Big Data Clusters instance, you can use multiple physical—or virtual—machines that can either be hosted on premises or in the cloud.

As we do not want you to carry the burden of providing the necessary infrastructure to host the Big Data Cluster instance yourself, you are going to make use of the **Azure Kubernetes Services** (**AKS**), hosted on a cluster of **Azure Virtual Machines** (**VMs**), providing data storage, computational capabilities, and connectivity, as well as management and monitoring.

The default **VM** size recommended to host a Big Data Cluster is the *ESv3* standard, memory-optimized Azure VM with *eight* CPU cores, running the Linux operating system. **Five** VMs are required to host an AKS instance used by a SQL Server 2019 Big Data Cluster instance.

> **Important note**
> Before using Azure VMs or setting up an AKS instance, you should also be familiar with the cost of hosting these resources in Azure. You can find more information at `https://azure.microsoft.com/en-gb/pricing/details/virtual-machines/linux/`.

Getting ready

The configuration and deployment of a Big Data Cluster hosted on AKS are fully integrated into **Azure Data Studio** (**ADS**); therefore, you will complete most of the following activities in ADS.

> **Important note**
> Due to the restrictions of the free trial subscription, you will also need access to a **Pay-As-You-Go** Azure subscription.

If you do not have access to a **Pay-As-You-Go** Azure subscription that you will be able to use for the recipes in this book, you can upgrade the free subscription that you created in *Chapter 1, Getting Started with Azure and SSIS 2019*.

1. To upgrade your free Azure subscription, log in to the Azure portal at `https://portal.azure.com/`.

2. On the **Home** page, select **Subscriptions**.

3. On the **Subscriptions** page, select the **Free Trial** subscription that you should have already created in *Chapter 1, Getting Started with Azure and SSIS 2019*.

4. On the subscription overview page, click **Upgrade** to start the upgrade procedure.

   It should take a few moments to check the state of your current subscription.

5. On the **Upgrade** page, enter a friendly name of your new **Pay-As-You-Go** subscription (for instance, `ETL in Azure Cookbook`), and then check the **No technical support** option, meaning that you do not want to add a support plan to your subscription.

> **Important note**
>
> The no-support plan should be good enough for typical development and testing purposes and is certainly good enough for the recipes in this book. However, for production use, and especially for enterprise-level development activities, one of the other plans would probably be much more appropriate.
>
> You can learn more about Azure subscription support plans from the vendor documentation, available at `https://azure.microsoft.com/en-us/support/plans/`.

When ready, click **Upgrade** to continue. Your payment information will be verified, and you might have to update it, so keep your credit card handy. When the upgrade is completed, a new message will appear in your **Azure Notifications** area.

Before even attempting to deploy a Big Data Cluster to Azure, you should also be familiar with the current resource restrictions in your region. As explained in the introduction to this recipe, you are going to need **five** standard *ESv3* VMs with *8* CPU cores each, for a total of *40* cores. You can check the resource quotas by following these steps:

6. On the Azure portal, open the **Azure PowerShell** pane by clicking the **Cloud Shell** icon, located to the right of the search text box, as shown in the following screenshot:

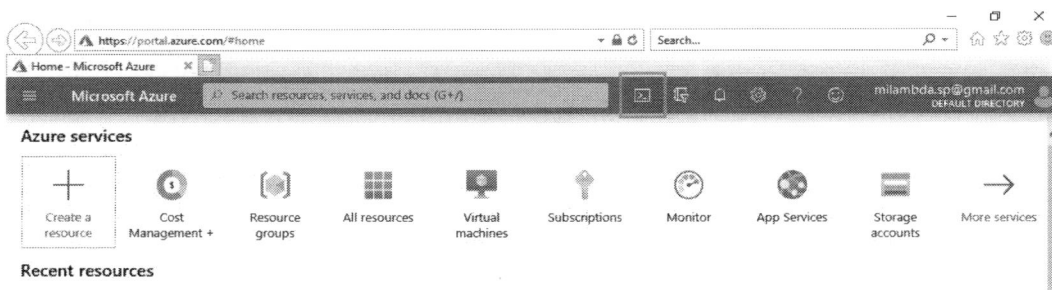

Figure 3.1 – Accessing PowerShell in the Azure portal

7. A Terminal pane should open at the bottom of the browser window, as shown in the following screenshot:

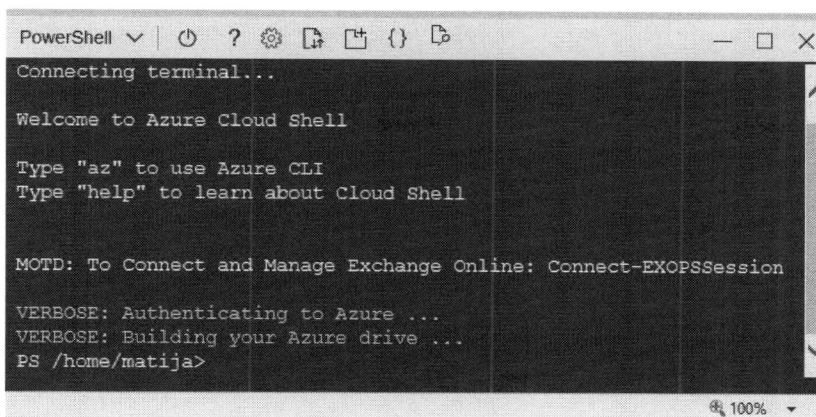

Figure 3.2 – The Azure PowerShell pane

If **PowerShell** is not the selected language, select it from the list box, located on the far left of the **Cloud Shell** menu.

8. Use the following PowerShell command to check the current quotas in the East US region:

```
Get-AzVMUsage -Location "East US"
```

These instructions assume that you are interested in the current quotas in this particular region, as they will also be used later in the recipe. To check the quotas in a different region, replace the value of the Location argument before executing the command.

9. In the results returned by the Get-AzVMUsage command, locate the Standard ESv3 Family vCPUs counter:

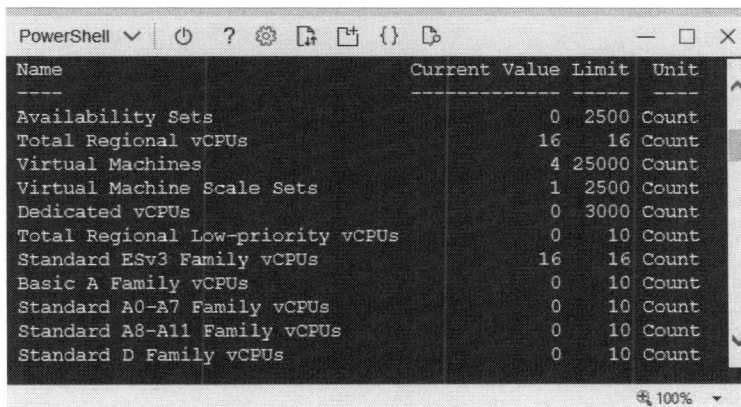

Figure 3.3 – The result returned by the Get-AzVMUsage command

> **Important note**
>
> If the `Limit` column value is less than *40*, you will have to request a quota increase by sending a support case request to the administrators. Relevant information about this is available in the online vendor documentation, at `https://docs.microsoft.com/en-us/azure/azure-portal/supportability/per-vm-quota-requests`.
>
> You only need to request a quota increase for the number of **virtual central processing units (vCPUs)** in the selected region (`eastus`, by default) to *40* for the *ESv3* family of Azure VMs for the subscription you created in *Chapter 1, Getting Started with Azure and SSIS 2019*. No other requests should be needed in order to complete the recipes in this chapter.

Until the current resource restrictions allow you to deploy the necessary number of VMs of the recommended size, you will not be able to continue with this recipe.

Support cases with a minimal-impact severity are resolved within 8 business hours, but are often resolved within minutes (of course, depending on how busy the support team is at the given time).

You are also going to need a place on your workstation where specific files needed in this chapter will be kept:

1. By using Windows Explorer, create a new folder named `ETL-with-Azure` on the `C:\` drive of your workstation.

2. Inside the new folder, create a folder for this chapter, named `Chapter03`, and inside that one, create two additional folders, named `BDC` and `Files`:

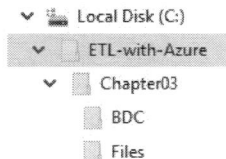

Figure 3.4 – The ETL-with-Azure folder and its contents

The preceding screenshot shows how the folders need to be organized.

3. Use your favorite internet browser, and connect to the GitHub location for this cookbook at `https://github.com/PacktPublishing/ETL-with-Azure-Cookbook`.

If you have not done so yet, clone the cookbook repository to the default location on your workstation.

4. Locate the `/Chapter03/Files` folder in your local clone of the cookbook repository and copy them to the `C:\ETL-with-Azure\Chapter03\Files` folder you created earlier.

You now have all the prerequisites in place to start with the first recipe.

How to do it...

You are going to use ADS to activate a new service in your Azure trial subscription—namely, an AKS cluster. You will then configure the newly created AKS cluster to host a SQL Server 2019 Big Data Cluster.

1. Start ADS, unless already open, and on the **Welcome** page, click **Deploy a server** to start the deployment procedure. If the **Welcome** page is closed, you can open it by using the `Welcome` command located in the **Help** menu.

2. In the **Select the deployment options** window, select **SQL Server Big Data Cluster** as the deployment type, **SQL Server 2019** as the **Version**, and **New Azure Kubernetes Service Cluster** as the **Deployment target**:

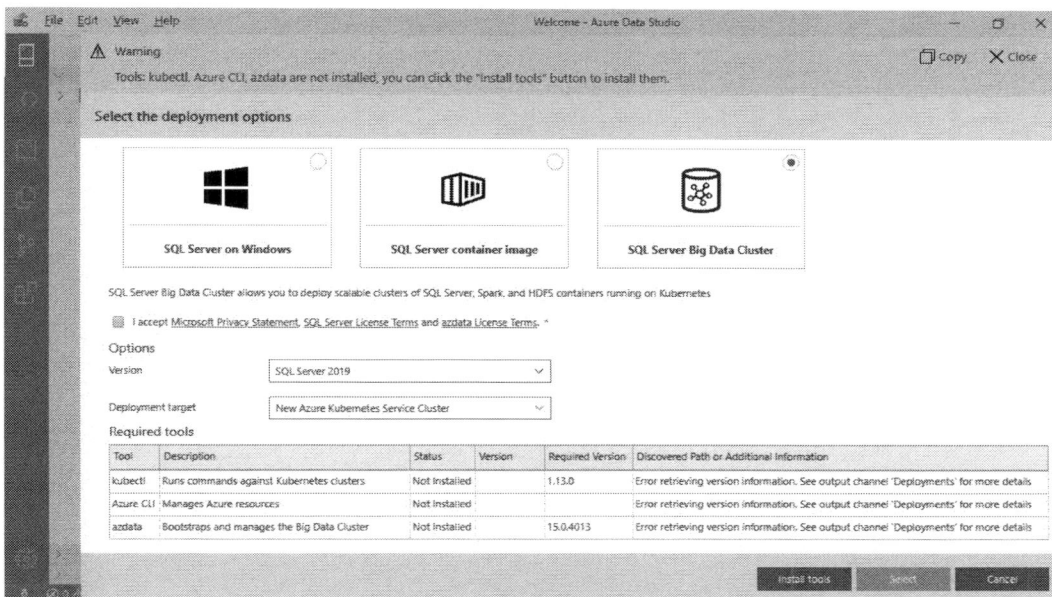

Figure 3.5 – The SQL Server 2019 Big Data Cluster deployment options

When deploying a Big Data Cluster for the first time, there should also be a warning displayed at the top of the window, saying that certain required tools have not yet been installed. If any tools are missing, as shown in the preceding screenshot, click **Install tools** to correct this, and then wait a few minutes for the installation to complete.

During the installation, when prompted by the **Windows User Account Control** to allow the applications to make changes to your device, click **Yes** to continue.

> **Tip**
> You should use this time to familiarize yourself with the Microsoft **Privacy Statement** and the **License Terms**. Follow the links above the deployment options to access the documents.

3. When all required tools have been installed successfully (marked by the status **Installed** in the **Required Tools** table), accept the privacy statement and license terms, and click **Select** to continue. It should take about a minute to load the deployment configurations and start the deployment wizard.

4. On the **Deployment configuration profile** page, make sure the **aks-dev-test** deployment configuration profile is selected. In this test deployment, you will not need any **High Availability (HA)** features.

    When ready, click **Next** to continue.

5. On the **Azure settings** page, leave the **Subscription id** text box empty so that the default Azure subscription will be used, and use the following values for the other settings:

    a) **New resource group name**: `etlinazure-ch-3`

    b) **Location**: `eastus`

    `East US` is the default location in the template; additional locations with the version of AKS on offer are available. You can access the complete list by clicking **View available Azure locations**.

> **Tip**
> Generally, the location should be determined based on its proximity to the location where the services you plan on hosting in Azure are going to be used—for instance, the proximity to the end users, if the services are to be accessed by the end users directly; or, the proximity of your on-premises location, if your organization is the principal consumer.

For development and testing purposes, the default location should be good enough, but you can select any other location if you prefer:

a) **AKS cluster name**: `etlinazure-ch-3-aks`

b) **VM count**: 5

c) **VM size**: `Standard_E8s_v3`

When ready, click **Next** to continue.

6. On the **Cluster settings** page, use `etlinazure-ch-3-aks-cluster` as the cluster name, leave **admin** as the administrator username, and assign a password for the administrator account.

   Leave all the **Docker settings** unchanged.

   When ready, click **Next** to continue.

7. On the **Service settings** page, leave all default settings unchanged.

   When ready, click **Next** to continue.

8. On the **Summary** page, review all the configuration settings, and make sure that they match the preceding instructions. Use the **Previous** and **Next** buttons to navigate through the pages of the wizard if you need to make any changes.

   If all the settings are correct, click **Save config files** to save the configuration to the local disk of your workstation. Save the files to the `C:\ETL-with-Azure\Chapter03\BDC` folder.

   When ready, click **Script to Notebook**, after which the wizard generates a new notebook with a script based on the configuration settings you provided earlier.

9. If this is the first time that you have used a Python Notebook, the **Configure Python for Notebooks** dialog should open.

   Either select **New Python installation** as the installation type or specify the folder where an existing Python installation is located.

   When ready, click **Install** to continue.

   The download and installation procedure should take a few minutes to complete.

   During the installation, you might be prompted to upgrade any installed Python packages.

   Click **Yes** to confirm the upgrade.

   When the installation completes, the results will be displayed in the **Tasks** pane.

10. The `deploy-bdc-aks` Python Notebook should now be open in ADS. Using the *Ctrl + S* shortcut on your keyboard, or by selecting **Save** from the **File** menu, save the Notebook to the `C:\ETL-with-Azure\Chapter03\BDC` folder.

    Inspect it, and then click **Run Cells** in the Notebook editor menu to execute the scripts.

    As no Azure subscription ID was supplied during the configuration, a browser window will open, prompting you to sign into your Azure account. Use the account you created in *Chapter 1, Getting Started with Azure and SSIS 2019*, with the corresponding credentials. The browser window might open in the background, so pay attention to that.

    The installation might take several minutes to complete; patience is advised.

    While the installation is in progress, the process might not return any messages; however, the first message returned should contain the command line that you can execute in a Windows Command Prompt window to track the current progress.

    After the installation has completed, the notebook should log you in to the newly created Big Data Cluster and retrieve the endpoint addresses. Some of the information returned in the results will be needed later; therefore, save the Notebook again—this time including the most recent results so that the information retrieved during the installation is now available in the Notebook for later use.

    > **Tip**
    >
    > One of the significant benefits provided by Notebooks is the ability to not only display the results of the operations inside the Notebook but also to have them saved into a file to be looked at later.

11. If the execution completed successfully, a new **Click here to connect to SQL Server Master instance** hyperlink should appear at the bottom of the Notebook, as shown in the following screenshot:

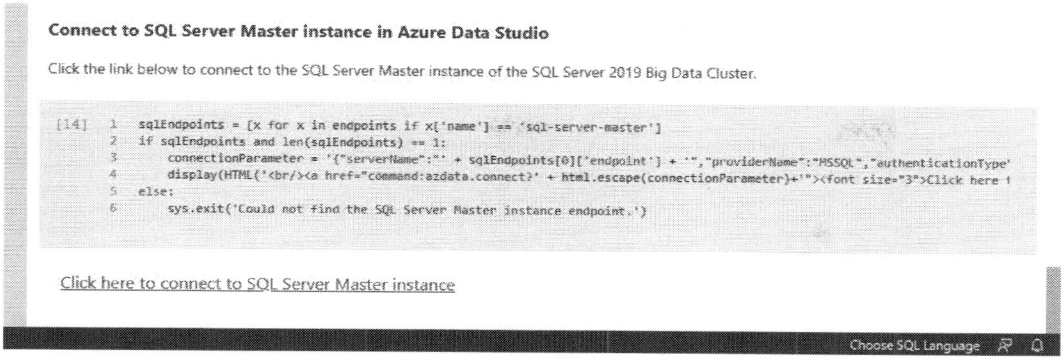

Connect to SQL Server Master instance in Azure Data Studio

Click the link below to connect to the SQL Server Master instance of the SQL Server 2019 Big Data Cluster.

```
[14]  1   sqlEndpoints = [x for x in endpoints if x['name'] == 'sql-server-master']
      2   if sqlEndpoints and len(sqlEndpoints) == 1:
      3       connectionParameter = '{"serverName":"' + sqlEndpoints[0]['endpoint'] + '","providerName":"MSSQL","authenticationType'
      4       display(HTML('<br/><a href="command:azdata.connect?' + html.escape(connectionParameter)+'"><font size="3">Click here 1
      5   else:
      6       sys.exit('Could not find the SQL Server Master instance endpoint.')
```

Click here to connect to SQL Server Master instance

Choose SQL Language

Figure 3.6 – Connecting to the SQL Server master instance from the deployment Notebook

Follow the link. It might take a few moments for the connection to be made, so patience is advised. Once the connection has been made, the information about the SQL Server master instance of your first Big Data Cluster should appear in a new ADS tab.

12. In the left column of the tab, under **Monitoring**, click **SQL Server Big Data Cluster** to view the properties of your Big Data Cluster, as shown in the following screenshot:

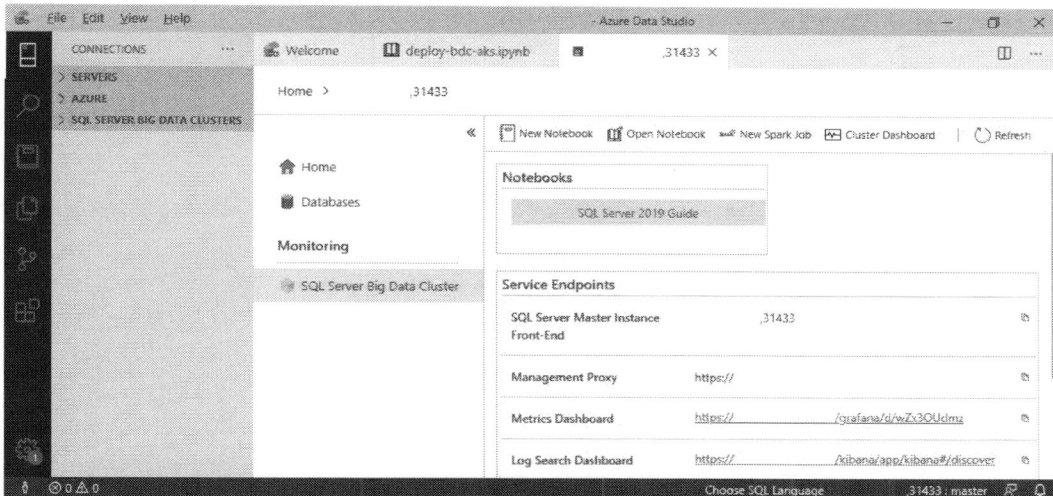

Figure 3.7 – Checking the Big Data Cluster instance after the deployment

13. In the window's menu ribbon, select **Cluster Dashboard**. After a few minutes, the current state of all of the parts of your newly created Big Data Cluster should be displayed, as shown in the next screenshot:

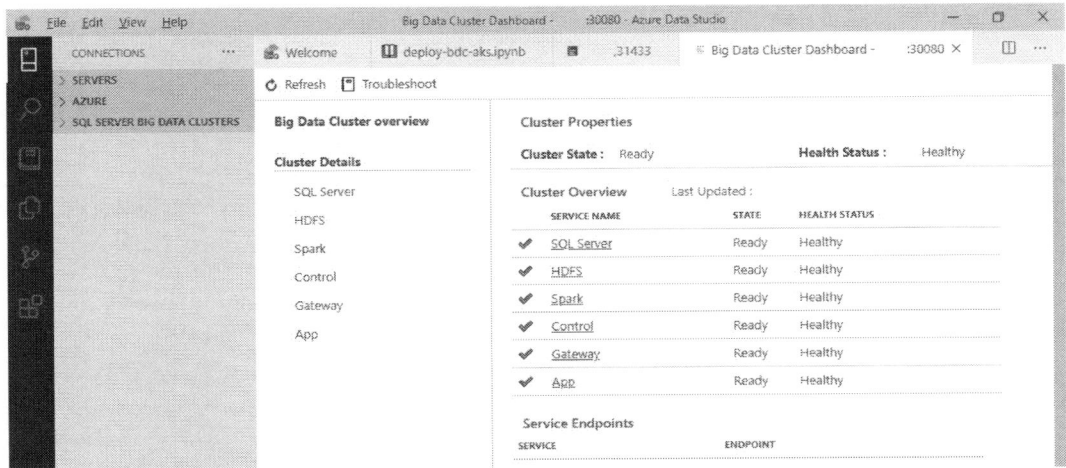

Figure 3.8 – The Big Data Cluster dashboard

In normal circumstances, all six elements should be in the **Ready** state, with a **Healthy** health status.

If this is not the case, you can try following the link to the problematic item and running a troubleshooting operation for it.

Depending on the exact situation, eventually the only successful remedy might be simply to remove the entire **Resource Group** from your trial subscription and start over.

14. Return to the ADS tab with the Big Data Cluster properties. As you can see in the ADS tab shown in *Figure 3.7*, all the endpoints use the **secure HTTP protocol (HTTPS)** in their **Uniform Resource Locators (URLs)**; however, no certificates are installed on these endpoints by default. This prevents client applications from connecting to the endpoints securely. In the **Notebooks** section of the current tab, click **SQL Server 2019 Guide** to open the **SQL Server 2019 Big Data Clusters Operations and Support** Jupyter Notebook. This Notebook provides access to a number of additional Notebooks that you can use to manage your SQL Server 2019 Big Data Clusters—for instance, to monitor, analyze, troubleshoot, and repair the installation.

15. In the **Chapters** section of the Notebook, click **Certificate Management** to open the set of notebooks used for **Certificate Management**.

16. In the **Notebooks in this Chapter** section of the **Certificate Management** notebook, locate the **CER100 - Configure Cluster with Self Signed Certificates** link, and follow the link to open the corresponding Notebook.

> **Tip**
>
> For development and testing purposes, you can safely use self-signed certificates to secure the communication between the server and the client applications; however, in a production environment, you would normally use a certificate issued by a **Root Certificate Authority** (**CA**). To use an existing Root CA certificate, you can use the **CER101 - Configure Cluster with Self Signed Certificates using existing Root** CA Python notebook, instead of the CER100 one.

17. When the CER100 - Configure Cluster with Self Signed Certificates Python notebook loads, inspect it, and then click **Run Cells** in the ADS tab menu to execute the script.

    Unfortunately, during the execution, you might run into one or more problems:

    a) If the execution of the main notebook (the **CER100**) should fail (for instance, when executing the Run the notebooks cell), you can work around this problem by executing each of the associated notebooks individually instead. They are listed in the correct order in the **Related** section of the main notebook; their names begin with **CER** (you can skip the **CAN100** notebook).

    b) If the execution of an individual notebook should fail, inspect the error messages returned by the failed cell execution. These might contain references to additional notebooks that you can use to solve the problem. After loading and running any additional notebooks, repeat the execution of the previously failed notebook—depending on the particular notebook, you might have to run all cells, or run each individual cell, starting with the one that originally failed.

    c) The Install the Root CA cell in the CER010 - Install generated Root CA locally notebook will use PowerShell to download the certificate to be installed on your workstation. Pay attention to the PowerShell window, as it might open in the background; it opens a dialog asking you to confirm the installation of the certificate. The execution will not continue until you respond.

    After all the notebooks have been executed successfully, the certificates will be installed on all the endpoints of your Big Data Cluster as well as on your workstation, which should now allow client applications to connect.

If by any chance you do get stuck when running the notebooks and find yourself unable to solve a particular problem, please contact Microsoft Support; they might be able to assist you further.

> **Important note**
>
> When using self-signed certificates to secure server resources (for instance, endpoints), such certificates are not trusted by client applications as their validity cannot be proven through an appropriate CA. This might prevent client applications from using the secured resource altogether.
>
> For instance, internet browsers or browser-based client applications will warn the user of these circumstances and might require user interaction before a connection can be made. Non-browser client applications, on the other hand, might be able to establish the connection with such a resource in a secure way, as long as they have access to the information needed in establishing trust.
>
> The **CER010** notebook installs the self-signed certificate on your workstation in a secure way, and thus makes the necessary information available to the client applications running on your workstation.

How it works...

You have just deployed a **SQL Server 2019 Big Data Cluster** to Azure, using AKS to host it. You will use this resource later in this chapter to load data into the cloud, process it, and then retrieve the results to be loaded into an on-premises database.

> **Important note**
>
> The resource that you just created in your Azure subscription **is not free**; you are already being charged for its use. To reduce the cost of your subscription, we recommend that you complete *Steps 1* through *4* of the next recipe, *Stopping and starting Azure resources*.

Stopping and starting Azure resources

As noted several times throughout this cookbook, not all Azure resources or services are free; in fact, most of them represent commercial services (after all, Azure is hosted by a private company that—just like your organization, or you personally—while offering services to its clients for payment, represents a client to numerous other vendors, who also expect to be paid for their services).

In a production environment, where services are delivered to paying customers, you would normally only stop your resources during maintenance, or when they have been discontinued. However, in a development and testing environment, with no paying customers, you may wish to stop your resources simply to reduce cost.

> **Important note**
>
> Not every Azure resource can be suspended—some can only be deallocated when the resource that they are part of is deallocated, and some will only be deallocated when the resource they are a part of is deleted, or when they themselves are removed completely.

Getting ready

You are going to sign into your Azure subscription, locate the VMs used by your Big Data Cluster, and suspend them. You will finish the recipe by learning how to start them again.

Right now, your principal objective is to learn how to suspend the VMs. You will follow the second part of this recipe only when you actually need access to the Big Data Cluster in later recipes.

How to do it...

Use your favorite internet browser to log in to the Azure portal at `https://portal.azure.com/`.

1. On the **Home** page of the subscription you used in the previous recipe, entitled *Creating a SQL Server 2019 Big Data Cluster,* open the menu on the left, and locate the **All resources** item:

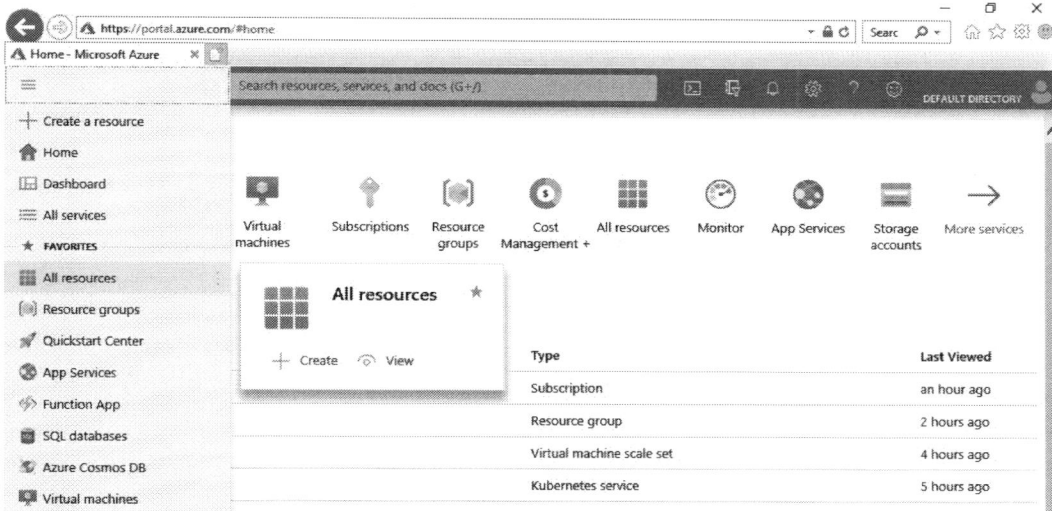

Figure 3.9 – Accessing All resources on the Azure portal

2. In the list of all your resources, locate the **VM Scale Set** (**VMSS**) that you created earlier (there should only be one) and follow the link to the resource's **Overview** page.

    The name of the VMSS used to host the Big Data Cluster that you created earlier in this chapter should begin with `aks-nodepool1-` and end with `-vmss`:

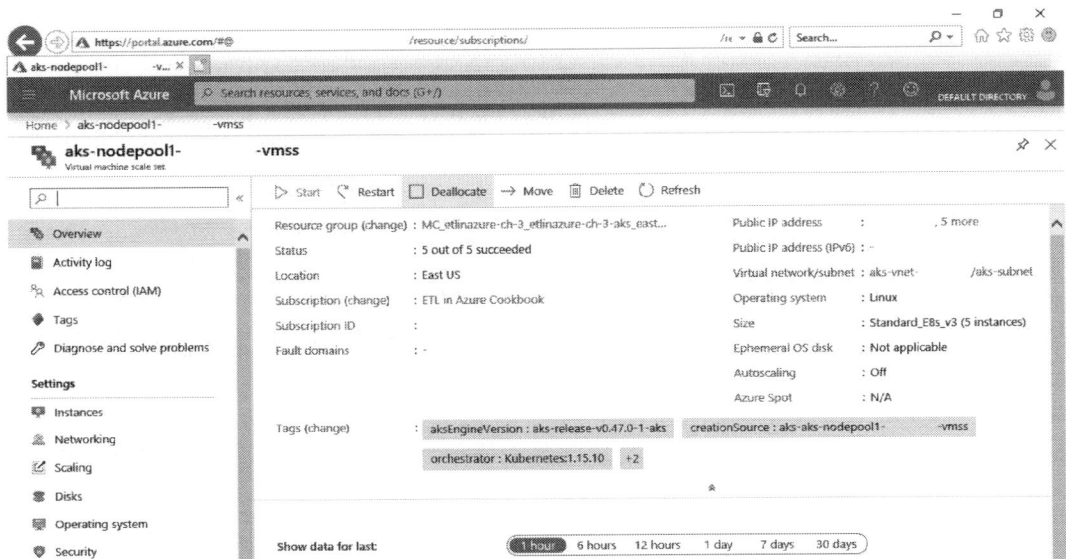

Figure 3.10 – Accessing the VMSS of an Azure Kubernetes installation

In the resource menu ribbon (not the browser menu, of course), click **Deallocate**.

3. A warning should appear, telling you that all of the VM instances will be deallocated when you deallocate the VMSS.

    As this is exactly what you want to do right now, click **Yes** to continue.

4. In the left column, under **Settings**, click **Instances**, to open information about the VM instances used by your Big Data Cluster.

    It should take a few minutes for the VMs to be suspended.

    In the resource menu, click **Refresh** to observe the current state of the instances:

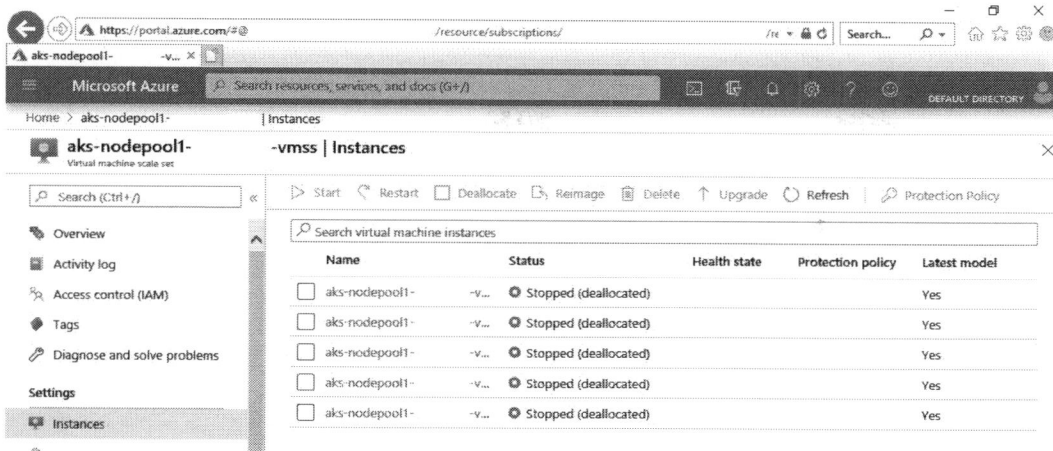

Figure 3.11 – The deallocated VM instances

Once the VMs have been suspended, their status should be **Stopped (deallocated)**. This means that your Big Data Cluster instance is offline and is no longer contributing to the cost of your subscription.

5. To start the Big Data Cluster again, you do this either by starting each of the VMs on the **Instances** page or by starting the entire VMSS on the **Overview** page.

   For instance, on the VMSS **Instances** page, check the box before each VM.

   Click **Start**, and the VMs should now return to their saved states. Depending on the size of the machines, it should take about a minute for them to return to a **Running** state.

> **Important note**
>
> By using the **Restart** command instead of **Start**, the VMs will be turned off and restarted, and will not return to the state they were in before being suspended; a restart might also take significantly longer to complete. Only use **Restart** if you want the machines to be restarted without returning to their saved states.
>
> For the purposes of this recipe, and most recipes in this cookbook for that matter, simply starting the VMs from their suspended state should be enough—after all, it was probably you who suspended them in the first place.

After the VMs have come back online, it might still take a few minutes until the services hosted on them come online as well. You can monitor those in ADS, by connecting to the Big Data Cluster. In the **Connections** pane, under **SQL Server Big Data Clusters**, right-click the node representing your Big Data Cluster instance and select **Manage** from the shortcut menu.

If your Big Data Cluster instance is not listed in the **Connections** pane, see *Step 11* of the first recipe in this chapter, entitled *Creating a SQL Server 2019 Big Data Cluster*, for further information.

How it works...

By deallocating Azure resources, all operations running on them will be suspended (or, depending on the individual resource, stopped altogether). This, of course, also affects all services and operations that depend on the deallocated resources—for instance, any dependent services or processes might fail when the resource becomes unavailable. Therefore, you should use caution when stopping Azure services or deallocating resources.

When a resource is deallocated, it will no longer use some of the resources assigned to it (such as CPUs or system memory) but might still use other resources (for instance, disk space). Suspended and deallocated resources no longer contribute to the cost of Azure subscriptions, whereas resources that cannot be suspended (and, therefore, not deallocated) will remain active, which will be reflected in the subscription cost.

> Tip
>
> More information about the costs associated with using Azure is available in the online documentation, at `https://azure.microsoft.com/en-us/pricing/`.

Setting up a Big Data Cluster

In this recipe, you are going to add data store objects to your Big Data Cluster instance— in a SQL Server database, as well as in the file store. You will also load a small data sample into the file store.

Getting ready

In the following recipe, you are going to create an **external table** in your Azure SQL Server instance by using the **Create External Table** wizard. The wizard is available in the **Data Virtualization** ADS extension.

1. In ADS, in the **View** menu, click **Extensions** to display the ADS extension explorer:

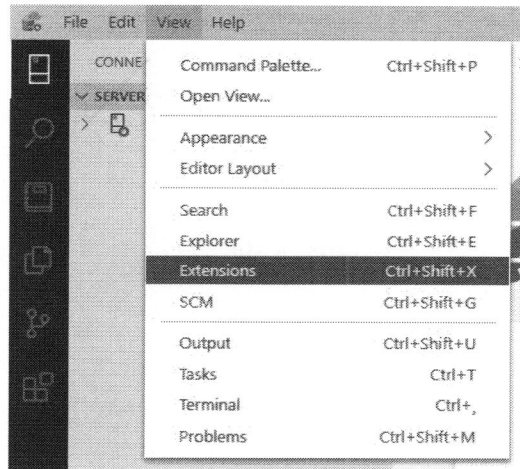

Figure 3.12 – Installing ADS extensions

Search for the phrase `data virtualization` to locate the extension in the collection.

2. Select the **Data Virtualization** extension from the list and click **Install** to start the installation. The download and the installation should complete within a few minutes, depending on your internet connection. You should also be notified of the progress and the completion of the installation in the **Output** pane at the bottom of the window. You are now ready to set up your Big Data Cluster. Before starting, make sure that your Big Data Cluster is up and running by checking the state of its VMSS on the Azure portal.

    If the VMs are stopped, follow *Steps 4* through *5* of the preceding *Stopping and starting Azure resources* recipe.

How to do it...

You are going to create data store objects in the Big Data Cluster, both in the **physical** sense, by creating a new Azure SQL Server database and HDFS folders, and in the **logical** sense, by creating an external table in the newly created database.

1. Start ADS, unless it is already open, and connect to the Big Data Cluster you created earlier in this chapter. It should be listed in the **Connections** tab, under **SQL Server Big Data Clusters**.

   If a connection is not available, then the quickest way to access the server is to open the Notebook you created in the first recipe of this chapter. It should be saved in the `C:\ETL-with-Azure\Chapter03\BDC` folder on your local drive.

   At the bottom of the Notebook, follow the **Click here to connect to SQL Server Master instance** link.

   The **Home** page of the Big Data Cluster should now open in a new ADS tab, and its connection should also be added to the **Connections** tab, under **SERVERS** and under **SQL Server Big Data Cluster**:

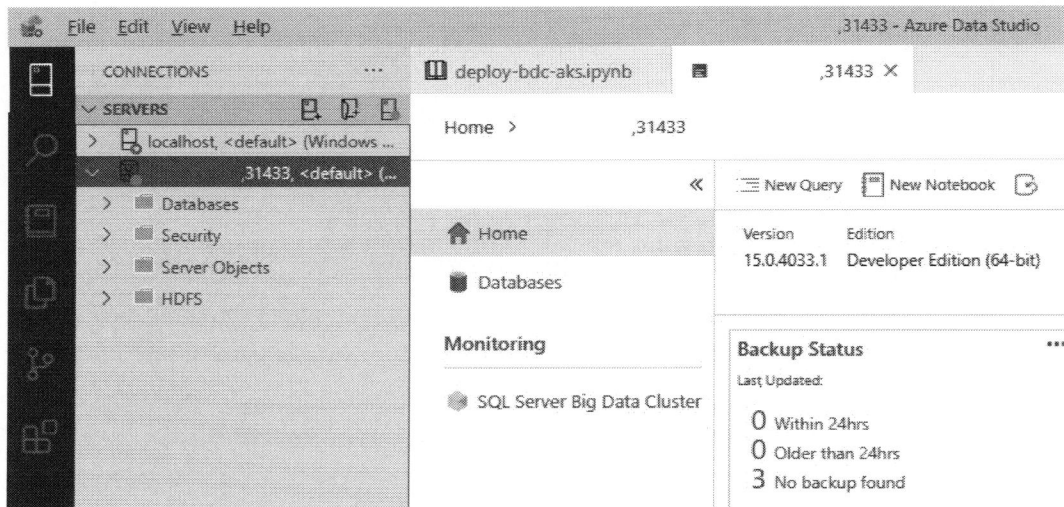

Figure 3.13 – Connection to a Big Data Cluster in ADS

2. In the **Connections** tab, right-click the SQL Server instance node represented by the IP address of your Big Data Cluster, and select **New Query** from the shortcut menu:

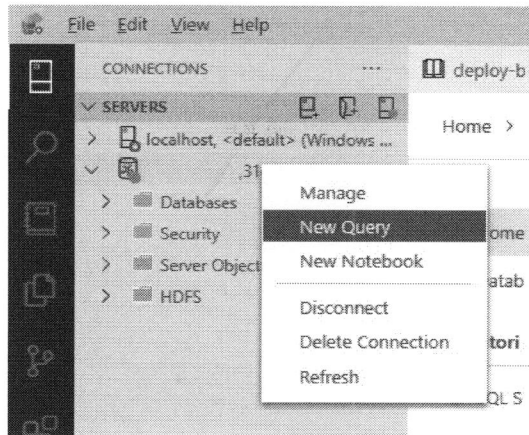

Figure 3.14 – Opening a New Query window in ADS

3. Use the following **Transact-SQL (T-SQL)** commands to create a new database:

```
USE master;
GO
```

```
CREATE DATABASE Staging;
GO
```

Execute the commands by clicking **Run** in the query editor tab, or by pressing *F5* on the keyboard.

In the **Connections** tab, expand the `Databases` node, under the Big Data Cluster instance. The new database should be listed there, as shown in the following screenshot:

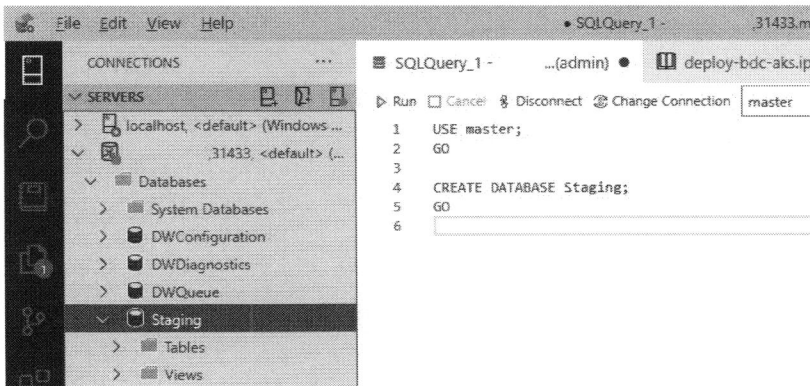

Figure 3.15 – The new database

You are going to use this database to host the data for the recipes in this chapter.

4. In the **Connections** tab, right-click the **HDFS** node, and then select **New directory** from the shortcut menu:

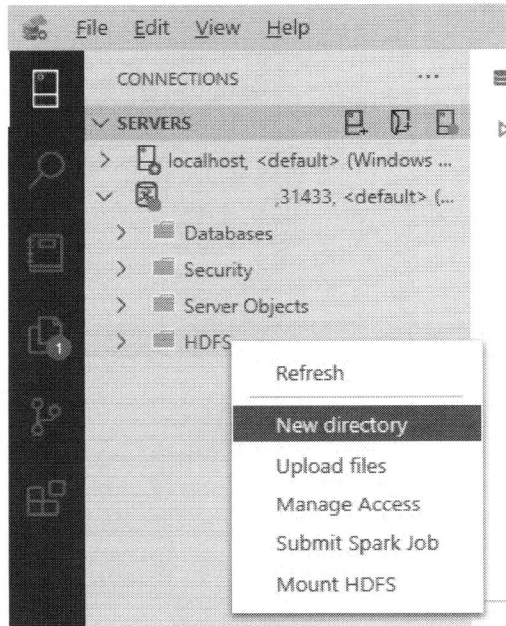

Figure 3.16 – Adding a new HDFS directory

In the **Enter directory name** dialog, use NewPeople as the directory name.

When ready, press **Return** to confirm the name.

The new directory should now appear in the **Connections** tab, under the **HDFS** node.

Create another folder, named UnknownPeople, by repeating the procedure.

5. Right-click the NewPeople folder, and this time select **Upload files** from the shortcut menu.

6. In the **Open** dialog, navigate to the `C:\ETL-with-Azure\Chapter03\Files` folder, select the `NewPeople.csv` file, and click **Upload** to start the process.

It should only take a moment to upload the 45-**kilobyte (KB)** sample file. Expand the `NewPeople` folder to see it. If the file is not listed, right-click the folder, and select **Refresh** from the shortcut menu to refresh its contents.

Once the file has been uploaded, you can make its contents available to the `Staging` database via an **external table**.

7. Right-click the folder again, and this time select **Create External Table From CSV Files** to start the **Create External Table** wizard:

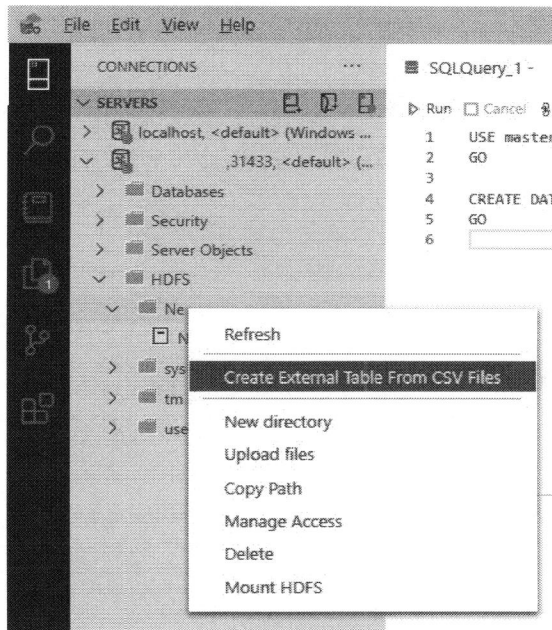

Figure 3.17 – Creating an external table from CSV files

It should take a few moments to load the wizard, including filling in all known settings into the fields of the **Select the destination database for your external table** page, as shown in the following screenshot:

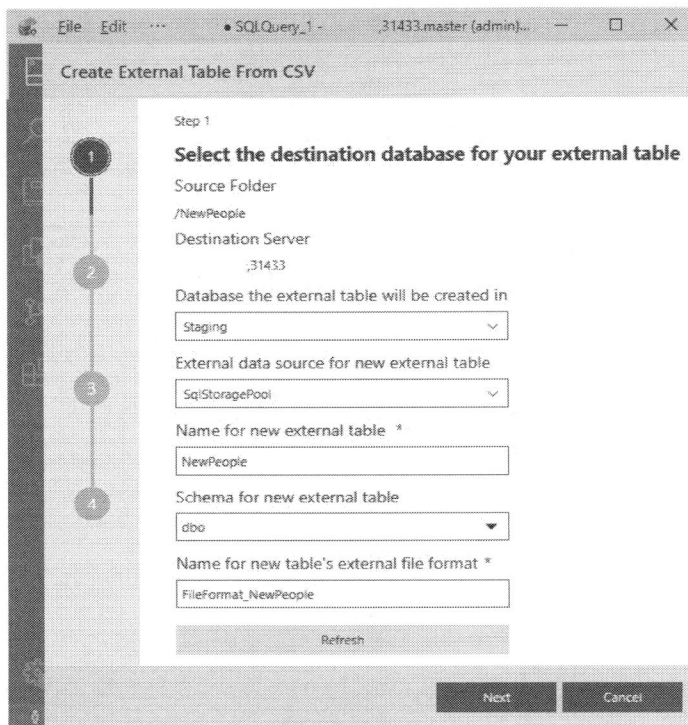

Figure 3.18 – The external table properties

Your Big Data Cluster instance should be selected as the destination server, and the Staging database should be used as the location of the external table.

By default, the directory name is also used as the external table name; dbo is used for the table schema; and the wizard also generates a name for the external file format object, based on the directory name.

Leave all the settings unchanged.

When ready, click **Next** to continue.

8. The first 50 rows of the file are displayed so that you can verify whether the column delimiters were recognized correctly:

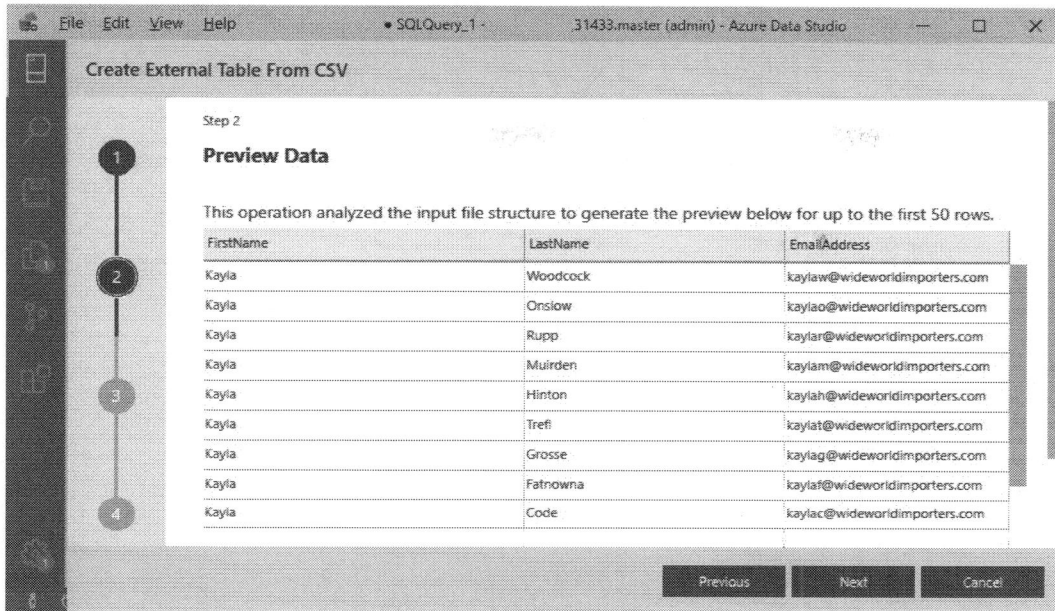

Figure 3.19 – The CSV file data

The same sample of rows is also used to determine the table schema—the column data types and dimensions, and whether a column allows NULL values or not.

> **Important note**
> If the first 50 rows do not contain a representative set of rows, the metadata might be determined incorrectly. Fortunately, you can make the necessary adjustments later before the table is actually created.

Typically, if a file uses standard delimiters—a comma (,) as the column delimiter; quotation marks for text delimiters ("); and the carriage-return line-feed combination as the row delimiter—the structure of the file should be recognized correctly.

When ready, click **Next** to continue.

9. On the **Modify Columns** page, you are presented with the external table schema as it was determined from the row sample:

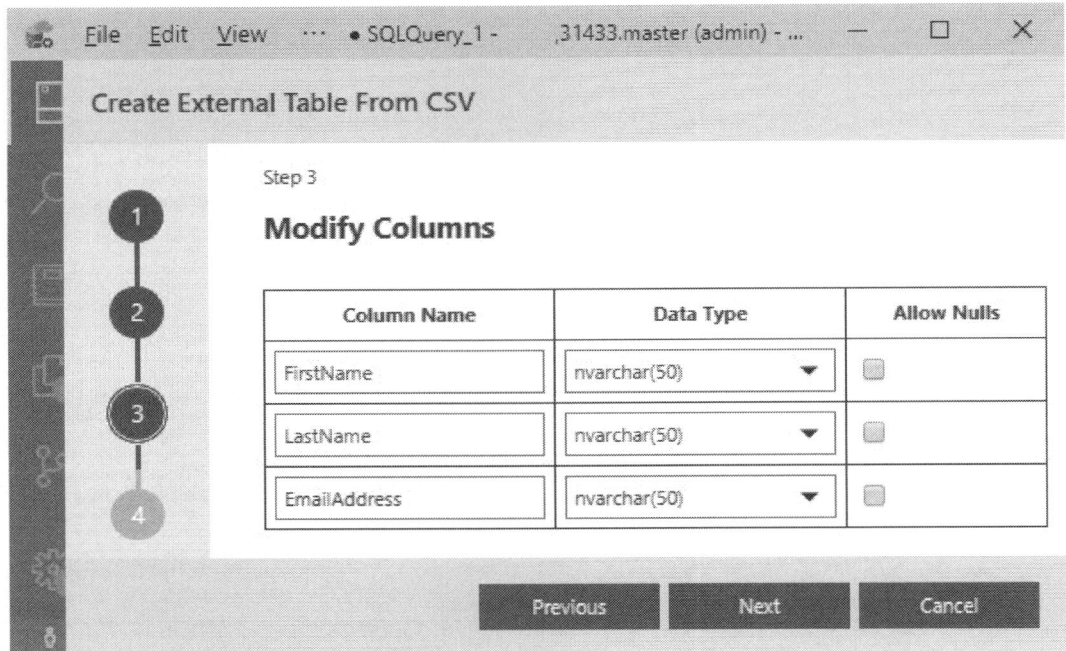

Figure 3.20 – The external table column definitions

In this particular case, column data types were determined correctly as nvarchar. None of the columns should allow NULLs. However, the length of the EmailAddress column will have to be adjusted later (it should be *256* characters, not *50*).

> **Important note**
>
> When it comes to string data types, the **Create External Table** wizard only supports two lengths: *50* characters or *max*; therefore, more often than not, you will have to make changes to the automatically generated script in order to correct the data types.

Click **Next** to continue.

10. On the **Summary** page, you can inspect the configuration. *Do not* click **Create Table**, as the table definition needs to be corrected manually before the table can be created:

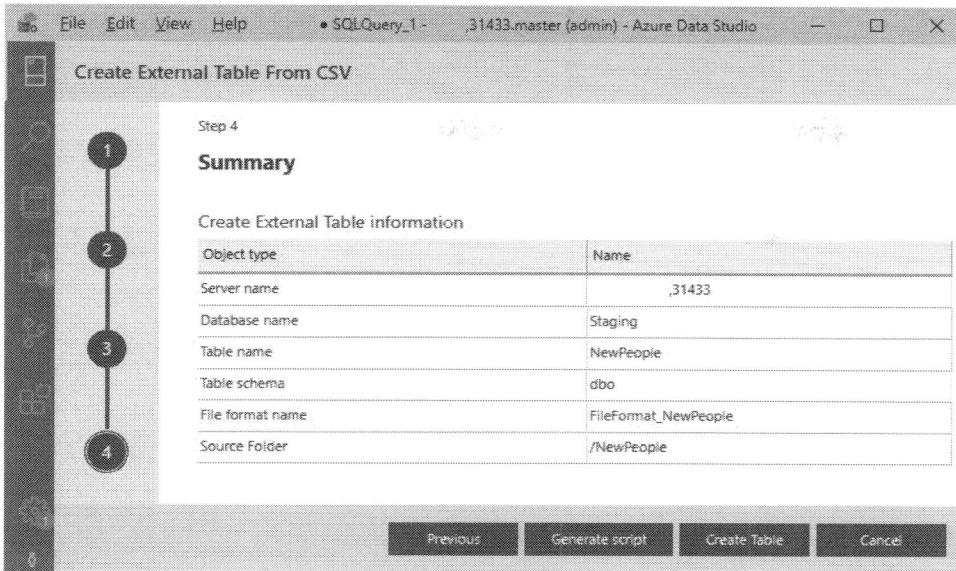

Figure 3.21 – The external table configuration summary

When ready, click **Generate script**, to instruct the wizard to prepare the T-SQL script with all the required object definitions.

Give it a moment, and then click **Cancel** to close the wizard.

The automatically generated T-SQL script should now be open in a new ADS tab.

11. In the script, locate the definition of the dbo.NewPeople external table, and in it the definition of the EmailAddress column:

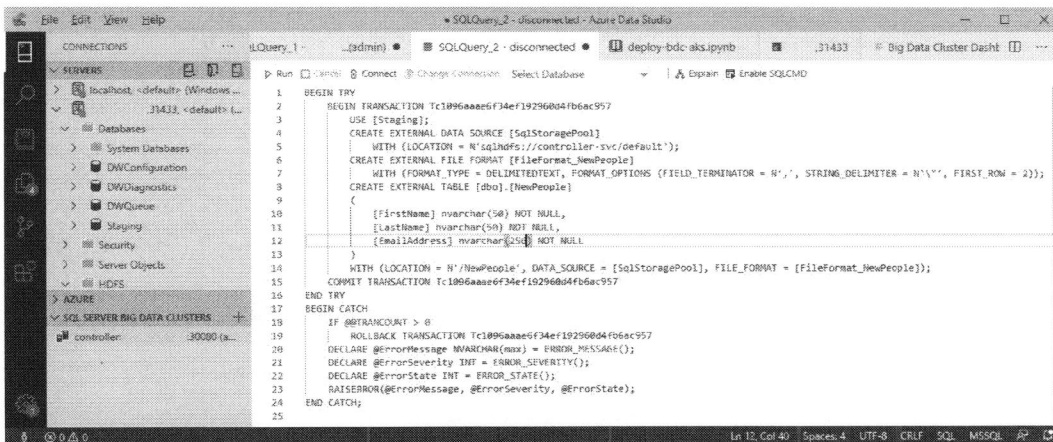

Figure 3.22 – The T-SQL script used to create the external table

Change the length of the `EmailAddress` column from `50` to `256`, as shown in the preceding screenshot.

12. Execute the script by clicking **Run** in the tab menu or by pressing *F5* on the keyboard to start the external table creation. By default, automatically created scripts are placed into a new ADS tab without establishing a connection:

Figure 3.23 – The ADS connection dialog

In the **Connection** dialog, select the connection to your Big Data Cluster instance from the list of recent connections. If the correct connection is not listed, you will have to provide the server name and the credentials.

Make sure that the `Staging` database is selected in the **Database** list box.

When ready, click **Connect** to continue the execution.

If the commands have completed successfully, the table should be listed in the **Connections** tab, under the **Tables** node of the `Staging` database of your Big Data Cluster instance, as shown in the following screenshot:

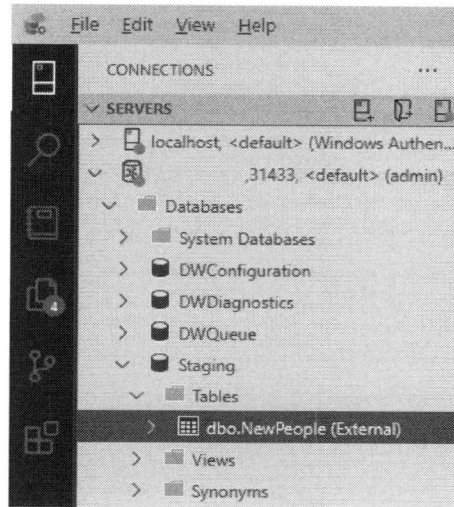

Figure 3.24 – The new external table

13. In **SQL Server Management Studio (SSMS)**, make sure the **Object Explorer** is connected to your local SQL Server instance (`localhost`, or `MSSQL2019`), and then select the `WideWorldImporters` database in the **Object Explorer**. Press *Ctrl + O* on your keyboard, or select **Open...** from the **File** menu, to open a new file.

14. In the **Open File** dialog, navigate to the folder you used when you downloaded a clone of the `ETL-with-Azure-Cookbook` repository. Locate the `\Chapter03\ ETLinAzure\Scripts` folder, and in it the `Chapter03_OnPremises.sql` file. Open it.

Inspect the T-SQL script; it is divided into two parts, marked with Roman numerals `I.` and `II.`: the first part contains T-SQL commands that you will use to create new objects, and a few T-SQL statements to test them, and the second part contains two commands that you should only use if you want to remove the database objects (for instance, if you need to create them again).

15. Make sure that you are connected to the `WideWorldImporters` database on the `localhost` server, and then carefully execute the following commands to create the following objects:

    a) `Application.NewPeople_List`—a procedure that uses data in the `WideWorldImporters` database to generate a list of names and email addresses

    b) `Application.UnknownPeople`—a new table

    After creating the procedure, you can test it by executing the `EXEC` command that follows the procedure definition.

16. In the **Object Explorer**, open another connection, this time to the master instance of your Big Data Cluster.

    For the server name, use the `SQL Server Master Instance Front-End` address that you can locate on the Big Data Cluster overview page in ADS.

    Select **SQL Authentication**, use `admin` as the username, and supply the password you created when deploying the instance to Azure.

17. In the **Object Explorer**, locate the `Staging` database of the remote SQL Server instance, and again press *Ctrl + O* on your keyboard, or select **Open…** from the **File** menu, to open a new file. In the **Open File** dialog, navigate to the `\Chapter03\ETLinAzure\Scripts` folder as before, and this time open the `Chapter03_Cloud.sql` file.

    This T-SQL script is also divided into two parts—the first is to create the objects, and the second is to remove them when they are no longer needed, or if they need to be recreated.

18. Make sure that you are connected to the `Staging` database on your remote SQL Server instance, and then carefully execute the commands to create two additional objects:

    a) `dbo.ExistingPeople`—a new database table

    b) `dbo.UnknownPeople`—another external table, hosted on the Big Data Cluster HDFS file store

19. Use the **Object Explorer** in SSMS to locate all the objects that you created in this recipe. Some of the Big Data Cluster features, such as the HDFS file store, can only be accessed through ADS.

How it works...

You created a new database on your remote SQL Server instance, and then created two **external** tables and a **regular** database table in this new database. You also loaded a data sample into the Big Data Cluster HDFS file store. By using a wizard, you created an **external** table based on the data sample you uploaded in a flat file. This **external** table now allows you to retrieve data from the HDFS file store by using T-SQL, as if the data were stored in a **regular** database table.

Loading data into a Big Data Cluster

In this recipe, you are going to design an SSIS package used to load data into a database hosted on the remote SQL Server instance.

The SSIS package contains two control flows:

- One extracts key information from the line-of-business database, and loads it into a `Staging` database hosted in Azure

- The other simulates a process that delivers data from a different source (for instance, managed by another department in your organization, or another organization altogether) and loads it into your Big Data Cluster that is also hosted in Azure

The objective of this SSIS package is to make the necessary data available at the remote location for further processing. The SSIS package that you are going to design in the last recipe of this chapter, entitled *Extracting data from a Big Data Cluster*, depends on the data made available by the package designed in this recipe.

Getting ready

We assume that you have already cloned the cookbook GitHub repository to your workstation, and that you have completed the first and the third recipe in this chapter, entitled *Creating a SQL Server 2019 Big Data Cluster* and *Setting up a Big Data Cluster*, respectively.

> **Important note**
> The SSIS package in this recipe uses the **curl** command-line utility to transfer data to the remote destination. This utility should already be available on Windows Server 2019 installations, as well as in the latest versions of Windows 10. If for some reason the utility is not available on your workstation, you can install the latest version from `https://curl.haxx.se/`.

How to do it...

Locate the clone of the cookbook GitHub repository that you deployed to your workstation.

1. Inside the local repository, locate the `\ETL-with-Azure-Cookbook\Chapter03\Starter` folder, and then open the `ETLinAzure.sln` solution in **SQL Server Data Tools** (**SSDT**) (Visual Studio 2019).

    It should take about a minute to load the solution into Visual Studio:

    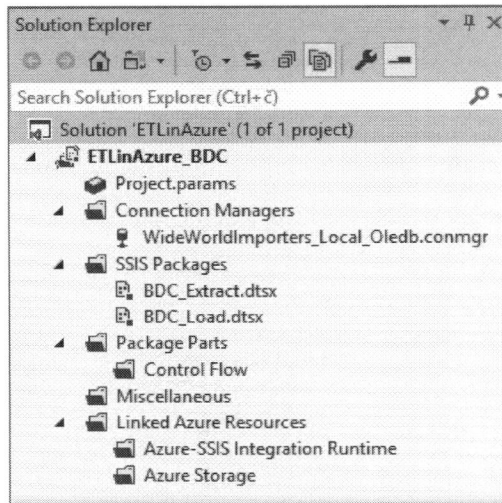

    Figure 3.25 – The ETLinAzure solution in the SSDT Solution Explorer

    In the **Solution Explorer**, you should see a single SSIS project, named `ETLinAzure_BDC`, containing the following two SSIS packages:

    a) `BDC_Load.dtsx`

    b) `BDC_Extract.dtsx`

2. Open the `BDC_Load.dtsx` package by double-clicking its node in the **Solution Explorer**, or by right-clicking it and selecting **Open** from the shortcut menu.

> **Important note**
>
> When the package is opened and validated, errors will be displayed, telling you that SSDT was unable to read sensitive information from the package file. You can safely ignore these errors, as you will provide all the sensitive information later.

The package contains the following two sequence containers:

a) **Simulate Loading Source Data into BDC**—this control flow will be used to load new data into the Big Data Cluster.

b) **Load Reference Data into Remote Database**—this control flow will be used to load existing data into a reference table in the Azure SQL Server instance.

You can see the control flow of the BDC_Load.dtsx package in the following screenshot:

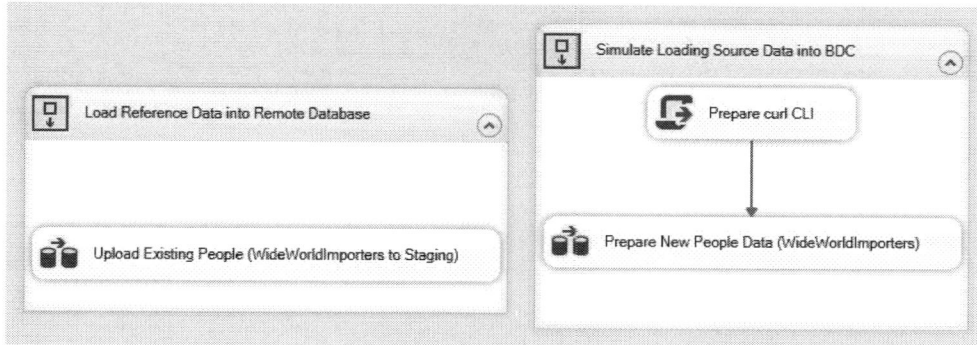

Figure 3.26 – The control flow of the BDC_Load.dtsx SSIS package

3.   On the **Parameters** tab of the package editor, you should see three parameters:

a) HDFSGatewayAddress—the address of the Big Data Cluster gateway to access HDFS files

b) HDFSRootPassword—the password of the administrator account you used when creating the SQL Server instance

c) NewPeopleFlatFilePath—the path and filename of a flat file used in the transfer of data from the local SQL Server instance to the Big Data Cluster instance:

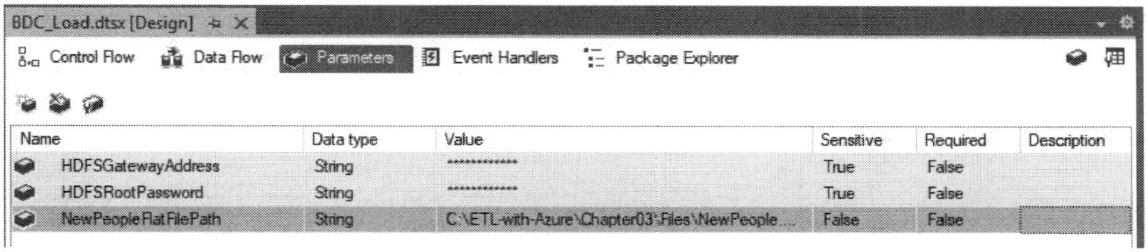

Figure 3.27 – The package parameters

The first two parameters are marked as sensitive, as they contain information that requires special protection. Change the values of these two parameters so that the `HDFSGatewayAddress` parameter contains the IP address of the gateway access to HDFS files on your Big Data Cluster, and the `HDFSRootPassword` parameter contains the password you used when you created the Big Data Cluster instance.

Leave the `NewPeopleFlatFilePath` parameter value unchanged.

Switch back to the **Control Flow** editor tab.

4. In the **View** menu, under **Other Windows**, select **Variables** to open the **Variables** pane.

    The package uses the following two variables:

    a) `CurlCliArgumentsPattern`—a string representing the arguments that are going to be used with the **curl** command-line utility with placeholders that will be replaced with actual values at runtime.

    b) `CurlCliArguments`—the string that will hold the complete collection of **curl** arguments determined at runtime. The default value of this variable is `--help` —purely to satisfy the validation of the **Execute Process** task:

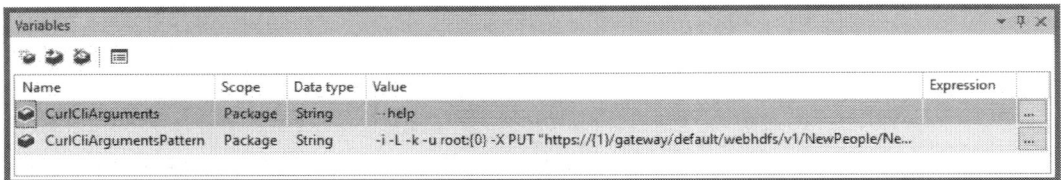

Name	Scope	Data type	Value	Expression
CurlCliArguments	Package	String	--help	...
CurlCliArgumentsPattern	Package	String	-i -L -k -u root:{0} -X PUT "https://{1}/gateway/default/webhdfs/v1/NewPeople/Ne...	...

Figure 3.28 – The package variables

Do not make any changes to the variables and close the **Variables** pane.

5. In the **Script Task Editor**, in the **Simulate Loading Source Data into BDC** container, open the **Prepare curl CLI** script task by double-clicking it, or by right-clicking it and selecting **Edit…** from the shortcut menu:

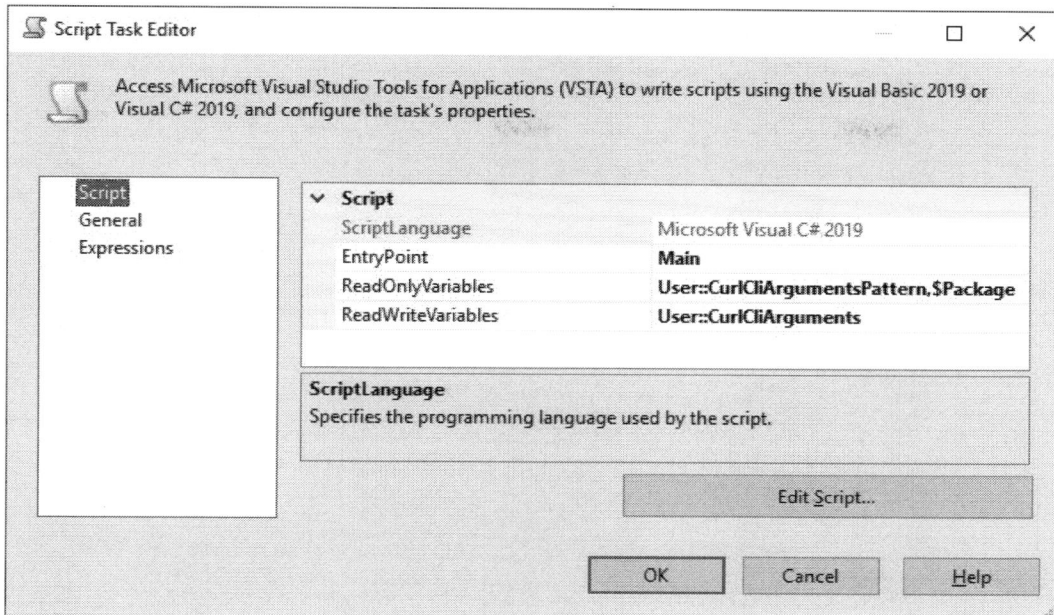

Figure 3.29 – The Script Task Editor

On the **Script** page of the **Script Task Editor**, inspect the read-only variables and the read/write variables that have been configured for use in the script task.

Do not make any changes to the configuration.

6. Click **Edit Script...** to open the script task definition and give **Visual Studio Tools for Applications** (**VSTA**) a few moments to start.

The script task definition should contain one method, named `Main`.

When the script task is run, this method will read the values from the specified package parameters and the `CurlCliArgumentsPattern` variable and use them to assign the value of the `CurlCliArguments` variable.

Close **VSTA**, and then click **Cancel** to close the **Script Task Editor**.

7. Open the **Prepare New People Data (WideWorldImporters)** data flow task in the
    Data Flow editor by double-clicking it, or by right-clicking it and selecting **Edit…**
    from the shortcut menu:

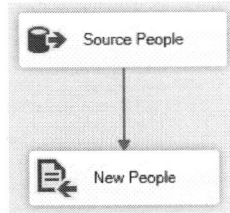

Figure 3.30 – The Prepare New People Data (WideWorldImporters) data flow task

This data flow task implements a simple data movement, where data is extracted
from a single source (**Source People**) and is then loaded into a single destination
(**New People**), without any additional transformations.

8. Double-click the **Source People** source component, or right-click it and select
    Edit… from the shortcut menu, to open the **OLEDB Source Editor**.

    On the editor's **Connection Manager** page, you can see that the source component
    connects to the WideWorldImporters_Local_Oledb connection manager,
    and that it uses the Application.NewPeople_List procedure to load the data
    into the data flow pipeline.

    Do not make any changes to the component, and then click **Cancel** to close the
    OLEDB Source Editor.

9. Open the **New People** destination component. On the **Connection Manager** page
    of the **Flat File Destination Editor**, you can see that this component connects
    to the NewPeopleFlatFile flat file connection manager, and that it is set to
    overwrite any existing contents with the data received from the data flow pipeline.

    Do not make any changes to the component, and then click **Cancel** to close the **Flat
    File Destination Editor**.

10. In the **Connection Managers** pane, below the editor pane, locate the `WideWorldImporters_Local_Oledb` connection manager. Open it.

    This provides a connection to the `WideWorldImporters` database on the local SQL Server instance.

    Click **Cancel** to close the connection manager, as no changes are needed.

11. Now, locate the `NewPeopleFlatFile` connection manager, and open it.

    This provides a connection to a flat file, located on your workstation. The file uses `UTF-8` encoding to store data in text format.

    Click **Cancel** to close the connection manager, as no changes are needed here either.

    Switch back to the **Control Flow** editor.

12. From the **SSIS Toolbox**, drag an **Execute Process** task to the **Simulate Loading Source Data into BDC** container, change its name to **Upload New People Data**, and then connect the precedence constraint from the **Prepare New People Data (WideWorldImporters)** data flow task to the newly added task.

13. Open the **Upload New People Data** Execute Process task by double-clicking it, or by right-clicking it and selecting **Edit…** from the shortcut menu.

    In the **Execute Process Task Editor**, on the **Process** page, set the following properties:

    a) **RequireFullName**: `false`

    b) **Executable**: `curl`

    Leave the rest of the properties unchanged.

14. On the **Expressions** page, open the **Property Expressions Editor**, by clicking the ellipsis symbol at the right side of the **Expressions** row.

    Select the **Arguments** property, and open the **Expression Builder**, by clicking the ellipsis symbol on the right side of the property row.

15. In the **Expression Builder**, drag the `CurlCliArguments` variable from the **Variables and Parameters** collection in the left column to the **Expression** text box:

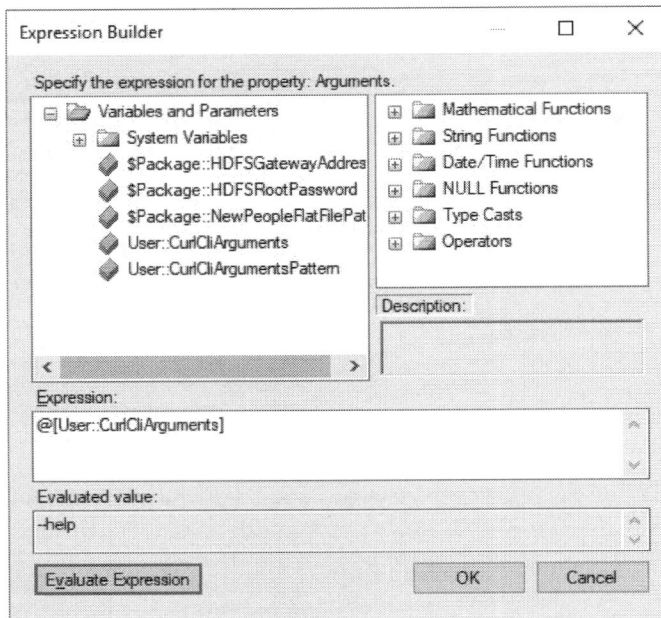

Figure 3.31 – The Expression Builder

Click **Evaluate Expression** to see whether the expression is correct and that it returns the current value of the corresponding variable.

When ready, click **OK** to confirm the expression.

At runtime, the **Arguments** property will be populated with the value of the `CurlCliArguments` variable. This variable is populated by the **Prepare curl CLI** script task.

16. If the expression configuration is complete, as shown in the following screenshot, click **OK** to close the **Property Expressions Editor**:

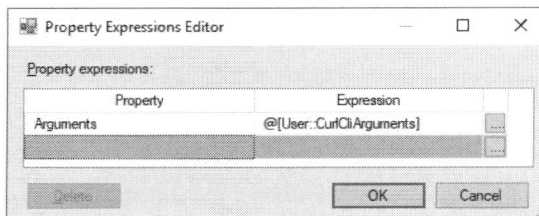

Figure 3.32 – The Property Expressions Editor

17. Back on the **Process** page, you can now verify the properties populated by literal values, and the properties populated by an expression:

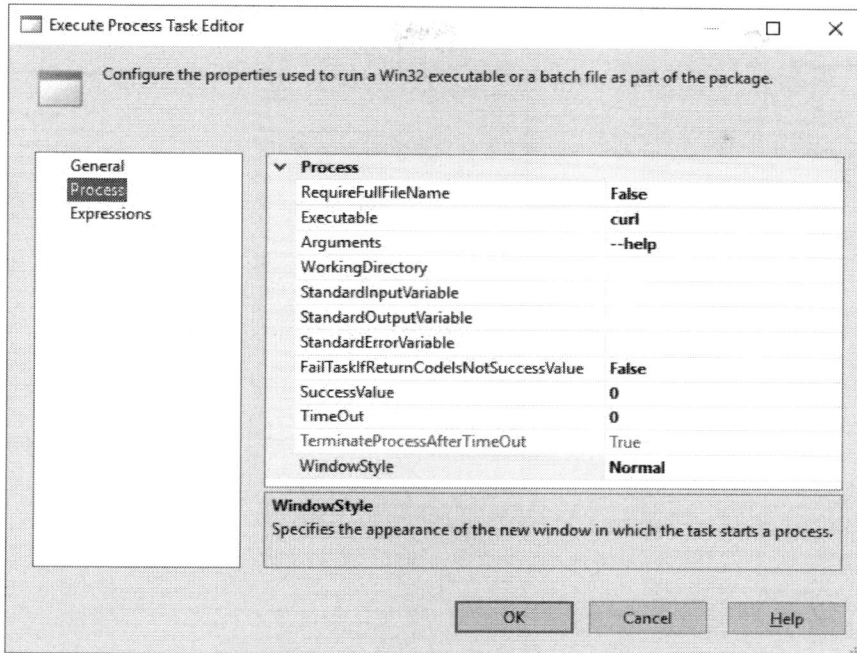

Execute Process Task Editor		□ ✕
Configure the properties used to run a Win32 executable or a batch file as part of the package.		

General	∨ **Process**	
Process	RequireFullFileName	**False**
Expressions	Executable	**curl**
	Arguments	**--help**
	WorkingDirectory	
	StandardInputVariable	
	StandardOutputVariable	
	StandardErrorVariable	
	FailTaskIfReturnCodeIsNotSuccessValue	**False**
	SuccessValue	**0**
	TimeOut	**0**
	TerminateProcessAfterTimeOut	True
	WindowStyle	**Normal**

WindowStyle
Specifies the appearance of the new window in which the task starts a process.

OK   Cancel   Help

Figure 3.33 – The Execute Process Task Editor

When ready, click **OK** to confirm the configuration.

Save the solution.

18. Create a new connection manager, by right-clicking the empty canvas of the **Connection Managers** pane and selecting **New OLEDB Connection...** from the shortcut menu.

In the **Configure OLEDB Connection Manager** dialog, click **New...** to create a new connection, and then, in the **Connection Manager** editor, make sure that **SQL Server Native Client** is selected as the provider.

Use the following settings for the rest of the properties:

a) **Server name**: **SQL Server Master Instance Front-End** address of your Big Data Cluster instance

b) **Authentication**: SQL Server Authentication

c) **User name**: admin

d) **Password**: The password you used for the admin account when you deployed the Big Data Cluster instance

e) **Save my password**: Checked

f) **Select or enter a database name**: Staging

Click **Test Connection** to verify the settings.

If the test is successful, click **OK** to confirm the settings; otherwise, make the necessary changes based on the information provided by any error messages.

> **Important note**
> The password will be saved in the SSIS package in encrypted form; however, you will have to enter it again whenever you want to make changes to this connection manager.

19. Change the name of the newly created connection manager to Staging_BDC_Oledb.

    Right-click the newly created connection manager and select **Convert to Project Connection** from the shortcut menu to promote the connection manager to a project resource.

20. From the **SSIS Toolbox**, drag an **Execute SQL** task into the **Load Reference Data into Remote Database** container, change its name to **Remove Existing Data (Staging)**, and then connect a precedence constraint from the new task to the existing **Upload Existing People (WideWorldImporters to Staging)** data flow task.

21. Open the newly added task, and on the **General** page, use the following settings to set the properties:

    a) **ConnectionType**: OLE DB

    b) **Connection**: Staging_BDC_Oledb

    c) **SQLSourceType**: Direct input

    d) **SQLStatement**: TRUNCATE TABLE dbo.ExistingPeople;

> **Tip**
>
> Rather than type the T-SQL statement into the `SQLStatement` text box, copy it from the `Chapter03_Cloud.sql` script that you used in the recipe entitled *Setting up a Big Data Cluster*, earlier in this chapter.

When ready, click **OK** to confirm the configuration.

Save the solution.

22. Open the **Upload Existing People (WideWorldImporters to Staging)** data flow in the Data Flow editor.

    Inspect the **Source Existing People (WideWorldImporters)** source component. You can see that it connects to the `WideWorldImporters_Local_Oledb` connection manager and extracts the `EmailAddress` data from the `Application.People` table.

    Leave the source component unchanged and click **Cancel** to close the editor.

23. From the **SSIS Toolbox**, drag an **OLE DB Destination** task to the data flow, change its name to **New Existing People (Staging)**, and connect the data path from the source component to the newly added destination component.

    On the **Connection Manager** page, use the following settings to configure the destination component:

    a) **OLE DB connection manager**: `Staging_BDC_Oledb`

    b) **Data access mode**: `Table or view – fast load`

    c) **Name of the table or the view**: `dbo.ExistingPeople`

    Leave the rest of the settings unchanged.

24. On the **Mappings** page, make sure that the source column is connected to the destination column.

    When ready, click **OK** to confirm the configuration.

    Save the solution.

25. If you have followed the instructions correctly, the `SSIS` package should now be ready for a test run.

First, switch to SSMS, and use the queries in the `Chapter03_OnPremises.sql` and `Chapter03_Cloud.sql` T-SQL scripts that you previously used in the *Setting up a Big Data Cluster* recipe, to check the state of the data in the local and the remote databases:

a) In the `WideWorldImporters` database on your local SQL Server instance, the `Application.UnknownPeople` table should be empty.

b) In the `Staging` database on your Big Data Cluster, both the `dbo.ExistingPeople` and the `dbo.UnknownPeople` tables should be empty, whereas the `dbo.NewPeople` table should contain 1,000 rows.

26. In SSDT, execute the `BDC_Load.dtsx` package in debug mode, and observe the execution of each data flow.

    When the flat file is processed by the **curl** utility, a Command Prompt window will open, allowing you to see the messages received from the execution.

    All operations should complete successfully within a few minutes.

    If there are errors, check the error messages and make the necessary corrections before repeating the debug mode execution.

27. Stop the execution, and inspect the tables again:

a) In the `WideWorldImporters` database, the `Application.UnknownPeople` table should still be empty, as you have not loaded any data into the local database.

b) In the `Staging` database, the `dbo.UnknownPeople` table should still be empty, whereas the `dbo.NewPeople` table should now contain 806,976 rows, and the `dbo.ExistingPeople` table should contain 1,029 rows.

    You can leave the tools open, as you will need them in the following recipe.

How it works...

You have added missing tasks to the existing SSIS package and created a new connection manager that connects to your Big Data Cluster, which you have then used in an SSIS data flow.

You have loaded data into the remote database table by using a regular data flow and have loaded data represented by a flat file into the Big Data Cluster HDFS file store by using the **curl** command-line utility.

Extracting data from a Big Data Cluster

In this recipe, you are going to complete the development of an SSIS solution used to extract data from a database hosted on a Big Data Cluster instance in Azure and load it into a database hosted on the local SQL Server instance.

The purpose of this package is to reduce the size of the data that actually needs to be transferred from the external source into the line-of-business database, by restricting the remote source set to only contain data that does not yet exist in the local database.

In general, **determining the delta** hardly represents a task worthy of the capabilities available in Big Data Clusters or a typical case for using Spark; however, it does represent a very significant element in efficient data warehousing.

Getting ready

This recipe assumes that you have completed the preceding recipe in this chapter, entitled *Loading data into a Big Data Cluster*, and that the expected data is available in the dbo.NewPeople external table and in the dbo.ExistingPeople database table on the Big Data Cluster instance.

How to do it...

In this recipe, you are going to use ADS to simulate a process hosted in your Big Data Cluster instance, and then use SSMS to check the results. In normal circumstances, the part of the operation performed in ADS would be performed automatically—either by another SSIS package or another control flow in the same package—or it would be performed by another application altogether (for instance, a scheduled Spark job set up at the Big Data Cluster). In this example, we want to show you how Spark processing can be performed interactively, and we also want you to examine the results as soon as they are ready. Most of the development activities in this recipe will take place in SSDT.

Make sure that the Chapter03\Starter\ETLinAzure\ETLinAzure.sln solution is open in SSDT; this is the same solution that you already used in the preceding recipe. Open ADS if it is not already open.

1. In ADS, in the **Connections** pane, expand the node representing your Big Data Cluster instance, and under **Databases**, select the Staging database.

   Press *Ctrl + O* on your keyboard, or select **Open File...** from the **File** menu, to open the **Open File** dialog. In the local clone of the cookbook GitHub repository, locate the Chapter03\Scripts folder, and in it the Chapter03_UnknownPeople.ipynb Python Spark Notebook. Open it.

2. Inspect the Notebook; it should contain a single cell.

    The script creates two data frames:

    a) newPeople, by extracting data from one or more **comma-separated values (CSV)** files in the NewPeople HDFS directory

    b) existingPeople, by extracting data from the dbo.ExistingPeople database table

    The script then displays 10 rows from each data frame.

    After that, the script creates a third data frame, named unknownPeople, by joining the first two data frames using a left anti-join on the EmailAddress column, which only returns rows from the first (left) data frame that do not exist in the second (right) data frame.

    Row counts from all three data frames are printed out next, followed by the FirstName, LastName, and EmailAddress columns of the unknownPeople data frame being written from one or more CSV files into the UnknownPeople HDFS directory on your Big Data Cluster instance.

3. Click **Run Cells** to execute the script. If prompted for a connection, make sure you connect to the Staging database on your Big Data Cluster instance.

    > **Important note**
    >
    > Occasionally, the execution might be interrupted by one or more errors (for instance, by "Error sending http request and maximum retry encountered." or by "Invalid status code '404' from … with error payload: {"msg":"Session '1' not found." }"errors".
    >
    > If you change the kernel used by the active ADS tab to any other one, and then back to **PySpark**, the underlying resources should be reloaded, so that the next attempt at running the cell will succeed.

    After a successful execution, you can save the Notebook with the results displayed for reference.

4. In ADS, in the **Connections** tab, locate the UnknownPeople directory under the HDFS node, and expand it to see its contents. If no files are displayed, right-click the directory node, and select **Refresh** from the shortcut menu to reload the data.

> **Important note**
>
> By default, Spark operations on big data result in multiple files when the data is persisted to the HDFS file store. Each file represents a single partition of data that was generated when the data frames were processed—**parallelism** represents an important aspect of the Big Data Clusters infrastructure. The **data virtualization** capabilities of this infrastructure also allow for data to be logically presented as a single set, even if it physically spans multiple files in the HDFS file store.

5. In SSMS or in ADS, open the `Chapter03_Cloud.sql` T-SQL script that you used in the preceding recipes in this chapter. Connect to the `Staging` database on your Big Data Cluster instance.

    In the script, execute the query that retrieves data from the `dbo.UnknownPeople` external table. This table should now contain 805,948 rows.

6. In SSDT, in the **Solution Explorer**, locate the `BDC_Extract.dtsx` SSIS package. Open it. The package should contain a single control flow inside the `Extract Data from BDC` sequence container, consisting of an **Execute SQL** task that truncates the `Application.UnknownPeople` table in the local `WideWorldImporters` database, and an incomplete data flow:

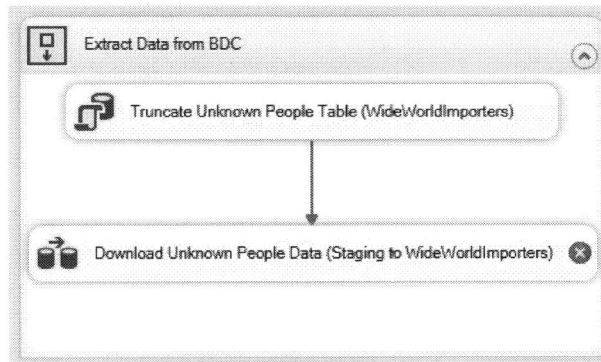

Figure 3.34 – The control flow of the BDC_Extract.dtsx SSIS package

7. Open the **Download Unknown People Data (Staging to WideWorldImporters)** data flow in the **Data Flow** designer. The data flow contains a transformation, and a destination component, but no sources.

    This is also the reason why the data flow task currently has an error and is even preventing the SSIS package from being executed.

8. From the **SSIS Toolbox**, drag an **OLE DB Source** component to the data flow; change its name to `Source Unknown People`, and open it.

    In the **OLE DB Source Editor**, on the **Connection Manager** page, use the following settings to configure the source component:

    a) **OLE DB connection manager**: `Staging_BDC_Oledb`

    b) **Data access mode**: `Table or view`

    c) **Name of the table or the view**: `[dbo] . [UnknownPeople]`:

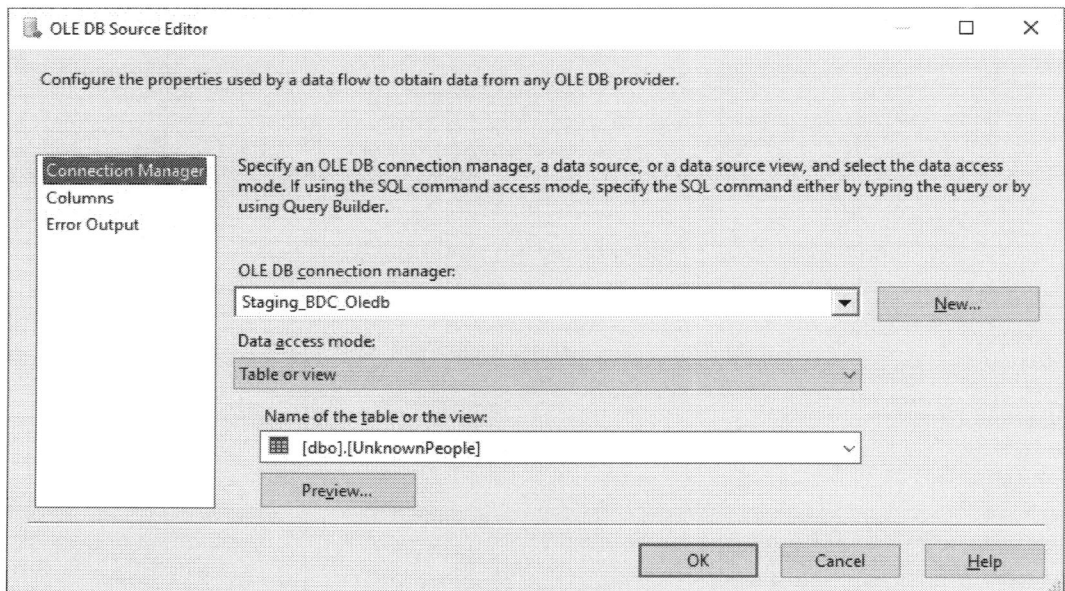

Figure 3.35 – The OLE DB Source Editor

The preceding screenshot shows the correct settings. You can click **Preview…** to check them by running the query and observing the first few rows.

9. On the **Columns** page, make sure that all three columns are selected.

    When ready, click **OK** to confirm the configuration.

10. In the **Data Flow** editor, connect the data path from the **Source Unknown People** component to the **Compute Full Name** transformation, and then open the transformation.

    This **Derived Column** transformation uses an expression that combines the values of the `FirstName` and `LastName` columns retrieved from the source component and adds a new `FullName` column to the data flow pipeline.

    Do not make any changes to the component's configuration and click **Cancel** to close the **Derived Column Transformation Editor**.

11. Open the **Unknown People** destination component. This component consumes the data from the data flow pipeline and places it into the `Application.UnknownPeople` table in the local `WideWorldImporters` data table.

    Do not make any changes to the component's configuration and click **Cancel** to close the **OLE DB Destination Editor**.

    Save the solution.

12. Execute the `BDC_Extract.dtsx` package in debug mode and observe the data flow execution.

    It should take about a minute to complete both operations.

13. Stop the execution, and then in **SSMS** or **ADS**, open the `Chapter03_OnPremises.sql` T-SQL script that you used in preceding recipes in this chapter. Connect to the `WideWorldImporters` database on your local SQL Server instance.

    In the T-SQL script, execute the query that retrieves data from the `Application.UnknownPeople` database table. The table should now contain 805,948 rows.

14. You can now close **SSDT**.

How it works...

You processed the data in your Big Data Cluster by using a PySpark script to execute commands against the Spark service, to examine the data and to place the processed results into the HDFS file store. Through the use of an **external** table in the database on the Big Data Cluster instance, you were able to query the data as if it were stored in a **regular** database table.

You then completed the development of an SSIS package that extracts the data from an **external** table on your Big Data Cluster instance and loads it into a **regular** table in your local database.

As you can see from this, and from the preceding recipe, when it comes to data retrieval (for instance, in SSIS), the data in Big Data Clusters is exposed in the standard way—as relational data—even though its physical storage, or the means used to process it, is non-relational in nature. From the perspective of SSIS data flows specifically, and the perspective of data warehousing and **Extract, Transform, Load** (ETL) in general, this approach to data access truly does allow for a (mostly) seamless transition between on-premises and cloud-based data management solutions.

4
Azure Data Integration

This chapter will teach you recipes for getting SSIS to interact with Azure services. Microsoft has created tools to enable SSIS to read, write, and call Apache Hive and Pig scripts in Azure. Performing all these tasks from an SSIS on-premises ETL server is not ideal in terms of security. You need to open multiple ports on the ETL server to access cloud services. A subsequent chapter will show you how to call those services from a cloud ETL tool known as **Azure Data Factory**.

This chapter will cover the following recipes:

- Setting up the Azure Feature Pack in SSIS
- Setting up a Java Runtime Environment
- Setting up an Azure storage account
- Creating an on-demand Azure HDInsight cluster
- Transforming data with Hive
- Transforming data with Pig

Let's get started!

Setting up the Azure Feature Pack in SSIS

This recipe is quite simple in terms of showing how to get Azure tasks and transforms. Let's start by setting up the Azure Feature Pack in SSIS. This will enable us to interact with Azure storage accounts and HDInsight compute services such as Hive and Pig.

Getting ready

In order to follow along with this recipe, you will need the following:

- An Azure subscription
- A computer with Visual Studio 2019 and the Integration Services extension installed

Refer to *Chapter 1, Getting Started with Azure and SSIS 2019*, for detailed recipe steps if you do not have the components listed here already set up.

How to do it...

Let's begin this recipe:

1. From a browser, navigate to the following link and download the Azure Feature Pack for SSIS. Select SQL Server 2019 if you installed Visual Studio 2019, as specified in *Chapter 1, Getting Started with Azure and SSIS 2019*: `https:// docs.microsoft.com/en-us/sql/integration-services/azure-feature-pack-for-integration-services-ssis?view=sql-server-ver15`.

2. Download and install the program.

3. Start Visual Studio and open any Integration Services project. In the SSIS toolbox, you should now see an Azure section, along with tasks, as shown in the following screenshot:

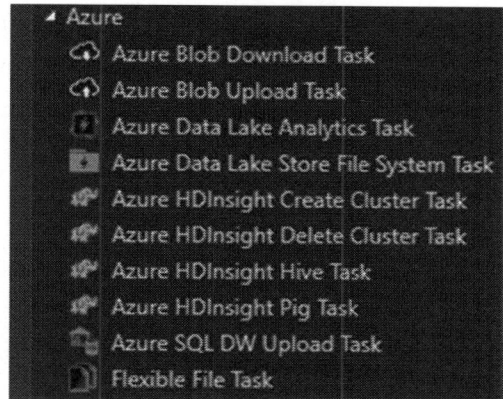

Figure 4.1 – The SSIS toolbox

4. Add a dataflow to the package and go inside it. You will now see some transforms in the SSIS toolbox, as shown in the following screenshot:

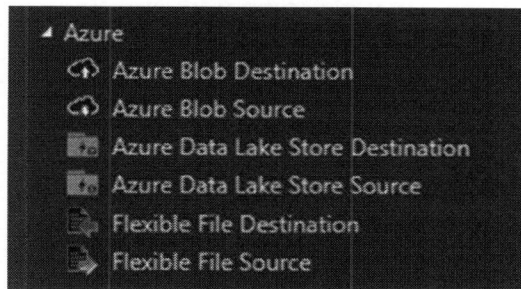

Figure 4.2 – The Azure transform options

That concludes this recipe. You have now installed the Azure Feature Pack in Visual Studio.

How it works...

SSIS is now ready to connect to Azure. This is useful when we want to connect our on-premises ETLs to Azure resources. The following recipes will use the Azure features available from SSIS.

Setting up a Java Runtime Environment

Some of the recipes in this chapter use the Parquet file format. This is a columnar file format that is widely used nowadays in cloud environments. The improvements that have been made to the format makes it an uncontestable choice, especially for files that contain large volumes of data. Reading from a Parquet file is much faster than reading from any other file formats. The following URL links to the Parquet website, where you can watch a video for more information on the Parquet file format: `https://parquet.apache.org/`.

Getting ready

We must install a **Java Runtime Environment** (**JRE**) to be able to use the Parquet file format. That's the first thing we'll do in this recipe.

How to do it...

Now, let's begin the installation process:

1. Go to the following website to download **Oracle JRE**. We're downloading version 8, which is compatible with the Microsoft Azure Feature Pack at the time of writing: `https://www.oracle.com/java/technologies/javase/javase8-archive-downloads.html`.

2. There are two versions of the JRE: 32-bit and 64-bit. Since Visual Studio is a 32-bit program, we need to install the 32-bit version to develop our SSIS packages. Once the packages have been deployed to the **SQL Server Integration Service Catalog** service, we need the 64-bit version of JRE to execute our package from there.

   Select **Windows X86 (32-bit) – Java Runtime Environment 8u202**, as shown in the following screenshot. Click on the link to the right to initiate the download process:

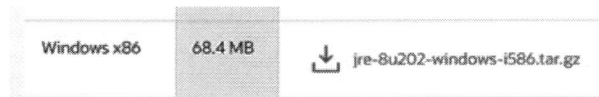

Windows x86	68.4 MB	↓ jre-8u202-windows-i586.tar.gz

   Figure 4.3 – Appropriate download option

3. You should be redirected to a web page that asks you to log in. If you do not have an Oracle account, create one – it's free to do so. Once it's downloaded, click on the **installation** file to install the `JRE 32-bit` file. You can optionally change the destination folder if desired. Click on **Install** to start the installation process.

4. For the 64-bit version of the JRE, go back to the download page and select the 64-bit version, as shown in the following screenshot:

Figure 4.4 – The 64-bit download option

5. Once it's downloaded, double-click on it to start the installation process.

That's it! We are now ready to start using the SSIS Azure Feature Pack!

How it works...

Now that we have set up the JRE, we can perform the rest of the recipes in this chapter.

Setting up an Azure storage account

This recipe will teach you how to set up a storage account in Azure. A storage account is a cheap resource for storing data that will be used by computing resources in Azure. There are two types of storage accounts:

- **Azure Blob Storage**: This is the basic storage type and can store petabytes of data for around 6 cents (USD $) per gigabyte. There are two types of block blobs: **Pages** and **Blobs**. Page blocks are mainly used for virtual machine disks. Blob blocks, on the other hand, are commonly for multi-purpose usage.

- **Azure Data Lake Gen2**: This storage is very similar to the preceding one except that the security is enhanced for advanced analytics purposes. **Azure Data Lake (ADL)** Gen2 has a folder hierarchy that does not exist in regular blob storage. This allows the security that's used to be role-based access control (**RBAC**), which means that we can use the credentials of the current user to authenticate to a specific folder in the storage account. This is the type of storage that is used by most Azure ETL services, such as **Data Factory** and **Databricks**.

Unfortunately, SSIS Azure Feature Pack tasks and transforms are not fully compatible with ADLS Gen2. We will therefore create a blob version for our storage in this chapter.

Getting ready

This recipe requires that you have the following:

- Visual Studio 2019 with the Integration Services extension installed

- Azure Feature Pack installed

- JRE installed

- Access to an Azure subscription

How to do it...

Let's get started:

1. From the Azure portal (`portal.azure.com`), navigate to the resource group we created in *Chapter 2, Introducing ETL*, that is, **ETLInAzureCookBook**. Click on **+Add** and type **Storage Account** into the search box. Then, click on **Create**, as shown in the following screenshot:

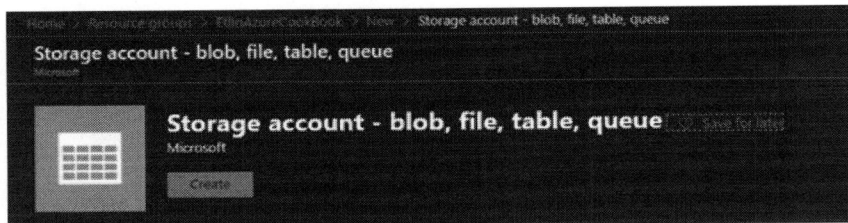

Figure 4.5 – Storage account creation

2. Fill in the fields that appear as follows and click on **Review + create** when you're done:

   a) **Subscription**: Select your Azure subscription from the drop-down list.

   b) **Resource group**: **ETLInAzureCookBook**.

   c) **Storage account name**: `<Your initials>ETLInAzure`. A storage account can only contain lowercase letters and numbers. It must also be unique. The following web page provides guidelines for storage account names: `https://docs.microsoft.com/en-us/azure/azure-resource-manager/management/resource-name-rules#microsoftstorage`.

d) **Location**: Select your location from the drop-down list. You should select the same region for all the services we are creating in this chapter, as well as throughout this book, to avoid supplemental charges. In Azure, there are some costs associated with moving data from one region to another.

e) **Performance**: Use the default; that is, **Standard**.

f) **Account kind**: Use the default; that is, **StorageV2 (general purpose V2)**.

g) **Replication**: Use the default replication value; that is, **Read-access geo-redundant storage (RA-GRS)**.

h) **Access tier (default)**: Use the default value; that is, **Hot**.

3. On the **Validation** page, click on **Review + Create** and then **Create** to create the storage account, as shown in the following screenshot:

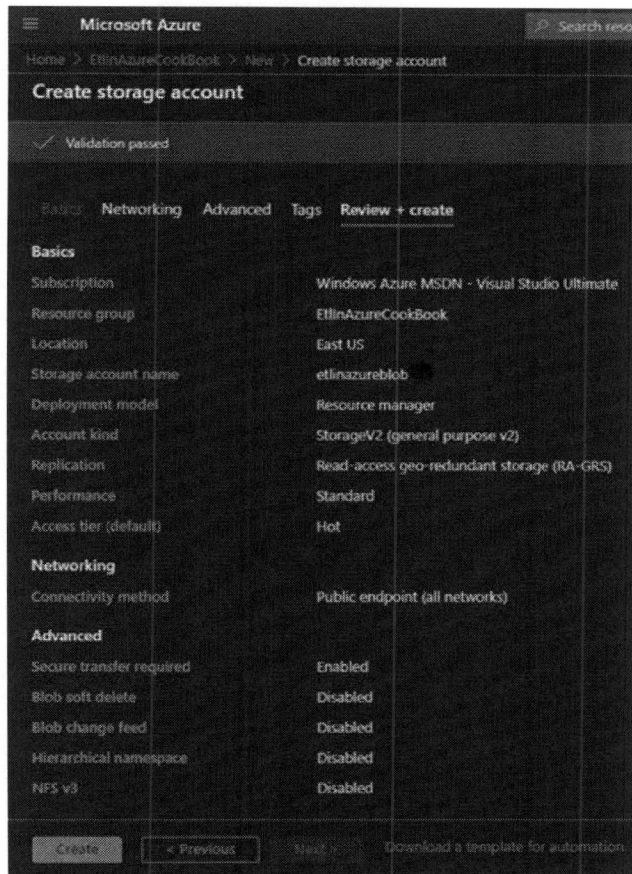

Figure 4.6 – The storage account validation step

4. With that, your storage account will be created, and you are almost ready to use it. We are only missing one piece of software on our PC: **Azure Storage Explorer**. From your internet browser, navigate to `https://azure.microsoft.com/en-us/features/storage-explorer/#overview` and download the version that's compatible with your system.

5. Once downloaded, install the program, and register your account. You should now see the blob you created previously, as shown in the following screenshot:

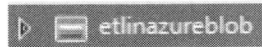

Figure 4.7 – The storage account created

We now have a storage blob set up. In the next recipe, we will use SSIS to interact with Azure services.

How it works...

We are now ready to do some coding! That's what we will be doing in the next few recipes.

Creating an on-demand Azure HDInsight cluster

So far, we have installed the Azure Feature Pack in SSIS and created a storage account. It is now time to create a compute service in Azure so that we can manipulate some data.

An **HDInsight** cluster is what we call a compute resource in Azure. It is essentially a Hortonworks (now Cloudera) service available in Azure. It is composed of Linux virtual machines that have Apache Hadoop or Spark installed on them. Hadoop has been around for more than a decade now and it was the first big data compute resource available. Hadoop writes (stages) the data to disk at almost all the stages of a program's execution. Spark is a newer technology. Instead of staging data on disks, it uses memory while a program executes. It's therefore much faster than Hadoop.

We will use Hadoop clusters in this chapter because SSIS uses this type of cluster. HDInsight clusters can be very expensive if we create them manually and leave them running continuously. This recipe will show you how to create an on-demand cluster; this cluster will be created just before its execution and released right after it is completed in order to reduce costs.

Getting ready

This recipe requires that you have the following:

- Visual Studio 2019 with the Integration Services extension installed
- Azure Feature Pack installed
- JRE installed
- Access to an Azure subscription

How to do it...

Let's get started:

1. Open Visual Studio and create a new SSIS project.
2. Rename the package something like **HiveSSIS.dtsx**.
3. From the SSIS toolbox, drag and drop an **Azure HDInsight Create Cluster Task**.
   Rename it **HDICC_etlinazure**. This task will create a cluster called **etlinazure**. Set
   the properties as shown in the following screenshot:

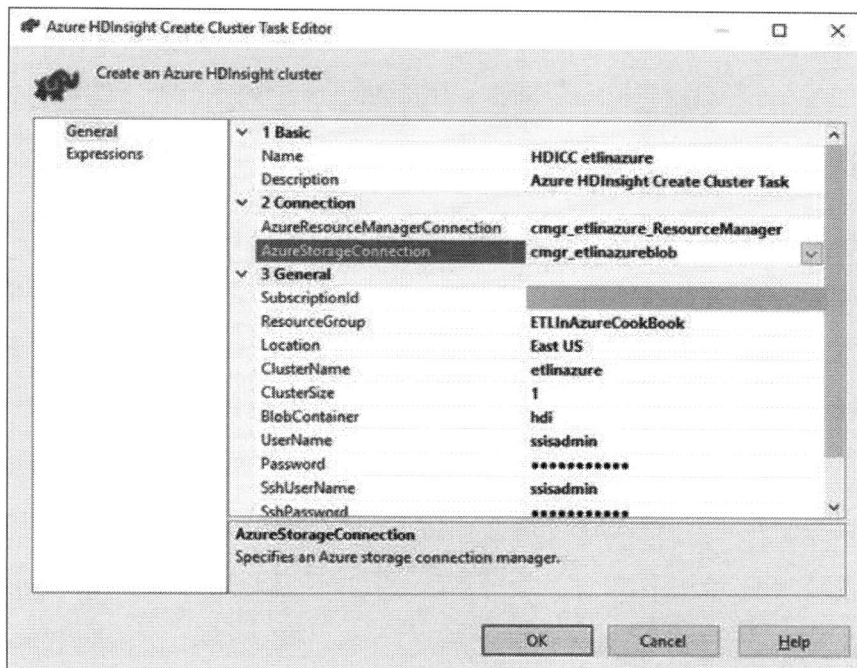

Figure 4.8 – HDInsight Create Cluster Task Editor

4. **Azure Resource Connection Manager** is a bit more complex. In a web browser of your choice, navigate to `https://docs.microsoft.com/en-us/azure/ active-directory/develop/howto-create-service-principal- portal` to learn how to get the necessary information, as shown in the following screenshot: Click on **OK** when you're done:

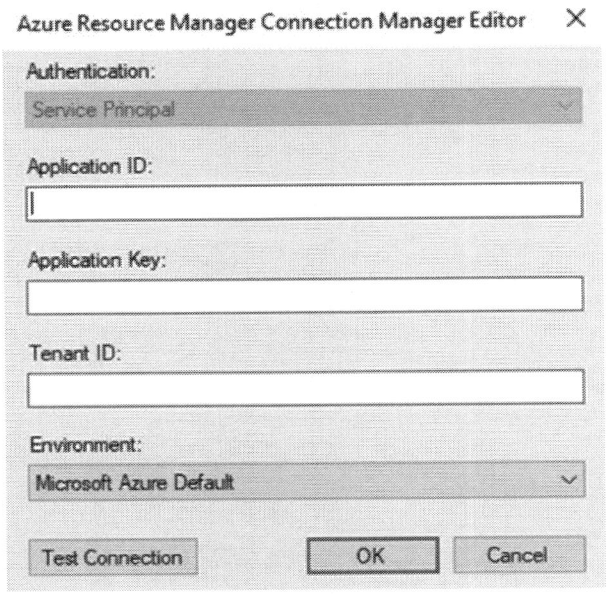

Figure 4.9 – Azure Resource Manager Connection Manager Editor

5. Rename the connection manager **cmgr_etlinazure_ResourceManager**.

6. From the drop-down menu for **Azure Connection**, select **<new connection>** and fill in the information boxes, as shown in the following screenshot:

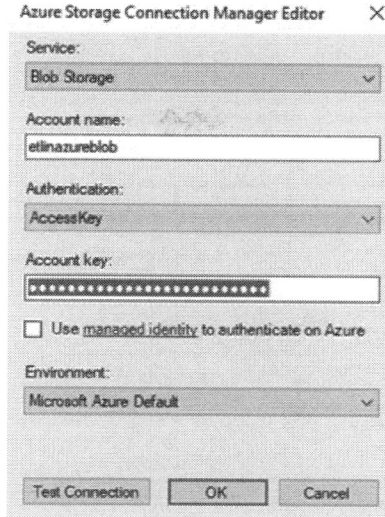

Figure 4.10 – The Azure Connection Manager Editor window with the properties filled in

7. The **Account key** information is available in the Azure portal. Navigate to your storage account and select **Access keys** from the leftmost panel. Copy the **key1** or **key2** information shown and paste in into the **Account key** textbox of the **Azure Storage Connection Manager Editor** window shown in *Step 6*:

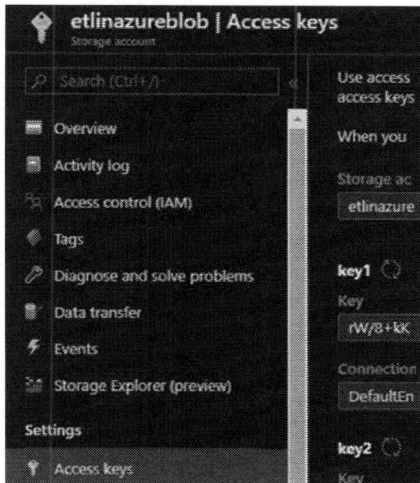

Figure 4.11 – Azure Storage Access keys

8. We do not need use the Managed Identity to authenticate. This setting can only be used when the package is run inside Azure Data Factory. We will talk about that in *Chapter 7, Azure Data Factory*. For now, click on **Test connection**, and then click **OK** when you're done.

9. Rename the connection manager **cmgr_etlinazureblob**.

10. Select the **EtlInAzureCookBook** resource group. Choose the same region you used when you created the storage account and use **etlinazure** for the cluster name if it is available. If it's not, you can use your initials to prefix or suffix it and make it unique.

11. Use 1 as the cluster size since our workload is small. This property determines how many workers (VMs) will be created to execute the script. If we had a big workload, we would increase this number.

    The blob container property is used to create a container in your storage account that will contain various pieces of cluster information, such as logs, scripts, and so on. The container will be created automatically.

12. Finally, enter a username and password for cluster administration (UserName) and SSH connections (SshUserName). We used the same username here, but in real life, they should differ for security purposes.

13. Leave the FailIfExists property set to **false**. This will allow us to reuse the cluster if it has already been created. Click on **OK** to create the task.

14. Now, right-click on the task and select **Execute** to ensure it works properly, as shown in the following screenshot:

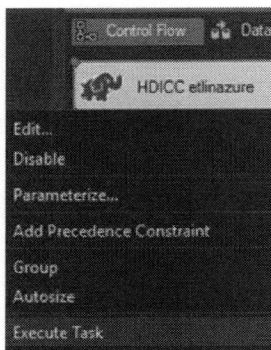

Figure 4.12 – Executing the HDI task

After several minutes (15-20), the task will complete successfully, as shown in the following screenshot:

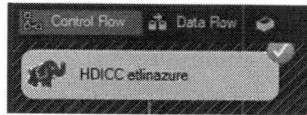

Figure 4.13 – The HDICC task completed successfully

15. Open Azure Storage Explorer and expand the **ETLInAzureBlob** storage account. You will see that the HDI container has been created, as shown in the following screenshot:

Figure 4.14 – The HDI container created

As I mentioned previously, this storage is permanent, even though the cluster has been dropped. This shows exactly how storage and compute resources are decoupled in the cloud.

With that, we have created an on-demand Azure HDInsight cluster. That concludes this recipe.

How it works...

Creating an HDInsight cluster is just the first step. It allows us to use services such as Hive or Pig to transform data with lots of resources. The next few recipes will teach you how to transform data using HDInsight services.

Transforming data with Hive

Now that we have some data copied to Azure, we'll transform it using a big data language called **Hive**. Hive is known by the big data community as being the data warehouse language in the cloud. It's essentially SQL, except we use it to transform data.

Getting ready

This recipe requires that you have the following:

- Visual Studio 2019 with the Integration Services extension installed.
- Azure Feature Pack installed.

- Java Runtime Engine installed.

- Access to an Azure subscription.

- An on-demand HDInsight cluster task in your package. Make sure you've completed the *Creating an on-demand Azure HDInsight cluster* recipe in this chapter.

How to do it...

Now, it's time to copy some data into a container in our storage account. This data will be used to make some transformations using Apache Hive. Let's get started:

1. From the SSIS toolbox, drag and drop a dataflow task. Rename it **DFT_Sales**.

2. Open it and drag an **OleDB Source transform** onto the dataflow surface. Name it **OLEDBSRC Sales**. Double-click on it to open **OLE DB Source Editor**. Click on **New** beside the connection manager property and click **New** in the **Configure OLE DB Connection Manager** window. Enter the required information, as shown in the following screenshot, and click on **OK** in all the windows to create the connection manager. Rename it **cmgr_ContosoRetailDW**:

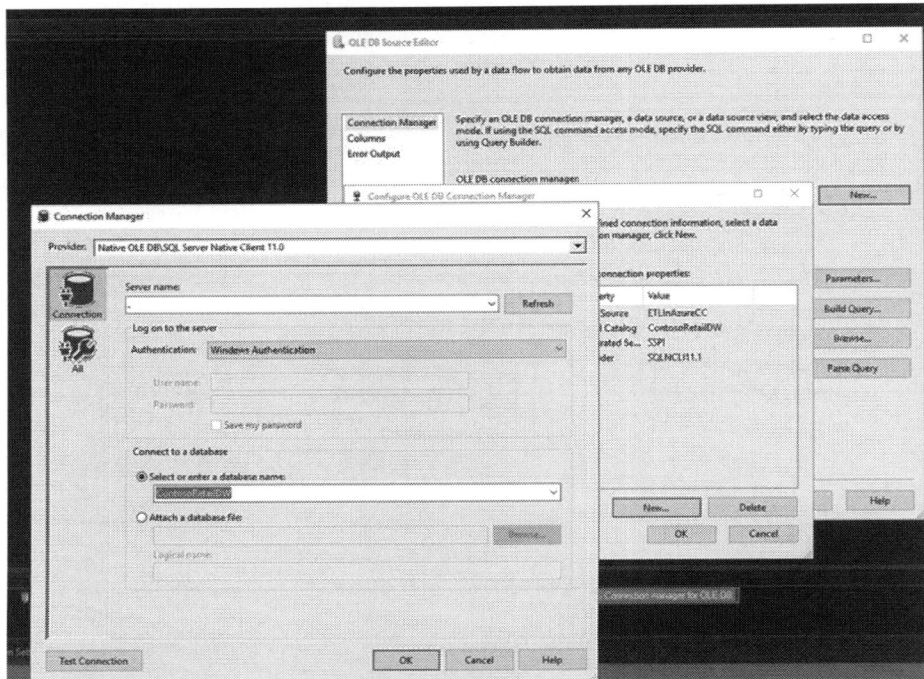

Figure 4.15 – Creating the connection manager for SQL Server

3. Right-click on **cmgr_ContosoRetailDW** and convert it into a project connection manager to make it available in all the subsequent packages we will create. The connection manager should look as follows:

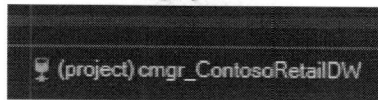

Figure 4.16 – The connection manager converted into a project connection manager

4. Go back to **OLE DB Source Editor** and make sure that **cmgr_ContonsoRetailDW** is selected under **OLD DB connection manager**. From the **Data access mode** drop-down, select **SQL command**. In the **SQL command text** box, type in the query shown in the following screenshot:

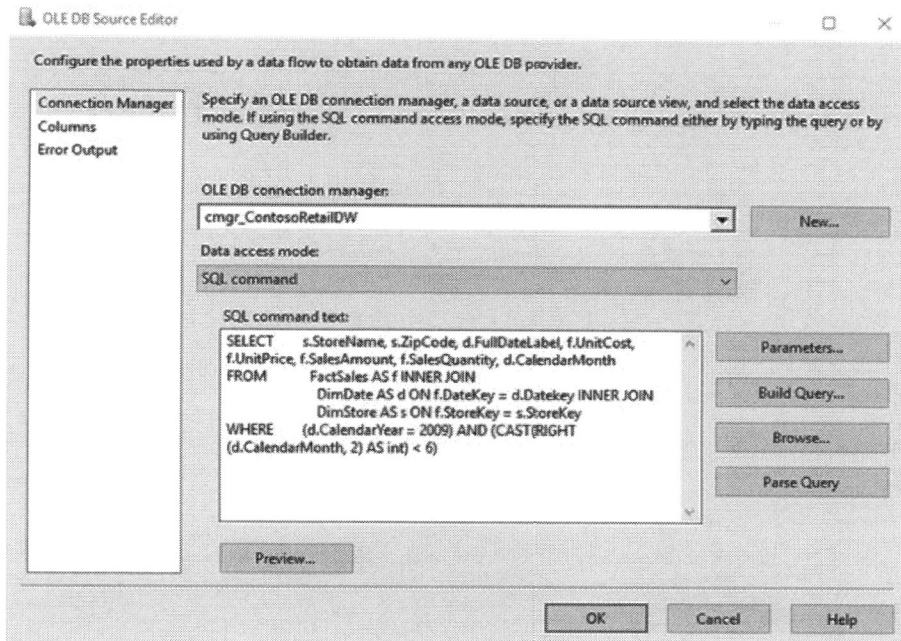

Figure 4.17 – OLE DB Source Editor

The command text shown in the preceding screenshot is as follows:

```
SELECT          s.StoreName, s.ZipCode, d.FullDateLabel,
f.UnitCost, f.UnitPrice, f.SalesAmount, f.SalesQuantity,
d.CalendarMonth
```
```
FROM FactSales AS f
   INNER JOIN    DimDate AS d
     ON f.DateKey = d.Datekey
```

```
      INNER JOIN DimStore AS s
          ON f.StoreKey = s.StoreKey
      WHERE           (d.CalendarYear = 2009)
      AND (CAST(RIGHT(d.CalendarMonth, 2) AS int) < 6)
```

Click on **OK** to close the editor.

5. Drag a Flexible Flat File Destination from the Azure section of the SSIS toolbox. Link it to the OLEDBSRC Sales source we just created. Rename it **FFD Sales**. Double-click on it to open the **Flexible File Destination Editor** window, as shown in the following screenshot:

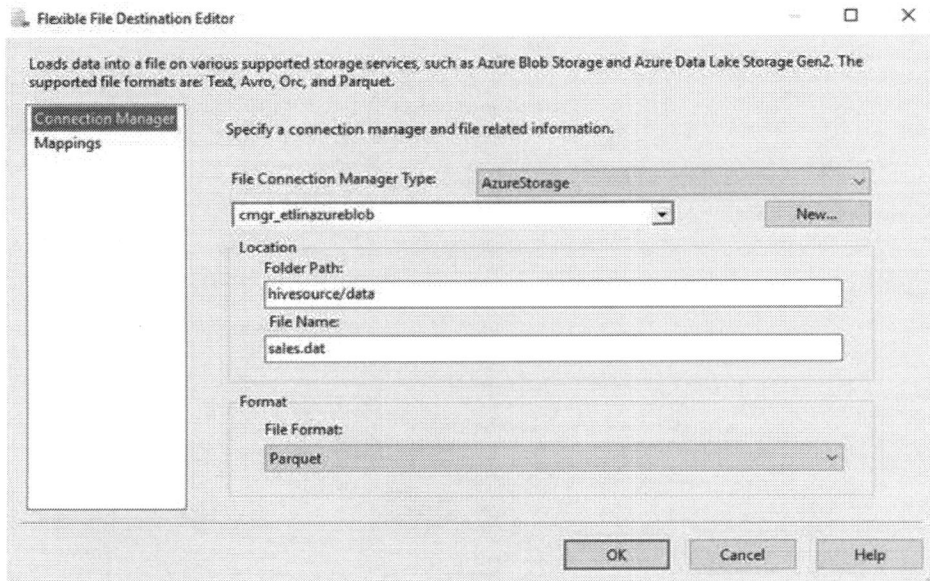

Figure 4.18 – Flexible File Destination Editor

Leave the default value for **AzureStorage** as **File Connection Manager Type**. Use the **cmgr_etlinazureblob** connection manager. For the location, use `hivesource` as **Folder Path** and `sales.dat` as **File Name**. Regarding the **File Format** dropdown, we will use `Parquet`. Go to the **Mapping** tab to create the mapping between the source and destination columns. Click **OK** to close the editor.

6. Go back to the control flow of the package. Right-click on the task and select **Execute** from the menu that appears.

7. Once completed, go to **Azure Storage Explorer**, and expand the `hivesource` container. Click on the folder called **data**. You should see the `sales.dat` file appear, as shown in the following screenshot:

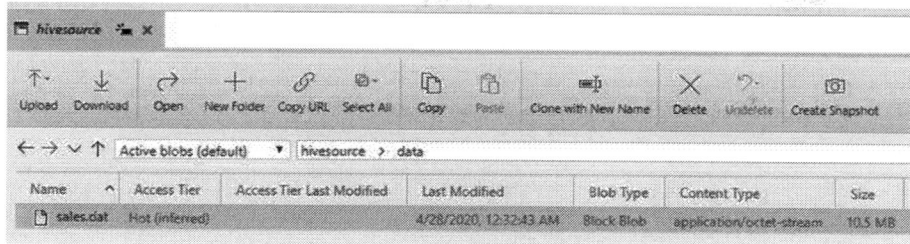

Figure 4.19 – The sales.dat file copied into the container

8. Now that we have copied some data in our storage account, it's time to apply some transformations to it. Go back to the control flow and add an **Azure HDInsight Hive Task**. Rename it **AHT_SalesAgg** and attach it to the `DFT Sales` dataflow we created previously.

9. Double-click on the task to open its editor. Set the properties shown in the following screenshot:

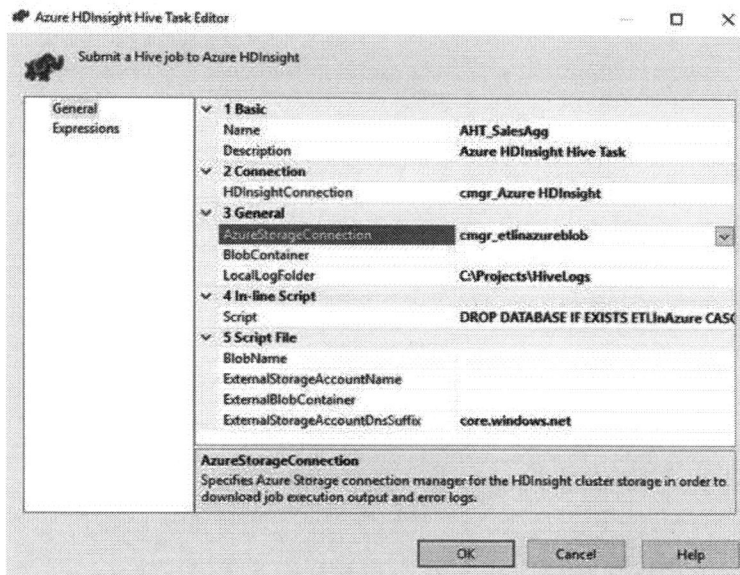

Figure 4.20 – Azure HDInsight Hive Task Editor

10. Now, we are going to create a connection manager that will interact with the HDInsight cluster we created in the *Creating an on-demand Azure HDInsight cluster* recipe. From the drop-down list near the **HDInsightConnection** property, select **<New Connection>**. **Azure HDInsight Connection Manager Editor** will appear. Here, you will need to fill in the textboxes with your cluster information, as shown in the following screenshot. The password property is protected, so we cannot see the text that's been entered in this textbox:

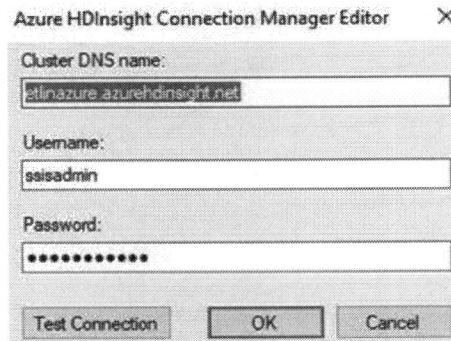

Figure 4.21 – Azure HDInsight Connection Manager Editor

11. Click **Test Connection** and then **OK** to close the window. Rename the connection manager **cmgr_AzureHdInsight** once you've finished configuring that task.

12. Set **cmgr_etlinazureblob** to **AzureStorageConnection**.

13. For **LocalLogFolder**, use a local path that will be used by HDInsight to store the logs.

14. Click on the ellipsis (…) button and enter the following script:

```
DROP DATABASE IF EXISTS ETLInAzure CASCADE;

CREATE DATABASE ETLInAzure;


CREATE EXTERNAL TABLE ETLInAzure.SaleSource(
                        storename string
                       , zipcode string
                       , fulldatelabel string
                       , unitcost decimal(12,4)
                       , unitprice decimal(12,4)
```

```
                                 , salesamount decimal(12,4)
                                 , salesquantity int
                                 , CalendarMonth int)
STORED AS PARQUET
LOCATION 'wasbs://hivesource@<your storage account name.
blob.core.windows.net/data/';


CREATE EXTERNAL TABLE  ETLInAzure.SalesAgg(
                                 storename string
                                 , zipcode string
                                 , unitcost decimal(12,4)
                                 , unitprice decimal(12,4)
                                 , salesamount decimal(12,4)
                                 , salesquantity int
                                 , CalendarMonth int)
STORED AS PARQUET
LOCATION 'wasbs://hivedest@<your storage account>.blob.
core.windows.net/etlinazure/';


INSERT OVERWRITE TABLE ETLInAzure.SalesAgg
SELECT storename , zipcode , SUM(unitcost) AS unitcost,
AVG(unitprice) AS unitprice, SUM(salesamount) AS
salesamount, SUM(salesquantity) AS salesquantity,
CalendarMonth
FROM etlinazure.salesource
GROUP BY storename, zipcode, CalendarMonth;
```

Leave the other properties empty and click on **OK** to close the task editor.

15. Right-click on the task and execute it. After 1 or 2 minutes, the task should complete successfully, as shown in the following screenshot:

Figure 4.22 – The Hive Task completed with success

16. Go into **Azure Storage Explorer**. Open the **hivedest** container and navigate to the **etlinazure** blob. You will see a file called **000000_0**, as shown in the following screenshot:

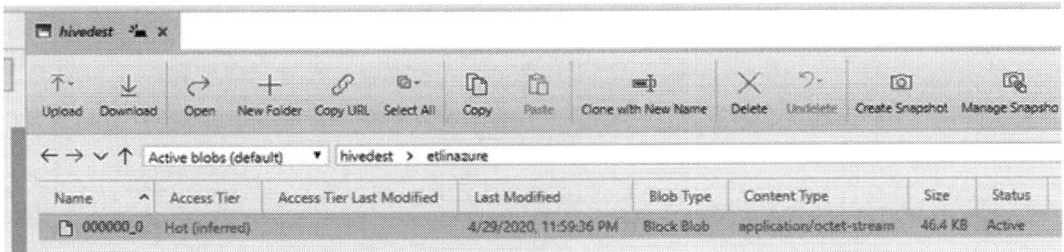

Figure 4.23 – The file created by Hive in Azure Storage Explorer

17. Double-click on the file to open it. The file will be downloaded to your `temp` folder. Click **Yes** on the security warning that appears. Then, choose **Notepad** (or another text editor of your choice) to open the file, as shown in the following screenshot.

The file will open, but since it's in Parquet file format, it won't make any sense when it's read:

Figure 4.24 – The file opened with Notepad

Close the text editor. The next recipe will show you how to read the file.

18. Now that we have transformed our data in our HDInsight cluster, we do not need our cluster anymore. Drag and drop an Azure HDInsight Delete Cluster Task from the SSIS toolbox. Rename it **HDIDC etlinazure** and attach it to the previous task on the package's control flow.

19. Double-click on the task to open its editor and set the properties, as shown in the following screenshot:

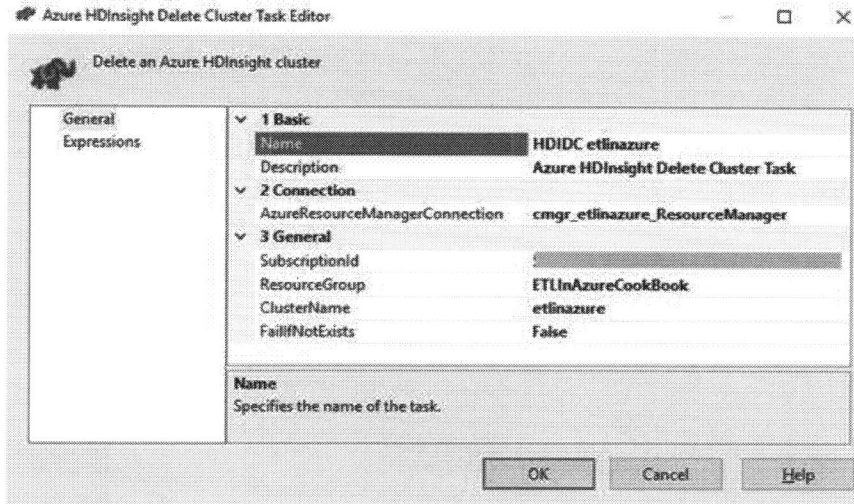

Figure 4.25 – Azure HDInsight Delete Cluster Task Editor

20. Use the **cmgr_etlinazure_ResourceManager** connection manager here, which is the same one we used for the create cluster task previously in this chapter. Set **SubscriptionId** to your Azure **SubscriptionId** and **ResourceGroup** to **ETLInAzureCookBook**. For **ClusterName**, make sure you use the cluster name we set up earlier in this chapter. Then, click on **OK** to close the editor.

21. Now, right-click on the task and select **Execute** from the menu that appears. Once the execution is completed – which might take a few minutes – you should see that the task completed with success.

> **Important note**
> It is very important to drop resources once we do not need them anymore. Since we're renting these resources, we are paying for them and they can become very expensive if we don't drop them when they are not being used. That's exactly what we'll do in the last step of this recipe.

22. Now that the data has been transformed with Hive, let's read it and insert it into a SQL Server table. From the SSIS toolbox, drag and drop an Execute SQL Task onto the control flow. Rename it **SQL Trucate SalesAgg**. Essentially, this task will be used to empty a table called **SalesAgg**. We will create this table later in this recipe. Double-click on the task to open the editor and set its properties, as shown in the following screenshot:

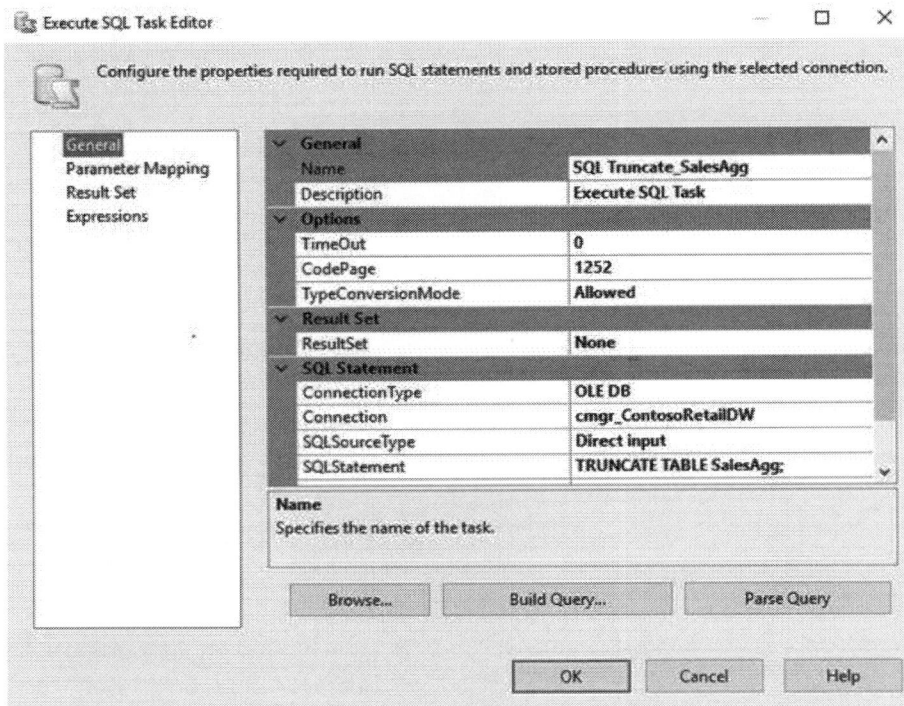

Figure 4.26 – Execute SQL Task editor

23. Set **ConnectionType** to **OLE DB** and use the **cmgr_ContonsoDW** connection manager to connect to the **ContonsoDW** database on our local machine.

24. The **SQLStatement** property is very simple:

```
TRUNCATE TABLE SalesAgg;
```

Click on **OK** to close the editor.

> **Important note**
> If you execute the task now, it will fail because we haven't created the table yet.
> We will create the table later in this recipe.

25. Drag and drop a For Each Loop container onto the control flow. Rename it FELC HiveDest. Attach it to the **SQL Trucate SalesAgg** table we created in *Step 22*.

26. Double-click on it to open its editor. Set its properties, as shown in the following screenshot:

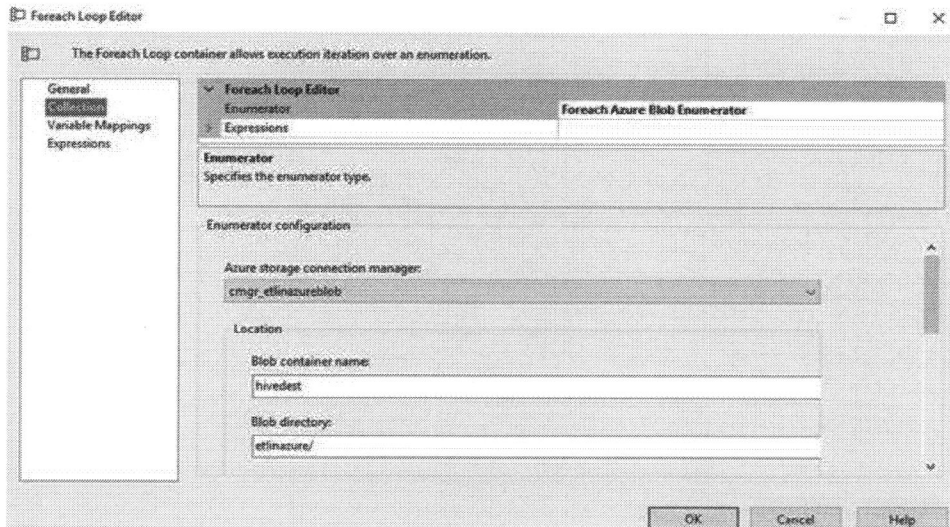

Figure 4.27 – Foreach Loop Editor

27. Click on the list beside the **Enumerator** property and select **Foreach Azure Blob Enumerator**. Use the **cmgr_etlinazureblob** connection manager. For the location information, type hivedest into the **Blob container name** textbox. Finally, type etlinazure/ into the **Blob directory** textbox.

28. Select **Variable Mappings** from the leftmost list box. Click on the drop-down list under **Variable Column** and select **<New Variable>**. The **Add Variable** window will appear.

29. Name the variable **Filename**. This will contain the name of the file that we're going to read from Azure. Click on **OK** to close the **Add Variable** window and **OK** again to close the **Foreach Loop Editor** window.

30. Drag and drop a dataflow task into the **FELC HiveDest** container. Rename it **DFT SalesAgg**.

31. Double-click on it to go inside it.

32. From the SSIS toolbox, drag and drop a **Flexible File Source**, name it FFS_
SalesAgg, and double-click on it to open its editor. Set the properties like so:

a) **File Connection Manager Type**: **AzureStorage**

b) Select **cmgr_etlinazureblob** as the connection manager.

c) Type **hivedest/** into the **Location property's Folder Path** textbox.

d) Type **000000_0** into the **File Name** textbox. Later, we will ensure that the filename is set dynamically via an expression.

e) **File Format: Parquet**.

33. Next, click on the **Columns** item in the leftmost list box. By doing this, you should see the column definitions, as shown in the following screenshot:

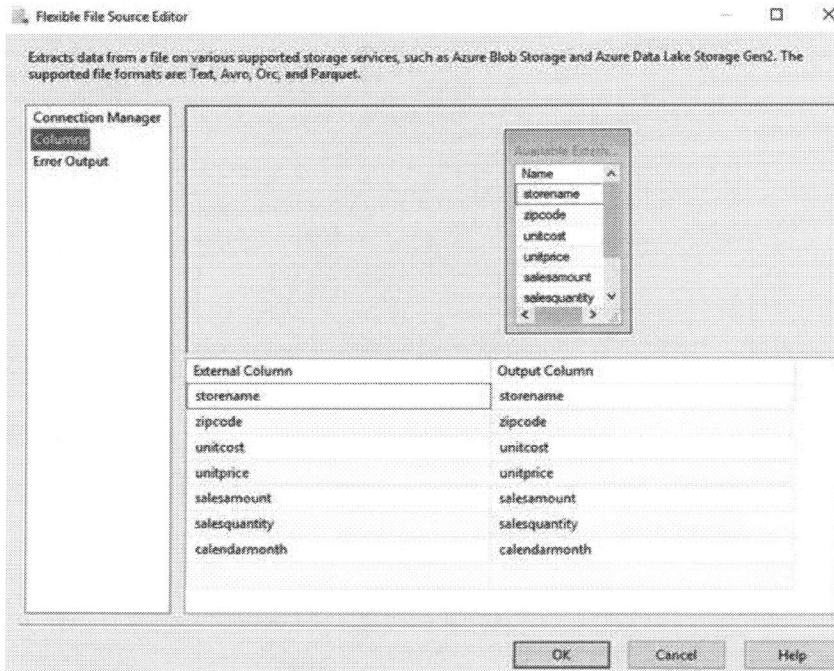

Figure 4.28 – Flexible File Source Editor

Click on **OK** to close the editor.

34. Now, in a production environment, we want to know the execution ID that inserted rows into our destination table. For that, we will use a SSIS system variable called **ServerExecutionID**. We will add it to our dataflow. Drag a **Derived Column transform** onto the dataflow, rename it **DER ServerExecutionID**, and attach it to the **Flexible File Source** component we created in *Step 32*. Double-click on it to open its editor. Set the **ServerExecutionID** column (from the system variables), as shown in the following screenshot:

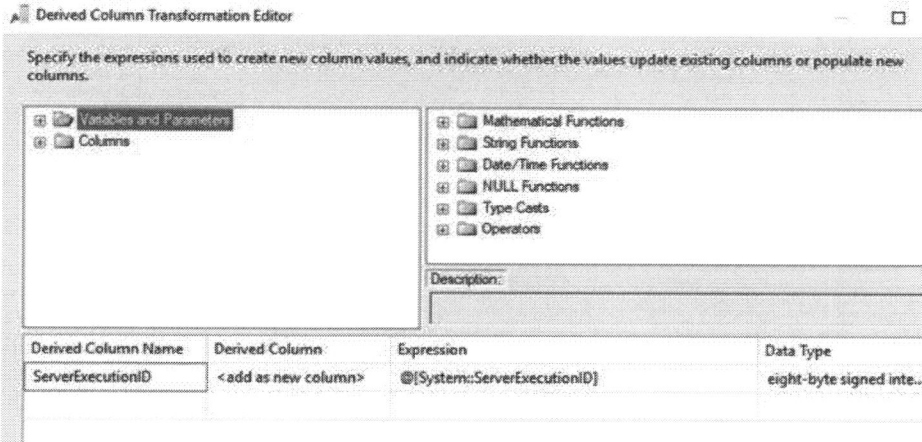

Figure 4.29 –Derived Column Transformation Editor

Click on **OK** to close the **Derived Column Transformation Editor** window.

35. Finally, drag and drop an **OLE DB Destination** onto the dataflow. Name it **OLEDBDST SalesAgg** and attach it to the **DER ServerExecutionID** derived column transform we created previously.

36. Double-click on it to open its editor. Set **OLE DB Connection Manager** to **cmgr_ContonsoRetailDW**. Click on the **New** button beside **Name of the Table** or **View**. A **Create Table** window will appear. Remove the **OLEDBDST** prefix and ensure that there is no whitespace left. Click on **OK** to create the table.

37. Click on the **Mappings** item in the leftmost list box to confirm the mappings between the source and destination columns. Your screen should look as follows:

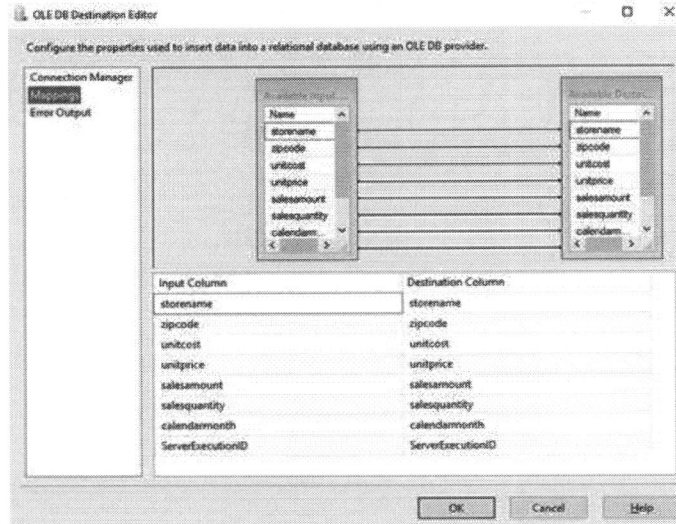

Figure 4.30 – The mappings editor in the OLE DB Destination Editor window

Click on **OK** to close the editor.

38. Now, there is a finishing touch that we need to add. Remember that our **Flexible File Source** has the name 000000_0 hardcoded? This name was set by the hive worker. Since we had only one worker, the name is 000000_0. If we had a bigger data load and many workers, we might have many files in the blob storage, and they might have different names. Previously, we set **Foreach Loop Container** so that it stores the filename in a package variable called Filename, but we haven't used it yet. Later in this recipe, will use it to set up the filename in the **Flexible File Source** component of the dataflow.

39. In the dataflow, click anywhere in its background and go to the **Properties** window to the right of the dataflow.

40. Scroll down to the **Expressions** property and click on the ellipsis button (...), as shown in the following screenshot:

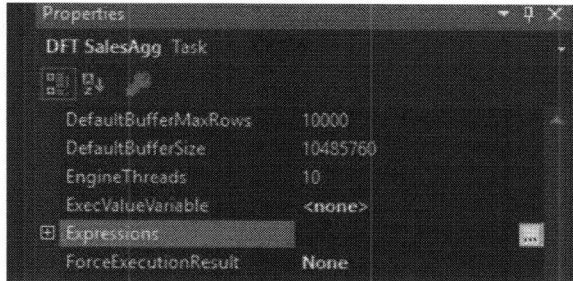

Figure 4.31 – The Expressions property in the Properties window

41. The **Property Expression Editor** will appear. Select the [**FFS_SalesAgg**][**FileName**] property in the left pane of the editor. In the expression, click the ellipsis button (…) and select the **Filename** variable. Click on **OK** in both the **Expression Builder** and **Property Expression** editor windows.

42. Now, when we run the package, the filename will be set by our **Foreach loop container** dynamically. But there is still a caveat. If the file does not exist in the blob storage, the package will not be validated when we execute it. To circumvent this issue, once again, click anywhere in an empty space of the dataflow and go the **Properties** window to the right.

43. Set the **DelayValidation** property to **True**, as shown in the following screenshot. This means that the package will not try to validate the dataflow when it opens. The dataflow will be validated only when it is executed:

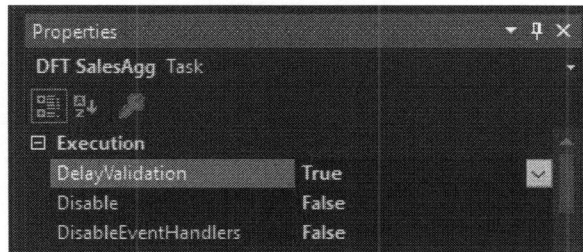

Figure 4.32 – The DelayValidation setting set to True

Now, go back to the control flow. Your package should look as follows:

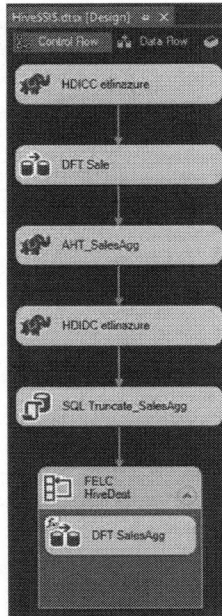

Figure 4.33 – The completed control flow

We can now execute the package. It will take several minutes to execute since we are creating and dropping an HDInsight cluster inside it.

44. Once the package has been executed, go to **SQL Server Management Studio**, and select the table's row, as shown in the following screenshot:

Figure 4.34 – Executing the query in SSMS

Here, we can see that Hive aggregated 358,697 rows down to 1,505 and that all the numeric columns have been summed, except for **unitprice**.

45. Go back into Visual Studio and promote all the connection managers to project connection managers. This will allow reusability if or when you want to create similar packages. To do so, right-click on each connection manager and select **Convert** to project connection from the menu that appears.

46. Your connections managers will have (**project**) in front of their names, as shown in the following screenshot:

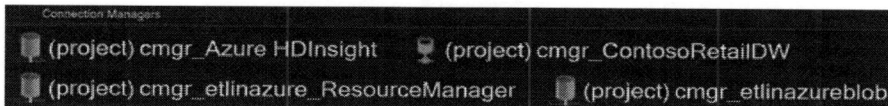

Figure 4.35 – The connection managers that were used in the package

Let's move on to the next section!

How it works...

The Hive script uses the SQL language to do the following:

First, it creates a database called **ETLInAzure**. It is dropped into the existing one if one already exists.

Next, it creates an external table, meaning a table that is managed outside the cluster. Dropping the cluster will not drop the table's data. The table points to the blob storage file where we copied the data previously.

Then, it creates a table called **SalesAgg**. Again, this is an external table that points to a container called **hivedest**. We will store our data into a blob called **etlinazure**.

Finally, it aggregates the data, removing the **fulldatelable** column and summing the data by **storename**, **zipcode**, and **CalendarMonth**.

This was quite a complex recipe. We created, used, and disposed of an Azure HDInsight compute resource to transform our data and then used the Hive language to aggregate this data. The next section will be very similar to this one, except we will use Pig instead of Hive.

Transforming data with Pig

This section is almost identical to the previous one. The only difference is that we're going to use Pig to do the transformations and use different containers in our storage.

Pig is a scripting language that can **eat** anything. This means that we can consume almost any type of file easily with Pig. However, there is a restriction on the file types we can use with the HDInsight version of Pig: The Parquet file cannot be used. This is because a library is missing in the out-of-the-box HDInsight cluster. For this reason, we will use a regular text file format in this recipe.

A lot of the steps in this section are similar to the steps shown in the previous recipe. If you completed all the recipes provided in the previous sections, some of them can be skipped. We'll indicate when this is the case.

Getting ready

This recipe requires that you have the following:

- Visual Studio 2019 with the Integration Services extension installed
- Azure Feature Pack installed
- Java Runtime Engine installed
- Access to an Azure subscription
- An on-demand HDInsight cluster task in your package

Make sure that you've completed the *Creating an on-demand Azure HDInsight cluster* recipe before starting this one.

How to do it...

Now that we have some data copied to Azure, let's transform it using **Apache Pig**.

Some of the steps in this recipe were explained in the *Transforming data with Hive* recipe when we copied data to an Azure storage account. What differs here is the **Flexible Flat File** destination.

We'll begin by copying some data into a container in our storage account:

1. In the **Solution Explorer** window, go to the SSIS packages folder, right-click on it, and select **New SSIS package** from the menu that appears. Rename it `PigSSIS.dtsx` and press Enter.

2. From the SSIS toolbox, drag and drop a dataflow task. Rename it **DFT Sales**.

3. Open it and drag an **OleDB Source transform** onto the dataflow surface. Name it **OLEDBSRC Sales**. Double-click on it to open the **OLE DB Source Editor** window. Click on **New** beside the connection manager property, and then click **New** in the **Configure OLE DB Connection Manager** window. Enter the required information, as shown in the following screenshot, then click on **OK** in all the windows to create the connection manager. Rename it **cmgr_ContosoRetailDW**.

4. Right-click on **cmgr_ContosoRetailDW** and convert it into a project connection manager to make it available in all subsequent packages we will create. The connection manager should look as follows:

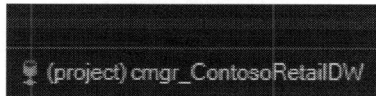

Figure 4.36 – The connection manager

5. Go back to the **OLE DB Source Editor** window and make sure that **cmgr_ContonsoRetailDW** is selected as **OLD DB connection manager**. In the **Data access mode**, select **SQL command**. Add the following SQL command text:

```
SELECT          s.StoreName, s.ZipCode, d.FullDateLabel,
f.UnitCost, f.UnitPrice, f.SalesAmount, f.SalesQuantity,
d.CalendarMonth
FROM FactSales AS f
    INNER JOIN DimDate AS d
        ON f.DateKey = d.Datekey
    INNER JOIN DimStore AS s
        ON f.StoreKey = s.StoreKey
WHERE           (d.CalendarYear = 2009)
    AND (CAST(RIGHT(d.CalendarMonth, 2) AS int) < 6)
```

Click on **OK** to close the editor.

6. Some zip codes are NULL. With Pig, they will be interpreted as return characters (\n), which will cause issues when we read the resulting file later. For this reason, we will make sure that the missing zip codes will be placed in a specific bucket; we will replace them with the "N/A" value. Drag a **Derived** column onto the dataflow and rename it **DER NULL**. Attach it to the OLEDBSRC_Sales source and double-click on it to get to the editor, as shown in the following screenshot:

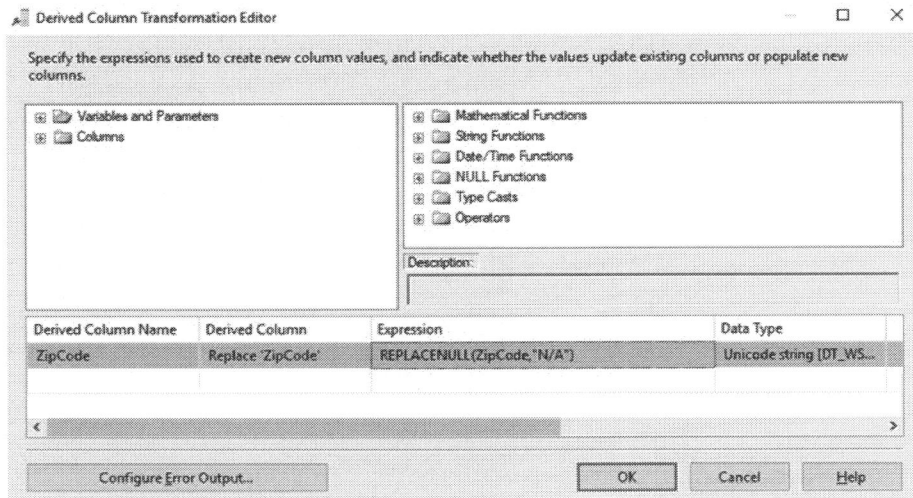

Figure 4.37 – The NULL replacement derived column

7. In the **Derived Column** section, select **Replace 'ZipCode'**. Type REPLACENULL(ZipCode, "N/A") as the expression. Click on **OK** to close the editor.

8. Drag a **Flexible Flat File Destination** from the Azure section of the SSIS toolbox. Link it to the OLEDBSRC Sales source we just created. Rename it **FFD Sales**. Double-click on it to open the **Flexible File Destination Editor** window, as shown in the following screenshot:

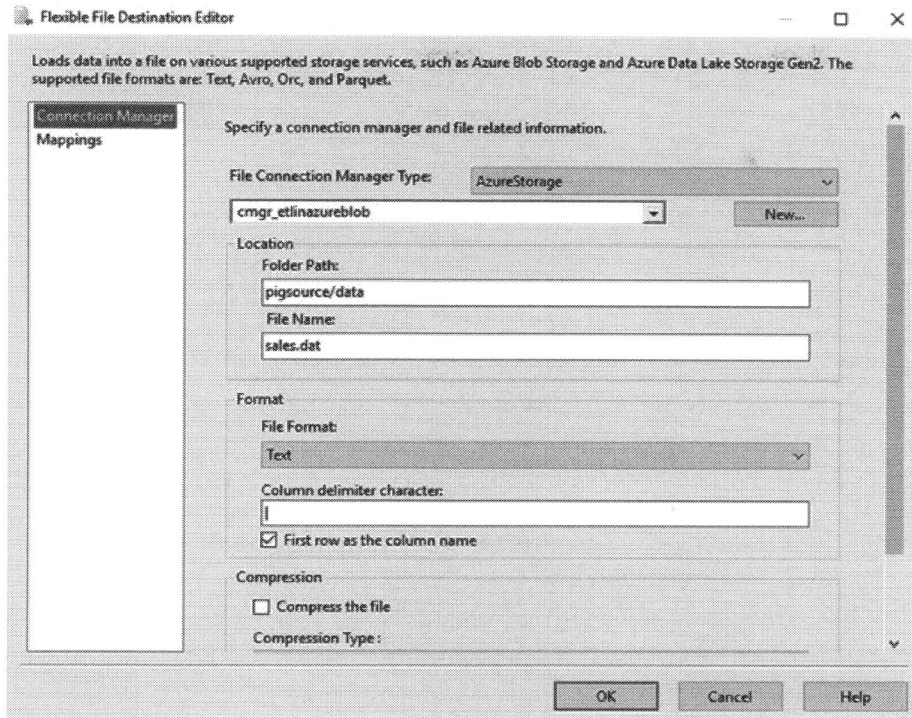

Figure 4.38 –Flexible File Destination Editor

9. Leave **AzureStorage** as **File Connection Manager Type**. Use the **cmgr_etlinazureblob** connection manager here. For the location, use **pigsource/data** as **Folder Path** and **sales.dat** as **File Name**. Pig does not support the Parquet format without supplemental libraries being installed, so for **File Format**, we will use **Text**, with a vertical bar (|) as a delimiter. Click on the **Mappings** tab to persist the column mapping. Then, click **OK** to close the editor.

10. Go back to the **Control Flow** section of the package. Right-click on the task and select **Execute** from the menu that appears.

11. Once completed, go to **Azure Storage Explorer**, and expand the **pigsource** container. Click on the folder called **data**. You should see the **sales.dat** file appear, as shown in the following screenshot:

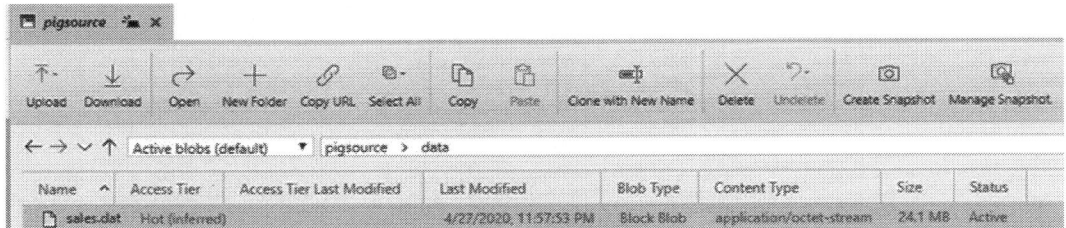

Figure 4.39 – The sale.dat file copied to the storage container

> **Important note**
> You might have noticed that the file size differs from the Parquet format. The Parquet format compresses data by columns. That is why the file is bigger here.

Now that we have some data copied to Azure, let's transform it using Pig. Pig is known to be a very flexible scripting language in the cloud since it was built based on the idea that it can ingest anything.

12. Open **Azure Storage Explorer** and create a container called **pigdest**, as shown in the following screenshot:

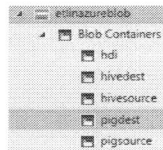

Figure 4.40 – The pigdest blob

13. Go back to Visual Studio and the package control flow and add an **Azure HDInsight Pig Task**. Rename it **APT_SalesAgg** and attach it to the DFT Sales dataflow we created previously.

14. Double-click on the task to open its editor and set its properties, as shown in the following screenshot:

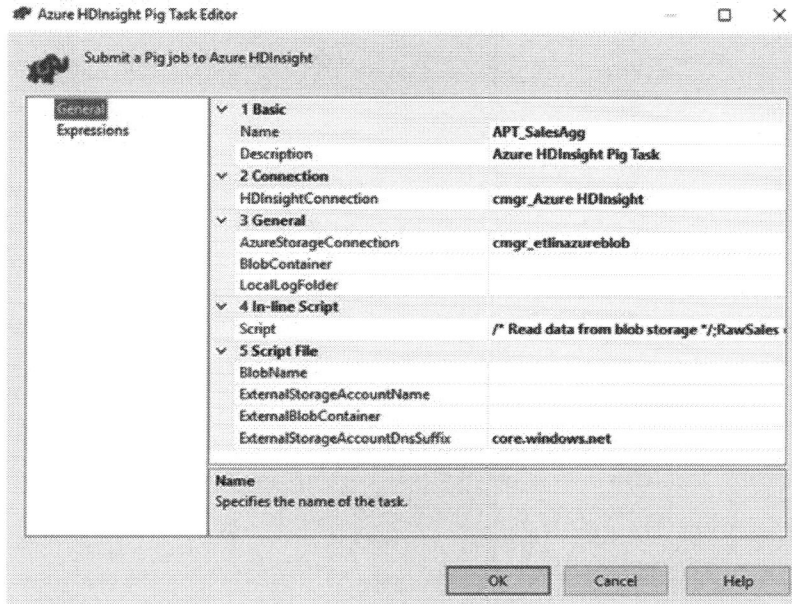

Figure 4.41 – Azure HDInsight Pig Task Editor

> **Tip**
> This step was explained in the *Transforming data with Hive* recipe.

15. In the *Transforming data with Hive* recipe, we created an on-demand HDInsight cluster. It was deleted at the end of the package, which means we need to recreate it. We are going to create a connection manager to interact with it. From the drop-down list near the **HDInsightConnection** property, select <**New Connection**>. An **Azure HDInsight Connection Manager Editor** window will appear. Fill in the required properties, as shown in the following screenshot:

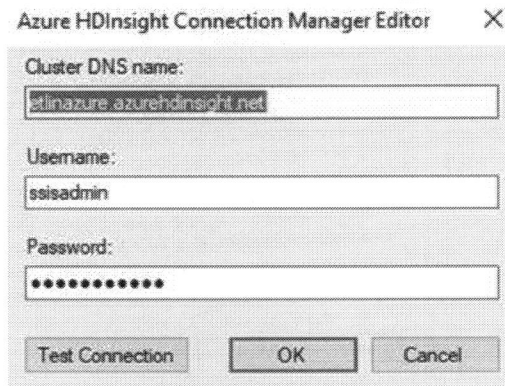

Figure 4.42 – Azure HDInsight Connection Manager Editor

16. Click **Test Connection** and then **OK** to close the window. Rename the connection manager **cmgr_AzureHdInsight** once you've finished configuring that task.

17. Set **cmgr_etlinazureblob** to **AzureStorageConnection**.

18. For **LocalLogFolder**, use a local path that will be used by HDInsight to store the logs.

19. In the **4-In-line Script** section, click on the three ellipsis (**...**) and copy and paste the following script:

```
/* Read data from blob storage */;
RawSales = LOAD 'wasbs://pigsource@etlinazureblob.
blob.core.windows.net/data/' USING PigStorage('|')
AS (StoreName:chararray, ZipCode:chararray,
FullDateLabel:chararray, UnitCost:double,
UnitPrice:double, SalesAmount:double, SalesQuantity:int,
CalendarMonth:long);
/* Remove header line */;
Sales = Filter RawSales by (StoreName != 'StoreName');
/* Group by dimensinal attributes */;
Sales_Group = Group Sales by (StoreName, ZipCode,
```

```
CalendarMonth);
/* Aggregate the data */;
AggSales = foreach Sales_Group generate FLATTEN((group)),
FLATTEN(( SUM(Sales.UnitCost), AVG(Sales.UnitPrice),
SUM(Sales.SalesAmount), SUM(Sales.SalesQuantity)));
/* Cleanup output directory */;
rmf wasbs://pigdest@<Your Storage account>.blob.core.
windows.net/etlinazure;
/* Store the result into a file */;
STORE AggSales INTO 'wasbs://pigdest@etlinazureblob.blob.
core.windows.net/etlinazure' USING PigStorage('|');
```

Leave the other properties empty and click on **OK** to close the task editor.

20. Right-click on the task and execute it. After 1 or 2 minutes, the task will complete successfully, as shown in the following screenshot:

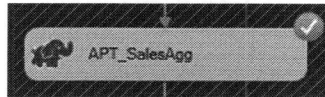

Figure 4.43 – The Pig task completed with success

21. Now, go into Azure Storage Explorer. Open the **pigdest** container and navigate to the **etlinazure** blob. You will see a file called **000000_0**, as shown in the following screenshot:

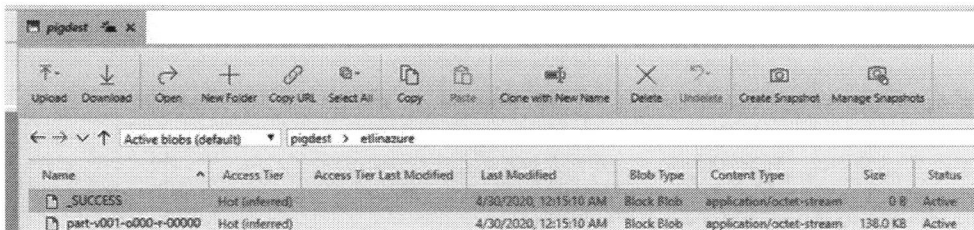

Figure 4.44 – The content of the etlinazure blob

There should be a file here called **_SUCCESS**. We'll have to get rid of it when we need to read the files in the container.

22. Double-click on the file to open it. The file will be download into your temp folder. Click on the **Open Folder** link from the **Activities** pane. Then, choose **Notepad** (or another text editor of your choice) to open the file.

23. The file will open. Since it is a text file format, we can see the transformed data as opposed to the Parquet format:

Figure 4.45 – The content of the file in Notepad

Close the text editor. The next recipe will show you how to read the file.

24. Now that we have transformed our data in our HDInsight cluster, we don't need it anymore. Drag and drop an **Azure HDInsight Delete Cluster Task** from the SSIS toolbox. Rename it **HDIDC etlinazure** and attach it to the previous task on the package's control flow.

25. Double-click on the task to open its editor and set its properties, as shown in the following screenshot:

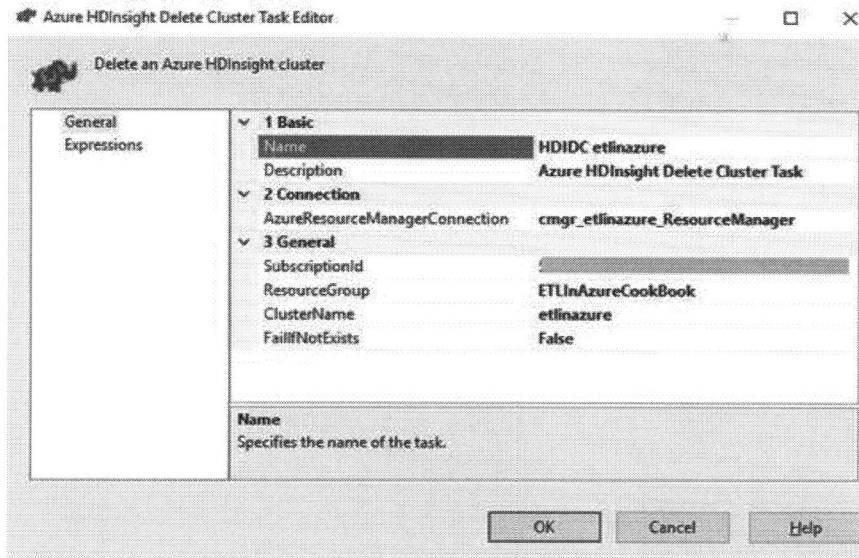

Figure 4.46 – Azure HDInsight Delete Cluster Task Editor

26. Use the **cmgr_etlinazure_ResourceManager** connection manager here, which is the same one we used previously in this chapter. Set **SubscriptionId** to your Azure **SubscriptionId** and **ResourceGroup** to **ETLInAzureCookBook**. For **ClusterName**, make sure you use the cluster name you set up previously in this chapter. Click on **OK** to close the editor.

27. Now, right-click on the task and select **Execute** from the menu that appears. Once the execution is completed – which might take a few minutes – you should see that the task completed with success, as shown in the following screenshot:

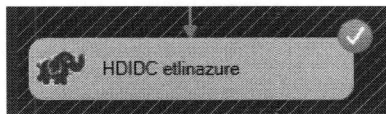

Figure 4.47 – The task completed with success

It is very important to drop resources once we do not need them anymore. Since we're renting these resources, we are paying for them and they can become very expensive if we don't drop them when they are not being used.

> **Important note**
> Most of the steps of this recipe were explained in a previous section. A few steps have been changed due to how Pig processes the destination folder's content.

Now that the data has been transformed with Pig, let's read it and insert it into a SQL Server table.

28. From the SSIS toolbox, drag and drop an **Execute SQL Task** onto the control flow. Rename it **SQL Trucate SalesAgg**. Essentially, this task will be used to empty a table called **SalesAgg**. We will create this table later in this recipe. Link the task to the previous one; that is, `HDIDC etlinazure`. Double-click on the task to open the editor for it and set the required properties, as shown in the following screenshot:

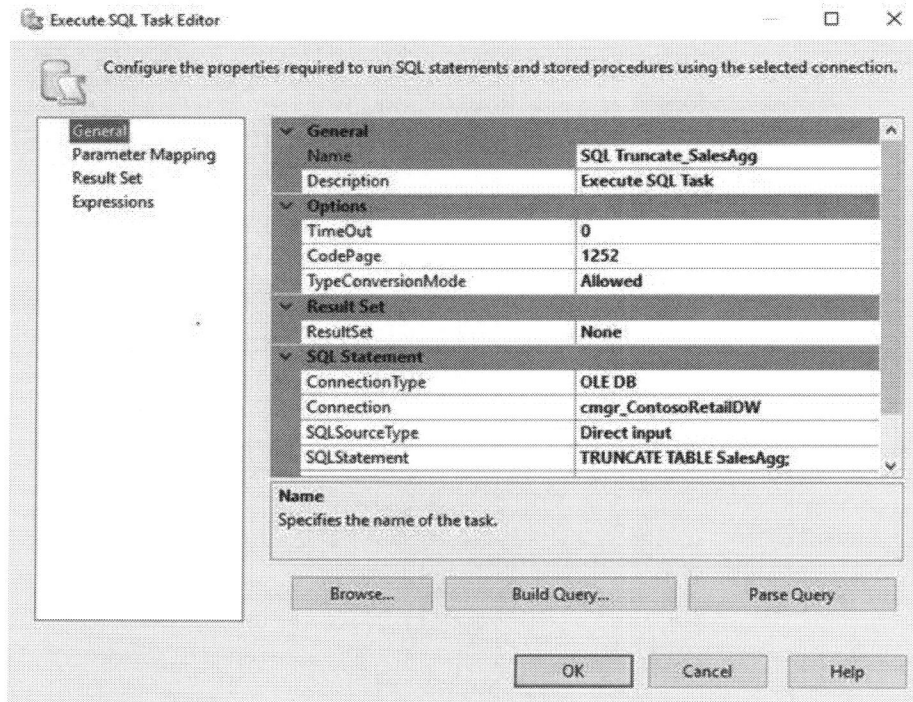

Figure 4.48 – Execute SQL Task Editor

Set **ConnectionType** to **OLE DB** and use the **cmgr_ContonsoDW** connection manager to connect to the **ContonsoDW** database on our local machine.

The code required for **SQLStatement** is very simple:

```
TRUNCATE TABLE SalesAgg;
```

Click on **OK** to close the editor. If you execute the task now, it will fail because we haven't created the table yet. Will do that later in this recipe.

29. Drag and drop a **Foreach Loop container** onto the control flow. Rename it **FELC PigDest**. Attach it to the **SQL Trucate SalesAgg** table we created previously in this recipe.

30. Double-click on it to open its editor. Set its properties, as shown in the following screenshot:

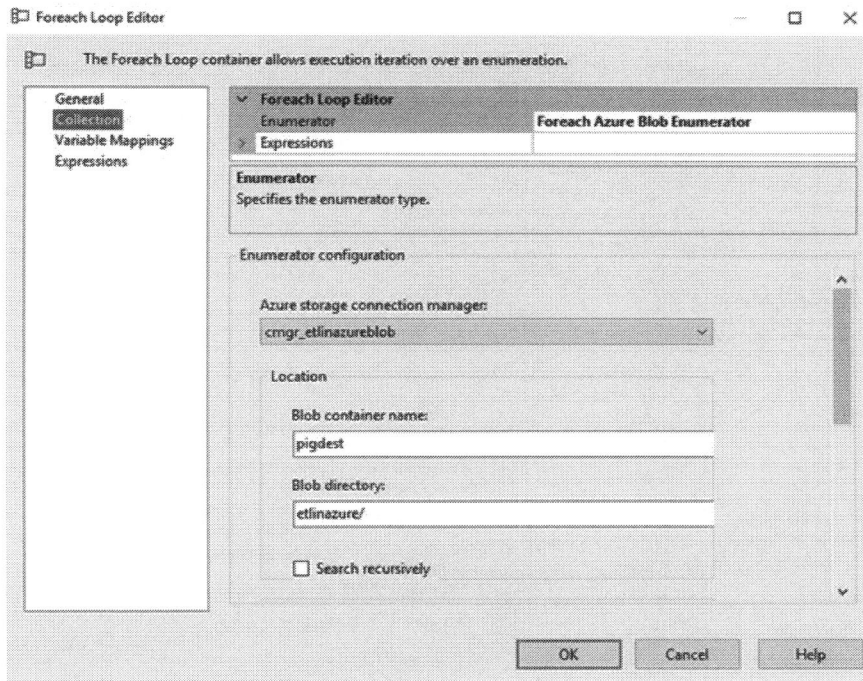

Figure 4.49 – Foreach Loop Editor

Click on the list beside the **Enumerator** property and select **Foreach Azure Blob Enumerator**. Use the **cmgr_etlinazureblob** connection manager here. For **Location**, type pigdest into the **Blob container name** text box. Finally, type etlinazure/ into the **Blob directory** text box.

31. Select **Variable Mappings** from the leftmost list box. Click on the drop-down list under the **Variable** column and select <**New Variable**>. The **Add Variable** window will appear, as shown in the following screenshot:

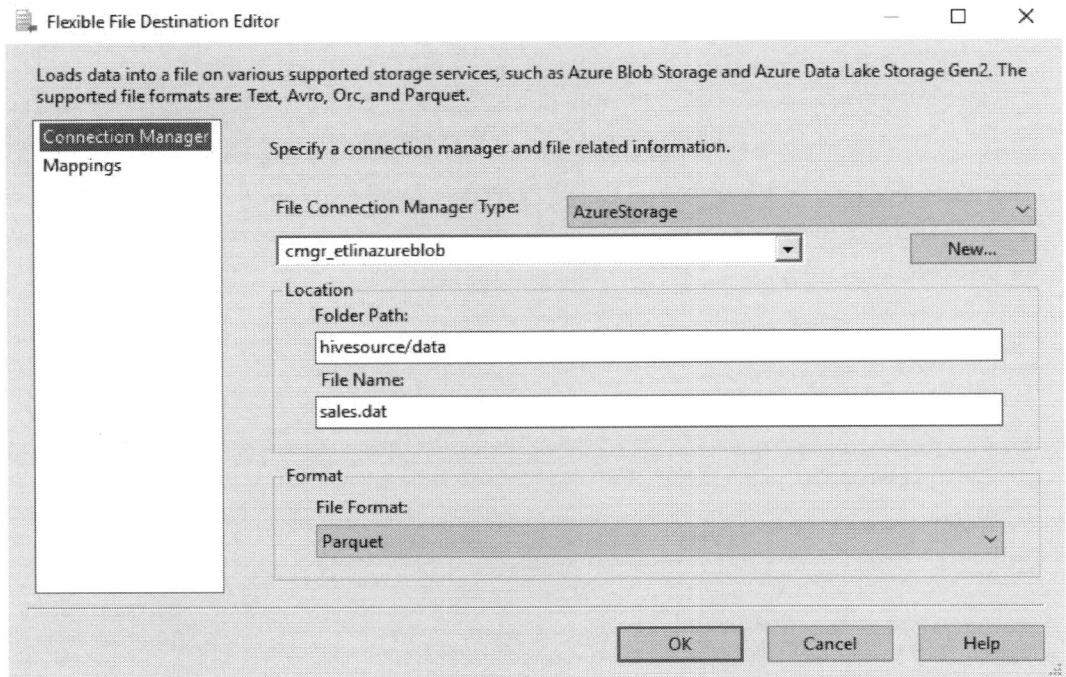

Figure 4.50 – The Add Variable window

32. Name the variable **Filename**. Then, click on **OK** to close the **Add Variable** window and **OK** again to close the **Foreach Loop Editor** window.

33. With Pig, there are two things we must be aware of. First, do not try to load the **_SUCCESS** file and remove the `etlinazure/` prefix in the filename. To do this correctly, we will use an **Expression Task**. Drag and drop an **Expression Task** onto the control flow surface. Rename it `EXPR Filename` and double-click on it to open its editor.

34. Type the following expression into the **Expression** box and click on **OK** to close the **Expression Builder** window:

```
@[User::Filename] =  REPLACE( @[User::Filename],
"etlinazure/", "")
```

This can be seen in the following screenshot:

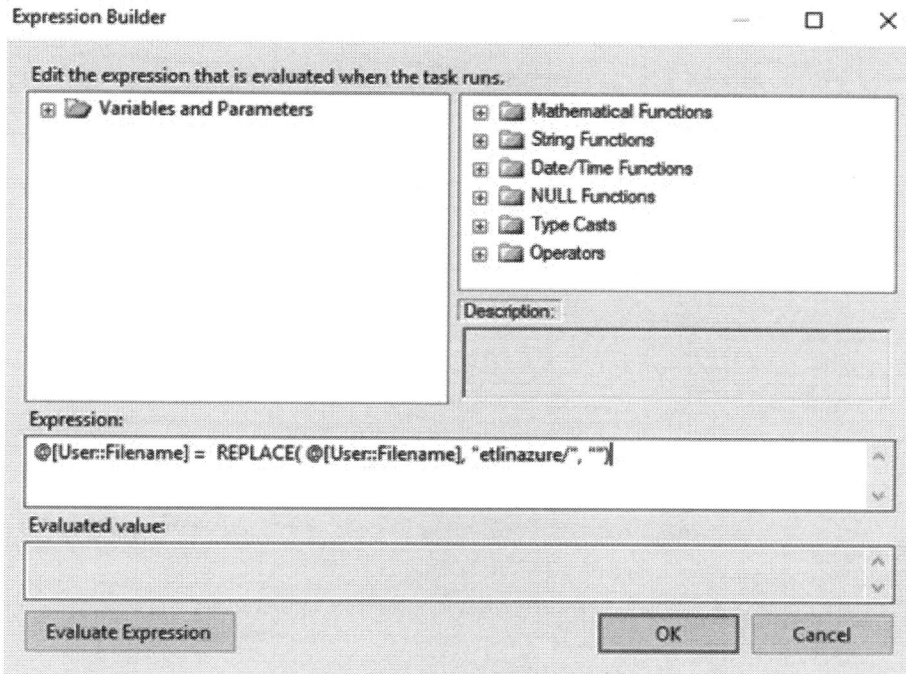

Figure 4.51 – Expression Builder

35. Drag and drop a dataflow task into the FELC PigDest container. Rename it DFT SalesAgg and attach it to the EXPR filename we created previously.

36. To ensure we don't load the _SUCCESS file created by Pig, double-click on the path; that is, the arrow between the expression task and the dataflow task. This will open the **Precedence Constraint Editor** window. We are using this to bypass the _SUCCESS file. As shown in the following screenshot, change **Evaluation operation** to **Expression and Constraint** and enter @[User::Filename] != "_SUCCESS" in the **Expression** box:

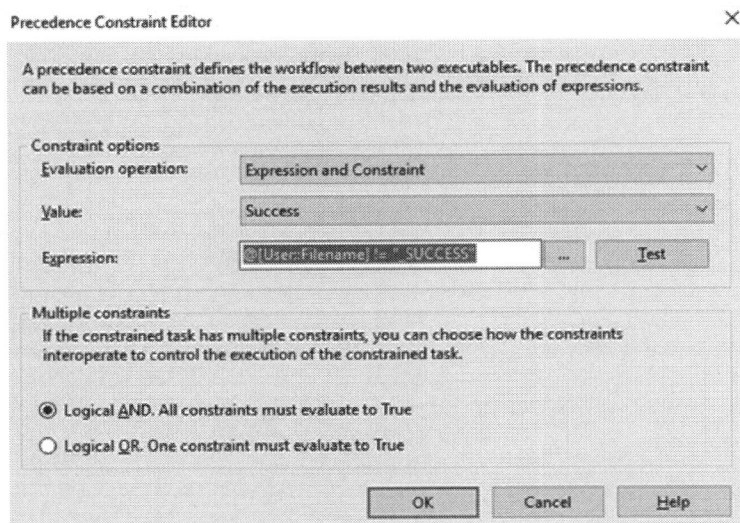

Figure 4.52 – The Precedence Constraint Editor window filled in

37. Click on **OK** to close the editor.

38. Double-click on the dataflow (**DFT SalesAgg**) to go inside it.

39. From the SSIS toolbox, drag and drop a **Flexible File Source**, rename it **FF_SalesAgg**, and double-click on it to open its editor. Set its properties like so:

   a) **File connection: AzureStorage**.

   b) Use **cmgr_etlinazureblob** as the connection manager.

   c) Type pigdest/etlinazure into the **Location** property's **Folder Path** text box.

d) For the **File Name** property, type in `part-v001-o000-r-00000`. Later, we will ensure that the filename is set dynamically via an expression.

e) Set **Text** as the **File Format** property.

f) Use a pipe (|) as the column delimiter character.

40. Next, click on the **Columns** item in the leftmost list box. As opposed to the Parquet format, we need to rename the columns since Pig has no concept of column names and they are all named `Prop1`, `Prop2`, and so on. Once you've renamed the columns, the final result should look as follows:

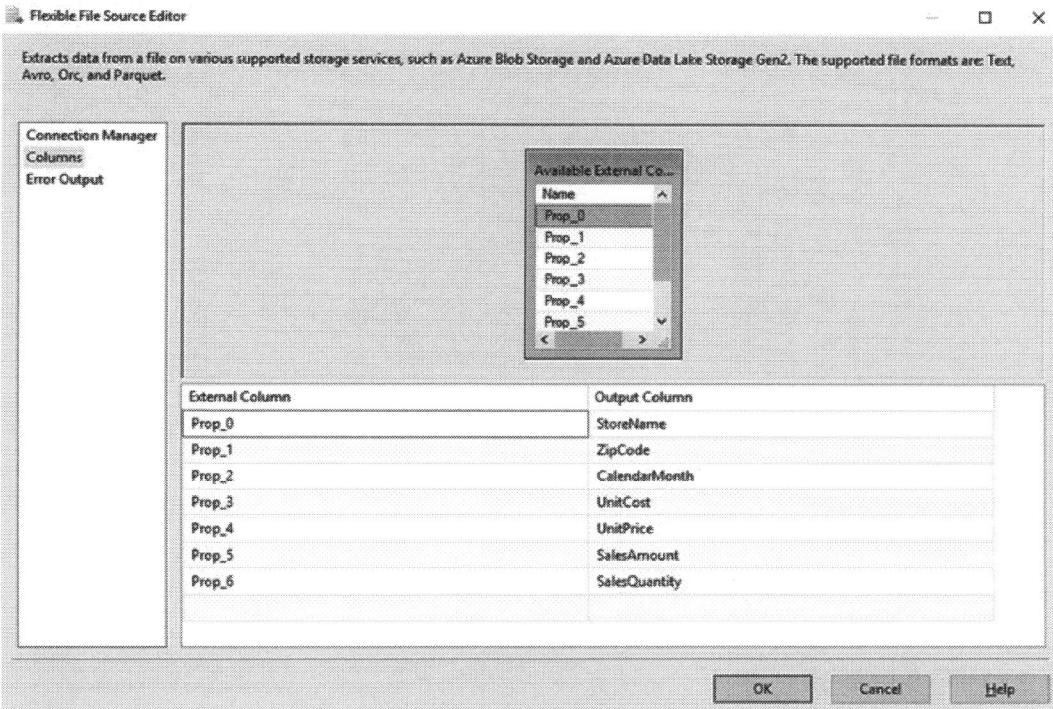

Figure 4.53 – The Columns editor in the Flexible File Source Editor window

41. Click on **OK** to close the editor.

42. Now, we want to know the execution ID that inserted rows into our destination table. We'll do this in a production environment. For this, we will use a SSIS system variable called **ServerExecutionID**. We will add it to our dataflow. Drag a **Derived Column** transform onto the dataflow, rename it **DER ServerExecutionID**, and attach it to the **Flexible File Source** component we created previously. Double-click on it to open its editor. Set the `ServerExecutionID` column from the System variables, as shown in the following screenshot:

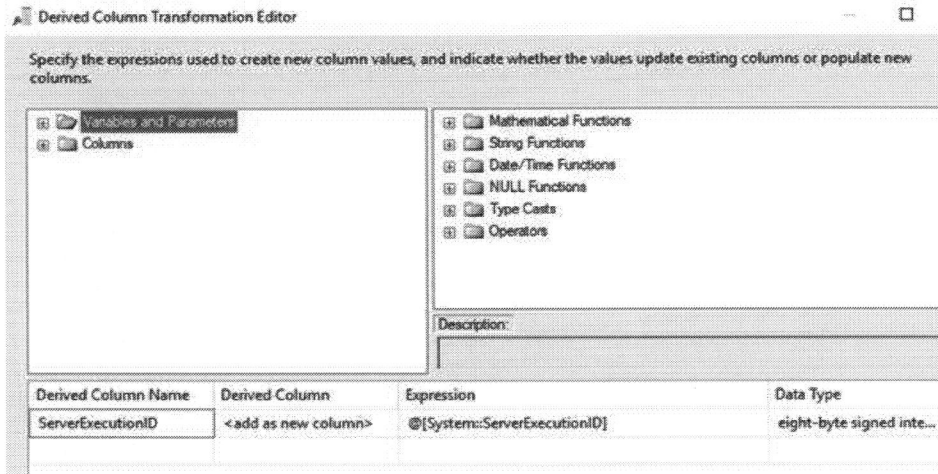

Figure 4. 54 –Derived Column Transformation Editor

Click on **OK** to close the **Derived Column Transformation Editor** window.

43. Finally, drag and drop an **OLE DB Destination** onto the dataflow. Name it **OLEDBDST SalesAgg** and attach it to the **DER ServerExecutionID** derived column transform we created previously.

> **Tip**
> We did this step in the *Transforming data with Hive* recipe.

44. Double-click on it to open its editor. Set **OLE DB Connection Manager** to **cmgr_ContonsoRetailDW**. Click on the **New** button beside **Name of the Table** or **View**. A **Create Table** window will appear. Remove the OLEDBDST prefix and ensure that there is no whitespace left. Your screen should look similar to the following:

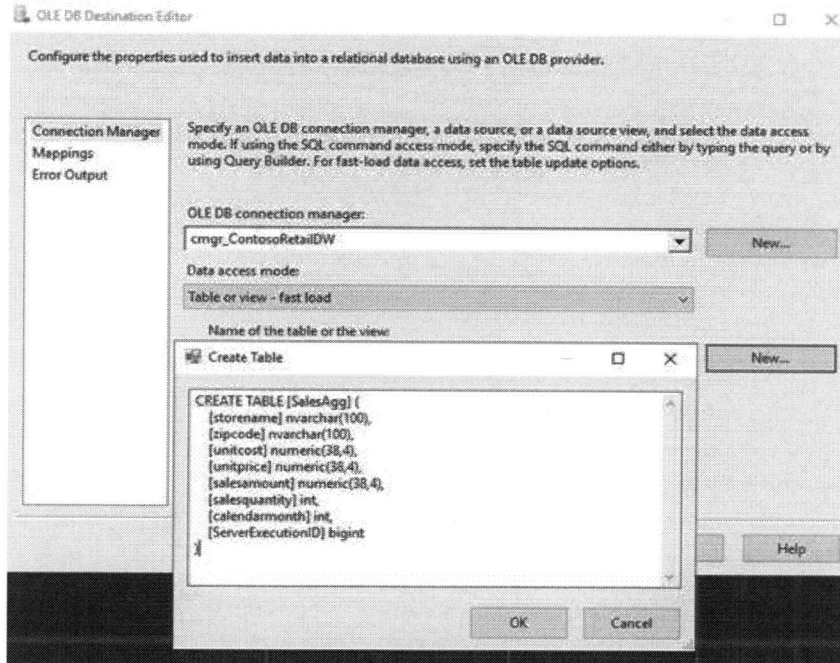

Figure 4.55 – The Create Table editor

45. Click on **OK** to create the table.

46. Click on the **Mappings** item in the leftmost list box to confirm the mappings between the source and destination columns. Your screen should look as follows:

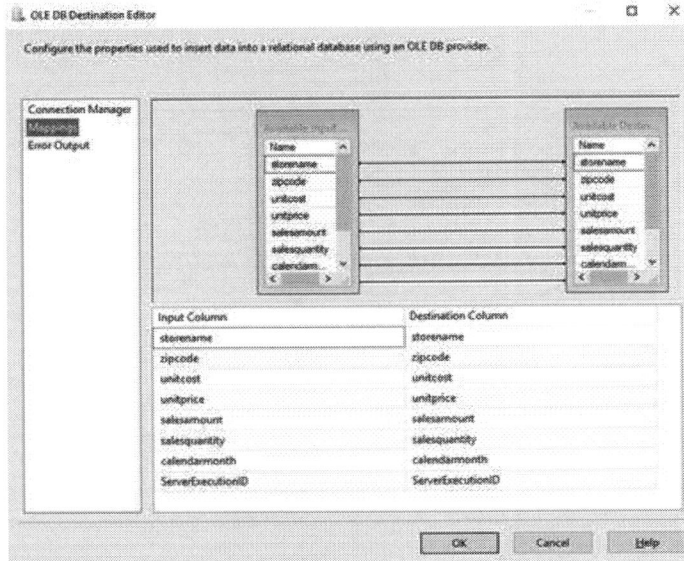

Figure 4.56 – The Mappings tab of the OLE DB Destination Editor window

Click on **OK** to close the editor.

47. There is one last finishing touch that we need to add. Remember that our **Flexible File Source** has the name part-v001-o000-r-00000 hardcoded. This name was set by the Pig worker since we had only one worker. If we had a bigger data load and many workers, we might have many files in the blob storage, and they might have different names. We set our **Foreach Loop Container** so that it stores the filename in a package variable called **Filename**, but we haven't used it yet. We will use this to set up the filename in the **Flexible File Source** component of the dataflow next.

48. In the dataflow, click anywhere in its background and go to the **Properties** window to the right of the dataflow.

49. Scroll down to the **Expressions** property and click on the ellipsis button (**...**), as shown in the following screenshot:

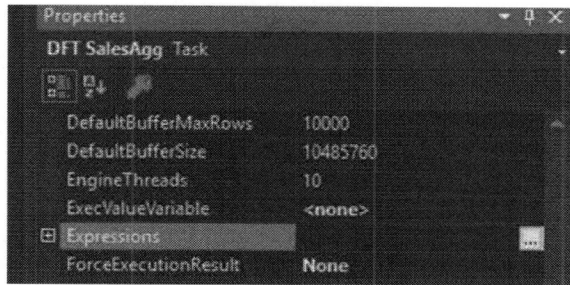

Figure 4.57 – The Expressions property

50. The **Property Expression Editor** window will appear. Select the [**FFS_SalesAgg**]
[**FileName**] property from the left pane of the editor. In the **Expression** box, click
the ellipsis button (…) and select the **Filename** variable, as shown in the following
screenshot:

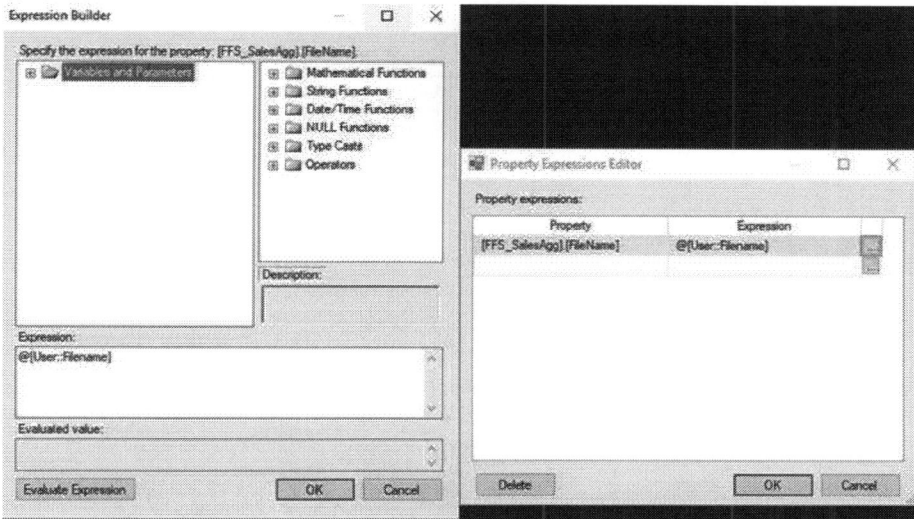

Figure 4.58 – Expression Builder

Click **OK** in both the **Expression Builder** and **Property Expression
editor** windows.

Now, when we run the package, the filename will be set by the Foreach loop
container dynamically. But there is still a caveat. If the file does not exist yet in the
blob storage, the package will not be validated when we execute it.

51. To circumvent this issue, once again, click anywhere in the dataflow's background and go the **Properties** window to the right.

52. Set the **DelayValidation** property to **True**, as shown in the following screenshot. This means that the package will not try to validate the dataflow when it opens. The dataflow will only be validated when it is executed:

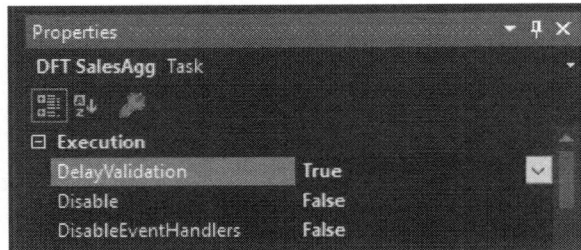

Figure 4.59 – The DelayValidation property

Now, go back to the control flow. Your package should look as follows:

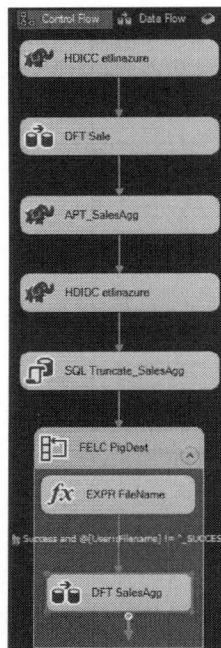

Figure 4.60 – The complete control flow

53. Now, we can execute the package. It will take several minutes to execute since we are creating and dropping an HDInsight cluster inside it.

54. Once the execution has completed, go to **SQL Server Management Studio**, and select the table's row, as shown in the following screenshot:

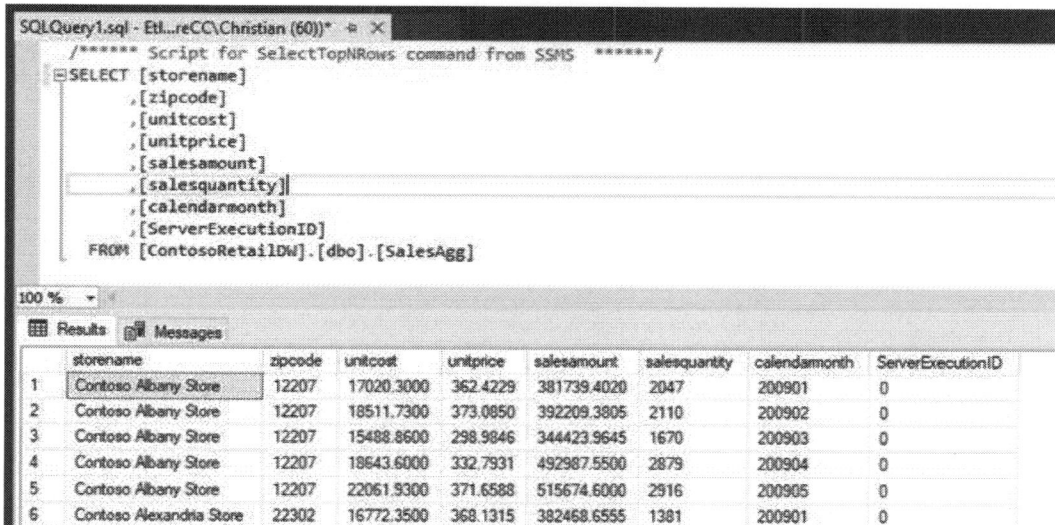

```
SQLQuery1.sql - Etl...reCC\Christian (60))*  ⊕ ×
        /****** Script for SelectTopNRows command from SSMS  ******/
    ⊟SELECT [storename]
          ,[zipcode]
          ,[unitcost]
          ,[unitprice]
          ,[salesamount]
          ,[salesquantity]
          ,[calendarmonth]
          ,[ServerExecutionID]
      FROM [ContosoRetailDW].[dbo].[SalesAgg]
```

	storename	zipcode	unitcost	unitprice	salesamount	salesquantity	calendarmonth	ServerExecutionID
1	Contoso Albany Store	12207	17020.3000	362.4229	381739.4020	2047	200901	0
2	Contoso Albany Store	12207	18511.7300	373.0850	392209.3805	2110	200902	0
3	Contoso Albany Store	12207	15488.8600	298.9846	344423.9645	1670	200903	0
4	Contoso Albany Store	12207	18643.6000	332.7931	492987.5500	2879	200904	0
5	Contoso Albany Store	12207	22061.9300	371.6588	515674.6000	2916	200905	0
6	Contoso Alexandria Store	22302	16772.3500	368.1315	382468.6555	1381	200901	0

Figure 4.61 – The executed query in SSMS

Here, we can see that Pig aggregated 358,697 rows down to 1,505 and that the numeric columns are all summed except for **unitprice**.

How it works...

Pig, as opposed to Hive, does not absolutely need databases to transform data. Another difference is that Hive works best with structured data, whereas Pig works best with semi-structured data. They also differ in terms of the language they use: Hive uses SQL, while Pig uses its own procedural language.

The Pig script allowed us to do the following in this recipe:

First, we created a variable called **RawSales** and loaded the content of the file we created previously into it. We removed the header line as this will only be in our way when we transform and group the data with the **Sales_Group** variable by using **StoreName**, **ZipCode**, and **CalendarMonth**.

We then aggregated the data in a variable called **AggSales**. Since this creates tuples in Pig, we flattened them to get a consumable result with the FLATTEN function. Pig cannot overwrite the destination file. We used the rmf command to erase the destination directory. Finally, we wrote the **SalesAgg** table into a file that will be stored in the eltinazure blob.

5

Extending SSIS with Custom Tasks and Transformations

In this chapter, you will learn how to extend the collection of natively provided SSIS Control Flow Tasks and Data Flow Components by designing a Custom Control Flow Task and a Custom Data Flow Component. By taking advantage of the built-in extensibility of **SQL Server 2019 Integration Services (SSIS)** you can implement your own solutions, or modules, to be used in SSIS control flows, or data flows. Furthermore, you can implement them in a way that makes them virtually indistinguishable from the natively provided ones.

This chapter covers the following recipes, aimed at introducing SSIS customization:

- Designing a Custom Control Flow Task
- Designing a Custom Data Flow Component
- Deploying SSIS customizations
- Upgrading a Custom Data Flow Component

Technical requirements

The recipes in this chapter assume that you already have an appropriate development environment in place on your workstation, including a SQL Server 2019 instance, with the administration and development tools installed. All these prerequisites are covered in *Chapter 1, Getting Started with Azure and SSIS 2019*. You do not need an Azure subscription to complete the recipes in this chapter.

Designing a Custom Control Flow Task

To determine whether, in a given situation, you actually need customization or not, you need to ask yourself two questions:

- Can the required operation be performed using one or more natively provided tasks or components in an efficient way that will remain scalable and not compromise the maintainability of the solution?

- Would the given operation only be needed in this one particular situation, or is it reasonable to expect that a similar operation might be required elsewhere, or at a later time?

If using the built-in features to address an otherwise unsupported requirement might negatively affect the efficiency of the solution, reduce its scalability, or increase its complexity, then customization should certainly be considered.

In SSIS, you can implement your own programmatic logic by using two different techniques – both built into the platform: by providing the custom code in a **Script Task** or a **Script Component**, or by designing a standalone **Custom Task** or **Custom Component**. **Scripting** allows you to customize an SSIS package as part of the package design with the script embedded in the package definition. The principal benefit of scripting is represented by the ability to address the problem right here and right now – as an integral part of package development. The principal drawback of scripting is in the very low, or at least very awkward, reusability of the resulting solution; in order for the same script to be used in more than one package, it needs to be physically copied into each one of them.

Typically, you would use scripting if the custom logic is needed in a single package, or – if it does eventually find its home in additional packages – when the life cycle (for instance, bug fixes, upgrades, or adjustments) of these separate instances can remain mutually independent (ideally, if later changes implemented in one copy do not have to be propagated to other copies).

If reusability is required, or can reasonably be expected, **customization** through the use of custom tasks, or custom components, should be preferred over scripting. This also allows the custom features to be developed, deployed, and maintained independently of the SSIS packages in which they are being used.

This recipe will guide you through the development of a rather simple, yet quite useful custom task. One of the problems that a database administrator has to face daily is resource usage monitoring. Knowing which processes use which resources at different times of the day is crucial to efficient operation and capacity planning. For instance, SQL Server supports the **Application Name** property, which client applications can use to identify themselves in the SQL Server activity logs. The property can be sent to the server inside the connection string when establishing the connection and is accessible to a variety of built-in monitoring features.

Typically, once an SSIS solution has been deployed to the target environment, the administrator of that environment has complete control of the configurations used by these solutions. For instance, to be able to distinguish between different connections, the administrator can add package names to connection strings used by different packages. On the other hand, package names might change over time, the same connection string might be used in more than one package, and so on.

To make it easier for the administrators to identify operations invoked by a particular SSIS package and allow them to be distinguished from other operations, you are going to create a custom task that will automatically amend the connection strings used by an SSIS package at runtime. The custom task is going to automatically add the SSIS package name into the connection string.

To design a Custom Control Flow Task, you need to design a .NET Class Library that contains a derivate of the `Task` base class, part of the `Microsoft.SqlServer.Dts.Runtime` namespace of the `Microsoft.SqlServer.ManagedDTS.dll` assembly. In this class, you need to provide the programmatic logic needed to perform the work at runtime, and you have to provide the logic that will allow the authors of SSIS packages to correctly configure the custom task at design time.

Getting ready

In *Chapter 3, Creating and Using SQL Server 2019 Big Data Clusters*, you were instructed to create the C:\ETL-with-Azure folder on the local drive of your workstation, and to clone the cookbook GitHub repository, located at https://github.com/PacktPublishing/ETL-with-Azure-Cookbook, to the default location on your workstation.

1. If you have not completed these tasks yet, do it now. The instructions are available in the *Getting ready* section of the first recipe, entitled *Creating a SQL Server 2019 big data cluster*, in *Chapter 3, Creating and Using SQL Server 2019 Big Data Clusters*.

    You do not have to perform any tasks associated with Azure at this time.

2. Inside the C:\ETL-with-Azure folder, create a folder for this chapter named Chapter05, and inside that one, create another subfolder named Files.

3. Locate the \Chapter05\Files folder in your local clone of the cookbook repository and copy all the files it contains to the C:\ETL-with-Azure\Chapter05\Files folder that you created earlier.

You now have all the prerequisites in place to start with the first recipe.

How to do it...

Start a new instance of Visual Studio 2019; you are going to create a new Visual Studio solution and create a new .NET Class Library by using the C# programming language:

1. In the **Open recent / Get started** dialog, select **Create a new project**.

2. In the **Create a new project** dialog, enter **C#** as the language, **Windows** as the platform, **Library** as the project type, and then select the **Class Library (.NET Framework)** template, and click **Next** to continue:

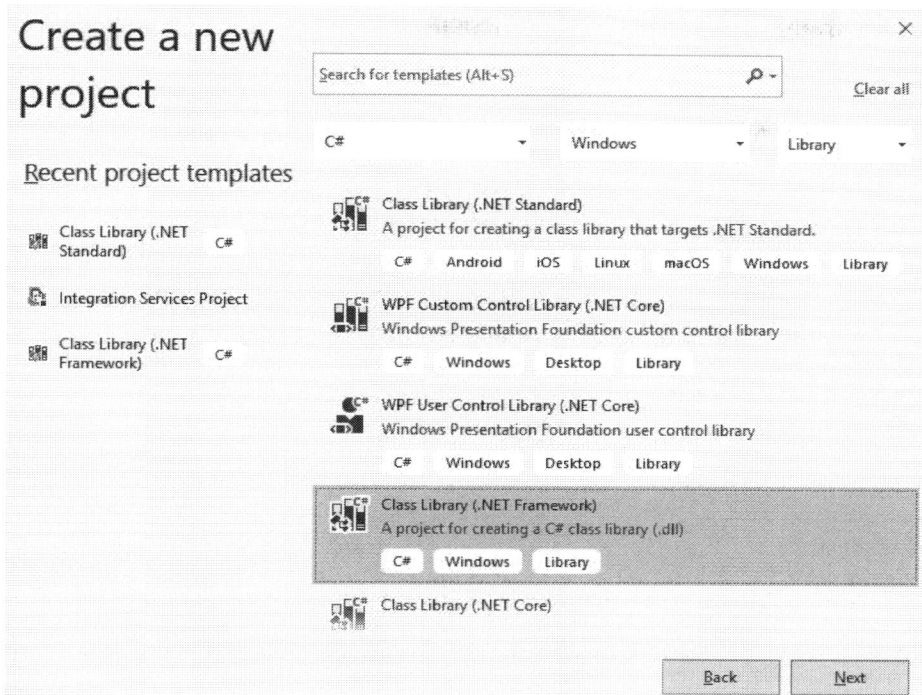

Figure 5.1 – Creating a new Class Library project

3. In the **Configure your new project** dialog, use the following settings:

    a) **Project name: ApplicationName**

    b) **Solution name: SSISCustomization**

    You can use the default location for the solution.

    Leave the **Place solution and project in the same folder** option unchecked and
    leave the default framework version selected – it should be the latest version.

    When ready, click **Create** to continue. It should only take a moment for the new
    solution to be created.

4. In the **Solution Explorer**, locate the Class1.cs file that was created by default,
    and change its name to ApplicationNameTask.cs.

When prompted by Visual Studio whether you would like to also change all references to the class, click **Yes** to confirm the rename:

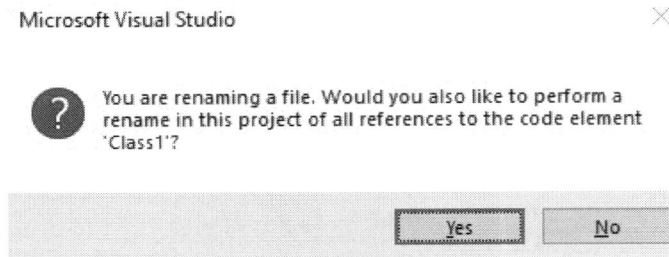

Microsoft Visual Studio   ×

? You are renaming a file. Would you also like to perform a rename in this project of all references to the code element 'Class1'?

Yes   No

Figure 5.2 – Renaming the file containing the class source code and the class itself

Save the solution.

5. In the **Solution Explorer**, right-click the **project** node, and select **Properties** from the shortcut menu.

On the **Application** page of the project properties, change the **Default namespace** setting to **EtlWithAzure**, as shown in the following screenshot:

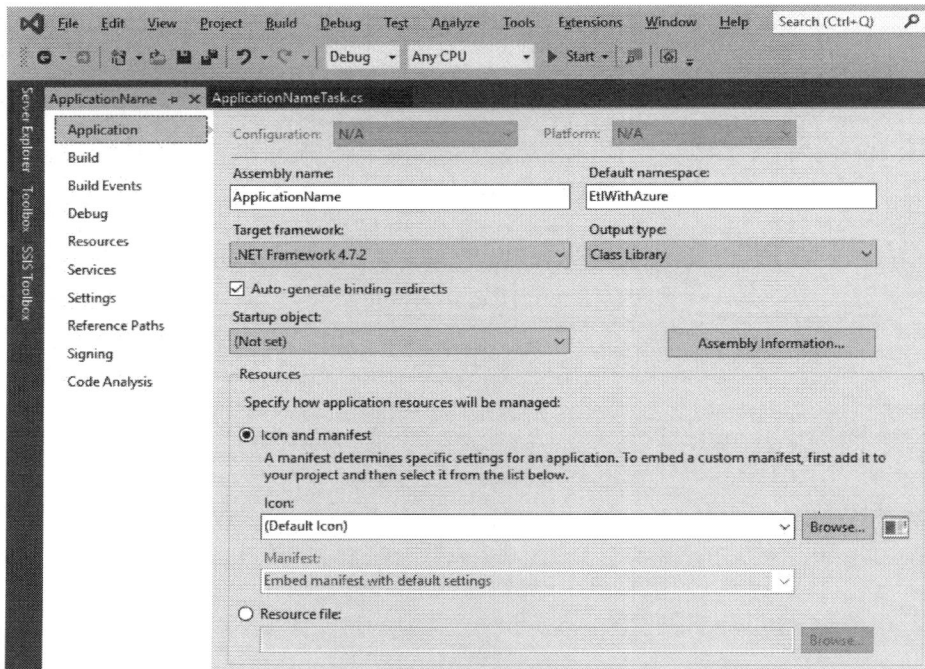

Figure 5.3 – Setting the project's Default namespace

Save the project.

6. On the **Build** page, make sure that **Release** is the selected configuration, and then, in the **Output** section, next to the **Output path** setting, click **Browse...** to open the **Select output path** dialog:

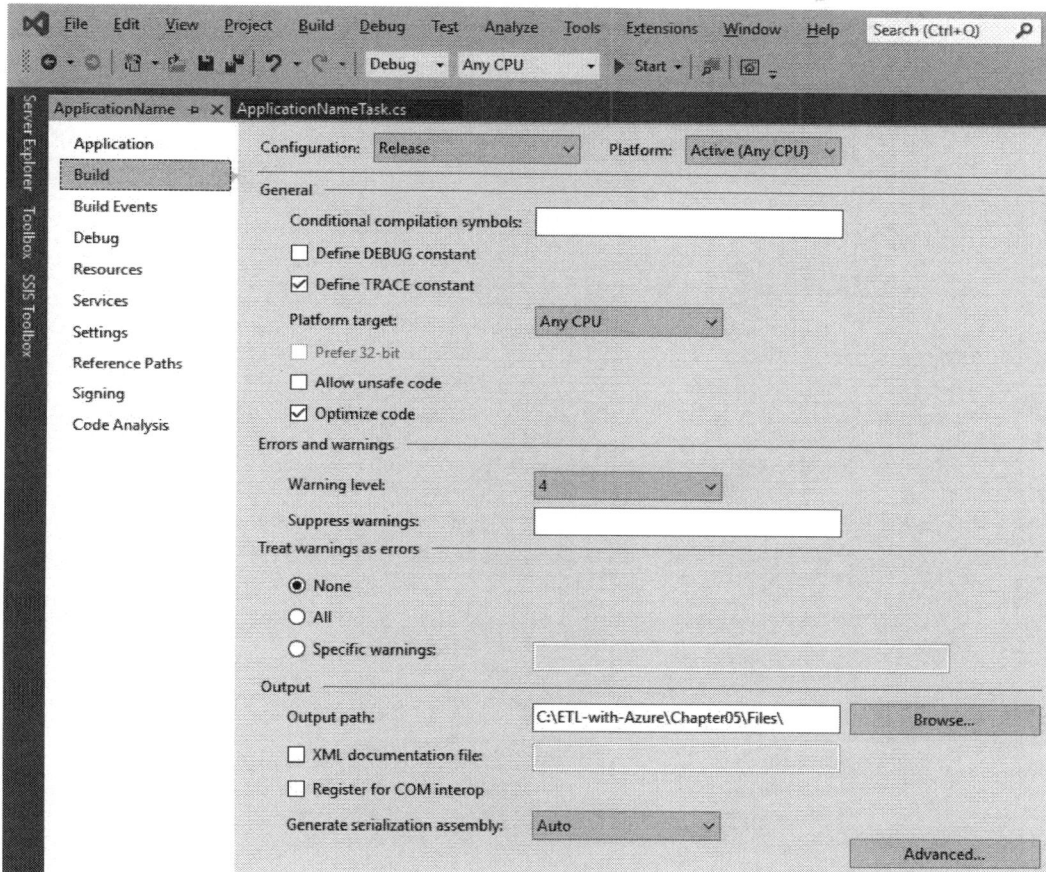

Figure 5.4 – Setting the release Output path

Navigate to the C:\ETL-with-Azure\Chapter05\Files folder, and then click **Select Folder** to confirm the selection.

The **Output path** setting should now contain the path to the C:\ETL-with-Azure\Chapter05\Files\ folder.

Save the project.

7. On the **Signing** page, check **Sign the assembly**, and then select **<Browse…>** from the **Choose a strong name key file** list box to open the **Select file** dialog.

Navigate to the `C:\ETL-with-Azure\Chapter05\Files` folder, select the `EtlWithAzure.snk` file, and click **Open** to confirm the selection:

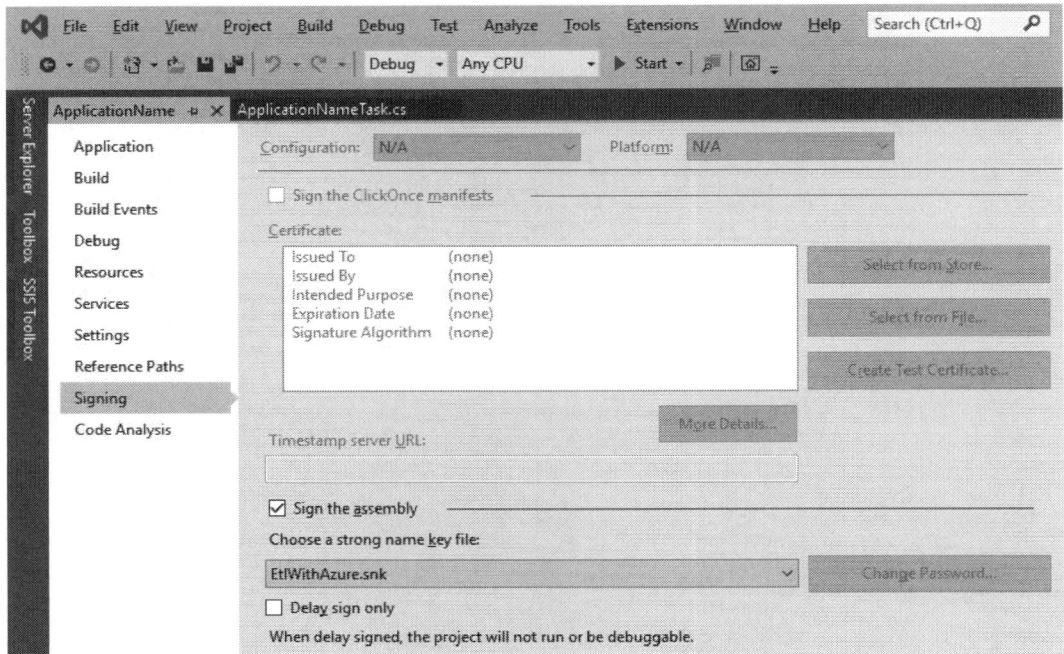

Figure 5.5 – Signing the assembly

Save the project, and close the **project properties** tab.

> **Tip**
> You can learn more about strong-named assemblies and assembly signing in the article entitled *Strong-named assemblies* at `https://docs.microsoft.com/en-us/dotnet/standard/assembly/strong-named`.

8. In the **ApplicationNameTask.cs** definition, change the namespace of the class to **EtlWithAzure**.

Save the solution.

9. In the **Solution Explorer**, under the **ApplicationName** project, right-click **References**, and select **Add Reference…** from the shortcut menu.

10. In the **Reference Manager**, under **Assemblies / Extensions**, check the following libraries:

a) `Microsoft.SqlServer.Dts.Design`

b) `Microsoft.SqlServer.ManagedDTS`

The following screenshot shows the selected references:

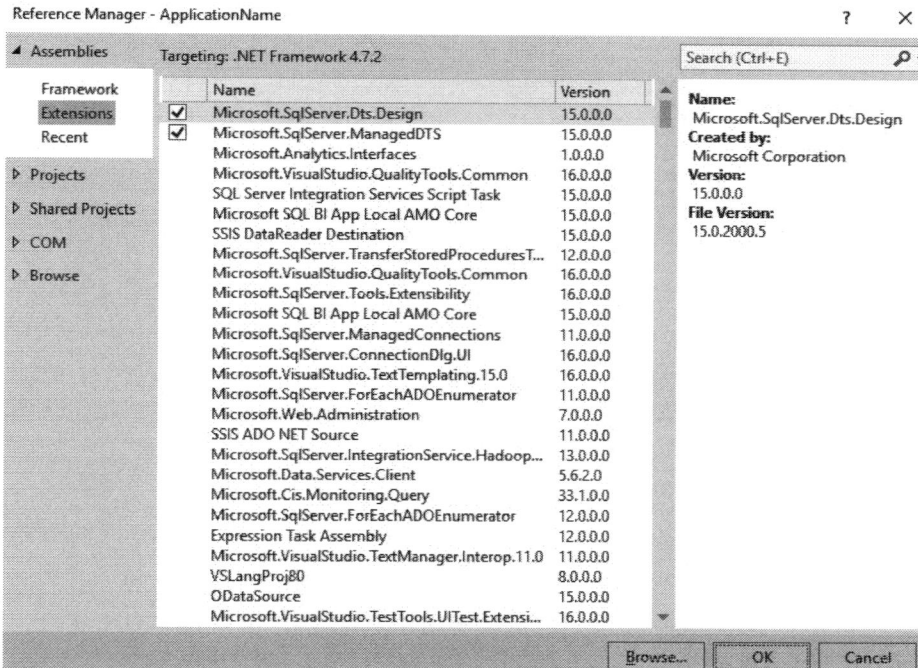

Figure 5.6 – Adding assembly references

When ready, click **OK** to confirm the selection.

Save the solution.

11. Use Windows Explorer to navigate to the `\Chapter05\Scripts` folder in your local clone of the cookbook GitHub repository, locate the `Chapter05_ApplicationNameTask.txt` file, and open it in a text editor (for instance, in Notepad).

> **Tip**
> This file contains all the C# source code needed to design the custom task. Use
> it to copy and paste the definitions into the class file, rather than typing them.
> Also, note that not all of the required source code is listed in this recipe, but it
> is available in the text file.

12. In Visual Studio, in the `ApplicationNameTask.cs` file, replace the existing
    references at the top of the definition with the following ones:

```
using Microsoft.SqlServer.Dts.Runtime;
using System;
using System.Collections.Generic;
using System.Data.Common;
```

The reference to the `Microsoft.SqlServer.Dts.Runtime` namespace
contains the `Task` base class.

13. Modify the `ApplicationNameTask` class definition so that it derives the `Task`
    base class:

```
public class ApplicationNameTask : Task
```

14. Implement `DtsTaskAttribute` by placing its definition just before the class
    definition:

```
[DtsTaskAttribute(
    Description = "Assign SSIS Package Name as
Application Name to Connection Strings.",
    DisplayName = "Application Name",
    TaskType = "Application Name Task",
    RequiredProductLevel = DTSProductLevel.None
    )]
public class ApplicationNameTask : Task
```

15. Copy and paste the following items from the text file into the class definition (each
    group is marked with a corresponding comment line):

a) **Private constants** – all fixed values used by the class are placed here for
   convenience.

b) **Private variables** – all variables used at the class level are also defined here.

c) **Public members** – configurable properties are exposed as public members.

16. Add an empty line after the public members and override the `InitializeTask` method by typing `override` into the editor, pressing the spacebar or *Tab* on the keyboard, and then selecting the method from the list of overridable methods.

Complete the method definition by copying and pasting the corresponding source code from the text file:

```
this.ApplicationName = String.Empty;
this.IsVerbose = true;
this.ResolveSystemVariables(ref variableDispenser);
base.InitializeTask(connections, variableDispenser,
events, log, eventInfos, logEntryInfos, refTracker);
```

These commands will be executed at design time when the task is placed into the control flow and will initialize the task – namely, setting the default values of both public members, exposed to the IDE as task custom properties.

17. Use the same approach as you used in *Step 16* to override the `Validate` method, and add the corresponding source code from the text file:

```
if (String.IsNullOrEmpty(_defaultApplicationName))
{
    componentEvents.FireError(0, _taskName,
    UNRESOLVED_APPLICATION_NAME_MESSAGE,
    String.Empty, 0);
    return DTSExecResult.Failure;
}
return DTSExecResult.Success;
```

These commands will be executed at design time when the task configuration is confirmed, and at runtime during package and task validation.

18. Next, override the `Execute` method. In this case, the definition is also enclosed in a `try...catch` block. It is located in the `Chapter05_ApplicationNameTask.txt` file, below the `Override Execute, and supply the following definition` comment.

19. Below the `Execute` method, paste the complete definitions of the following private methods from the text file:

a) `ResolveSystemVariables`

b) `GetApplicationName`

c) `GetConnectionManagerType`

d) `GetEnhancedConnectionString`

e) `FireInformation`

The method definitions are listed in the `Chapter05_ApplicationNameTask.txt` file, below the `Private Methods (to be placed inside the main class)` comment.

20. Just below the `ApplicationNameTask` class (that is, outside the `ApplicationName` class), copy and paste the `ConnectionManagerType` enumeration from the text file:

```
internal enum ConnectionManagerType : Byte
{
    Unsupported = 0,
    OleDb = 1,
    AdoNet = 2,
    ODBC = 3
}
```

21. Save the solution, and then build the project in debug mode by pressing *Ctrl + B* on the keyboard or by selecting **Build ApplicationName** from the **Build** menu.

The library should build without errors; however, if any errors do occur, review the error messages, make the necessary corrections, and try again.

22. Once the debug build is completed successfully, change the configuration to **Release** by selecting this option from the **Solution Configurations** list box in the Visual Studio toolbar:

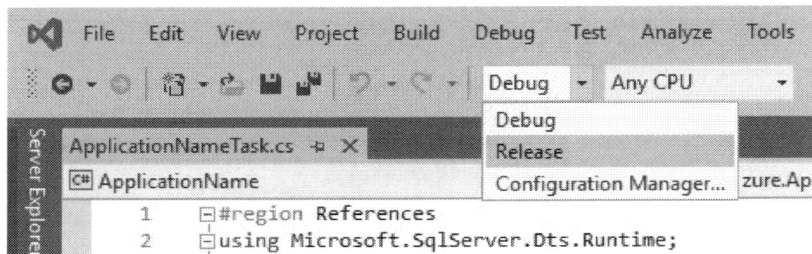

Figure 5.7 – Compiling the Release version of the assembly

Build the solution by pressing *Ctrl + Shift + B* on the keyboard or by selecting **Build Solution** from the **Build** menu.

After a successful release build, the compiled library should be available in the `C:\ETL-with-Azure\Chapter05\Files` folder. In order for the custom task to be available in SSDT and to the SSIS runtime, the files must also be copied to the correct locations and registered in the **Global Assembly Cache** (**GAC**), which you are going to do in the third recipe, *Deploying SSIS customizations*, in this chapter.

You can leave Visual Studio open.

How it works...

You have just designed a very simple yet effective SSIS custom task. When used in an SSIS package, this task will amend the connection strings used by the package's connection managers when connecting to supported data stores.

At runtime, the `Execute` method is called by the SSIS execution engine. The main `foreach` loop of this method traverses the collection of connection managers available to the package, checks whether they are compatible with the underlying functions, and amends their connection strings so that these also contain the package name as the application name.

The individual tasks are performed by the following private methods:

- `ResolveSystemVariables`: The method retrieves the values of the system variables and assigns them to local variables for later use.

- `GetApplicationName`: The method determines the application name to be used in the connection strings. By default, the SSIS package name is used, but the author of the SSIS package can also supply a different value through the task's `ApplicationName` property. For instance, a literal value determined at design time can be used, or the value can be assigned via an expression at runtime.

- `GetConnectionManagerType`: The method identifies the type of the connection manager; ADO.NET, OLE DB, and ODBC connection managers are supported.

- `GetEnhancedConnectionString`: The method amends the connection string used by a supported connection manager.

- `FireInformation`: The method is a simplification of the built-in method used to emit informational messages recorded in the SSIS activity log.

When the value of the task's `IsVerbose` property is `true`, the task reports all details of its progress to the SSIS activity log. If the value is `false`, the task only reports the default actions.

When this task is used in an SSIS package, each connection string includes the package name, which a compatible datastore is going to pick up and expose through a variety of system views and functions. This should make it much easier for the administrators to distinguish between operations performed against the databases by the SSIS packages using this task and any other concurrent operations.

By placing the task at the very beginning of the package's control flow, you can make sure that the correct application name is reported to the target server(s) as soon as the package starts running.

Designing a Custom Data Flow Component

This recipe demonstrates the design of a Custom Data flow transformation. Efficient resource use represents one of the principal objectives in ETL development. Being able to determine which data extracted from the source actually needs to be loaded into the destination is probably the most important capability of any ETL solution. Determining whether an incoming row contains data that is different from the corresponding existing row can be performed by comparing each source column with the corresponding destination column. Such comparisons can be costly as they require all relevant data to be loaded from the destination table to perform the comparison.

By creating a single **hash value** based on the values of all the columns in the incoming row, and comparing only this single value with the one stored in the destination table, resource use can be reduced significantly. Of course, the hashed values are restricted in size and none of the algorithms typically used to calculate them can guarantee that two different sets of source values will not produce the same hash value.

> **Tip**
>
> You can find more information about SHA1, the algorithm used in this recipe, and other algorithms available in .NET Framework in the online documentation at, https://docs.microsoft.com/en-us/dotnet/api/system.security.cryptography.hashalgorithm.
>
> The algorithm used in this recipe might not represent the ultimate in .NET hashing capabilities but should be good enough for this demonstration.

You are going to design a custom transformation that will retrieve the values from one or more columns of each pipeline row, create a single composite value, and use it to calculate a single hash value, which will then be placed into the pipeline in a new column. The transformation is going to support any number of columns of all the supported SSIS pipeline data types, specified by the author of the SSIS package at design time.

To design a Custom Data Flow Component, you need to design a .NET Class Library that contains a derivate of the `PipelineComponent` base class, part of the `Microsoft.SqlServer.Dts.Pipeline` namespace of the `Microsoft.SqlServer.PipelineHost.dll` assembly. In this class, you need to provide the programmatic logic needed to perform the work at runtime, and you have to provide the logic that will allow the authors of SSIS packages to correctly configure the custom component at design time.

Getting ready

This recipe assumes that you have finished the previous recipe in this chapter, entitled *Designing a Custom Control Flow Task*, or at the very least completed *Steps 1* through *4* of that recipe.

How to do it...

Make sure that the **SSISCustomization.sln** solution is open in Visual Studio 2019 on your workstation. You are going to add another project to the same solution, which will allow you to maintain both of these SSIS customizations as part of the same solution:

1. In the Solution Explorer, right-click the **Solution** node and select **Add | New Project...** from the shortcut menu, or select **Add | New Project...** from the **File** menu while the **Solution** node is selected, to add a new project to the existing solution.

    Select the `Class Library (.NET Framework)` template, as shown in *Figure 5.1* in the *Designing a Custom Control Flow Task* recipe.

    When ready, click **Next** to continue.

2. On the **Configure your new project** page, enter `RowHash` as the project name, and leave all the other settings unchanged.

    When ready, click **Create** to complete the operation.

3. In the **Solution Explorer**, locate the `Class1.cs` file that was created by default, and change its name to `RowHashTransformation.cs`.

    When prompted by Visual Studio whether you would like to also change all references to the class, click **Yes** to confirm the rename.

    Save the solution.

4. Follow *Steps 5* through *7* of the *Designing a Custom Control Flow Task* recipe in this chapter to set the project properties for the newly added project. The same default namespace, build, and signature settings, can also be used for this project.

5. In the `RowHashTransformation.cs` definition, change the namespace of the class to `EtlWithAzure`.

6. Follow *Steps 9* through *10* of the *Designing a Custom Control Flow Task* recipe in this chapter to add the following assembly references to the `RowHash` project:

    a) `Microsoft.SQLServer.DTSPipelineWrap`

    b) `Microsoft.SQLServer.PipelineHost`

    c) `Microsoft.SQLServer.DTSRuntimeWrap`

    Use **Windows Explorer** to navigate to the `\Chapter05\Scripts` folder in your local clone of the cookbook GitHub repository, locate the `Chapter05_RowHashTransformation.txt` file, and open it in a text editor (for instance, in Notepad).

> **Tip**
>
> This file contains all the C# source code needed to design the custom component. Use it to copy and paste the definitions into the class file, rather than typing them. Also, note that not all the required source code is listed in this recipe, but it is available in the text file.

7. In Visual Studio, in the `RowHashTransformation.cs` file, replace the existing references at the top of the definition with the following ones:

```
using Microsoft.SqlServer.Dts.Pipeline;
using Microsoft.SqlServer.Dts.Pipeline.Wrapper;
using Microsoft.SqlServer.Dts.Runtime.Wrapper;
using System;
using System.Collections.Generic;
using System.IO;
using System.Linq;
using System.Security.Cryptography;
using System.Text;
```

8. Modify the `ApplicationNameTask` class definition so that it derives the `PipelineComponent` base class:

```
public class RowHashTransformation : PipelineComponent
```

The base component contains all the methods and interfaces needed to interact with the SSIS runtime, allowing you to perform custom operations inside the SSIS data flow, and to interact with the data flow pipeline, which provides you with access to the data being sent through the data flow.

9. Implement `DtsPipelineComponentAttribute` by placing its definition just before the class definition:

```
[DtsPipelineComponentAttribute(
    ComponentType = ComponentType.Transform,
    DisplayName = "Row Hash",
    Description = "Generates a hash of selected columns
                  in the pipeline row.",
    NoEditor = false,
    RequiredProductLevel = DTSProductLevel.DTSPL_NONE
    )]
public class RowHashTransformation : PipelineComponent
```

This attribute will allow the SSIS runtime, as well as the SSIS development environment, to understand how the component is to be used in the data flow.

10. Copy and paste the following items from the text file into the class definition (each group is marked with a corresponding comment line):

a) **Private constants** – the fixed values used throughout the class definition are available in one place.

b) **Private variables** – the variables used at the class level are also defined in one place.

Save the solution.

11. Add an empty line after the private variables and override the ProvideComponentProperties method by typing override into the editor, pressing the spacebar or *Tab* on the keyboard, and then selecting the corresponding method from the list of overridable methods. Complete the method definition by copying and pasting the source code from the text file:

```
base.ProvideComponentProperties();
IDTSInput100 input = ComponentMetaData.
InputCollection[0];
input.Name = INPUT_NAME;
IDTSCustomProperty100 isInternal;
IDTSOutput100 output = ComponentMetaData.
OutputCollection[0];
output.Name = OUTPUT_NAME;
output.SynchronousInputID = ComponentMetaData.
InputCollection[INPUT_NAME].ID;
isInternal = output.CustomPropertyCollection.New();
isInternal.Name = IS_INTERNAL_CUSTOM_PROPERTY_NAME;
isInternal.State = DTSPersistState.PS_PERSISTASDEFAULT;
isInternal.TypeConverter = typeof(Boolean).
AssemblyQualifiedName;
isInternal.Value = true;
IDTSOutputColumn100 rowHashColumn = output.
OutputColumnCollection.New();
rowHashColumn.Name = ROW_HASH_COLUMN_NAME;
rowHashColumn.SetDataTypeProperties(DataType.DT_BYTES,
20, 0, 0, 0);
isInternal = rowHashColumn.CustomPropertyCollection.
New();
isInternal.Name = IS_INTERNAL_CUSTOM_PROPERTY_NAME;
isInternal.State = DTSPersistState.PS_PERSISTASDEFAULT;
isInternal.TypeConverter = typeof(Boolean).
AssemblyQualifiedName;
isInternal.Value = true;
```

This method provides the metadata needed to configure the component at design time and to provide the essential functionalities needed to perform the work at runtime.

A single input, and a single output, synchronized with the input, are created when the component is added to the data flow.

Use the same approach as you used in *Step 12* to override the `Validate` method, and add the source code from the text file:

```
IDTSInput100 input = ComponentMetaData.
InputCollection[INPUT_NAME];
if (input == null ||
    ComponentMetaData.InputCollection.Count == 0)
{
    ComponentMetaData.FireWarning(0, ComponentMetaData.
Name, NO_INPUT_MESSAGE, String.Empty, 0);
    return DTSValidationStatus.VS_ISBROKEN;
}
else
{
    if (ComponentMetaData.InputCollection.Count > 1)
    {
        ComponentMetaData.FireWarning(0,
ComponentMetaData.Name, TOO_MANY_INPUTS_MESSAGE, String.
Empty, 0);
        return DTSValidationStatus.VS_ISBROKEN;
    }
    if (input.InputColumnCollection.Count == 0)
    {
        ComponentMetaData.FireWarning(0,
ComponentMetaData.Name, NO_INPUT_COLUMN_MESSAGE, String.
Empty, 0);
        return DTSValidationStatus.VS_ISVALID;
    }
}
if (ComponentMetaData.OutputCollection.Count > 1)
{
    ComponentMetaData.FireWarning(0, ComponentMetaData.
Name, TOO_MANY_OUTPUTS_MESSAGE, String.Empty, 0);
    return DTSValidationStatus.VS_ISBROKEN;
}
return base.Validate();
```

At design time, this method will be used by Visual Studio to help the author of the SSIS package to correctly configure the component. At runtime, the method will allow the SSIS execution engine to determine whether the component can be executed as intended.

> **Tip**
>
> Of course, in neither case does the successful result of the validation mean that the component will deliver the expected result. However, you should use this method to check the settings and properties of the component that are, or might be, relevant to the execution of the operations that you designed.
>
> Keep in mind that the methods used to determine the state of the custom component represent your only way of communicating your intentions to the authors of SSIS packages who are using this component. From their perspective, if the validation succeeds, it is reasonable to expect that the execution will succeed as well. Think about what could go wrong in the execution of the custom operations, and try to prevent it by reporting any relevant inconsistencies.

Save the solution.

12. Override the `PreExecute` method by copying its definition from the text file:

```
IDTSInput100 input = ComponentMetaData.
InputCollection[INPUT_NAME];
_columnCollection = new List<IDTSInputColumn100>();
foreach (IDTSInputColumn100 inputColumn in input.
InputColumnCollection)
{
    _columnCollection.Add(inputColumn);
}
base.PreExecute();
```

This method is used to simplify access to the pipeline metadata by storing the essential properties of the pipeline columns in a variable for later use. Compared to the `PipelineComponent.ComponentMetaData` property, which provides access to **all** of the component's metadata, the private variable will only contain the **subset** of metadata related to the component's input columns.

> **Tip**
>
> You can reduce the size of this variable even further by using it to store only the input column properties that are actually required by the `ProcessInput` and `GetColumnValueBytes` methods.

13. Override the `ProcessInput` method with the corresponding definition:

```
IDTSInput100 input = ComponentMetaData.InputCollection.
GetObjectByID(inputID);

IDTSOutput100 output = ComponentMetaData.
OutputCollection[OUTPUT_NAME];

IDTSOutputColumn100 rowHashColumn = output.
OutputColumnCollection[ROW_HASH_COLUMN_NAME];

Int32 rowHashColumnIndex = BufferManager.
FindColumnByLineageID(input.Buffer, rowHashColumn.
LineageID);

while (buffer.NextRow())
{
    List<Byte[]> columnBytesCollection = new
List<Byte[]>();

    foreach (IDTSInputColumn100 inputColumn in _
columnCollection.OrderBy(c => c.LineageID))
    {
        Int32 inputColumnIndex = input.
InputColumnCollection.GetObjectIndexByID(inputColumn.ID);

        columnBytesCollection.Add( this.
GetColumnValueBytes(buffer, inputColumn,
inputColumnIndex));
    }

    buffer.SetBytes(rowHashColumnIndex, this.
ComputeHash(columnBytesCollection));
}
```

The `ProcessInput` method contains the programmatic logic needed to perform work against the data in the pipeline.

Save the solution.

14. Add the following private methods to the component class by copying their definitions from the text file:

a) `GetColumnValueBytes`

b) `ComputeHash`

15. Add the event handlers in the same way:

a) `OnInputPathAttached`

b) `OnInputPathDetached`

c) `OnOutputPathAttached`

d) `OnDeletingInputColumn`

Do the same for the metadata maintenance methods:

a) `InsertInput`

b) `InsertOutput`

c) `InsertOutputColumnAt`

d) `DeleteInput`

e) `DeleteOutput`

f) `DeleteOutputColumn`

Save the solution.

16. Build the project using the **Debug** configuration. If any errors are raised, inspect the error messages, make the appropriate corrections, and repeat the build.

17. Once the debug build has succeeded, change the configuration to **Release**, and build the solution.

You can leave Visual Studio open.

How it works...

You have designed an SSIS data flow transformation that can be used to simplify change management in data warehousing solutions – namely, to determine which rows that already exist in the destination table really need to be updated. It uses a hash value to determine whether the new values are different from the existing ones, without actually comparing each destination column value with the corresponding source column value.

The programmatic logic of this custom component is divided into **design-time methods** that will be used by Visual Studio during SSIS package development and **runtime methods** that will be used by the SSIS runtime during package execution.

At design time, the following event handlers will assist the developer of the SSIS package in configuring the component as intended, as well as helping them to prevent a fatal misconfiguration that might require them to remove the component from the data flow altogether and start over:

- `OnInputPathAttached`: The method is called when the data path from another component is connected to this component's input.

- `OnInputPathDetached`: The method is called when the data path to the component's input is detached.

- `OnOutputPathAttached`: The method is called when this component's output path is attached to the input of another component.

- `OnDeletingInputColumn`: The method is called when the author of the SSIS package attempts to remove an input column.

The following methods will also be used at design time, assisting the SSIS package developer in successfully completing the configuration of the component's inputs and outputs:

- `InsertInput`: This method is called when the author of the SSIS package attempts to create a new input.

- `InsertOutput`: This method is called when the author of the SSIS package attempts to create a new output.

- `InsertOutputColumnAt`: This method is called when the author of the SSIS package attempts to create a new output column.

- `DeleteInput`: This method is called when the author of the SSIS package attempts to remove an input.

- `DeleteOutput`: This method is called when the author of the SSIS package attempts to remove an output.

- `DeleteOutputColumn`: This method is called when the author of the SSIS package attempts to remove an output column.

In this particular transformation, most of these methods simply raise exceptions, and with this, effectively prevent the base operations from being executed. Each exception contains a message that will help the developer of the SSIS package to understand how the component should be configured.

At runtime, the `ProcessInput` method is called by the execution engine. The transformation extracts values from all the columns that the author of the SSIS package has specified at design time, and gathers them in a single large binary object. This composite value is then used to calculate the hash value. The resulting value is then placed into a new column in the pipeline and made available to the following components in the data flow.

The following methods contain the logic needed to compute the hash value:

- `GetColumnValueBytes`: This method extracts the value of the specified column(s) using a retrieval function that corresponds to the column data type and returns it as a binary array.

- `ComputeHash`: This method calculates a hash value from the supplied binary array containing the column values using the `SHA1Managed` hashing algorithm.

In the recipe entitled *Deploying SSIS customizations* in this chapter, you are going to use a Conditional Split transformation in the data flow to compare the calculated hash value with the existing value of the corresponding row extracted from the destination table. If the hash value that was stored in the destination table during a previous run is different from the hash value calculated during this execution, this means that at least the value of one of the columns is different, and therefore qualifies the row for the update operation. Based on this, the Conditional Split transformation only redirects the changed rows to the intended destination component; rows that have not changed since the last execution are not used in the rest of the data flow.

There's more...

The algorithm used to calculate the hash value guarantees that even a minute difference in source values will be reflected in a dramatic difference in the result value. Of course, if the 20-byte data space used by the algorithm might not provide the accuracy required in your particular business case, you should replace it with a different one.

Simply replace the `SHA1Managed` class in the `ComputeHash` method with one that better suits your needs – for instance, the `SHA256Managed` class. After replacing the algorithm, you will also have to adjust the length of the `rowHashColumn` defined in the `ProvideComponentProperties` method, and the length of the `RowHash` columns in the `DW.PurchaseOrders`, `ETL.PurchaseOrders_New`, and `ETL.PurchaseOrders_Modified` tables of the `WideWorldAnalysis` database.

Deploying SSIS customizations

In this recipe, you are going to deploy the custom task and custom component that you created in the previous recipes in this chapter to the SQL Server instance on your workstation. You are going to copy the assembly files to the destinations used by the SSIS runtime and register them in the Windows **Global Assembly Cache (GAC)**.

You will finish this recipe by implementing both of these customizations in two SSIS packages. You are going to see them in action – at design time, and at runtime.

Getting ready

This recipe depends on the results of the previous two recipes, *Designing a Custom Control Flow Task*, and *Designing a Custom Data Flow Component*, in this chapter. You need to complete both previous recipes successfully before you can complete this recipe.

How to do it...

You are going to start these tasks in the file system of your workstation, and then continue in SSDT by completing an existing SSIS solution:

1. Use Windows Explorer to locate the `C:\ETL-with-Azure\Chapter05\Files` folder, and in it, the `DeployCustomizations.bat` file. Right-click the file and then select **Edit** from the shortcut menu to open it in your default batch file editor. Inspect the commands.

    When the batch file is run, the assemblies that you designed in the first two recipes of this chapter will be copied to the SSIS 2019 locations on the `C:\` drive, and then registered in the **GAC** by the **gacutil** command-line utility. Close the batch file editor.

2. In **Windows Explorer**, right-click the file again, and then select **Run as administrator** from the shortcut menu to execute the commands with elevated privileges.

    > **Important note**
    > Administrator privileges are required to access the folders where the SSIS binaries are kept, and to make changes to the **GAC**.

3. Use Windows Explorer to locate the \Chapter05\Starter folder in your local clone of the cookbook GitHub repository, and open the SSISCustomizationTest.sln solution.

The solution contains two SSIS packages:

a) ApplicationNameTaskTest.dtsx: The package will help you test the custom task.

b) RowHashTest.dtsx: The package will help you test the custom component.

4. Open the ApplicationNameTaskTest.dtsx package:

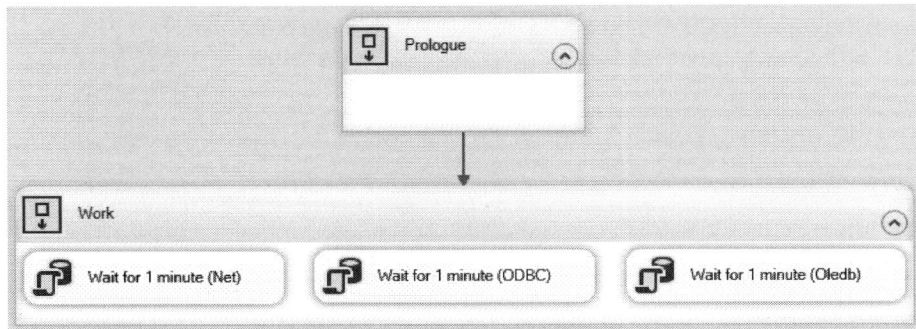

Figure 5.8 – The ApplicationNameTaskTest.dtsx control flow

The package contains a rather simple control flow – two containers set to execute in sequence:

a) An empty sequence container, named **Prologue**, with which the execution begins.

b) A second sequence container, named **Work**, containing three **Execute SQL Tasks**, each configured to run concurrently for 1 minute, connected to the WideWorldImporters database on the local SQL Server instance using three different connection managers: ADO.NET, OLE DB, and ODBC.

5. Inspect the configuration of each **Execute SQL Task**. After that, inspect the connection managers, and the package parameters used to configure them.

In each connection string, you can see different application names.

> **Important note**
>
> When a connection manager is created in SSIS, a default application name might be added to the connection string automatically. Depending on the connection manager, you can access this value on the **All** page of the connection manager editor. Alternatively, you can control the value by parameterizing the connection string property. The value can either be assigned at design time or after deployment.
>
> Not all connection managers support this property.

6. In SSMS, connect to the `WideWorldImporters` database on your local SQL Server instance, and then use the **Open File** dialog to navigate to the `\Chapter05\Scripts` folder in your local clone of the cookbook GitHub repository. Open the `Chapter05.sql` file. The file is made up of six parts, marked with Roman numerals. For this demonstration, you are only going to use the three commands in `Part I`.

7. In **SSDT**, execute the package in debug mode, and then return to **SSMS**.

    While connected to the `master` database, execute the two `SELECT` statements reading from the `sys.dm_exec_sessions` data management view.

    While the package is running, inspect the query results. The first query should not return any rows, whereas three rows should be returned by the second query.

    The `program_name` column contains the application name reported by each connection manager.

8. In SSDT, wait for the operations to complete, and then stop the debug mode execution. While the control flow editor is active, in the SSIS Toolbox, locate the **Application Name** task.

> **Important note**
>
> As you have just recently started this instance of Visual Studio, the new task should have been loaded automatically and should be listed in the **Common** task group.
>
> If, for some reason, the task is missing, right-click the empty canvas of the SSIS Toolbox, and then select **Refresh Toolbar** from the shortcut menu to reload the available Control Flow Tasks.

9. Drag the **Application Name** task to the **Prologue** sequence container.

> **Important note**
>
> Unfortunately, on a fresh installation of SQL Server and Visual Studio 2019 with SSDT and the Integration Services templates, the following error might occur when trying to place the custom task into the control flow:
>
> *Cannot create a task from XML for task "", type "" due to error 0x80070057 "The parameter is incorrect."*
>
> This very likely signifies corruption in one of the SQL Server shared features and can only be corrected by repairing the SQL Server installation. Note that only the shared features need to be repaired, not the entire SQL Server installation.
>
> You can find more information about SQL Server repairs online, in the documentation article entitled *Repair a Failed SQL Server Installation*, at `https://docs.microsoft.com/en-us/sql/database-engine/install-windows/repair-a-failed-sql-server-installation`.

10. If you try to open this task's editor (for instance, by double-clicking it), the following message will be displayed, informing you that no editor has been provided for this particular task:

    This task does not have a custom editor. Use the Properties window to edit properties of this task.

> **Important note**
>
> By default, custom tasks do not have a generic editor associated with them, and unless you design a custom editor and associate it with the custom task at design time, no editor will be available for it.
>
> You can find more information about custom task editors online, in the article entitled *Developing a User Interface for a Custom Task*, at `https://docs.microsoft.com/en-us/sql/integration-services/extending-packages-custom-objects/task/developing-a-user-interface-for-a-custom-task`.

All public properties of a custom task are exposed to the development environment as task properties, accessible through the **Properties** pane in SSDT when the task is selected in the control flow designer.

Therefore, a custom editor might not really be needed at all; especially for a simple task such as this one where, in most cases, nothing will actually need to be configured anyway.

11. Execute the package in debug mode again, switch back to **SSMS,** and execute the two SELECT statements again.

    This time, the first query should return three rows, one for each connection, and the program_name column should now contain the package name in all three cases.

12. Switch back to **SSDT,** wait for the operations to complete, and then stop the debug mode execution.

13. You can now close the ApplicationNameTaskTest.dtsx package but leave SSDT open.

14. Before you can test the custom component, you need to create a new database with three new tables.

15. In SSMS, locate Part II of the Chapter05.sql script. Inspect the statements, and then execute them, one by one, to create the WideWorldAnalysis database, and in it two new schemas, DW and ETL, followed by these three tables:

 a) *DW.PurchaseOrders* – the final destination table

 b) *ETL.PurchaseOrders_New* – a staging table to hold new data before the final insert

 c) *ETL.PurchaseOrders_Modified* – a staging table to hold modified data before the final update

16. In SSDT, open the `RowHashTest.dtsx` package:

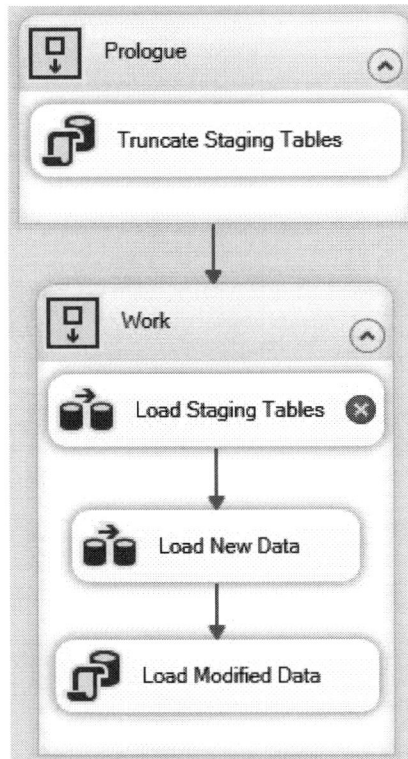

Figure 5.9 – The RowHashTest.dtsx control flow

You can see that the package starts with an **Execute SQL Task** used to truncate the two staging tables in the destination `WideWorldAnalysis` database, followed by two data flows, and another Execute SQL Task.

The first data flow, which is currently in error, is supposed to extract the source data from the `WideWorldImporters` database and then, based on whether the rows already exist in the destination table or not, load the new data into one staging table, and modified data into another one.

The second data flow simply loads all new rows from the new data staging table into the final destination.

The final Execute SQL Task is supposed to update the final destination table with data that has changed since the last time the process was run.

17. Take a closer look at the **Load Staging Tables** data flow by opening it in the data flow editor. It is in error, as it needs to be completed:

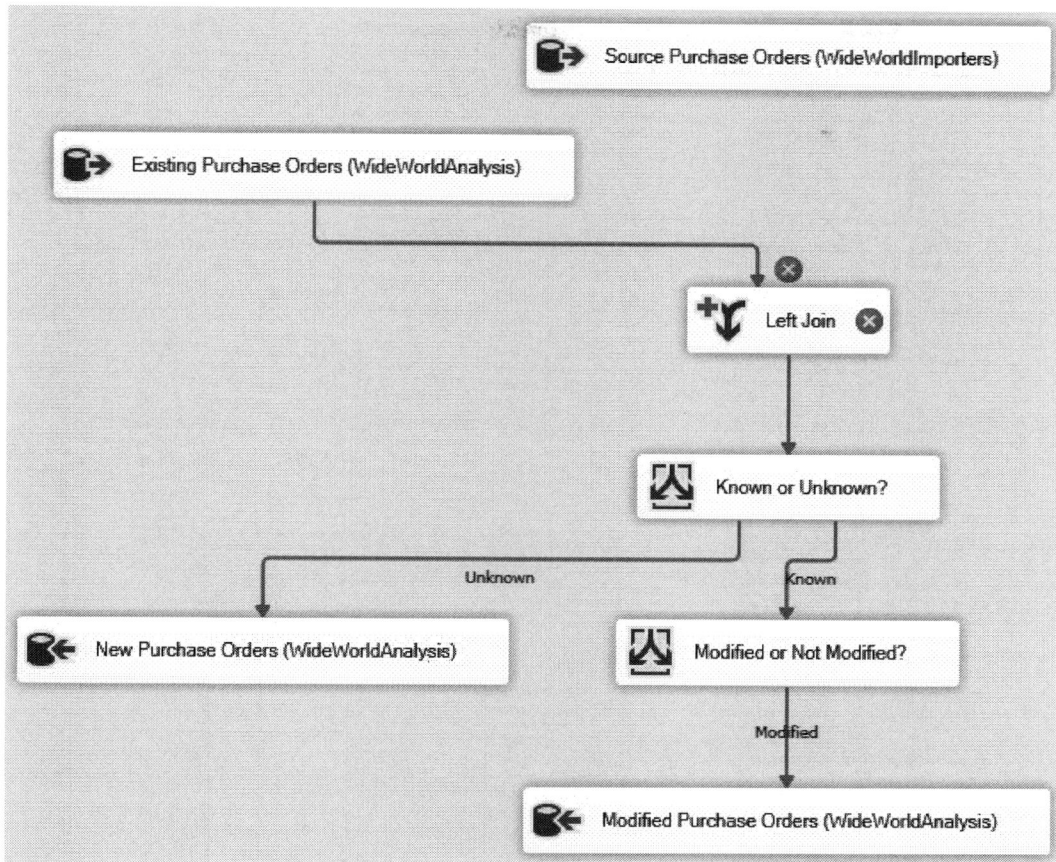

Figure 5.10 – The Load Staging Tables data flow

The data flow uses two sorted sources, one loading the data from the source table, and the other from the final destination table. The **Merge Join** transformation with a left outer join is used to place all source rows into the pipeline together with any associated destination rows based on the common key column.

After that, two Conditional Split transformations are used: one to differentiate between unknown rows that need to be **inserted** into the final destination table and known rows that might have to be used to **update** the rows of the final destination table.

Unknown rows are redirected to one staging table, and known rows are redirected to another one. However, to keep resource use at a minimum, only known source rows that are **actually** different from the existing destination rows should be considered for the update.

18. In the SSIS Toolbox, locate the **Row Hash** transformation; it should be located in the **Common** component group.

> **Important note**
>
> If you cannot find the **Row Hash** transformation in any of the data flow component groups, right-click the empty canvas of the SSIS Toolbox, and then select **Refresh Toolbar** from the shortcut menu to reload all available data flow components.

19. Drag the transformation into the data flow designer. Immediately, a warning is returned by the component. Examine it by hovering the mouse over the exclamation mark displayed in the component image, or by opening the **Error List** pane.

> **Tip**
>
> If the **Error List** pane is not visible, you can access it through the **View** menu.

20. Connect the output data path of the **Source Purchase Orders (WideWorldImporters)** source component to the **Row Hash** component.

    The warning should now disappear.

21. Double-click the **Row Hash** transformation, or right-click it and select **Edit...** from the shortcut menu, to open the **Advanced Editor**.

> **Tip**
>
> The **Advanced Editor** is used by default for all components that do not have a custom editor defined. If you prefer for a custom editor to be used instead, you can design one as a separate class library, associate it with the component at design time, and deploy it together with the component.
>
> You can find more information about custom component editors online, in the article entitled *Developing a User Interface for a Data Flow Component*, at `https://docs.microsoft.com/en-us/sql/integration-services/extending-packages-custom-objects/data-flow/developing-a-user-interface-for-a-data-flow-component`.

22. On the **Input Columns** tab, all the columns should already be selected, which means that when the data flow is executed, the data in **all** of them will be used to compute the row hash. This is not actually needed: the PurchaseOrderID column is the primary key in the source, and the destination, tables, and the LastEditedBy and LastEditedDate columns are not significant when the data is transferred from the source database to the destination database.

23. Uncheck all three columns, as shown in the following screenshot:

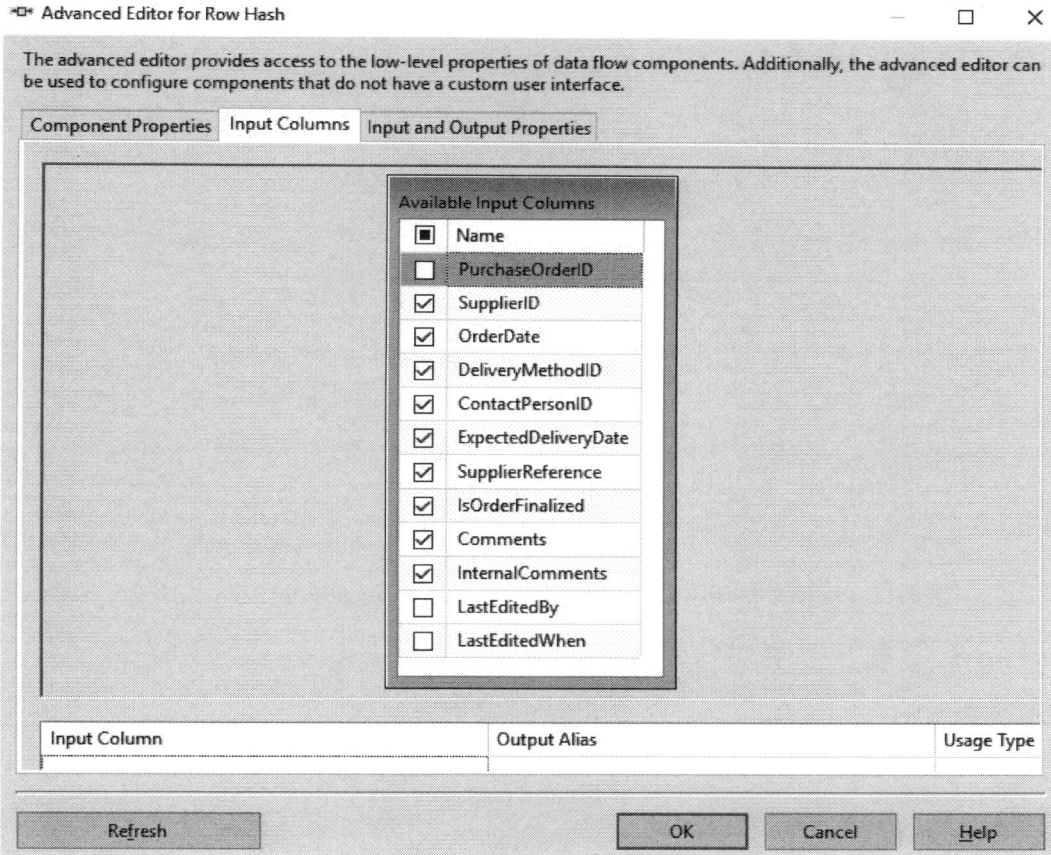

Figure 5.11 – Selecting the row hash transformation input columns

24. When ready, click **OK** to confirm the changes.

25. Connect the output path of the **Row Hash** transformation to the **Left Join** transformation. The data flow should now be complete and no longer in error.

26. Inspect the **Left Join**, **Known or Unknown?**, and **Modified or Not Modified?** transformations to see how the pipeline has been implemented to distinguish between known and unknown rows, as well as between changed and unchanged rows.

27. Check the destination components to see where the pipeline data is sent. You can see that the hash values, computed during the execution in the **Row Hash** transformation, are inserted into the destination tables as well.

    Save the package.

28. Execute the package in debug mode and observe the `Load Staging Tables` data flow. During the initial run, all rows will be considered unknown, directed to the `ETL.PurchaseOrders_New` staging table, and then all of them will be inserted into the `DW.PurchaseOrders` table.

    In SSMS, you can use the queries in `Part III` of the `Chapter05.sql` script to inspect the data in detail; however, to understand the SSIS package, it should suffice to simply look at the row numbers in the active data flow.

29. When all the operations have finished, stop the debug mode execution. In SSMS, locate `Part IV` of the `Chapter05.sql` script. Use the three UPDATE statements to modify the source data in the `WideWorldImporters` database. Altogether, five rows should be affected by the updates.

30. In SSDT, run the package again in debug mode, and observe the `Load Staging Tables` data flow once more. All five rows that you modified in the previous step should now be redirected to the `ETL.PurchaseOrders_Modified` staging table.

    When all the operations have finished, stop the debug mode execution.

    If you plan to work on the final recipe in this chapter, *Upgrading a Custom Data Flow Component*, you should now close the `SSISCustomizationTest.sln` solution.

How it works...

You have now deployed both the custom task as well as the custom component that you created earlier in this chapter to the local SQL Server instance. To deploy the components to other environments, copy the files to each target environment, adjust the `DeployApplicationNameTask.bat` command file so that the commands reference the correct folders, and run it.

After a successful deployment, you have implemented the **Application Name** task in one SSIS package, which made it easier to identify operations invoked by the package on the target SQL Server instance. After that, you implemented the **Row Hash** transformation in another SSIS package to deliver an efficient data flow capable of detecting which data is actually needed in the final destination.

Upgrading a Custom Data Flow Component

When you determine that a custom component that might have already been deployed to production use needs to be modified – for instance, to implement a bug fix, to add an improvement, or simply to extend its capabilities – you can take advantage of a built-in feature of the `PipelineComponent` class to automate the upgrade.

> **Tip**
>
> In general, all the changes needed by the upgrade should be delivered without the need for user intervention – for instance, if the new version uses properties that were not available in the previous version(s), then default values should be provided as well.

After the new version of the component has been deployed to the target environment, the upgrade is performed automatically:

- At design time when the package that implements the component is opened in SSDT
- At runtime when the package that implements the component is executed

> **Important note**
>
> If the upgrade cannot be completed successfully, the component, as well as the SSIS package implementing it, can be left in an unusable state.

Getting ready

This recipe depends on the results of two previous recipes in this chapter, *Designing a Custom Data Flow Component*, and *Deploying SSIS customizations*, which need to be completed before you can start working on this recipe.

How to do it...

The `SSISCustomization.sln` solution should be open in **Visual Studio**:

1. Use Windows Explorer to navigate to the `\Chapter05\Scripts` folder in your local clone of the cookbook GitHub repository, locate the `Chapter05_RowHashTransformation_Upgrade.txt` file, and open it in a text editor (for instance, in Notepad).

   In Visual Studio, open the `RowHashTransformation.cs` class file.

2. You will now make changes to the class definition that are needed to add new design-time and runtime functionalities and to make changes to the existing ones. You will also provide the means to upgrade the previous version of the component to the new version.

3. Start by amending the `DtsPipelineComponentAttribute` definition; add the new version information, or replace the entire attribute:

```
[DtsPipelineComponentAttribute(
    ComponentType = ComponentType.Transform,
    DisplayName = "Row Hash",
    Description = "Generates a hash of selected columns
in the pipeline row.",
    NoEditor = false,
    RequiredProductLevel = DTSProductLevel.DTSPL_NONE,
    CurrentVersion = 2
    )]
```

   The version information will be used by the SSIS runtime to detect whether an upgrade is needed or not.

4. Add two more private constants; you can place them below the existing ones:

```
private const String COLUMN_ORDER_CUSTOM_PROPERTY_NAME =
"Ordinal";
```

```
private const String DUPLICATE_ORDINAL_VALUE_MESSAGE =
"Ordinal values must be unique. Duplicate ordinal values
encountered: {0}.";
```

5. Change the data type of the `_columnCollection` private variable:

```
private SortedList<Int32, IDTSInputColumn100> _
columnCollection;
```

In the original version, this variable used the generic `List` type, whereas in the new version it is going to use the `SortedList` type. The new type automatically sorts all values placed into the list by their keys. More on this later.

Save the solution.

6. In the `Validate` method, locate the following test:

```
if (input.InputColumnCollection.Count == 0)
{
    ComponentMetaData.FireWarning(0, ComponentMetaData.
Name, NO_INPUT_COLUMN_MESSAGE, String.Empty, 0);
    return DTSValidationStatus.VS_ISVALID;
}
```

Replace it with the extended version, located in the `Chapter05_RowHashTransformation_Upgrade.txt` file, below the `Validate - extend input column count check` comment.

The additional rule will check whether the new input column custom properties contain unique values for each selected input column.

7. In the `PreExecute` method, replace the existing commands used to initialize and populate the `_columnCollection` variable with the following:

```
_columnCollection = new SortedList<Int32,
IDTSInputColumn100>();
foreach (IDTSInputColumn100 inputColumn in input.
InputColumnCollection)
{
    _columnCollection.Add( (Int32)inputColumn.
CustomPropertyCollection[COLUMN_ORDER_CUSTOM_PROPERTY_
NAME].Value, inputColumn);
}
```

The new input column custom property will be used as the column sorting key in the `_columnCollection` variable. More on this later.

8. In the `ProcessInput` method, change the way the `_columnCollection` variable is used when processing the columns of the given pipeline row:

```
foreach (IDTSInputColumn100 inputColumn in _
columnCollection.OrderBy(c => c.LineageID))
```

This:

```
foreach (IDTSInputColumn100 inputColumn in _
columnCollection.Values)
```

When a variable of type SortedList is enumerated, the items are returned in ascending order of the keys, by default.

9. Create some more space after the ProcessInput method, and override the ReinitializeMetaData base method with the following definition:

```
this.CreateInputCustomProperties();
base.ReinitializeMetaData();
```

10. Next, override the PerformUpgrade base method using the following definition:

```
DtsPipelineComponentAttribute pipelineComponentAttribute
= (DtsPipelineComponentAttribute)Attribute.
GetCustomAttribute(this.GetType(),
typeof(DtsPipelineComponentAttribute), false);
Int32 componentLatestVersion = pipelineComponentAttribute.
CurrentVersion;
if (pipelineVersion < componentLatestVersion)
{
    this.CreateInputCustomProperties();
}
ComponentMetaData.Version = componentLatestVersion;
```

This is the method that facilitates the automatic upgrade of an older version of the component to the latest version.

11. In the OnInputPathAttached method, locate the foreach loop that is used to automatically select all input columns when the component's input is attached:

```
foreach (IDTSVirtualInputColumn100 inputColumn in input.
VirtualInputColumnCollection)
{
    Int32 inputColumnLineageID = inputColumn.LineageID;
    input.SetUsageType(inputColumnLineageID,
DTSUsageType.UT_READONLY);
}
```

Amend the loop so that it now includes the creation of the input column custom property:

```
foreach (IDTSVirtualInputColumn100 inputColumn in input.
VirtualInputColumnCollection)
{
    Int32 inputColumnLineageID = inputColumn.LineageID;
    input.SetUsageType(inputColumnLineageID,
DTSUsageType.UT_READONLY);
    this.CreateInputColumnCustomProperties(n,
inputColumnLineageID);
}
```

12. Add the following three new private methods into the class definition; you can place them below the existing private methods:

   a) `InputColumnCustomPropertyExists`

   b) `CreateInputCustomProperties`

   c) `CreateInputColumnCustomProperties`

   Save the solution.

13. Build the project using the **Debug** configuration, and if successful, change the configuration to **Release** and build the solution again.

   In case of any errors, inspect the error messages, make any necessary corrections, and repeat the build.

14. Run the `DeployCustomizations.bat` file, located in the `C:\ETL-with-Azure\Chapter05\Files` folder, to deploy the new version of the `Row Hash` component.

15. In SSDT, open the `SSISCustomizationTest.sln` solution. If you left the `RowHashTest.dtsx` package open when you last edited this solution, the `Row Hash` component should upgrade automatically.

   If the package is closed, the component will be upgraded as soon as you open it.

If you followed the instructions in this and the previous recipes, the upgrade should succeed without any problems. However, in case of any errors, inspect the error messages, make the necessary corrections, and repeat the deployment.

> **Important note**
>
> Any Visual Studio 2019 solution that contains a project that implements custom tasks or components needs to be closed and reopened every time you redeploy said tasks or components. Otherwise, the latest versions of the customizations will not be loaded automatically. Simply refreshing the SSIS Toolbox will not help, unfortunately.

16. After the upgrade has succeeded, open the `Load Staging Tables` data flow and double-click the **Row Hash** transformation to review its state. On the **Input Columns** tab, there should be no changes. The settings that you used when you last edited the component should still be in place. On the **Input and Output Properties** tab, expand the **RowHashInput** node, under it the **Input Columns** node, and then select one of the input columns:

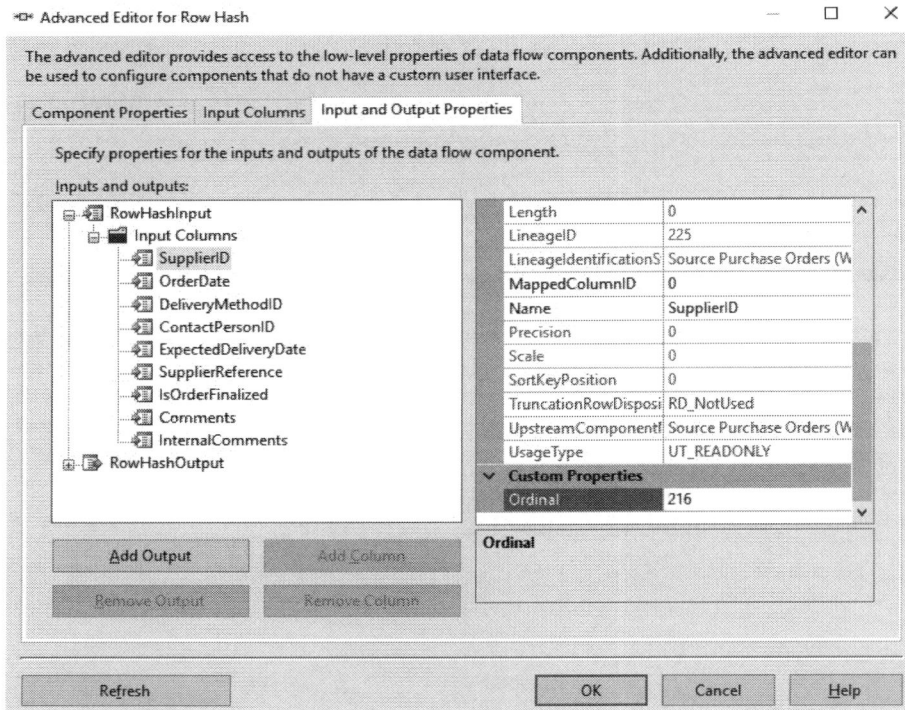

Figure 5.12 – Locating the new input column custom property

17. Scroll down the input column property list in the right column. At the bottom, in the **Custom Properties** section, you should see the **Ordinal** input column custom property. The authors of SSIS packages can now use this property to specify the order in which the columns should be processed when calculating the row hash value.

18. For fun, switch the **Ordinal** values of two columns of your choice.

19. When ready, click **OK** to confirm the settings. If the **Ordinal** values are not unique, an error will be reported, preventing you from running the package until the values are corrected. Save the solution.

20. Execute the package in debug mode and observe the **Load Staging Tables** data flow. Observe the execution results:

a) How many rows were identified as changed?

b) How many rows did you actually change before this last execution?

You can now close both instances of Visual Studio.

How it works...

You have implemented an upgrade of a Custom Data Flow component. You made the necessary changes to the component's definition to introduce new features and change the behavior of some of the existing features. You also implemented the `PerformUpgrade` method of the `PipelineComponent` base class that facilitates an automated upgrade of an older version of the component in the target environment.

When the `PerformUpgrade` method is called at design time or at runtime, the upgrade begins by retrieving the new version number from `DtsPipelineComponentAttribute`. If the current version of the component is lower, the method then performs the feature upgrade by adding new custom properties on the input columns.

At the end of the upgrade, the current version number is replaced with the new one, which signifies a successful upgrade and prevents the upgrade from being attempted again.

The following methods provide the programmatic logic needed to make sure that all the input columns selected at design time contain the custom property used to determine the order in which the columns should be processed at runtime when the pipeline data is processed in the `ProcessInput` method:

- `InputColumnCustomPropertyExists`: The method is used to check whether a custom property with a specific name already exists on the given input column of the given input.

- `CreateInputCustomProperties`: The method is used to add custom properties to the given input.

- `CreateInputColumnCustomProperties`: The method is used to add custom properties on a given input column of the given input.

Version 2 of the transformation allows the SSIS package developer to determine the order in which the values of the selected columns are to be concatenated into a single binary array that is used in computing the hash value. In version 1, the columns were processed in the order determined when columns were selected at design time. In version 2, the columns will be processed in the order specified by the **Ordinal** input column custom property. The correct order is guaranteed by the `SortedList` data type used by the variable.

6
Azure Data Factory

Azure Data Factory (**ADF**) is a de facto ETL/ELT tool in Azure. The service is very popular for dealing with data load and transformations. This chapter will show you how Data Factory can be used as a central orchestration service and how some of its toolset can be used to transform data.

We will cover the following Azure Data Factory recipes in this chapter:

- Data factory creation
- Copying data from the internet
- Moving and transforming data
- Triggering and monitoring our pipeline

Let's begin by creating our data factory.

Data factory creation

This is our first recipe in this chapter. We will create and explore the various Data Factory components. The following recipes will use the same data factory to move and transform data.

As shown in the following diagram, a data factory contains the following components. Azure Storage and SQL Database are not part of the factory; they are just an example of a simple copy activity that Data Factory can do:

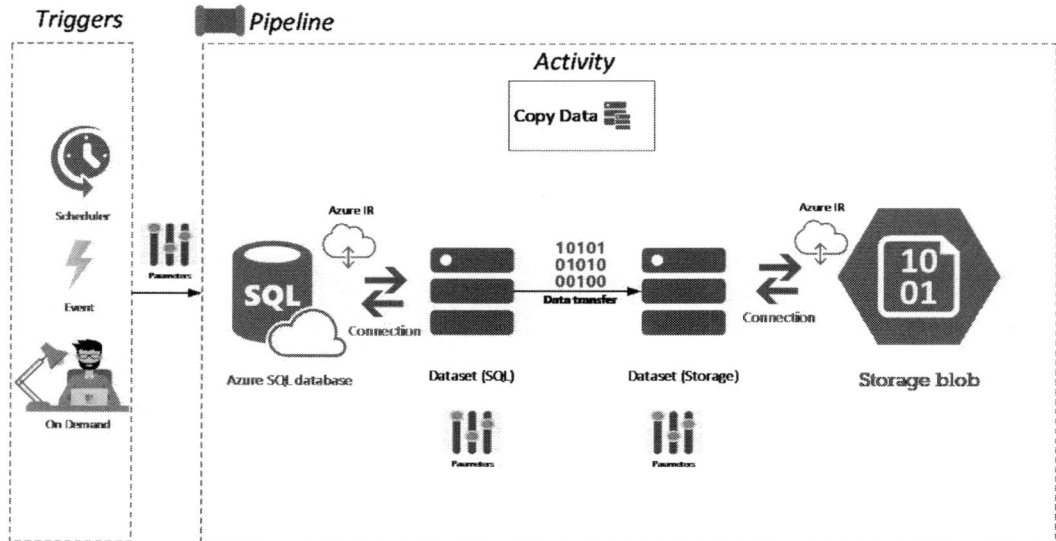

Figure 6.1 – An overview of Azure Data Factory

The two main components are **triggers** and **pipelines**.

A trigger is essentially a mechanism that starts a pipeline execution. There are three types of triggers:

- **Scheduler**: Can be based on a wall clock schedule or based on tumbling windows. A tumbling window essentially triggers the pipeline execution every **n** time: for example, every 5 minutes, hours, and so on.

- **Event**: Detects the presence of a file in an Azure Storage account. Once the file is detected, the pipeline is executed.

- **Manual**: Can be executed in an ad hoc manner. A user will launch the pipeline manually every time.

A pipeline is a container for activities. In the preceding diagram, we can see a copy activity that takes data from an Azure SQL database and copies it to a storage account. The other components of a pipeline are the following:

- **Linked Services (Connection)**: Like SSIS connection managers, they are used to connect the factory to various resources that can either be storage or compute services.

- **Dataset**: A dataset is the schema representation of the data connected via a linked service. This is how an activity knows how to map data from a source to the target (sink).

- **Azure Integration Runtime (IR)**: Used to connect the Data Factory linked services to different Azure services.

- **Parameters**: Like SSIS parameters, we can use them to change the behavior of a factory pipeline execution.

Now that we know the major components of a data factory, let's create one.

Getting ready

This recipe assumes that you have access to an Azure subscription. It can be a free trial one as described in the recipe *Creating an Azure subscription*, in *Chapter 1, Getting Started with Azure and SSIS 2019*.

How to do it...

Let's start creating the data factory!

1. From your Azure Subscription, click on + **Create a resource**.

2. From the Azure blade that appears, select **Integration** on the left and **Data Factory** on the right, as shown in the following screenshot:

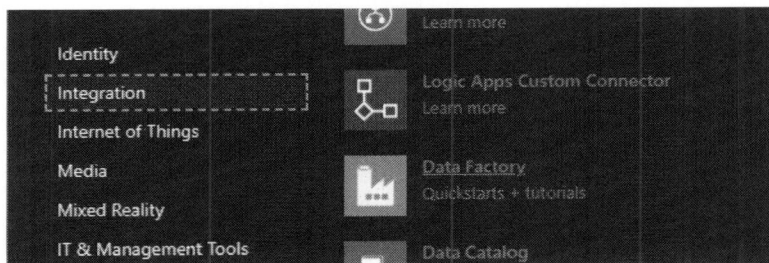

Figure 6.2 – Add a new data factory

3. Name the factory ETLInAzure preceded or followed by your initials as the name **ETLInAzure** will probably not be available. The data factory's name must be unique in Azure. As shown in the following screenshot, select the **V2** version, your subscription name, **ETLInAzureCookBook,** and your desired region. Uncheck the **Enable GIT** property. We will not use Git, a source control service, for the recipes in this book:

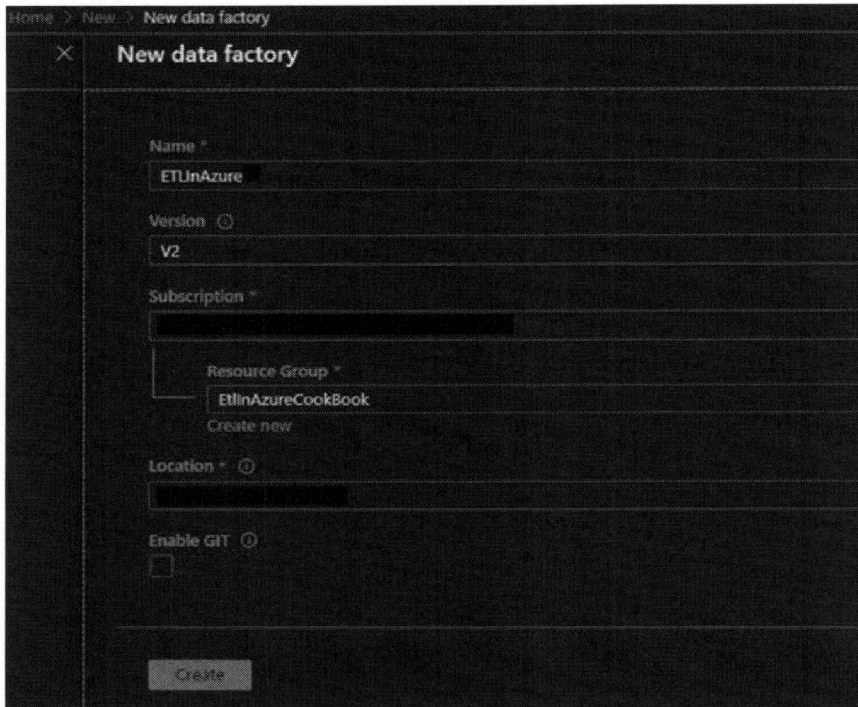

Figure 6.3 – New data factory blade

4. Click **Create** at the bottom of the screen to create the data factory.

5. Once the data factory is created, navigate to it. As shown in the following screenshot, there are many components in the **Data Factory** blade:

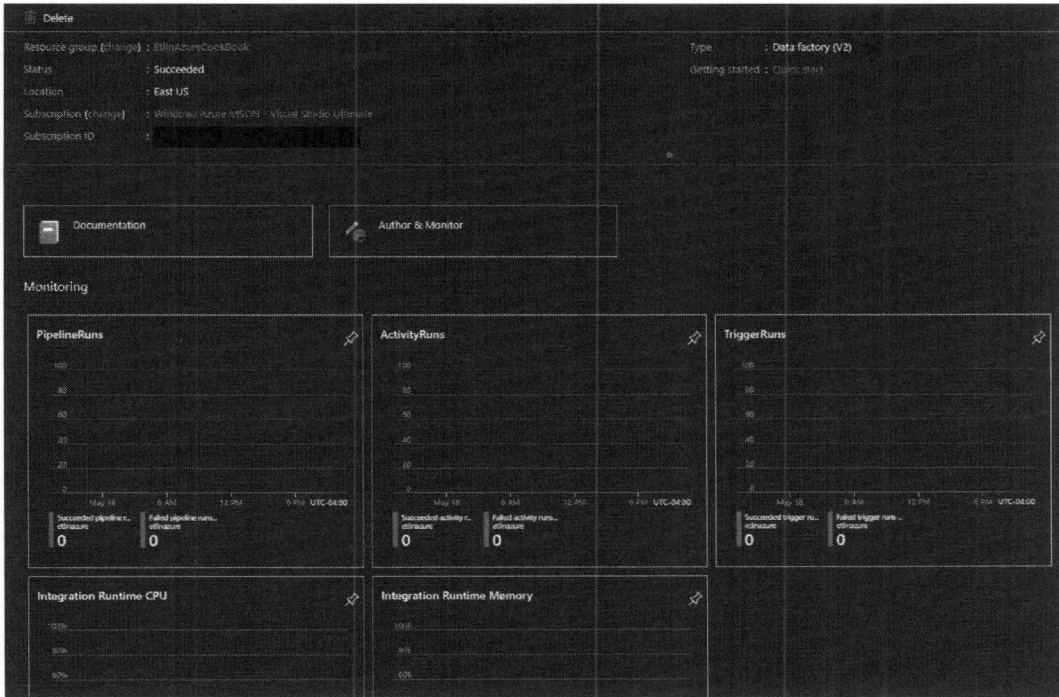

Figure 6.4 – Azure Data Factory blade in the portal

6. Here is the description of the default graphs:

    a) **Documentation**: Clicking on it will navigate to Data Factory documentation pages on the Microsoft Azure documentation website.

    b) **Author and Monitor**: This is the tool that will allow us to add and modify (author) the factory.

    c) **PipelineRuns**, **ActivityRuns** and **TriggerRuns**: A graph that shows how many pipelines activities or triggers ran and whether they succeeded or failed. As we will see later; pipelines are the main components.

    d) **Integration Runtime CPU** and **Integration Runtime Memory**: How much CPU and memory an integration runtime is using. This is for **Self-Hosted Integration Runtime (SHIR)** usage. A SHIR is a small program that is installed on a PC (or VM) in an enterprise network. They allow safe and encrypted communication between the factory in Azure and the enterprise network. For more information on integration runtimes, navigate to https://docs.microsoft.com/en-us/azure/data-factory/concepts-integration-runtime.

That's it! We have created our data factory!

How it works...

As stated before, a data factory is composed of many elements. What we've done in the recipe is to create the shell of a factory. The next recipe will copy some data from an Azure SQL database to a storage account.

Copying data from the internet

This recipe will teach you how we can connect to a data source from a public internet URL. We're going to use demographic income **Status of Income (SOI)** data from the **Internal Revenue Service (IRS)**. We will explore and transform this data with our Databricks workspace environment.

We will get data from the following links:

- `https://www.irs.gov/pub/irs-soi/17zpallnoagi.csv`: This is a CSV file that contains the year 2017 incomes per state per zip code.

- `https://worldpopulationreview.com/static/states/abbr-name.csv`: This CSV file contains state abbreviations (codes) and state names.

The first file contains income data and state codes. We will use the second file to augment the first one with state names. We will also aggregate the state income file to get one state income per state instead of zip code.

Getting ready

This recipe assumes that you have access to an Azure subscription. It can be a free trial one as described in the recipe *Creating an Azure subscription*, in *Chapter 1, Getting Started with Azure and SSIS 2019*.

How to do it...

This recipe requires us to create the following items, which represent the plumbing of our factory:

a) Two linked services, one for each file we're going to retrieve from the internet.

b) One linked service that points to an Azure storage.

c) Four datasets: two for the internet files and two more for the destination files in the storage account.

Once the plumbing is in place, we're able to create a pipeline. So, let's start with the plumbing!

1. From the Azure portal (`portal.azure.com`), go to the data factory we created in the first recipe of this chapter, *Data factory creation*. Click on **Author & Monitor** to access the design pane of the factory as shown in the following screenshot:

Figure 6.5 – Data Factory – Author & Monitor

2. To create linked services, we need to create a blank pipeline first. From the **Data Factory** landing page, click on the **Author** pipeline icon as shown in the following screenshot:

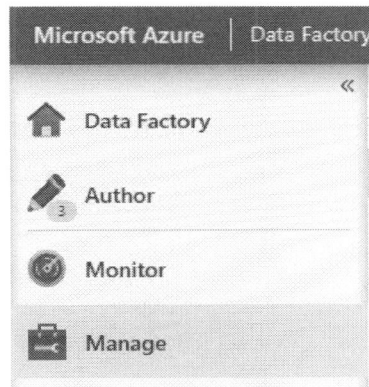

Figure 6.6 – Data Factory Author pipeline icon

3. Once in the **Author** pipeline pane, we're faced with a blank pipeline. We're going to add linked services (connections) to the internet files. Click on the **Connections** link at the bottom left of the **Author** pane as shown in the following screenshot:

Figure 6.7 – Data Factory pipeline Connections icon

4. Two different tabs are available here: **Linked services** and **Integration runtimes**. The first allows us to connect to different data store and compute services. The former is used to enable us to connect to on-premises, SSIS packages in Azure or Azure-specific regions and compute capacities. For now, we will use **Linked services**. As shown in the following screenshot, click on the + sign to add a new connection:

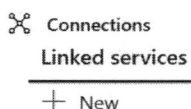

Figure 6.8 – Data Factory pipeline – add connection

5. The **New linked service** blade appears on the right. Again, we have two options here. We can create a linked service to connect to a **Data store** or to a **Compute** capacity. A connection to a **Data store** allows us access to a stored file. A **Compute** connection allows us to connect to compute capacity such as Azure HDInsight, Azure Databricks, and so on. There are over 90 data store connections. For now, we're going to connect to an internet data store. Click on **File** and select **HTTP** and click on **Continue** as shown in the following screenshot:

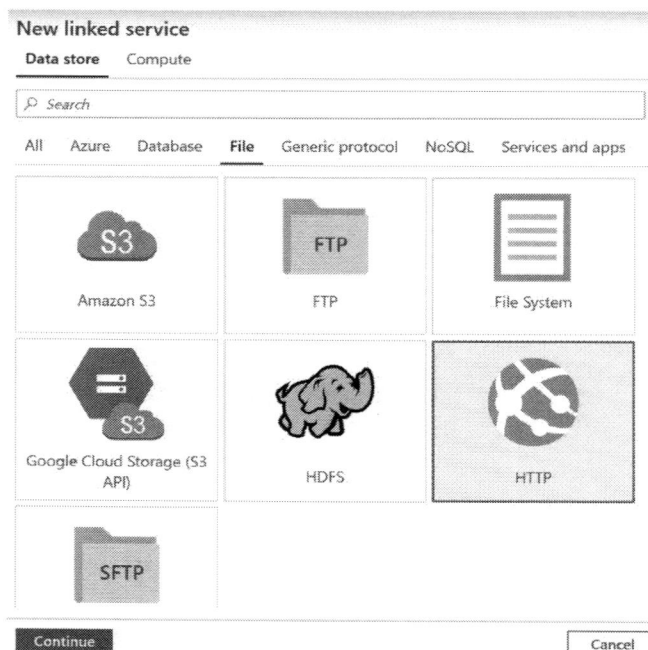

Figure 6.9 – Data Factory – adding an HTTP data store

6. The **New linked service (HTTP)** page is displayed – enter **LNK_Abbreviations**
    for the **Name** property, `https://worldpopulationreview.com/static/`
    `states/abbr-name.csv` for **Base URL**, and use **Anonymous** as **Authentication**
    type. Click on **Test connection** as shown in the following screenshot. Click on
    Create once the connection tests successfully:

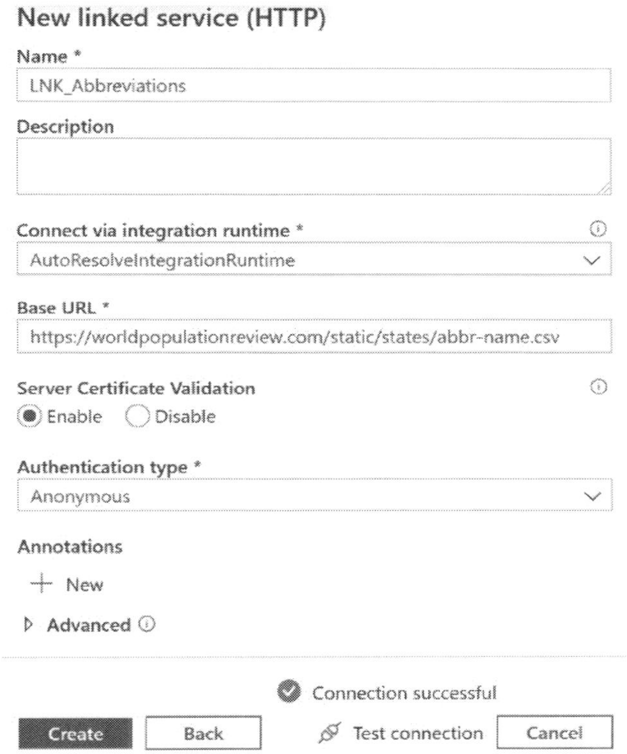

New linked service (HTTP)

Name *

LNK_Abbreviations

Description

Connect via integration runtime *   ⓘ

AutoResolveIntegrationRuntime   ⌄

Base URL *

https://worldpopulationreview.com/static/states/abbr-name.csv

Server Certificate Validation   ⓘ
◉ Enable   ◯ Disable

Authentication type *

Anonymous   ⌄

Annotations

+ New

▷ Advanced ⓘ

✓ Connection successful

Create   Back   ⚡ Test connection   Cancel

Figure 6.10 – Data Factory abbreviations – HTTP data store details

7. Add another **HTTP** linked service. This time call it **LNK_StatesIncomeData**. Use
    `https://www.irs.gov/pub/irs-soi/17zpallnoagi.csv` for **Base URL**
    and **Anonynous** as **Authentication type**. Click on **Test connection** and **Create** to
    create the linked service.

8.   You should now have two linked services created, as shown in the following
     screenshot:

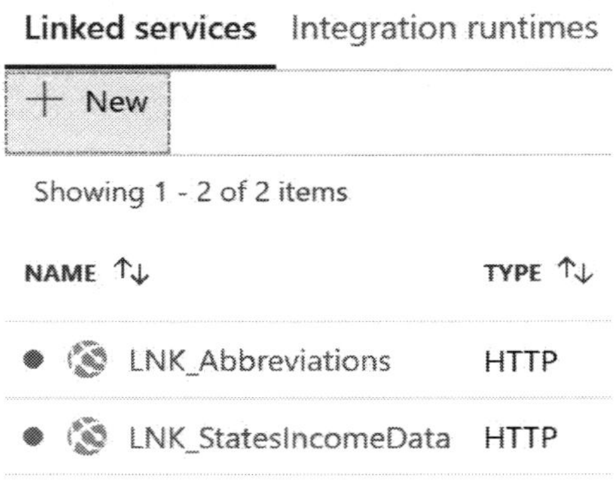

Figure 6.11 – Data Factory abbreviations – HTTP data store created

9.   Now that we have created our two source linked services, we're going to create our
     target or sink linked services. Add another linked service using **Azure Blob Storage**
     as shown in the following screenshot. Click on **Create**:

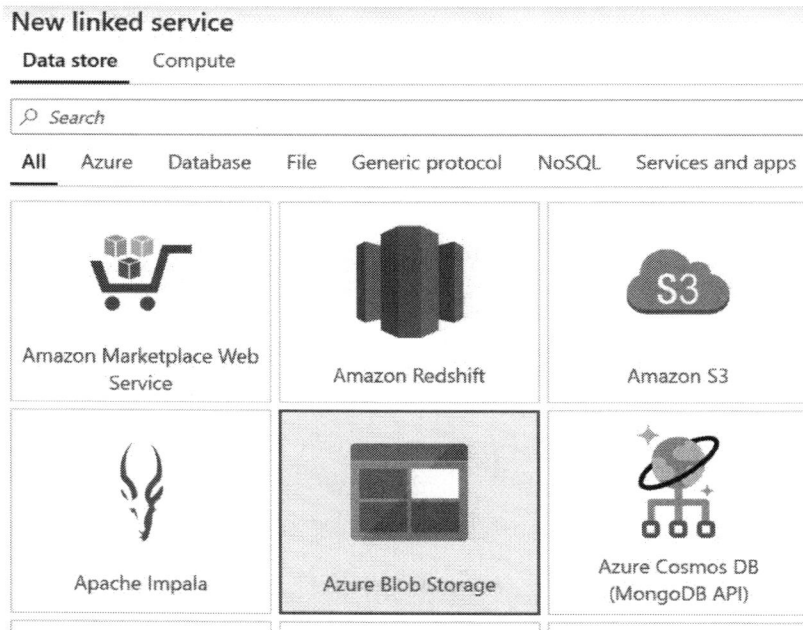

Figure 6.12 – Data Factory – add a blob storage data store

10. Use **LNK_ETLInAzure** for the name, select your subscription, and use **etlinazure** for **Storage account name**. Click on **Test connection** and **Create** to create the linked service as shown in the following screenshot:

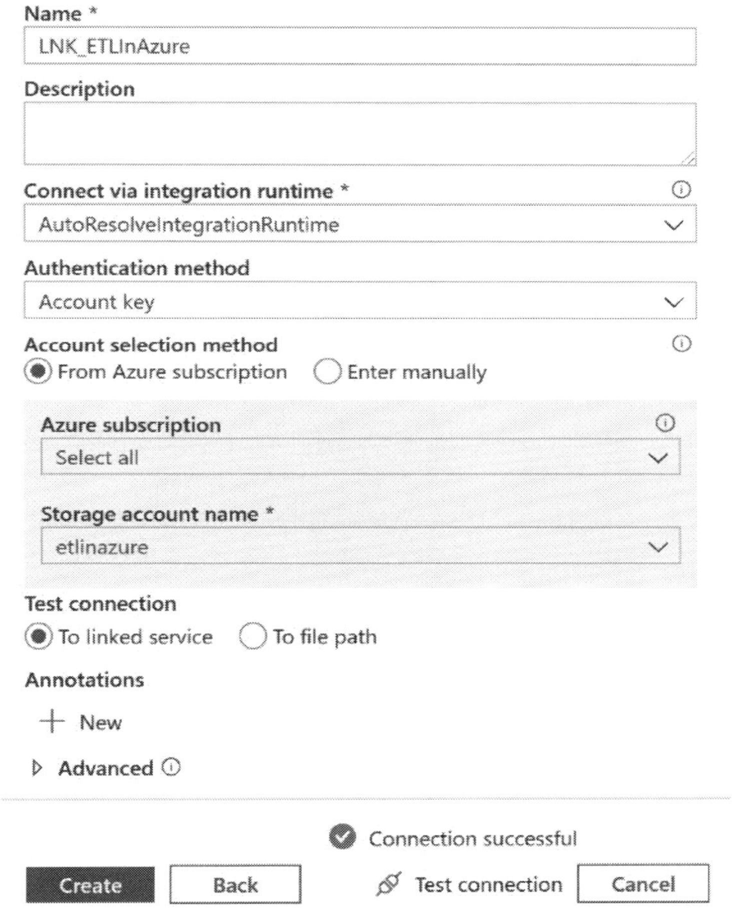

Figure 6.13 – Data Factory – add blob storage data store details

11. We now have created our connections. The next step is to create datasets on top of them. Datasets are the schema definitions of our data, the contract we have between the source and sinks. Sources provide columns and data types and targets agree to this contract. Make sure you are on the **Author** tab. From the **Factory Resources** section, click on the + sign and select **Dataset** from the menu that appears, as shown in the following screenshot:

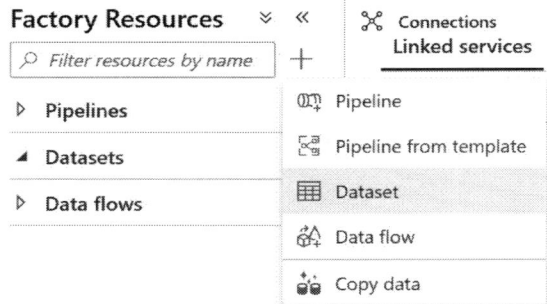

Figure 6.14 – Dataset creation

12. From the **New dataset** blade that appears at the right of the screen, select the **File** tab and **HTTP** as shown in the following screenshot. Click on **Continue**:

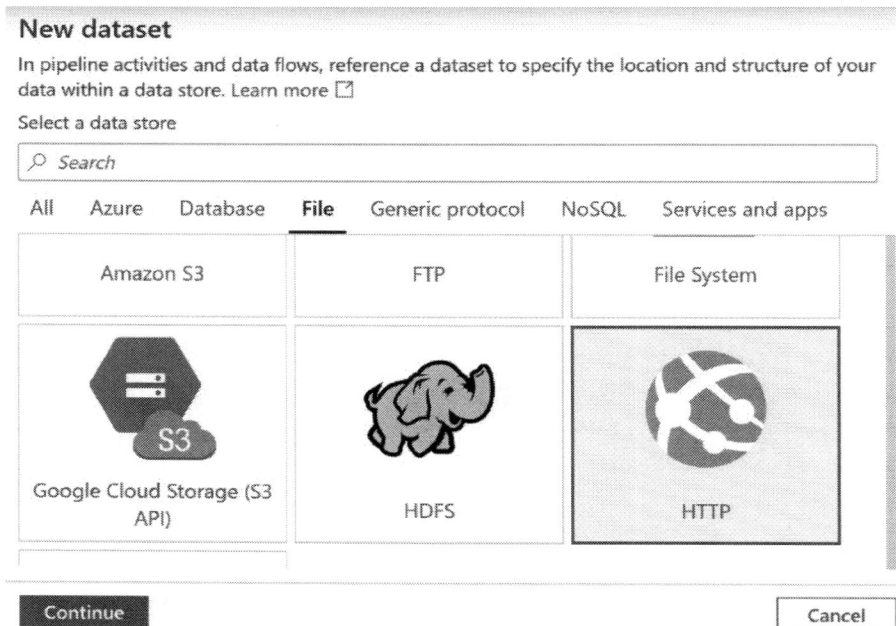

Figure 6.15 – Data Factory – add an HTTP dataset

13. Select **DelimitedText** as the format and click on **Continue** as shown in the following screenshot. Use **DelimitedText1** for **Name**, **LNK_Abbreviations** for **Linked service**, **From connection/store** for **Import schema**, and **GET** for **Request method**. Click on **OK** to save the dataset as shown in the following screenshot:

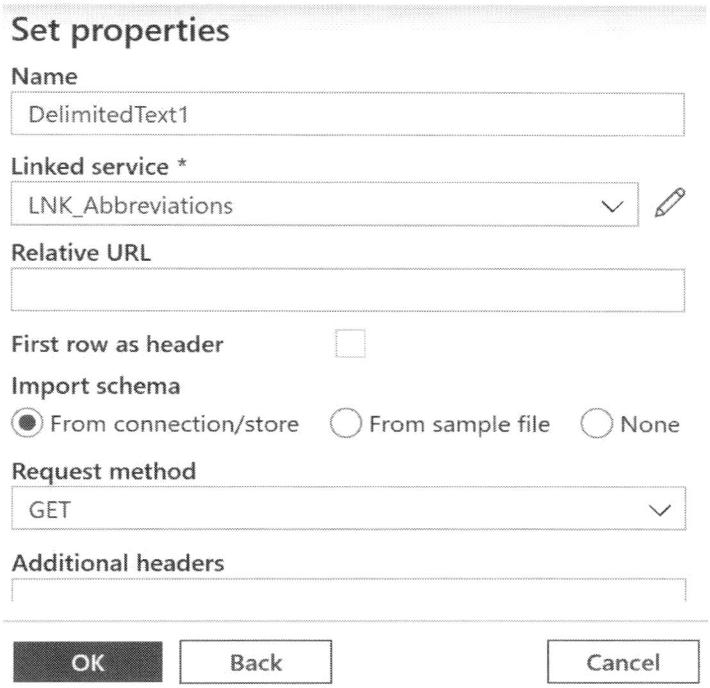

Figure 6.16 – Data Factory – add HTTP dataset properties

14. Rename the dataset DS_StateAbbreviationHTTP.

15. Go to the **Schema** tab, click on **Import schema**, and select **From connection/store** from the submenu that appears, as shown in the following screenshot:

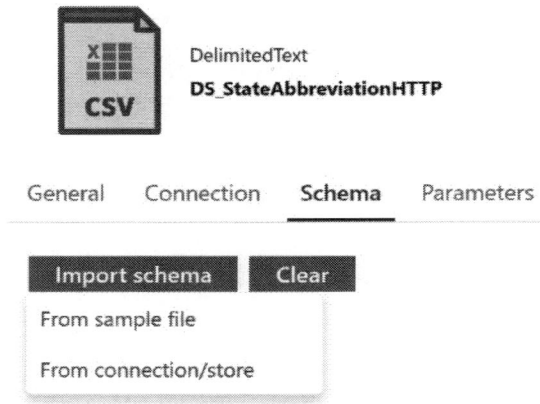

Figure 6.17: Data Factory – add an HTTP dataset properties import schema

16. The data store read settings appear. Click on **Finish**. Your screen should look like the following screenshot:

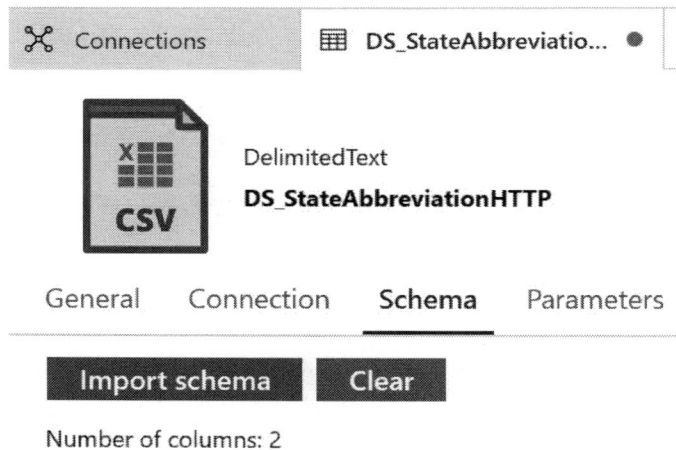

Figure 6.18 – Data Factory – HTTP dataset properties schema imported

17. We will now repeat the same *steps (11 to 15)* for the **State Income Data**. Add a new dataset, name it **DS_ StateIncomeDataHTTP, use LNK_StateIncomeData** for **Linked service, From connection/store** for **Import schema**, and finally, **GET** for **Request method**. On the **Connection** tab, make sure you have checked **First row as header**.

18. Import the schema. You should have 153 columns.

19. Next, we're going to create two datasets for the sinks. Add a new **Azure Blob Storage** dataset, and this time, choose **Parquet** as the file format. **Parquet** compresses data by column. It makes files smaller and data retrieval from them very efficient. Name the dataset **DS_StateAbbreviationParquet**, and select **LNK_ETLInAzure** for the **Linked service** property. For the **File path,** enter **adf/abbreviations/stateAbbreviations.parquet**. Since we do not have a file created for now, we'll use **None** for the **Import schema** property as shown in the following screenshot. Click **OK** to create the dataset:

Set properties

Name

DS_StateAbbreviationParquet

Linked service *

LNK_ETLInAzure

File path

adf / abbreviations / stateAbbreviations.par [Browse ▾]

Import schema

◯ From connection/store   ◯ From sample file   ⦿ None

[OK] [Back]   [Cancel]

Figure 6.19 – Data Factory – add blob dataset properties

20. Add another **Azure Blob Storage** dataset, name it **DS_StateIncomeDataParquet,** use **LNK_ETLInAzure** for **Linked service, adf/stateIncomeData/stateIncomeData.parquet** for **File path**, **None** for the **Import schema** property, and check **First row as header**. Click **OK**.

21. We have now created our two sink schemas created. It's now time to use them. From the **Factory Resources** section, click on the + sign and add a new pipeline. Name it **P_StateIncomeMappingDataflow** as shown in the following screenshot:

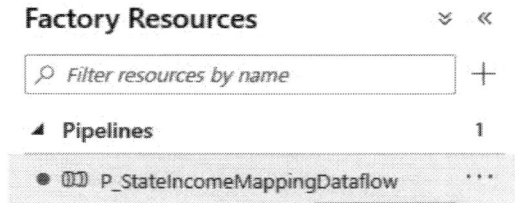

Figure 6.20 – Data Factory – new pipeline

22. From the **Activities** section, expand the **Move & transform** section. Drag and drop a **Copy data** activity on the pipeline. Name it **ACT_CPY_StateAbbreviations** as shown in the following screenshot:

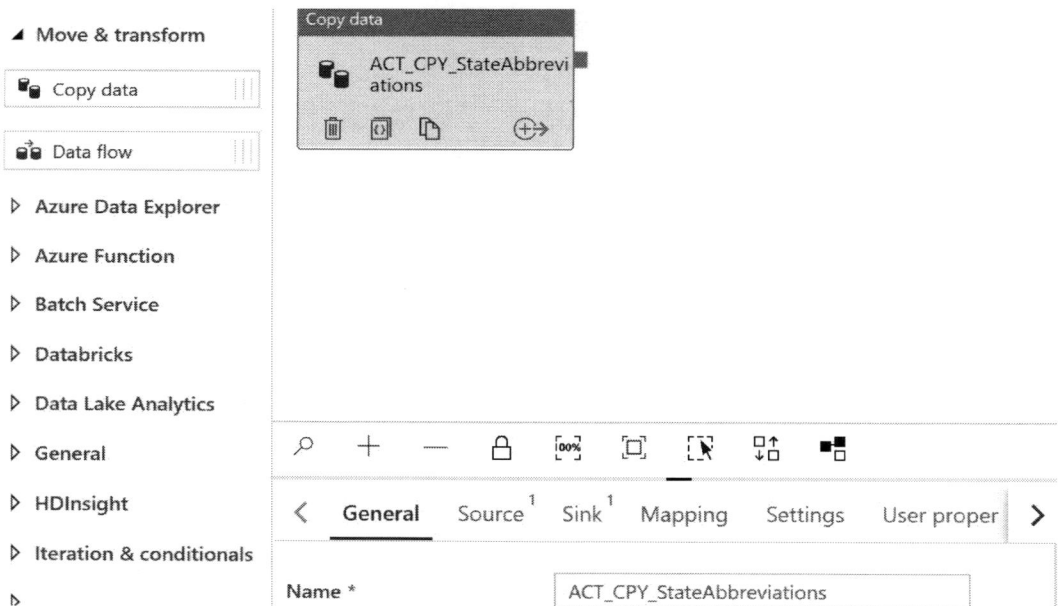

Figure 6.21 – Data Factory new copy activity

23. Click on the **Source** tab and select the **DS_StateAbbreviationHTTP** dataset.

24. Click on the **Sink** tab and select **DS_StateAbbreviationParquet**.

25. Click on the **Mapping** tab and click on **Import schemas**. Rename the sink column names as shown in the following screenshot:

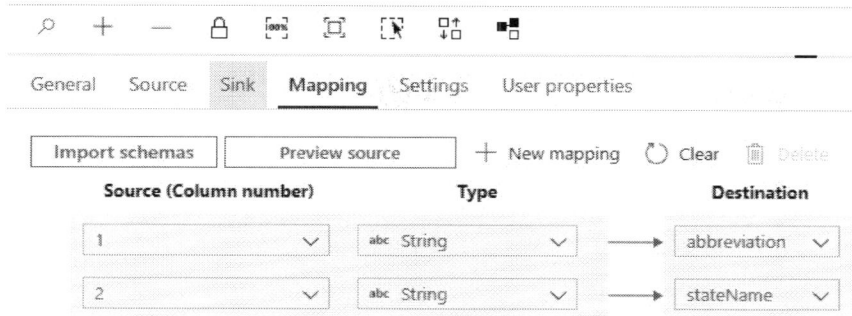

Figure 6.22 – Data Factory new copy activity Mapping tab

26. Let's test our new copy activity now. From the top of the pipeline, click on **Debug**. The copy activity will copy the data successfully, as shown in the following screenshot:

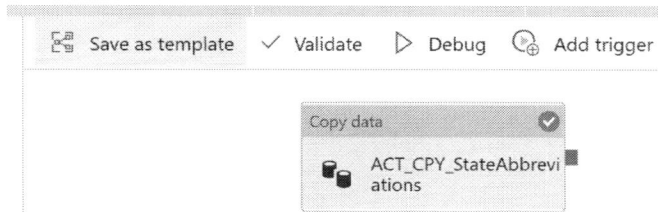

Figure 6.23 – Data Factory new copy activity debug success

27. Open Azure Data Explorer and navigate to the container `adf/abbreviation` blob. You will see that a file called **stateAbbreviations.parquet** has been created as shown in the following screenshot:

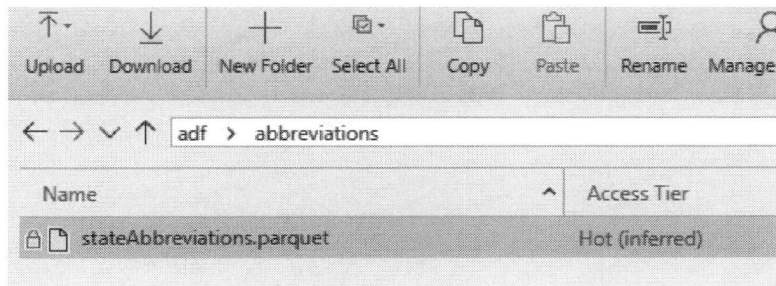

Figure 6.24 – Data Factory new copy activity – stateAbbreviations.parquet

28. Add a new **Copy** activity and name it **ACT_CPY_StateIncomeData**.

29. Select **DS_StateIncomeDataHTTP** as the source dataset and **DS_StateIncoemDataParquet** as the sink dataset.

30. On the **Mapping** tab, select **Import mapping**. Remove all columns except **STATE** and **A02650** as shown in the following screenshot:

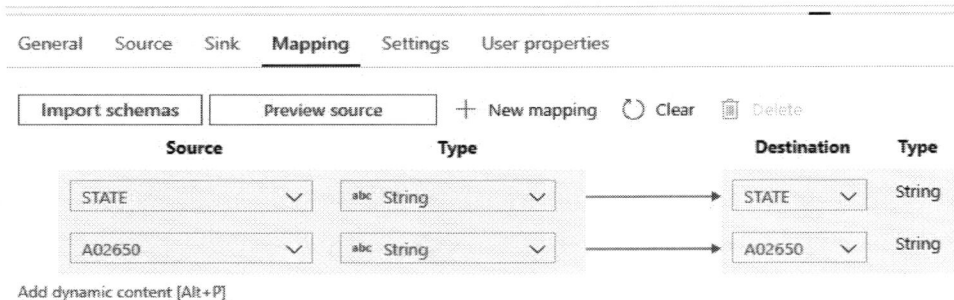

Figure 6.25 – Data Factory – new copy activity stateIncomeData on the Mapping tab

31. Click **Debug** at the top of the pipeline. The two copy activities will run successfully, as shown in the following screenshot:

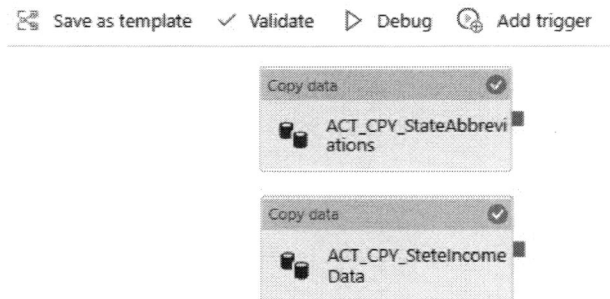

Figure 6.26 – Data Factory – new copy activity stateIncomeData execution

32. Go back into **Azure Storage Explorer** to verify that the file was copied successfully, as shown in the following screenshot:

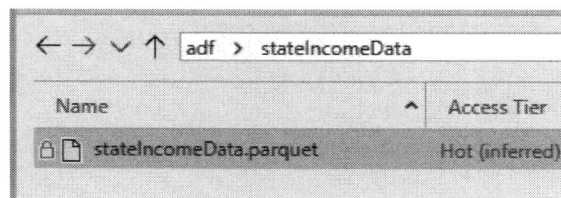

Figure 6.27 – Data Factory – new copy activity stateIncomeData parquet file

33. Now, it's time to publish our factory to ensure we will not lose anything when we close the browser. Click on the **Publish all** icon at the top of the factory as shown in the following screenshot:

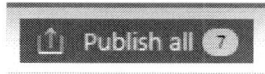

Figure 6.28 – Data Factory Publish all icon

34. A summary of the changes appears at the right of the factory. Click on **Publish** to save the changes.

35. Within a few seconds, you will get a message telling you that the data factory has been successfully published.

That's it! We have completed our first pipeline.

How it works...

Copying data from a URL is quite easy with Data Factory. We created a linked service to both URLs that allowed us to download two CSV files: StateAbbreviations and StateIncomeData. These files were then transferred to an Azure storage account using a copy activity.

Editing a data factory is done via a web browser. This allows to us to work from multiple devices without having to install Visual Studio as we did for the on-premises SSIS ETLs. Publishing the factory to the live environment is the simplest method. In real-life scenarios, you would use source control such as Git to save your factory changes. The live environment would contain managed changes from Git, the master branch. For simplicity in this recipe, we did not use source control but it's a must in real-world scenarios.

Moving and transforming data

We copied data in our storage account in the previous recipe, *Copying data from the internet*. In this recipe, we will join and transform the two datasets using a mapping data flow. They contain many tools that help us join, map, and aggregate our source datasets to produce another output (sink) dataset.

Mapping dataflows are a new addition for Data Factory. They were not part of the initial Data Factory v2 that was available in July 2018. The ADF team added the mapping data flows about a year later. For those who are familiar with SSIS, they will understand how to work with them in no time.

So, let's dig into our recipe!

Getting ready

This recipe assumes that you have access to an Azure subscription. It can be a free trial one as described in the recipe *Creating an Azure subscription*, in *Chapter 1, Getting Started with Azure and SSIS 2019*. It also assumes that you have created some Data Factory artifacts such as linked services, datasets, and so on, from the previous recipe, *Copying data from the internet*.

How to do it...

OK, let's dig into it!

1. Open the Data Factory designer from the Azure portal by clicking on the **Author & Monitor** link.

2. Go the pipeline we created in the previous recipe: **P_ StateIncomeMappingDataflow**. From the **Activities** section, expand **Move & Transform**. Drag and drop a **Data flow** activity to the pipeline. From the pane that appears at the right of the designer, select **Create new data flow**, choose **Mapping Data Flow**, and click on **OK** as shown in the following screenshot:

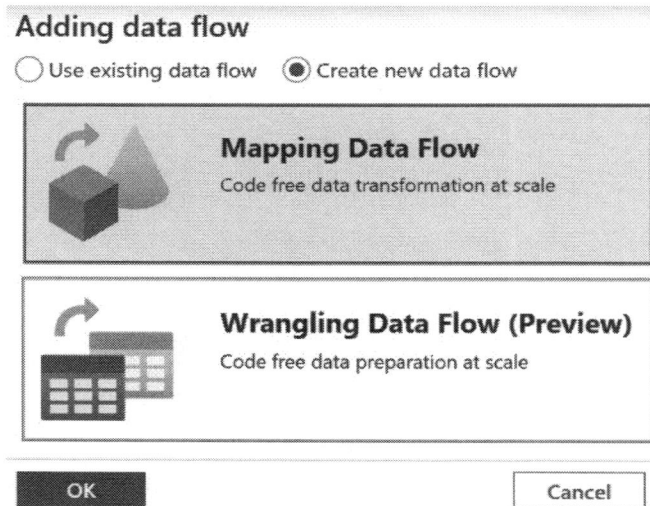

Figure 6.29 – Data Factory – adding a mapping data flow

3. In the **General Properties**, name the data flow **DFT_ StateIncomeMappingDataflow**, as shown in the following screenshot:

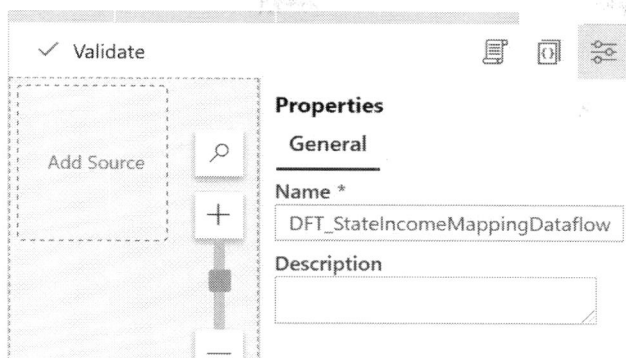

Figure 6.30 – Data Factory – naming a mapping data flow

4. Turn on **Data flow debug**. At the top of the data flow, slick on the **Data flow debug** icon, as shown in the following screenshot:

Figure 6.30a – Data Factory – turn on debug

5. A pop-up window appears and asks us to select an integration runtime. Use **AutoResolveIntegrationRuntime** and click on **OK** as shown in the following screenshot. Data Factory will start a Databricks cluster to get some computation resources for the operation. It might take up to 5-10 minutes to start the cluster.

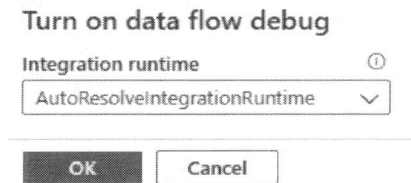

Figure 6.30b – Data Factory – turn on debug and select Integration runtime

6. Now, click on **Add source**. If a help tutorial appears, click **Next** and **Finish** to pass the steps. In the **Source settings** section, use **StateAbbreviation** for **Output stream name**. Select **DS_StateAbbreviationParquet** for the **Dataset** property. Uncheck the **Allow schema drift** option. Schema drift allows us to allow schema changes from the source dataset. For example, we could have a source that contains an **EmployeeName** column and another file could have the same column called **Name**. Allowing schema drifting would allow us to map those two columns to the same input column without failing our data flow. Ensure that the **Sampling** property is set to **Disable**. We do not need to sample our data because our data sources are very small. Your screen should look like the following screenshot:

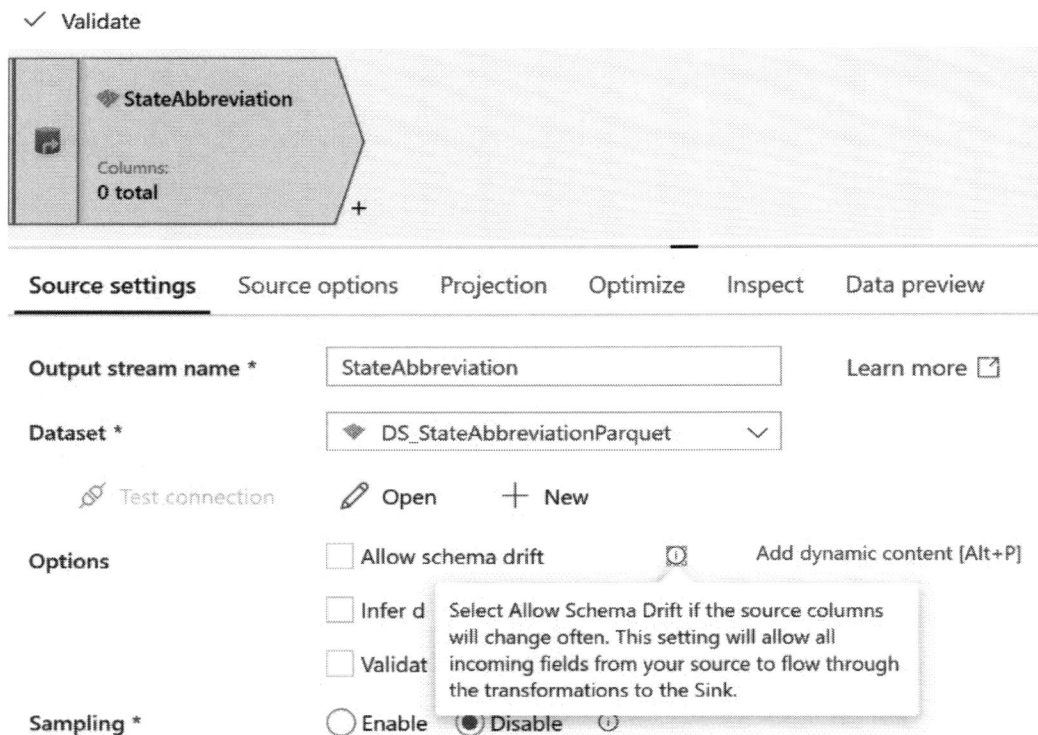

Figure 6.31 – Data Factory – adding a source to a mapping data flow

7. For **Source options**, leave the default properties. We do not have anything special to do here for our recipe.

8. The **Projection** tab allows us to get the schema from our source. Click on **Import projection**. We can see the schema on the screen shown in the following screenshot. The **StateAbbreviation** source has been updated to **2 total** columns:

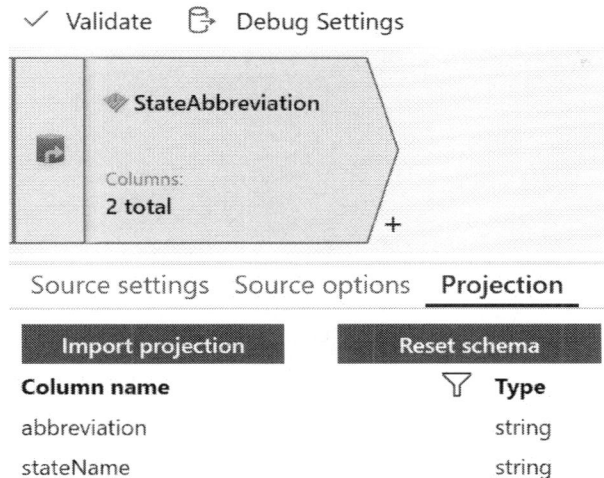

Figure 6.32 – Data Factory – retrieving a schema for a source in the mapping data flow

9. The **Optimize** tab allows us to set the partitioning for the source. For very large data sources, using partitioning will greatly improve the performance of our data flow. Transforming data requires compute resources and we must rent (and pay for) them. The less time we spend transforming the data, the less it will cost. Since we have a very small source and it's not partitioned, we do not see any partitions here. Leave **Partition option** set to **Use current partitioning** as shown in the following screenshot:

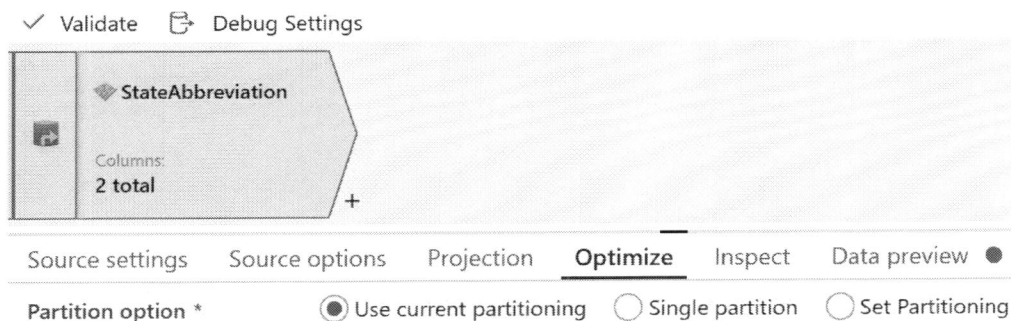

Figure 6.33 – Data Factory – the Optimize tab for a source in mapping data flow

10. The **Inspect** tab will show us the schema and allow us to sort on the columns **Order**, **Name** and **Type**. It can be helpful to use that tab when we have a data source with many columns. The **Inspect** tab is shown in the following screenshot:

Source settings	Source options	Projection	Optimize	**Inspect**	Data preview ●

Number of columns **Total** 2		
Order ↑↓	Column ↑↓	Type ↑↓
1	abbreviation	abc string
2	stateName	abc string

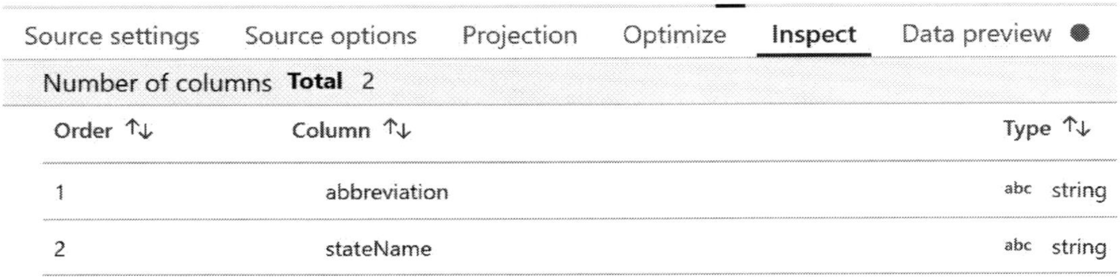

Figure 6.34 – Data Factory Inspect tab for a source in mapping data flow

11. The **Data preview** tab allows us to see the data in the source. Click on the **Refresh** icon as shown in the following screenshot:

Source settings	Source options	Projection	Optimize	Inspect	**Data preview** ●

Number of rows	✦ **INSERT** N/A	✳ **UPDATE** N/A	✕ **DELETE** N/A	✦ **UPSERT** N/A	⌕ **LOOKUP**

◌ **Refresh**

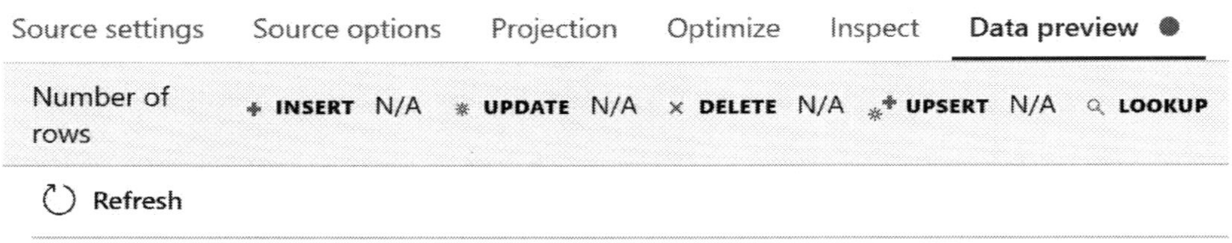

Figure 6.35 – The Data Factory Preview tab for a source before
refreshing in mapping data flow

12. We can now see our data source's data in the pane shown in the following screenshot. The + sign before the **abbreviation** column means that we are inserting the data:

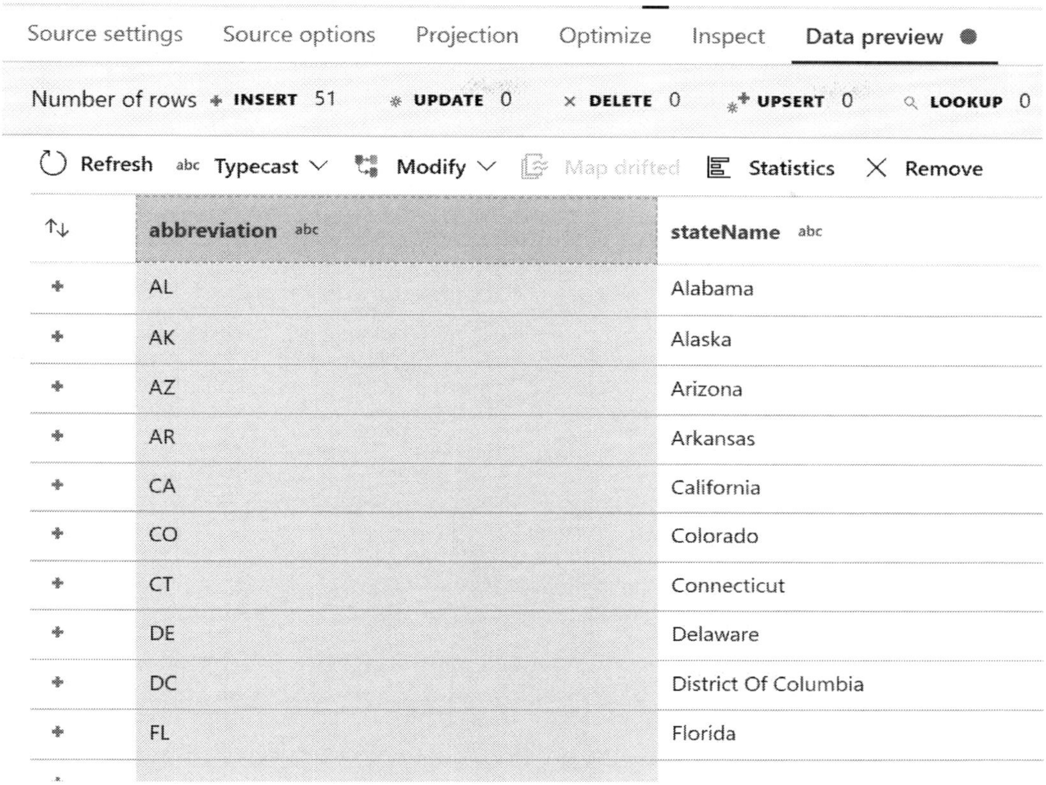

Source settings   Source options   Projection   Optimize   Inspect   **Data preview** ⬤

Number of rows ✦ **INSERT** 51   ✻ **UPDATE** 0   ✕ **DELETE** 0   ✦⁺ **UPSERT** 0   ⚲ **LOOKUP** 0

◯ Refresh   abc Typecast ∨   🖳 Modify ∨   📄 Map drifted   📊 Statistics   ✕ Remove

↑↓	abbreviation abc	stateName abc
✦	AL	Alabama
✦	AK	Alaska
✦	AZ	Arizona
✦	AR	Arkansas
✦	CA	California
✦	CO	Colorado
✦	CT	Connecticut
✦	DE	Delaware
✦	DC	District Of Columbia
✦	FL	Florida

Figure 6.36 – The Data Factory Data preview tab for a source after
refreshing in mapping data flow

13. We can change the type of the column if necessary, by clicking on **Typecast** as shown in the following screenshot:

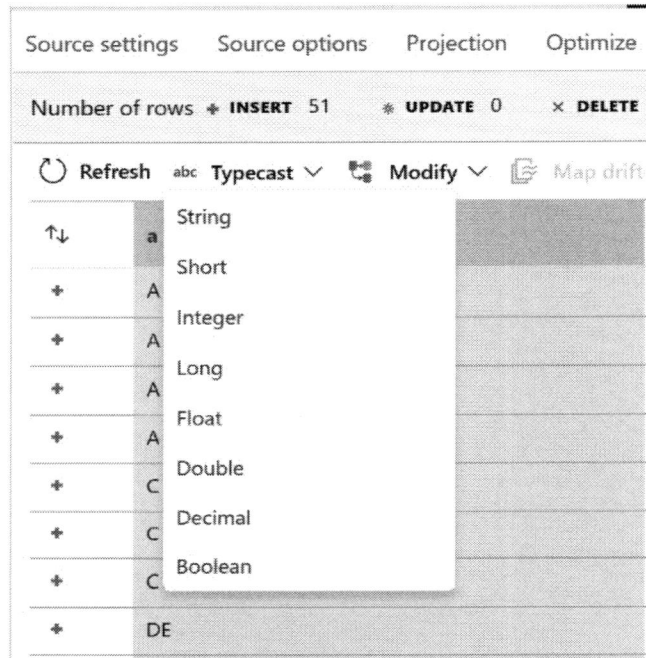

Figure 6.37 – The Data Factory Preview tab for a source with
Typecast in mapping data flow

14. We can also apply transformations to the column's data by clicking on the **Modify** button at the top of the column, as shown in the following screenshot:

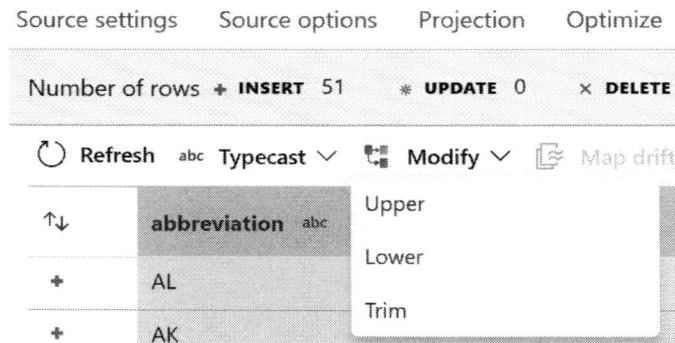

Figure 6.38 – The Data Factory Preview tab for a source with the
Modify column's data in mapping data flow

15. There's also a **Statistics** button that allows us to see some basic data profiling information on the column, as shown in the following screenshot:

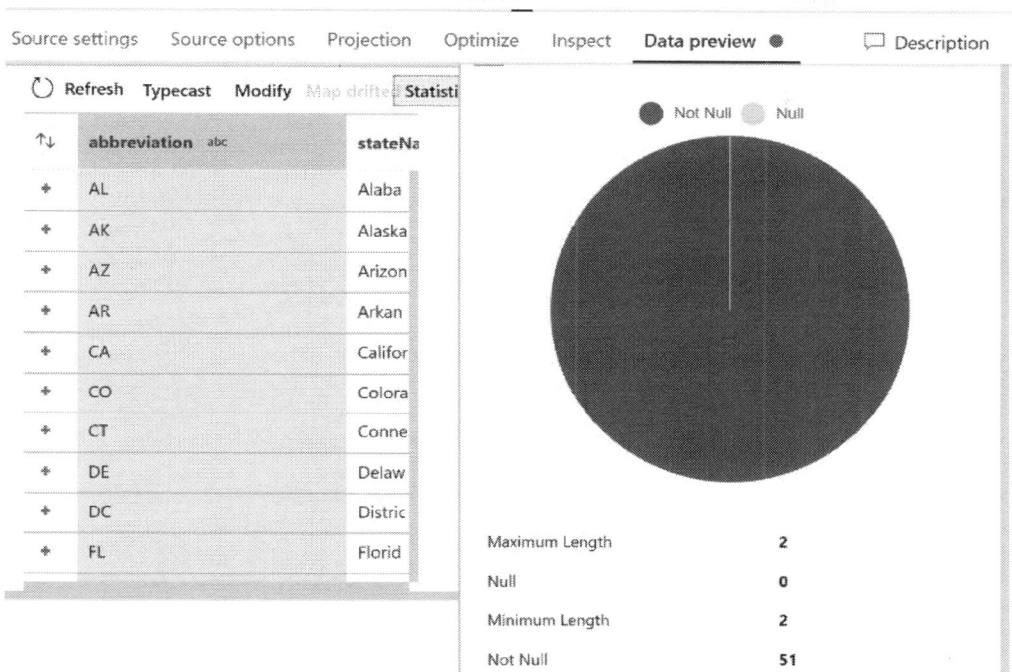

Figure 6.39 – The Data Factory Preview tab for a source with the Statistics column's data in mapping data flow

16. Click on the data flow designer. Your screen should look like the following screenshot:

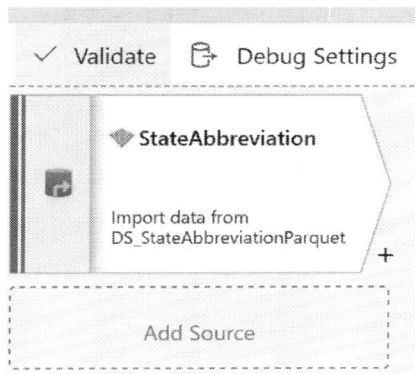

Figure 6.40 – Data Factory – add a new source in mapping data flow

17. Click on **Add Source** to add our **StateIncomeData** parquet file. Follow the same steps as we did for the **StateAbbreviation** source. The **Projection** tab should look like the following screenshot:

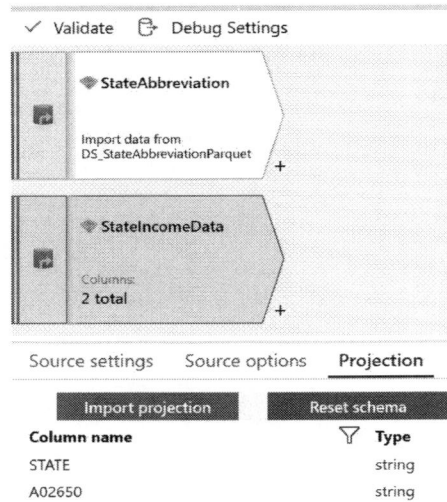

Figure 6.41 – The Data Factory Project tab for the StateIncomeData source in mapping data flow

18. The refreshed **Data Preview** tab will show us the data in the source. Select the **A02650** column and click on **Statistics** at the top of the **Preview** tab to see its statistics. As shown in the following screenshot, the stats are based on **1000** rows:

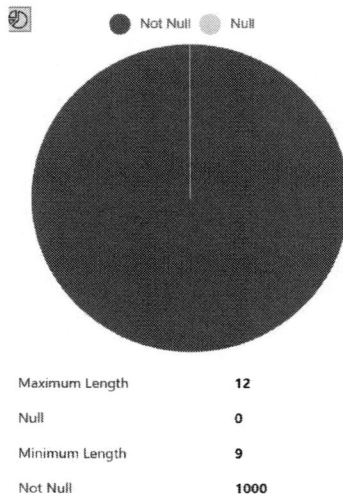

Figure 6.42 – The Data Factory Statistics tab for the StateIncomeData source in mapping data flow

19. To get them for the entire data source, **27760** rows, we need to change some settings. Click on **Debug Settings** at the top of the data flow. A blade appears and we can see the settings for each item we have in our data flow so far. As shown in the following screenshot, change **Row limit** for the **StateIncomeData** source to **30000** and click **Save** at the bottom of the blade to save our settings and close it:

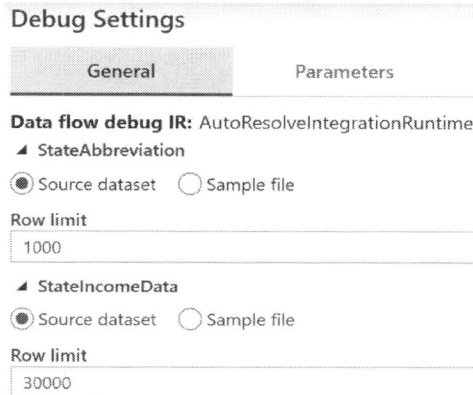

Figure 6.43 – Data Factory Debug Settings for mapping data flow

20. Next, hit the **Refresh** button to refresh the previewed data and click on **Statistics** again. We see that the statistics are now calculated on **27760** rows, as shown in the following screenshot:

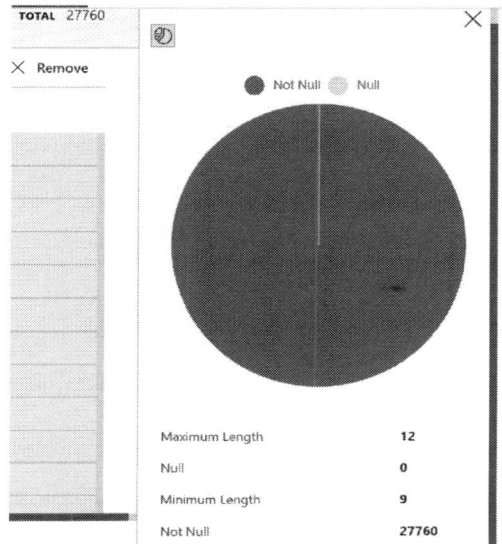

Figure 6.44 – Data Factory Statistics on the entire dataset for mapping data flow

21. We are now going to enrich our **StateIncomeData** source with the **stateName** column from **StateAbbreviation**. Click on the + sign of the **StateIncomeData** source and select **Lookup** from the submenu that appears, as shown in the following screenshot:

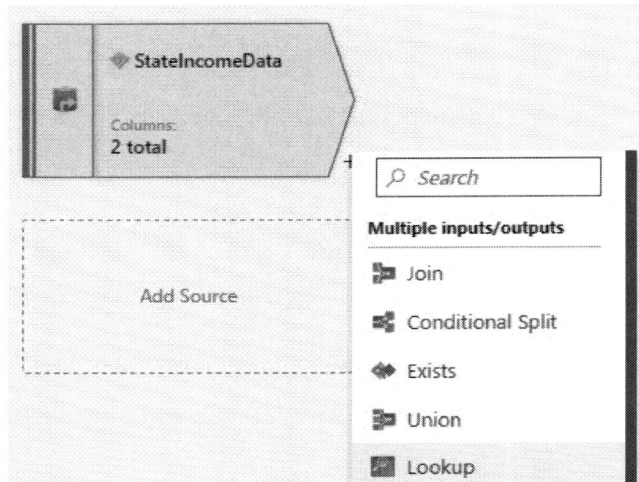

Figure 6.45 – Data Factory Lookup transform for the mapping data flow

22. A **Lookup** transformation is added to the data flow. In the **Join Lookup** settings pane, set **Output Stream Name** to **LKPStateAbbreviation**. **Primary stream** is already set to **StateIncomeData** because we added the lookup transformation from there. Set **Lookup stream** to the **StateAbbreviation** source. Set the other lookup conditions as shown in the following screenshot:

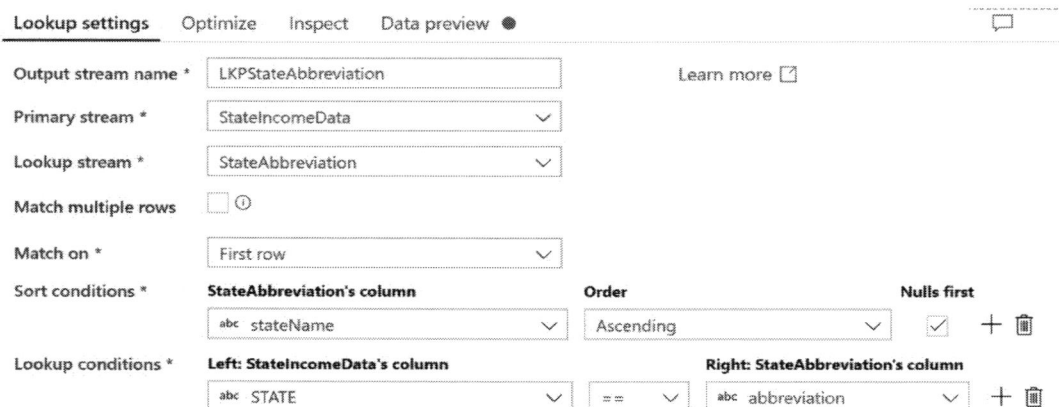

Figure 6.46 – Data Factory Lookup settings for mapping data flow

23. Click on the **Optimize** tab. Set the **Broadcast** property to **Fixed**. This will ensure that the smallest data source will be replicated to all worker nodes in the cluster. This give us a performance improvement if we have larger data sources that want to look up the **StateAbbreviation** source, and the data can fit in the worker node memory. Check **Right: 'StateAbbreviation'** in **Broadcast options** and leave the partitioning setting as it is, as shown in the following screenshot:

Lookup settings	**Optimize**	Inspect	Data preview ●		
Broadcast	○ Auto ⓘ		◉ Fixed ⓘ		○ Off ⓘ
Broadcast options *	☐ Left: 'StateIncomeData'	ⓘ			
	☑ Right: 'StateAbbreviation'	ⓘ			
Partition option *	◉ Use current partitioning	○ Single partition		○ Set Partitioning	

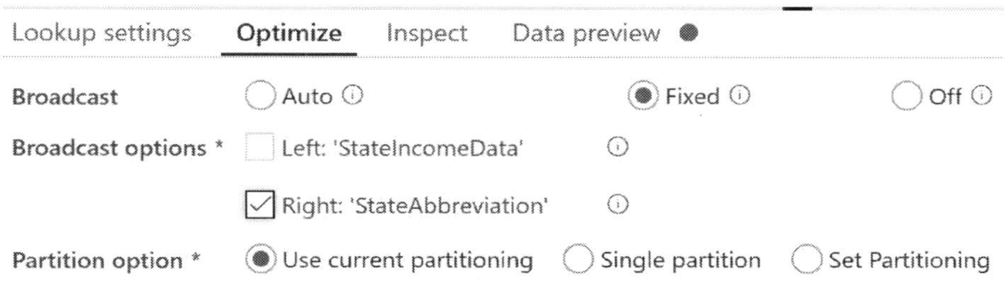

Figure 6.47 – Data Factory Lookup Optimize tab for mapping data flow

24. Click the **Inspect** tab. There is nothing to set there. You will only notice that the two columns we used (**STATE** and **abbreviation**) are marked as **Used in Lookup** as shown in the following screenshot:

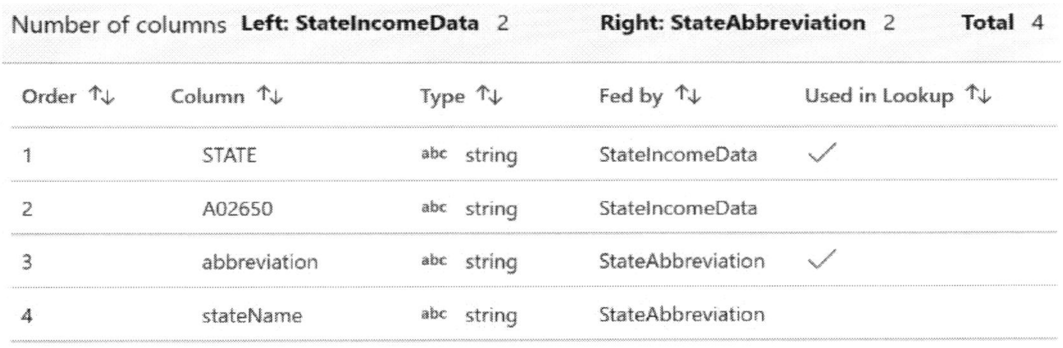

Number of columns **Left: StateIncomeData** 2			**Right: StateAbbreviation** 2	**Total** 4
Order ↑↓	Column ↑↓	Type ↑↓	Fed by ↑↓	Used in Lookup ↑↓
1	STATE	abc string	StateIncomeData	✓
2	A02650	abc string	StateIncomeData	
3	abbreviation	abc string	StateAbbreviation	✓
4	stateName	abc string	StateAbbreviation	

Figure 6.48 – Data Factory Lookup Inspect tab for mapping data flow

25. Click on the **Data preview** tab and refresh it. Select the **stateName** column and click on **Statistics**. We can see the **stateName** information distribution after the lookup as shown in the following screenshot. What's more important is that we can see that we have a perfect match as we get **27760 Not Null** values:

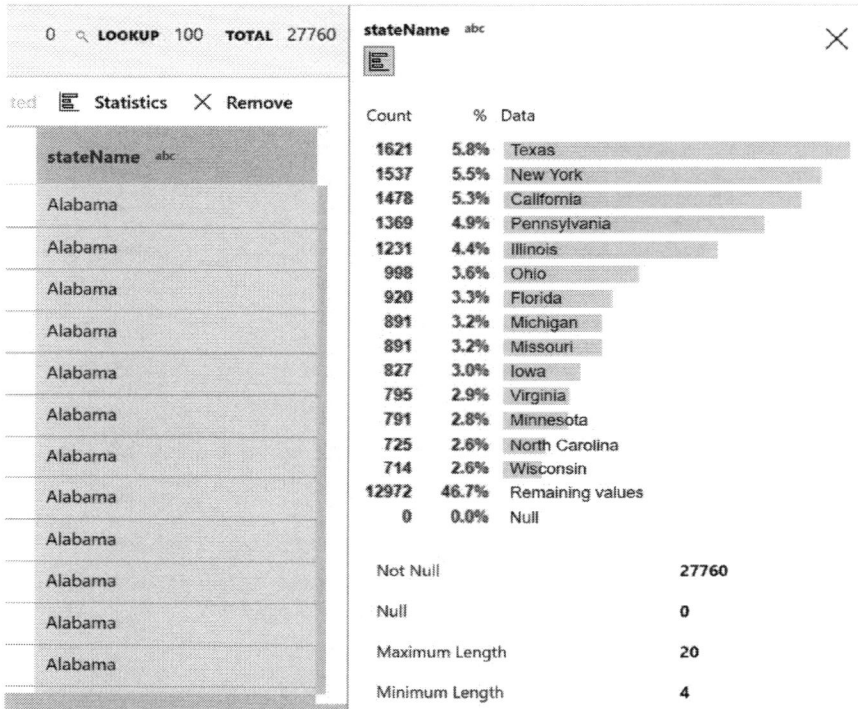

Count	%	Data
1621	5.8%	Texas
1537	5.5%	New York
1478	5.3%	California
1369	4.9%	Pennsylvania
1231	4.4%	Illinois
998	3.6%	Ohio
920	3.3%	Florida
891	3.2%	Michigan
891	3.2%	Missouri
827	3.0%	Iowa
795	2.9%	Virginia
791	2.8%	Minnesota
725	2.6%	North Carolina
714	2.6%	Wisconsin
12972	46.7%	Remaining values
0	0.0%	Null

Not Null	27760
Null	0
Maximum Length	20
Minimum Length	4

Figure 6.49 – Data Factory Lookup Data preview tab with Statistics for mapping data flow

26. Next, we're going to add a parameter to our pipeline: **RunID**. This is useful to relate a row inserted or updated to a specific pipeline run. Click anywhere in the data flow designer and go to the **Parameters** tab. Click on **+ New** to add a parameter. As shown in *Figure 6.51*, type **PipelineRunID** for **NAME** and leave **TYPE** as string.

27. Next, click on **DEFAULT VALUE** and the **Visual expression builder** will show up. Type **"No parameter value"** as the default parameter value, as shown in the following screenshot:

Visual expression builder

UNCTIONS   «

🔍 Filter...

All   Functions   Input schema   Parameters

abc   stateName

"No parameter value"

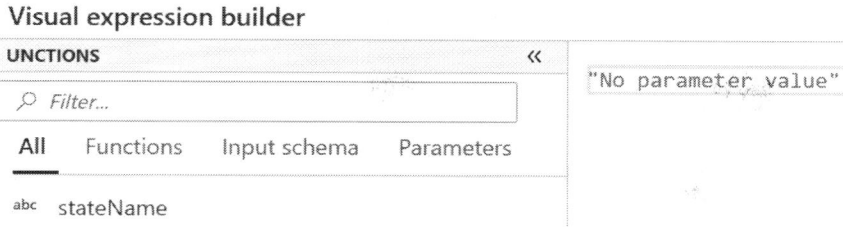

Figure 6.50 – Data Factory Mapping parameter Visual expression builder

28. Click on **Save and finish**. You should have something like the following screenshot:

General   **Parameters**   Settings

+ New | 🗑 Delete

	NAME	TYPE	DEFAULT VALUE	
	PipelineRunID	abc string ∨	"No parameter value"	🗑

Figure 6.51 – Data Factory Mapping parameter

29. Now, click on the **+ New** sign after the lookup to add a **Derived Columns** transform. In **Derived column's settings**, set **Output stream name** to **DERStateIncomePipelineRunID**. In the **Columns** section, type **StateIncome** and click on the textbox on the right to enter the **Visual expression builder**. Type **toLong(A02650)** to cast the column to a long data type. Click on **Save and finish**. Your screen should look like the following screenshot:

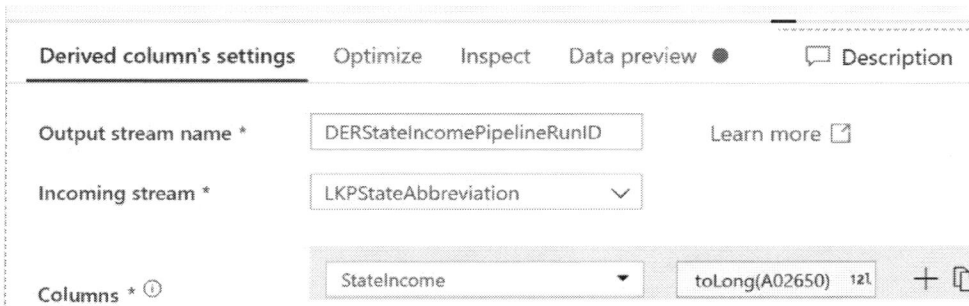

Derived column's settings   Optimize   Inspect   Data preview ●   💬 Description

Output stream name *   DERStateIncomePipelineRunID   Learn more 🗗

Incoming stream *   LKPStateAbbreviation   ∨

Columns * ⓘ   StateIncome   ▾   toLong(A02650) 12l   + 📋

Figure 6.52 – Data Factory Derived column's settings – add a StateIncome column

30. Click the **+** sign at the right of the **StateIncome** column and select **Add column** to add a new derived column as shown in the following screenshot:

Figure 6.53 – Data Factory Derived column's settings – add a new column

31. Type **PipelineRunID** and click to get the **Visual expression builder**. In the **FUNCTIONS** blade, go to the **Parameters** tab and click on **PipelineRunID** to add the expression **$PipelineRunID**, as shown in the following screenshot:

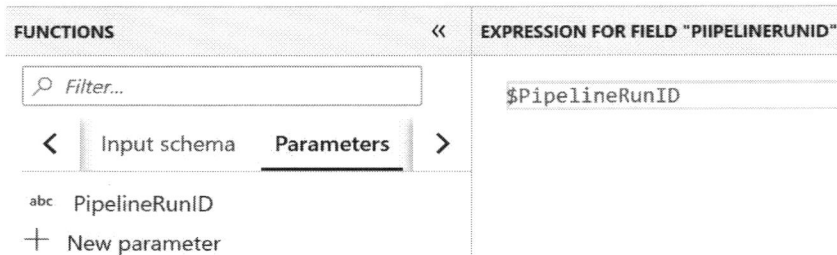

Figure 6.54 – Data Factory Derived column's settings – add a parameter column

32. Click on **Save and finish**. As shown in the following screenshot, you should now have added two columns:

Figure 6.55 – Data Factory Derived column's settings with two columns

33. Next, click on the **+** sign from the derived column transformation we just added. This time select a **Select** transformation. This transformation allows us to remove unused columns that would take up unnecessary resources at runtime. Use **SELRemoveUnusedColumns** for **OutputStreamName**. Remove the **STATE** and **A02650** columns. Your screen should look like the following screenshot:

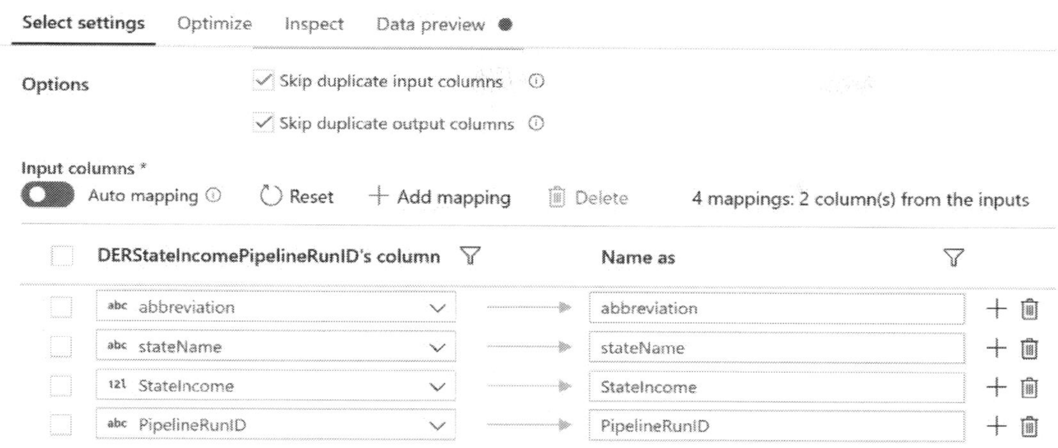

Figure 6.56 – Data Factory Select setting with four columns

34. Now, we are going to aggregate the **StateIncome** column by state. To do so, add an aggregate transform to the data flow. Name it **AGGStateIncome**. We now have two settings where we can select columns: **Group by** and **Aggregates**. In the **Group by** setting, select **abbreviation** and add two other columns: **stateName** and **PipelineRunID**, as shown in the following screenshot:

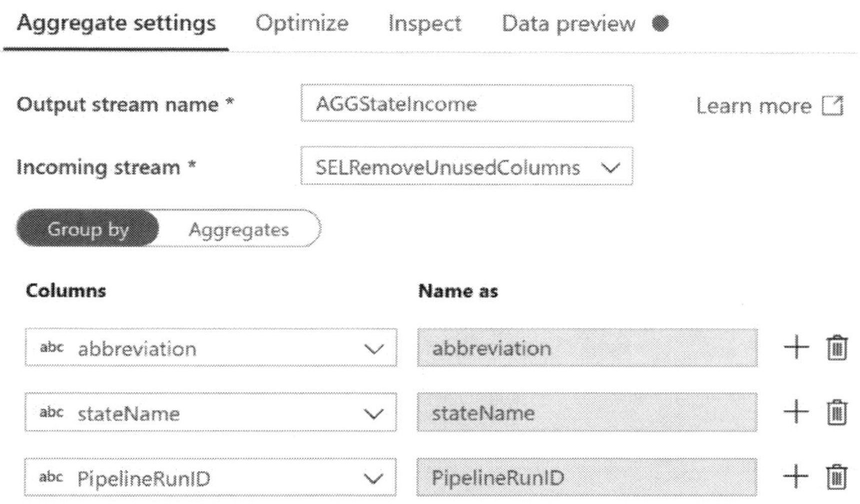

Figure 6.57 – Data Factory Aggregate settings – Group by tab setting with three columns

35. Now, click on **Aggregates**. Add the **StateIncome** column and use **sum (StateIncome)** for the expression, as shown in the following screenshot:

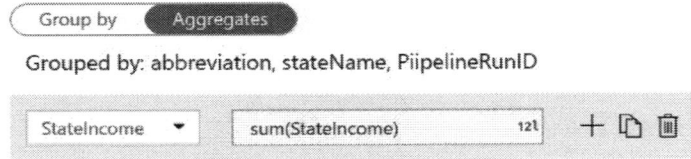

Figure 6.58 – Data Factory Aggregates tab setting with a StateIncome column

36. Now, go to the **Data preview** Tab and refresh it. We now have **51** rows instead of **27760**. The **StateIncome** column has been aggregated by state as shown in the following screenshot:

Figure 6.59 – Data Factory Aggregates Data preview tab

37. We now have all the transformations we need. We are ready to insert our data into an Azure SQL Server table. Open **SQL Server Management Studio (SSMS)**. Connect to the **AdventureWorksLT** database we created in *Chapter 2, Introducing ETL*, in the recipe *Creating a SQL database*. Type and run the following SQL statements. This will create a table named **SalesLT.IncoesPerStates**:

```
DROP TABLE IF EXISTS   [SalesLT].[IncomesPerStates];
CREATE TABLE [SalesLT].[IncomesPerStates]
(
    StateAbbreviation NVARCHAR(10) NULL,
    StateName NVARCHAR(100) NULL,
    StateIncome BIGINT NULL,
    BatchID NVARCHAR(100) NOT NULL
);
```

38. Go back to the data factory's data flow. Add a **Sink** named `SINKSalesLT` as shown in the following screenshot:

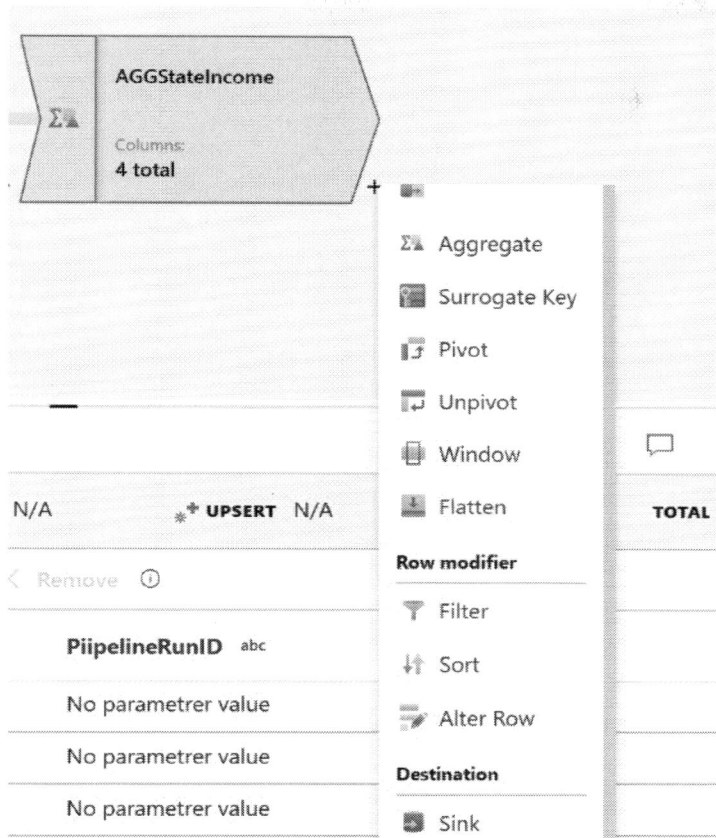

Figure 6.60 – Data Factory – adding a sink

39. In the **Sink** tab, click on + at the right of the **Dataset** property to add a new **Dataset**. Choose **Azure SQL Database** as shown in the following screenshot and click on **Continue**:

New dataset

In pipeline activities and data flows, reference a dataset to specify the location and structure of your data within a data store. Learn more

Select a data store

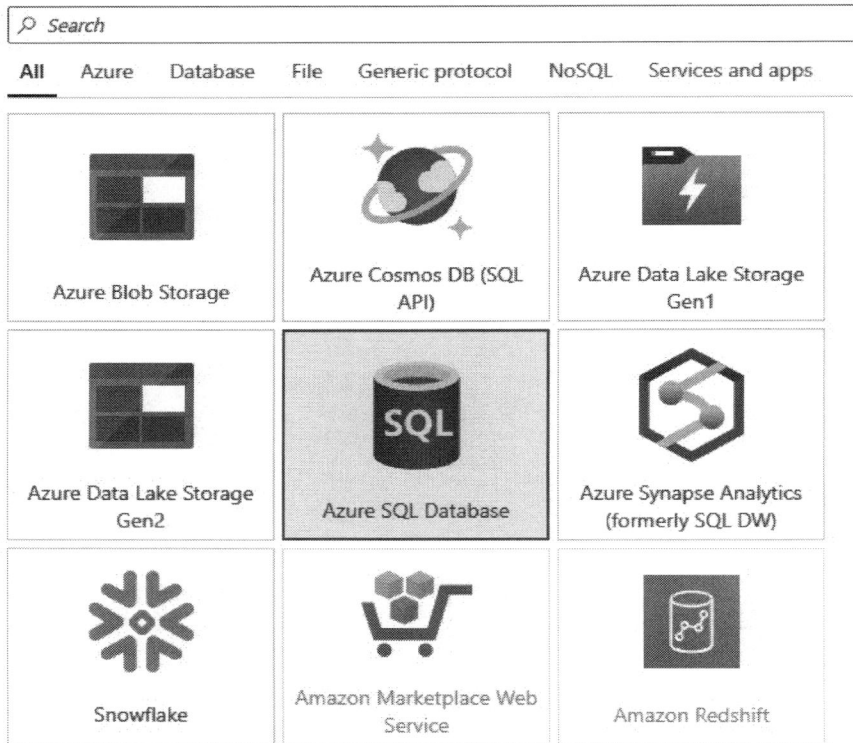

Figure 6.61 – Data Factory – adding an Azure SQL Database dataset

40. Name it **DS_SalesLTIncomesPerStates**. Select **+ New** from the linked service combo box. Create a new **Azure SQL Linked** service as shown in the following screenshot:

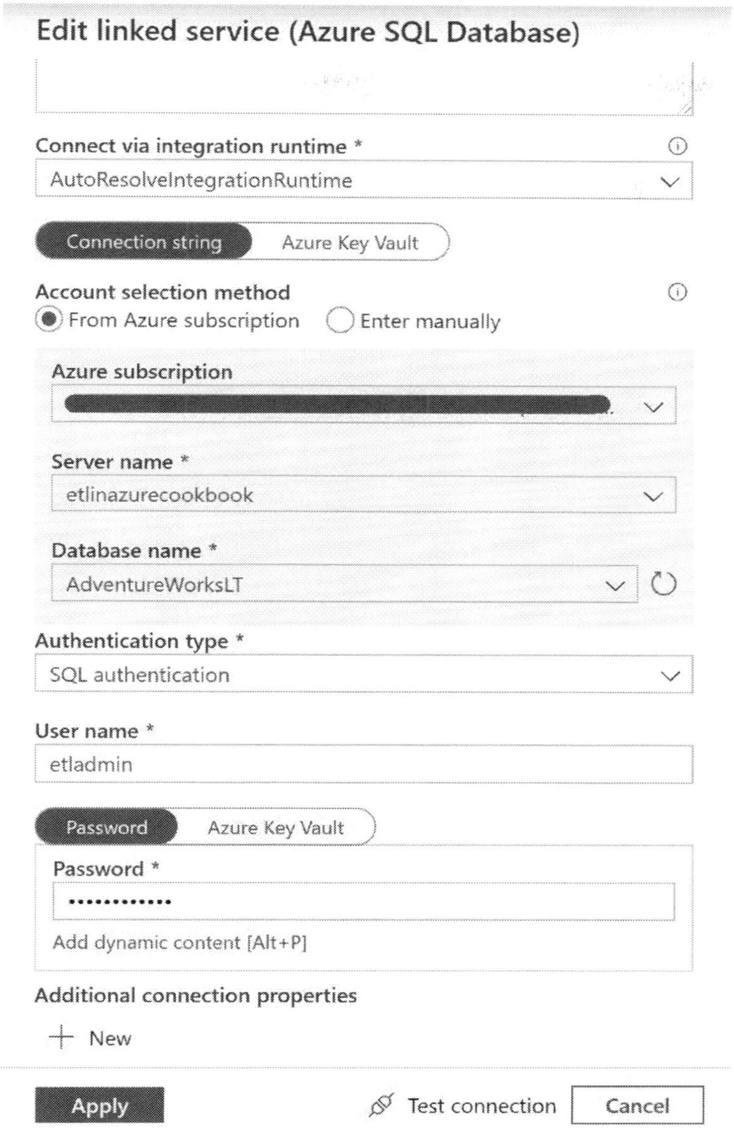

Edit linked service (Azure SQL Database)

Connect via integration runtime * ⓘ

AutoResolveIntegrationRuntime ⌄

(**Connection string** | Azure Key Vault)

Account selection method ⓘ
⦿ From Azure subscription ◯ Enter manually

Azure subscription

▬▬▬▬▬▬▬▬▬▬▬▬▬▬▬▬▬▬▬▬ ⌄

Server name *

etlinazurecookbook ⌄

Database name *

AdventureWorksLT ⌄ ↻

Authentication type *

SQL authentication ⌄

User name *

etladmin

(**Password** | Azure Key Vault)

Password *

••••••••••••

Add dynamic content [Alt+P]

Additional connection properties

╋ New

[Apply]   ✐ Test connection [Cancel]

Figure 6.62 – Data Factory – adding an Azure SQL Database linked service

41. Click on **Test connection** and **Save** to save the new linked service. Back to the dataset properties, select **Create new table**, use **SalesLT** for the schema name and **IncomesPerStates** for the table name, as shown in the following screenshot:

Set properties

Name

DS_SalesLTIncomesPerStates

Linked service *

LNK_AdventireWorksLT

⚪ Select from existing table   ⦿ Create new table

Schema and table name

SalesLT   .   IncomesPerStates

▷ Advanced

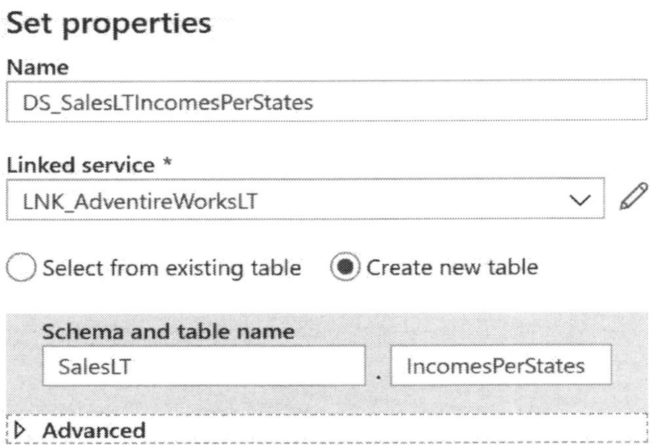

Figure 6.63 – Data Factory – adding an Azure SQL Database dataset

42. Click on **OK** to save the changes. Back in the data flow, uncheck the **Allow schema drift** property. Go to the **Settings** tab and set **Table action** to **Truncate table** as shown in the following screenshot:

Sink   **Settings**   Mapping   Optimize   Inspect   Data preview ⦿

Update method   ☑ Allow insert

☐ Allow delete

☐ Allow upsert

☐ Allow update

Table action   ⚪ None   ⚪ Recreate table   ⦿ Truncate table

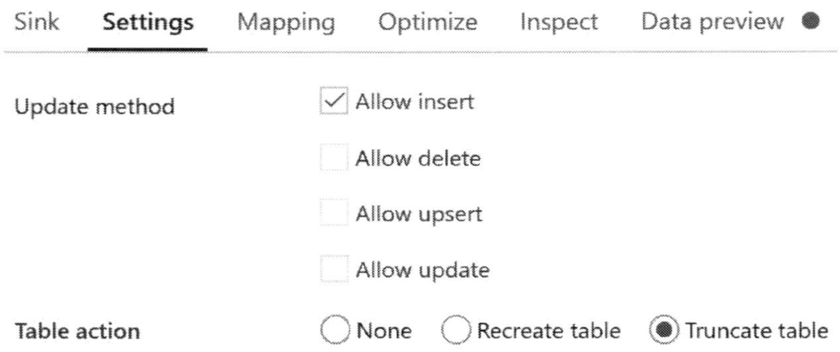

Figure 6.64 – Data Factory Sink Settings tab

43. Go to the **Mapping** tab. Turn **Auto mapping** off. Select and move the **StateIncome** column above the **PipelineRunID** column as shown in the following screenshot. Rename the columns in the **Output columns** window:

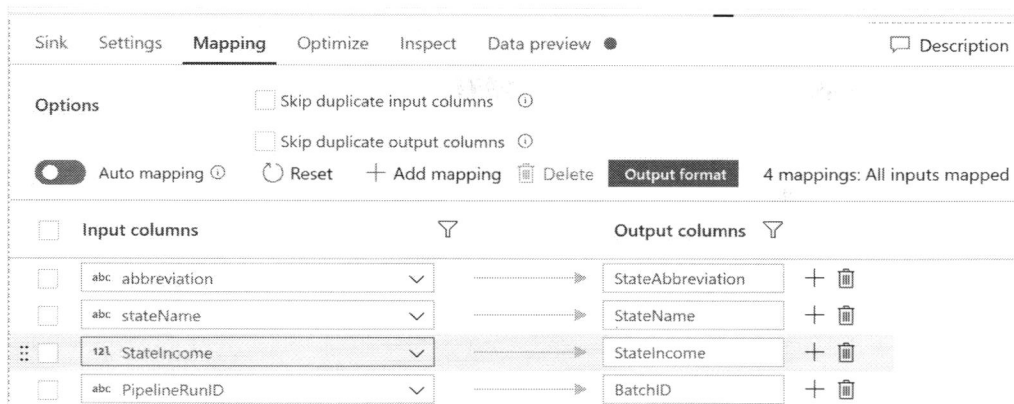

Figure 6.65 – Data Factory Sink Mappings tab – move StateIncome up

44. Now, go back to the **P_StateIncomeMapping** pipeline and link it to the two **Copy data** activities.

45. Select the **Mapping Data Flow** and click on the **Parameters** tab. Click on the textbox at the right of **PipelineRunID**. This will open a blade called **Add dynamic content**. As shown in the following screenshot, select **Pipeline run ID** from the **System variables** section and click on **Finish**:

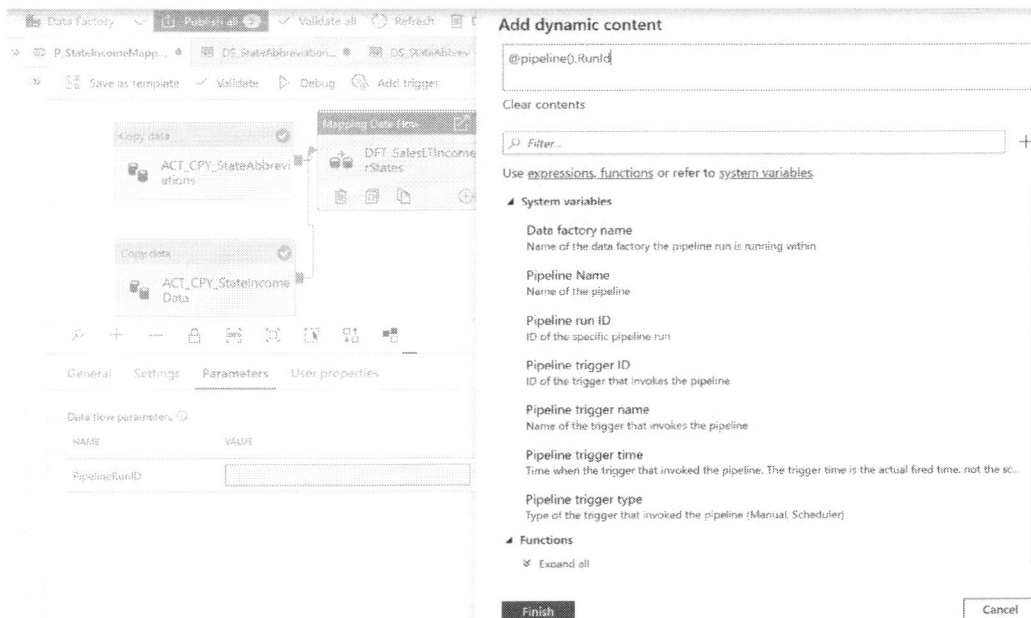

Figure 6.66 – Data Factory Sink Mapping data flow parameter addition

46. Our data flow is now complete. Name it **DFT_StateIncomeMappingDataflow**. Attach both copy activities we created before to it. Click on the **Debug** button at the top of the pipeline to run it. After a few minutes, you should have something like what's shown in the following screenshot:

Figure 6.67 – Data Factory pipeline execution

47. Now, hover the mouse over the **DFT_SalesLTincomesPerStates** component. As shown in the following screenshot, click the **glasses** icon to see the detailed execution of the data flow:

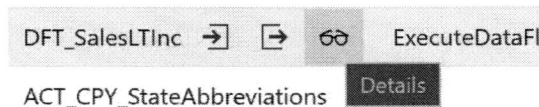

Figure 6.68 – Data Factory pipeline mapping execution detail icon

48. We are now presented with a screen that shows us the data flow execution details as shown in the following screenshot:

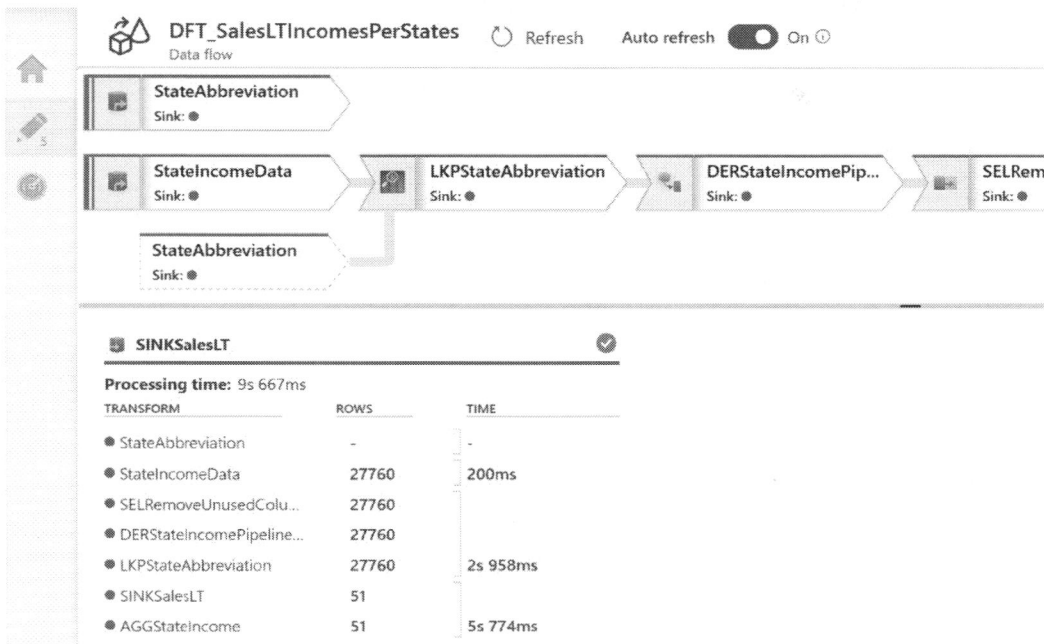

Figure 6.69 – Data Factory pipeline mapping execution details

49. Now, go back to the Azure portal and select the **AdventureWorksLT** database. Click the **Query editor (preview)** icon. Click on the ellipsis icon (**...**) and click on **Select Top 1000 Rows**, as shown in the following screenshot:

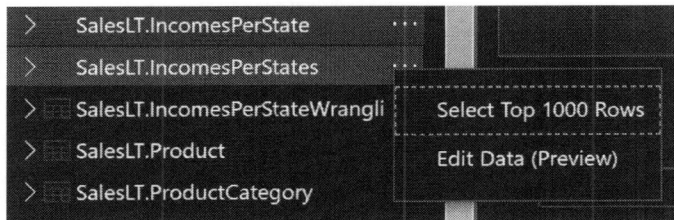

Figure 6.70 – Query editor – select top 1000 rows from SalesLT.IncomesPerStates

This will issue the following query:

```
SELECT TOP (1000) * FROM [SalesLT].[IncomesPerStates]
```

50. And we get the following `resultset`. If you look at the `BatchID` column, you can see that we now have a real `PipelineRunID` value in it:

StateAbbreviation	StateName	StateIncome	BatchID
CA	California	3131748846	14639a40-fc7b-4eaf-91bb-75b557091762
VA	Virginia	631796888	14639a40-fc7b-4eaf-91bb-75b557091762
KS	Kansas	176080188	14639a40-fc7b-4eaf-91bb-75b557091762
OK	Oklahoma	200317260	14639a40-fc7b-4eaf-91bb-75b557091762
NM	New Mexico	99934078	14639a40-fc7b-4eaf-91bb-75b557091762
RI	Rhode Island	73652196	14639a40-fc7b-4eaf-91bb-75b557091762
MD	Maryland	480338040	14639a40-fc7b-4eaf-91bb-75b557091762
TX	Texas	1834322462	14639a40-fc7b-4eaf-91bb-75b557091762
NV	Nevada	196389184	14639a40-fc7b-4eaf-91bb-75b557091762
LA	Louisiana	237122122	14639a40-fc7b-4eaf-91bb-75b557091762
NH	New Hampshire	110973138	14639a40-fc7b-4eaf-91bb-75b557091762

Figure 6.71 – Query editor – Select Top 1000 Rows result

That's it! We have created our mapping data flow!

How it works...

We joined the data from the two sources using a lookup transform. This transform is very efficient and usually everything is done in memory in the workers. We then aggregated the pipeline by summing the incomes grouped by every state and inserted it into an Azure SQL Server table.

Data flows rely on a compute resource – a Databricks Spark cluster. Data flows allow us to write Spark code without any code. They rely on Azure Integration Runtime to connect to the compute service, the Databricks cluster. We can create our own Azure integration runtimes with more compute options, such as memory, nodes (machines), and the CPU. We used the default (smallest) possible cluster in the recipe as we don't need anything else in terms of capacity as the recipe was pretty simple and did not involve large volumes of data.

Triggering and monitoring our pipeline

We have created our first pipeline and ran it manually in a debug environment. In real-life scenarios, we would schedule a trigger for our pipeline to run. Once the pipeline is scheduled, we want to monitor its runs such as status, row counts, and runtimes. We also want to be alerted when a run fails.

This recipe will show you how it can easily be done with Azure Data Factory. It will teach you how to perform specific actions:

- Load metadata and accumulate it into a storage account

- Schedule a trigger to run our pipeline

- Create an alert for any pipeline failure

Getting ready

This recipe assumes that you have access to an Azure subscription. It can be a free trial one, as described in the *Creating an Azure subscription recipe*, in *Chapter 1, Getting Started with Azure and SSIS 2019*. It also assumes that you have created a pipeline from the previous recipe, *Moving and transforming data*.

How to do it...

Let's load some metadata!

1. Open the pipeline we created in the previous recipe, *Moving and transforming data*, **P_StateIncomeMappingDataflow**. Add a new Azure SQL Server dataset to the factory. Name it **DS_LoadMetadata**, and select **LNK_AdventureWorksLT** as the **Linked service** and no **Table name** (**None**), as shown in the following screenshot. Click on **OK**:

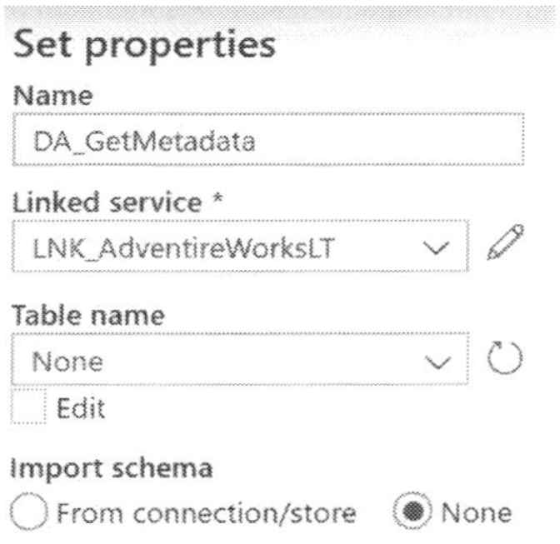

Figure 6.72 – Data Factory – new dataset for metadata collection

2. Create another dataset based on an Azure Blob storage. Choose **DelimitedText** as the format type. Name it **DS_WriteLoadMetadata**. Set the properties as the following: **metadata/@{pipeline().Pipeline}/@{pipeline().RunId}.csv** for **File path**; make sure that **First row as header** is selected and select **None** for **Import schema**:

3. Set the **Connection** properties as shown in the following screenshot:

General   **Connection**   Schema   Parameters

Linked service *	📇 LNK_ETLInAzure ⌄	🖉 Test connection 📝 Open ＋ New

File path *	metadata / @{pipeline().Pipeline} / @{pipeline().RunId}.csv Browse ⌄ 👓 Preview data

Compression type	none ⌄
Column delimiter	Comma (,) ⌄ ☐ Edit
Row delimiter	Auto detect (\r,\n, or \r\n) ⌄ ☐ Edit
Encoding	Default(UTF-8) ⌄
Escape character	Backslash (\) ⌄ ☐ Edit
Quote character	Double quote (") ⌄ ☐ Edit
First row as header	☑

Figure 6.73 – Data Factory dataset connection properties for the metadata collection

4. Add a **Copy activity** to the right of the mapping data flow. Rename it **ACT_CPY_WriteLoadMetadata** and link it to **DFT_SalesLTIncomePerState**.

5. Go to the **Source** tab of the copy activity we just added. Set the **Source dataset** to **DS_LoadMetadata**. Set the **Use query** property to **Query**. Copy and paste the following query into the **Query** textbox:

```
SELECT '@{pipeline().DataFactory}' as DataFactory_Name,
'@{pipeline().Pipeline}' as Pipeline_Name,
'@{pipeline().RunId}' as RunId,
'@{pipeline().TriggerType}' as TriggerType,
'@{pipeline().TriggerId}' as TriggerId,
'@{pipeline().TriggerName}' as TriggerName,
'@{pipeline().TriggerTime}' as TriggerTime,
'ACT_CPY_StateAbbreviations' AS ActivityName,
```

```
'@{activity('ACT_CPY_StateAbbreviations').output.
rowsRead}' as RowsRead,
'@{activity('ACT_CPY_StateAbbreviations').output.
rowsCopied}' as RowsWritten,
'@{activity('ACT_CPY_StateAbbreviations').
output.effectiveIntegrationRuntime}' as
effectiveIntegrationRuntime,
'@{activity('ACT_CPY_StateAbbreviations').output.
executionDetails[0].source.type}' as Source_Type,
'@{activity('ACT_CPY_StateAbbreviations').output.
executionDetails[0].sink.type}' as Sink_Type,
'@{activity('ACT_CPY_StateAbbreviations').output.
executionDetails[0].status}' as Execution_Status,
'@{activity('ACT_CPY_StateAbbreviations').output.
executionDetails[0].start}' as Activity_Start_Time
UNION ALL
SELECT '@{pipeline().DataFactory}' as DataFactory_Name,
'@{pipeline().Pipeline}' as Pipeline_Name,
'@{pipeline().RunId}' as RunId,
'@{pipeline().TriggerType}' as TriggerType,
'@{pipeline().TriggerId}' as TriggerId,
'@{pipeline().TriggerName}' as TriggerName,
'@{pipeline().TriggerTime}' as TriggerTime,
'ACT_CPY_StateIncomeData' AS ActivityName,
'@{activity('ACT_CPY_StateIncomeData').output.rowsRead}'
as RowsRead,
'@{activity('ACT_CPY_StateIncomeData').output.
rowsCopied}' as RowsWritten,
'@{activity('ACT_CPY_StateIncomeData').
output.effectiveIntegrationRuntime}' as
effectiveIntegrationRuntime,
'@{activity('ACT_CPY_StateIncomeData').output.
executionDetails[0].source.type}' as Source_Type,
'@{activity('ACT_CPY_StateIncomeData').output.
executionDetails[0].sink.type}' as Sink_Type,
'@{activity('ACT_CPY_StateIncomeData').output.
executionDetails[0].status}' as Execution_Status,
'@{activity('ACT_CPY_StateIncomeData').output.
executionDetails[0].start}' as CopyActivity_Start_Time
UNION ALL
SELECT '@{pipeline().DataFactory}' as DataFactory_Name,
'@{pipeline().Pipeline}' as Pipeline_Name,
'@{pipeline().RunId}' as RunId,
'@{pipeline().TriggerType}' as TriggerType,
'@{pipeline().TriggerId}' as TriggerId,
```

```
'@{pipeline().TriggerName}' as TriggerName,
'@{pipeline().TriggerTime}' as TriggerTime,
'DFT_SalesLTIncomesPerStates' AS ActivityName,
'@{activity('DFT_SalesLTIncomesPerStates').output.
runStatus.metrics.SINKSalesLT.sources.StateIncomeData.
rowsRead}' as RowsRead,
'@{activity('DFT_SalesLTIncomesPerStates').output.
runStatus.metrics.SINKSalesLT.rowsWritten}' AS
RowsWritten,
'N/A' as effectiveIntegrationRuntime,
'N/A' AS Source_Type,
'N/A' AS Sink_Type,
'N/A' AS Execution_Status,
'0' AS Activity_Start_Time
```

6. Your screen should look like the following screenshot:

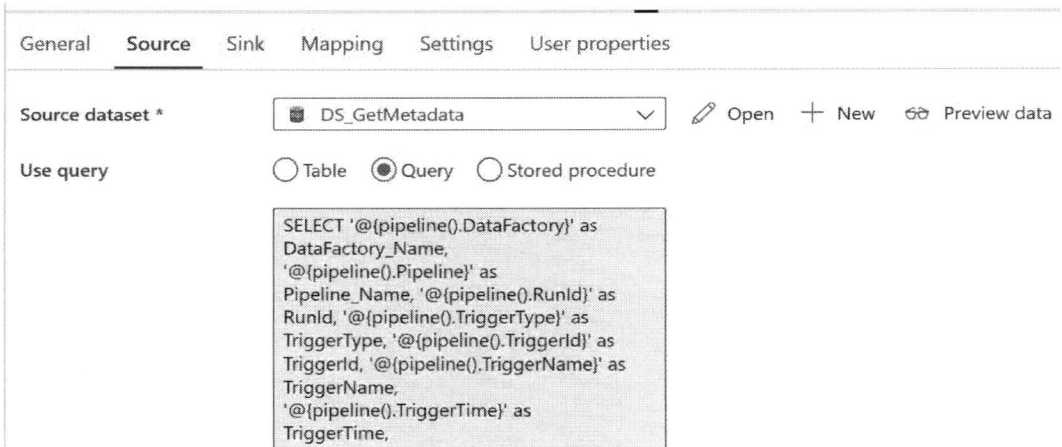

Figure 6.74 – Data Factory Copy data activity source tab for the metadata collection

7. Go to the **Sink** tab. Set **Sink dataset** to **DS_WriteLoadMetadata**. Leave all other properties as their default values.

8. Now, run the pipeline using the **Debug** button at the top. Once it completes, your screen should look like the following screenshot:

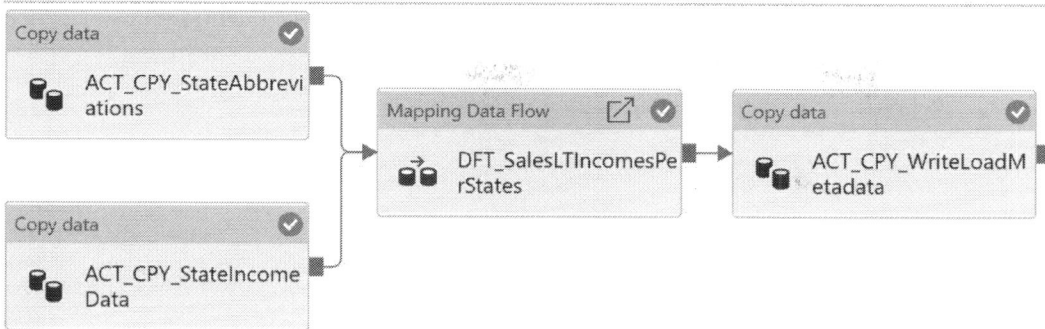

Figure 6.75 – Data Factory pipeline executed with the metadata collection activity

9. Now, go to your storage account. Navigate to **metadata / P_ StateIncomeMappingDataflow**. If you open the **P_ StateIncomeMappingDataflow** directory, you should see a CSV file named **<your run id>.csv** as shown in the following screenshot:

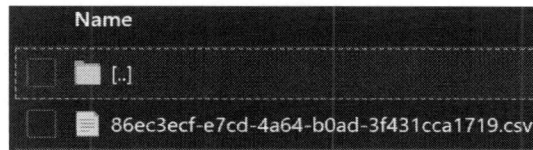

Figure 6.76 – Storage account blob with metadata

10. Click on it and click on **Edit** in the blade that opens. Scroll to the right to see the load metrics, as shown in the following screenshot:

Figure 6.77 – Storage account blob metadata content

11. Using blob storage gives us more flexibility in term of structure. If we were using a SQL Server table, we would have to modify its structure every time we added or removed a column in the copy activity query.

12. Go back to the pipeline we just modified – **P_StateIncomeMappingDataflow**. Click on **Add trigger** to open the trigger menu. As shown in the following screenshot, we have two choices: **Trigger now**, which will run the pipeline outside the debug environment and **New/Edit**, which allows us to create or edit a trigger:

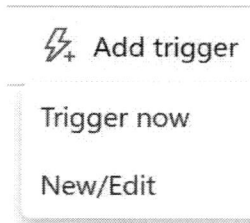

Figure 6.78 – Trigger submenu for a pipeline

13. Let's choose the latter option to create our trigger. The **Add triggers** blade appears. Click **+ New** from the dropdown, as shown in the following screenshot:

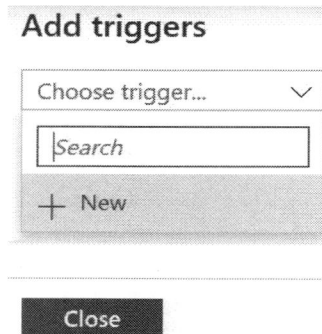

Figure 6.79 – Choose a new trigger

14. The **New trigger** blade appears. Set **Name** to **TRG_DailyLoad**, **Type** to **Schedule**, and **Start Date (UTC)** to any date you want. Set **Recurrence** to **Every 1 Day(s)**. **Execute at these times**: **Hours (UTC) 21**, **Minutes (UTC) 00**, as shown in the following screenshot. Click on **OK** twice to save it:

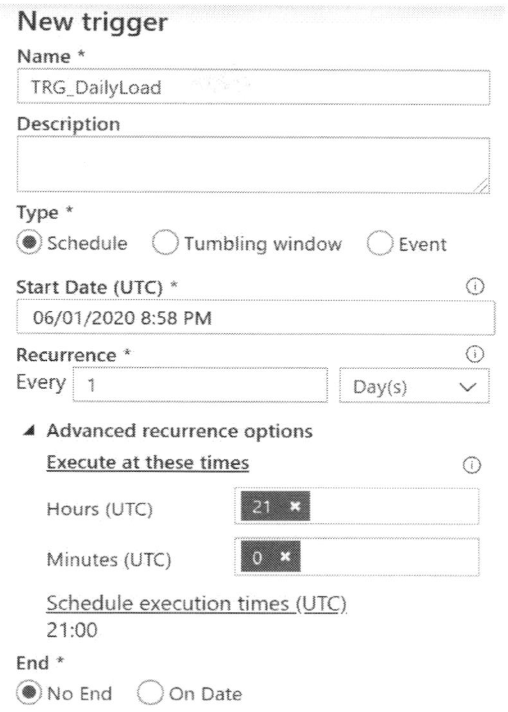

New trigger

Name *

TRG_DailyLoad

Description

Type *

◉ Schedule   ◯ Tumbling window   ◯ Event

Start Date (UTC) *   ⓘ

06/01/2020 8:58 PM

Recurrence *   ⓘ

Every 1   Day(s)   ∨

▲ Advanced recurrence options

Execute at these times   ⓘ

Hours (UTC)   21 ✕

Minutes (UTC)   0 ✕

Schedule execution times (UTC)
21:00

End *

◉ No End   ◯ On Date

Figure 6.80 – New trigger details

15. Now, click on **Publish all** to save our factory and make it available to the production environment. A blade opens and you should see the following **Pending changes**, which will be published. Click on **Publish**:

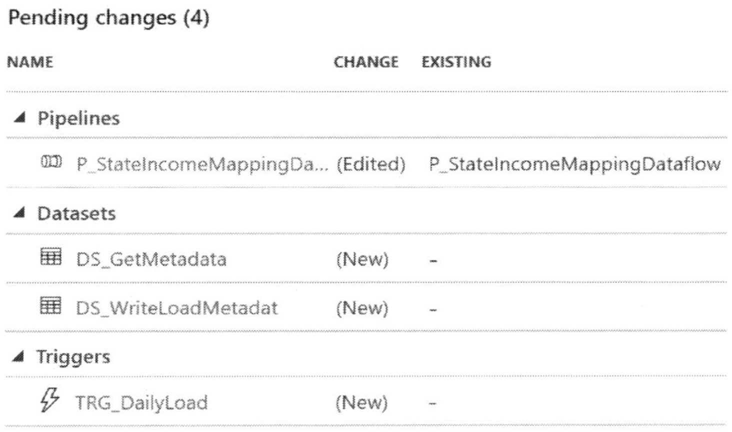

Pending changes (4)

NAME	CHANGE	EXISTING
▲ Pipelines		
⚬⚬⚬ P_StateIncomeMappingDa...	(Edited)	P_StateIncomeMappingDataflow
▲ Datasets		
▦ DS_GetMetadata	(New)	-
▦ DS_WriteLoadMetadat	(New)	-
▲ Triggers		
⚡ TRG_DailyLoad	(New)	-

Figure 6.81 – New trigger details

16. Now, click on the **Manage** tab and click on **Triggers** in the **Data Factory** section. You should see that the trigger is ready to start, as shown in the following screenshot:

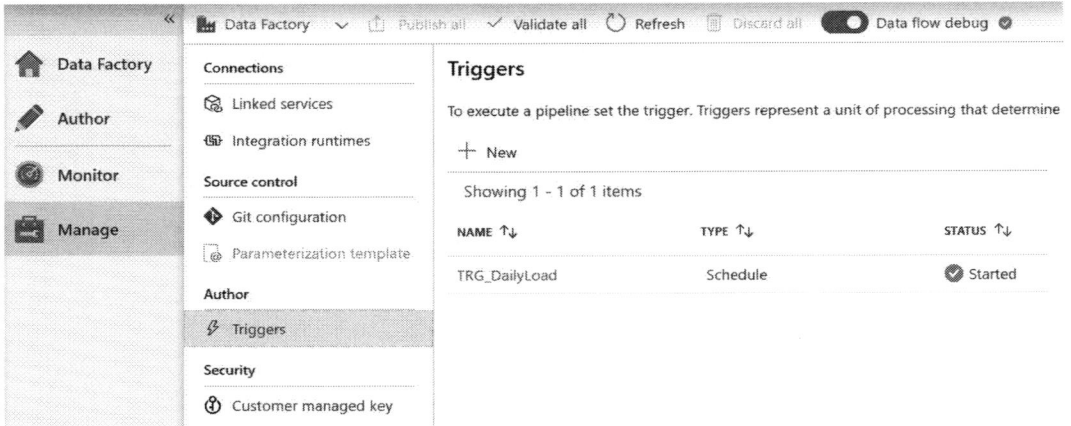

Figure 6.82 – Published trigger details

17. Lastly, we're going to create an alert that will send us an email if the factory fails.

18. Click on the **Monitor** tab on the left side of the browser screen to enter that section. Click on **Alerts & metrics** as shown in the following screenshot:

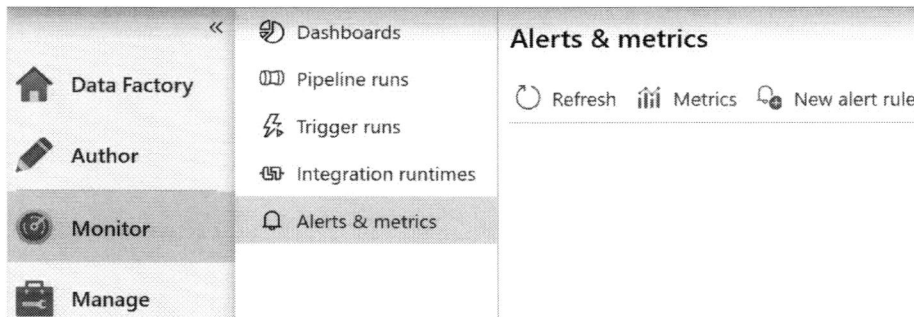

Figure 6.83 – The Alerts & metrics section

19. Click on **New alert rule** at the top to open the **New alert rule** blade at the right of the screen. Type **PipelineFails** and set **Severity** to **Sev0**. Now, click on **Add criteria**.

20. The **Add criteria** blade appears. Select the **Failed pipeline runs** metric.

21. The **Configure alert logic** pane opens. As shown in the following screenshot, select all pipelines from **DIMENSION Name** and select all failure types from the **FailureType** dropdown. Set **Alert logic** to **Greater than** and **Threshold count** to **0**. The alert will fire every time there's a failure. Set **Period** to **Over the last 6 hours** and **Frequency** to **Every 15 minute** in the **Evaluate based on** section. Click on **Add criteria** to save the changes:

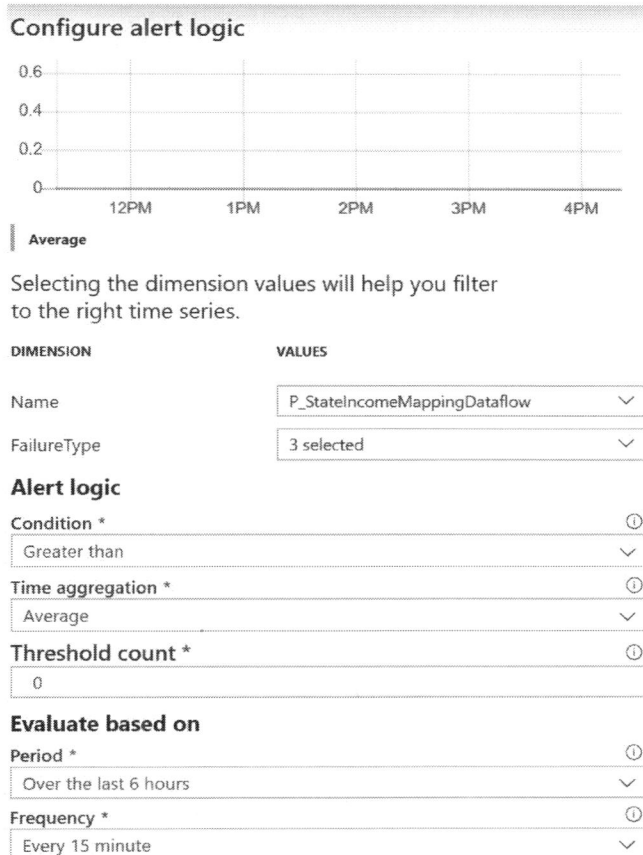

Figure 6.84 – Configuration of the alert logic

22. Now, click on **+ Configure notification** to open the **Configure notification** blade. Type **IT** in both **Action group name** and **Short name**, as shown in the following screenshot:

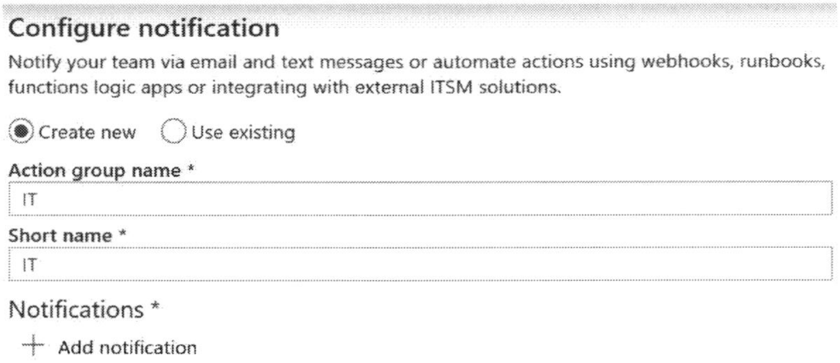

Figure 6.85 – Configuration of the notification

23. Click on **+ Add notification** to open the **Add notification** blade. As shown in the following screenshot, enter **Send email** for **Action Name**. Check the **Email** checkbox and enter a valid email address. Click on **Add notification** when complete:

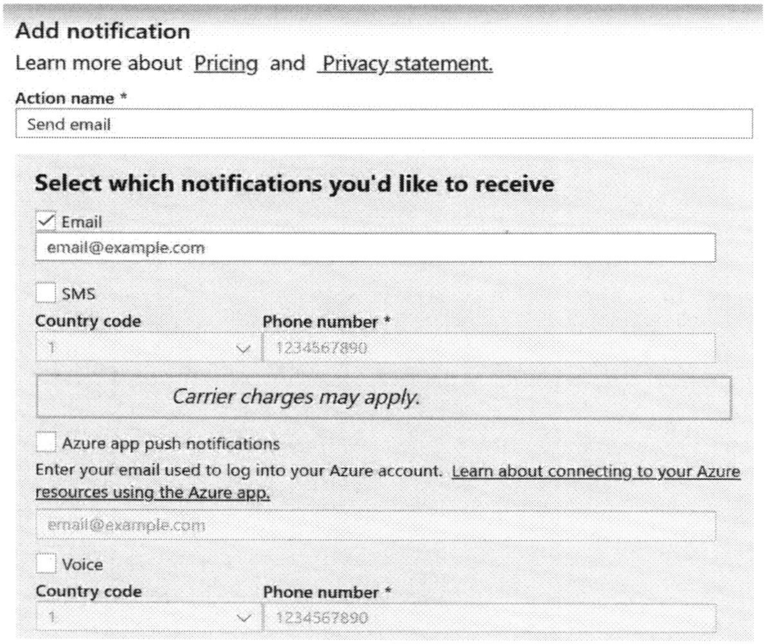

Figure 6.86 – Add notification

24. Click on **Add action group** to save the notification.

25. Back to the **Alert rule name** blade, your screen should look like the following screenshot. Click on **Create alert rule** to create the alert:

Alert rule name *

PipelineFails

Description

Severity *

Sev0

TARGET CRITERIA	ACTIONS
Whenever Pipeline Failed Runs metric is Greater Than to 0	🖊 🗑

+ Add criteria

ℹ *There will be a monthly rate for the configured criteria. Learn more about* *Pricing*

NOTIFICATIONS	ACTION GROUP TYPE	ACTIONS
IT	1 Email	🗑

+ Configure notification

Enable rule upon creation

On

Create alert rule   Cancel

Figure 6.87 – Add notification

26. After a few seconds, we're back to the **Alerts & metrics** blade. We now see that we have created an alert, as shown in the following screenshot:

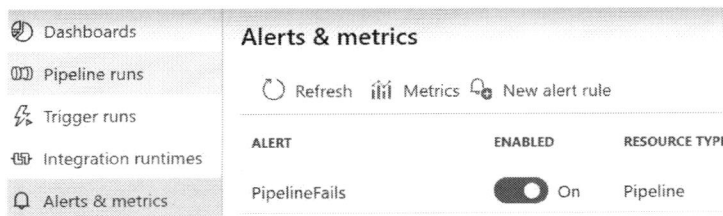

🕘 Dashboards

Alerts & metrics

⚙ Pipeline runs

🕘 Refresh 📊 Metrics 🔔 New alert rule

⚡ Trigger runs

ALERT	ENABLED	RESOURCE TYPE

🔧 Integration runtimes

🔔 Alerts & metrics | PipelineFails | On | Pipeline |

Figure 6.88 – Alert created

27. To test the alert, we need to modify the pipeline to have it fail. Go back to the pipeline. Select the **ACT_CPY_WriteLoadMetadata** activity. Click on the **Source** tab and modify the query to get only the following query text. Since **output.executionDetails[0].end** does not exist, the activity will fail:

```
SELECT '@{activity('ACT_CPY_StateAbbreviations').output.
executionDetails[0].end}' as Activity_End_Time
```

28. Publish the pipeline. Once done, click on **Trigger > Trigger now** to execute the pipeline outside the sandbox (debug) environment. Click on **OK** in the **Pipeline run** blade that appears at the right of the screen to start the pipeline execution.

29. Click on the **Monitor** tab at the left of the factory. Select **Pipeline runs**. Click on the pipeline link as shown in the following screenshot:

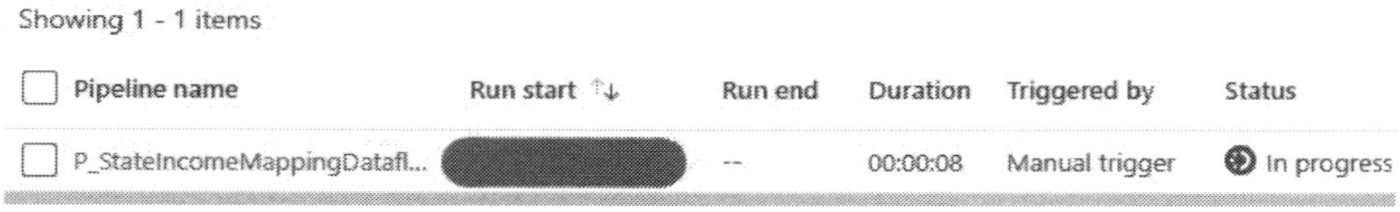

Figure 6.89 – Pipeline running

30. The pipeline execution screen opens as shown in the following screenshot:

P_StateIncomeMappingDataflow

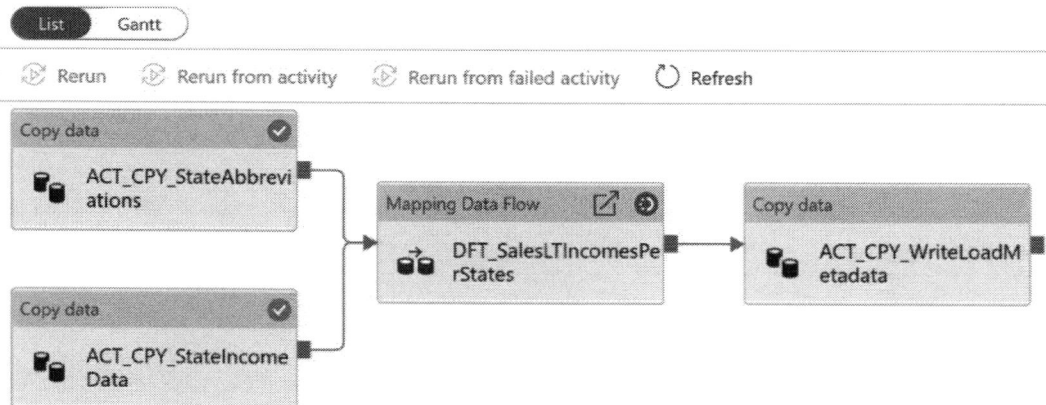

Figure 6.90 – Pipeline running

31. In **Activity** runs, hover the mouse over the **DFT_SakesLTIncomesPerStates** data flow and click on the binoculars icon. The data flow execution details open and we can see how the data flow executed, as shown in the following screenshot:

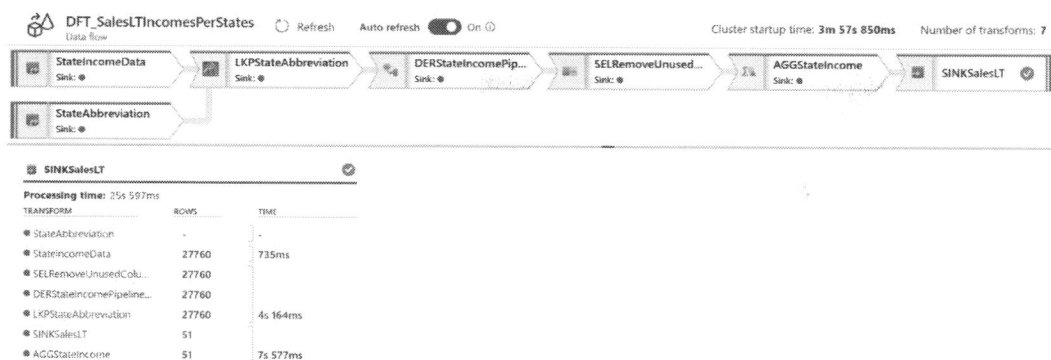

Figure 6.91 – Pipeline data flow running

32. Don't worry if it takes time to complete. The trigger starts a new cluster and it takes a while to start and execute the pipeline.

33. Close the data flow execution screen by clicking on the **X** at the top right. Back on the pipeline run, we now see that **ACT_CPY_WriteLoadMetadata** failed, as shown in the following screenshot:

Activity runs

Pipeline run ID 702591bb-63d0-4e00-9ea8-1209ef0fa8b5

All status ∨

Showing 1 - 4 of 4 items

ACTIVITY NAME	ACTIVITY TYPE	RUN START ↑↓	DURATION	STATUS	INTEGRATION RUNTIME
ACT_CPY_WriteLoadMetadata	Copy	6/6/20, 5:56:41 PM	00:00:01	✖ Failed	Unknown

Figure 6.92 – Pipeline data flow running

34. An email will be sent to the address we configured before within the next 15 minutes. Go to your mailbox and you should have received an email as shown in the following screenshot:

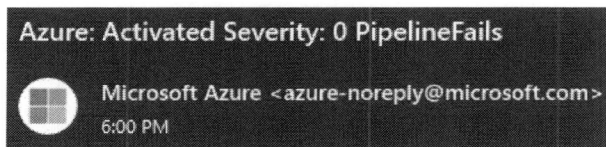

Figure 6.93 – Pipeline failure notification email

35. Perfect! Our alert works! Now, let's go back to the pipeline and fix the query that we modified in **ACT_CPY_WriteLoadMetadata**. Publish the pipeline when done.

36. If you do not want the pipeline to execute every day from now on, click on the **Manage** tab at the left of your screen and click on **Triggers** to go to the triggers section. Hover your mouse over the **TRG_DailyLoad** trigger and click on **Deactivate** (||), as shown in the following screenshot:

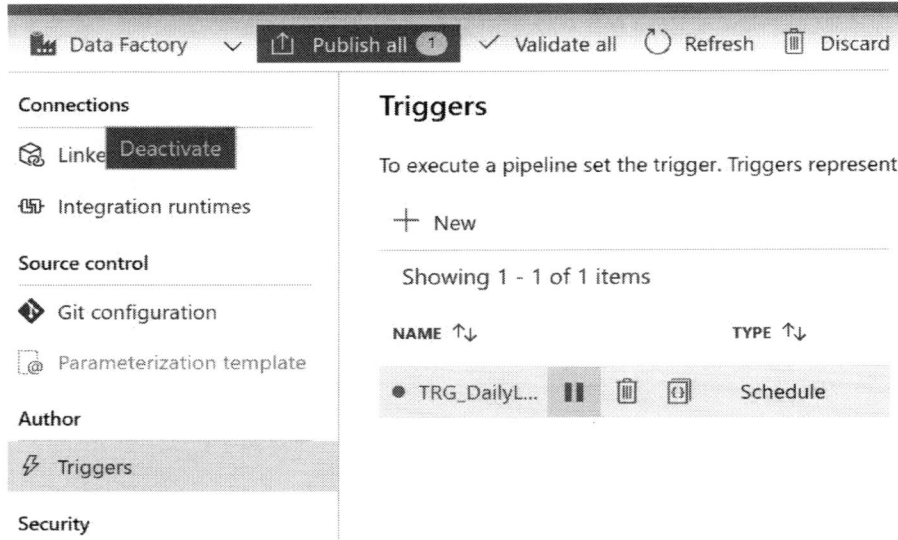

Figure 6.94 – Deactivating a trigger

37. The trigger status is now set to stopped. Click on **Publish all** again to persist the change to the factory run environment. *Failure to do this will prevent the trigger from being stopped; it will then run every day and will cost you money.*

That's it! We've now industrialized our factory!

How it works...

In this recipe, we retrieved row counts from the mapping data flow. We also created a trigger to execute the pipeline. We then created an alert that sent us an email indicating that the pipeline failed.

Azure Data Factory has all the necessary components to create an ETL or ELT solution in the cloud. The fact that we schedule a pipeline, get the load statistics, and generate a variety of alerts makes this service the perfect tool to ingest data in the cloud.

7
Azure Databricks

Azure Databricks has become the de facto ETL tool in the cloud. It's a Unified Data Analytics Platform, meaning that it's more than an ETL tool. It can have access to many libraries that will allow a data engineer or a data scientist to work collaboratively and perform a wider task range; from ETL to machine learning and AI analysis.

Like Azure Data Factory, it's a Platform as a Service development and deployment environment. Unlike Data Factory, Databricks is not Azure specific. It is available on Microsoft Azure as well as the **Amazon Web Services (AWS)** platform. The main difference between Data Factory and Databricks from an ETL point of view is that Data Factory is a no-code environment. We basically use activities to do our ETL.

Databricks uses code and notebooks to achieve the same result. And as we will see later, it is the ETL tool when it comes to big data, whether it's measured in exabytes or petabytes. It is usually used in conjunction with Azure Data Factory when we have such data loads, as Azure Data Factory has a Databricks activity to trigger Databricks notebooks.

This chapter will cover the following recipes:

- Creating a Databricks workspace
- Creating a cluster in our workspace
- Connecting to an internet data source

- Using Delta Lake
- Writing in Azure SQL Server

Let's start with our first recipe!

Creating a Databricks workspace

A Databricks workspace is an environment that contains Databricks assets such as the following:

- **Notebooks**: A notebook is an interface that contains a series of runnable commands. It's a placeholder for code, visualizations, and narrative text.

- **Libraries**: Can be third-party or locally based. They contain code that can be used in notebooks.

- **Experiments**: Used primarily by **machine learning**, they allow the visualization of an MLflow run.

- **Clusters**: Virtual machines in Azure that act as a compute service. They execute the code we write in notebooks.

- **Jobs**: A job is used to run Databricks commands without using the notebook UI. A job is called via a scheduler or data factory.

Now that we have a better idea of the Databricks components, let's dig into it.

Getting ready

If you are using a trial Azure subscription, you will need to upgrade it to a **Pay-As-You-Go** subscription. Azure Databricks requires eight cores of computing resources. The trial Azure subscription has only four computing resource cores. If you are using an Enterprise or MSDN Azure subscription, it should contain enough resources for Azure Databricks.

Important note

Make sure to remove the resources after you have completed all the recipes to reduce the cost of your subscription.

How to do it...

OK, enough theory, let's prepare our Azure Databricks workspace:

1. From the Azure portal, click on **+ Create a resource** and, from the **Analytics** menu, select an **Azure Databricks Service**.

2. In the **Azure Databricks Service** blade, fill in the properties as shown in the following screenshot:

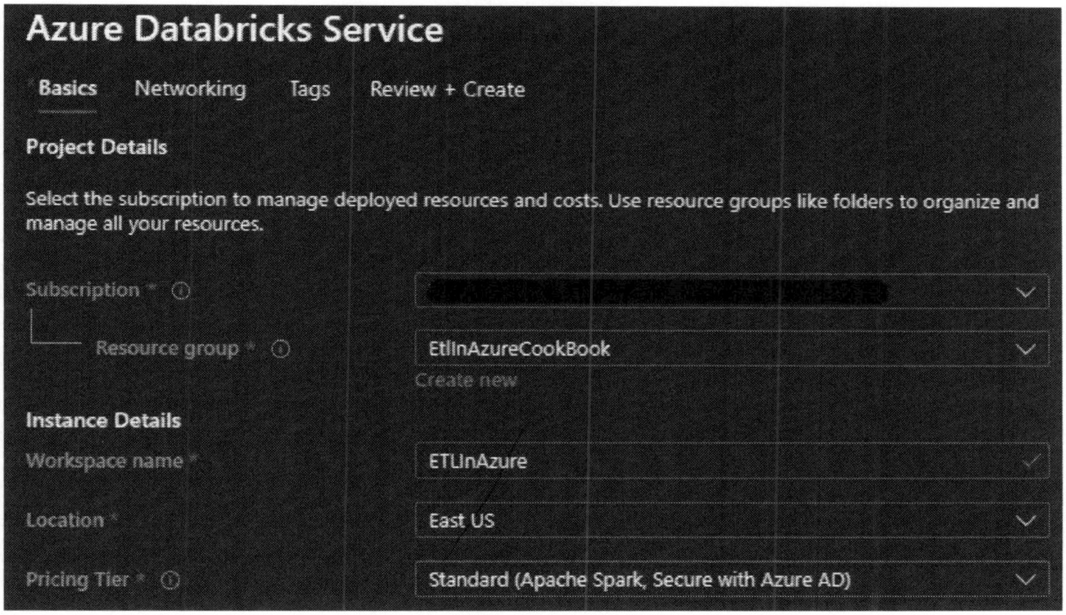

Figure 7.1 – Databricks workspace creation

3. We're going to connect to our Azure SQL Server later in this chapter. Choose the same region as the SQL server that we created in *Chapter 2, Creating an Azure SQL Database*.

4. If you want the workspace to have access to your company resources, you can click on **Networking** to add the workspace in an **Azure Virtual Network** and configure subnets. Otherwise, click on **Review + Create** and you will get the following screenshot:

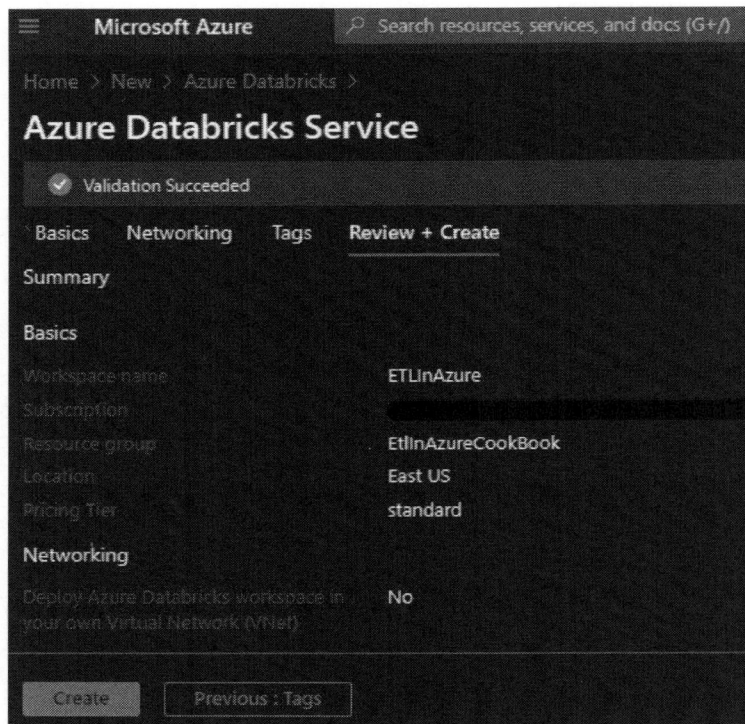

Figure 7.2 – Databricks workspace validation

5. Click on **Create** at the bottom of the browser screen to create the Databricks workspace.

6. Once the deployment is completed as shown in the following screenshot, click on **Go to resource** to access the Databricks workspace blade:

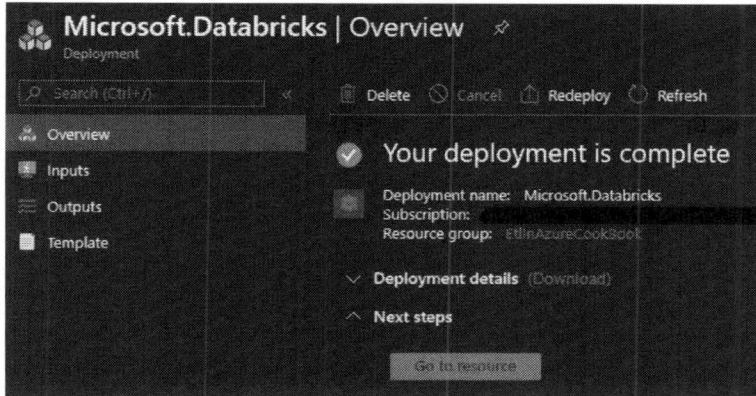

Figure 7.3 – Databricks workspace created

7. In the blade, click on **Launch Workspace** as shown in the following screenshot to open the Databricks environment:

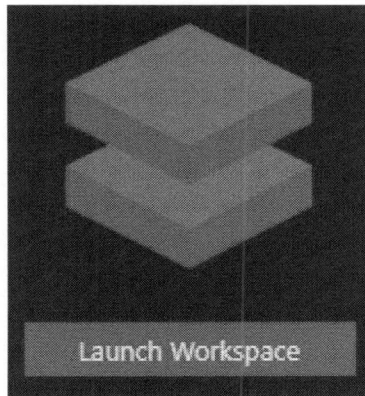

Figure 7.4 – Databricks workspace launch

8. You will land in the Databricks workspace as shown in the following screenshot:

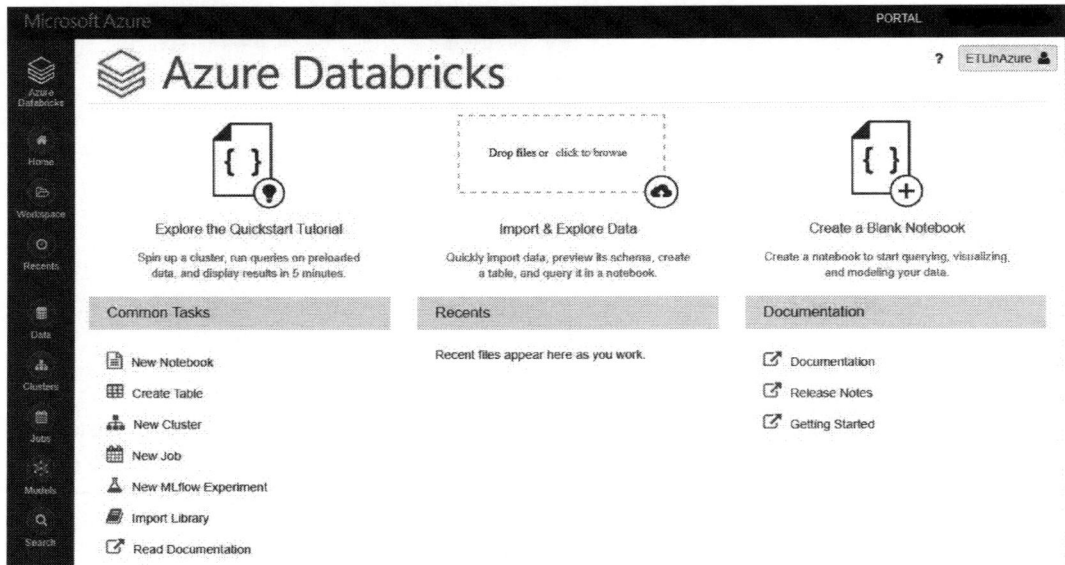

Figure 7.5 – Databricks workspace

9. We have several items available in the workspace, such as **Home**, **Data**, **Clusters**, **Jobs**, and so on. We will use several of them in the following recipes.

That's it! We now have a working Azure Databricks environment!

How it works...

We created the basic Databricks component in this recipe. We will now be able to create other artifacts such as clusters and notebooks to write code in. As stated before, a workspace is an environment that allows you to develop ETLs in a Spark environment.

Creating a cluster in our workspace

A cluster is necessary to manipulate and transform data with Databricks. It is composed of a minimum of two machines:

-   **A driver node**: Receives the commands and dispatches them to a worker.

-   **A worker node**: Receives and executes the commands. We can use multiple workers that will execute the command in parallel.

There are also two types of clusters:

- **Interactive**: A cluster that is started manually. It is used to do interactive queries in a notebook, or another program connected to it, such as Power BI.
- **Automated**: A cluster created automatically to run a job and stopped after it. For example, this type of cluster is used when we use a Databricks activity in Azure Data Factory.

Let's create a cluster in our Databricks workspace now.

Getting ready

As with every recipe in this chapter, you will need to upgrade your trial Azure subscription to a **Pay-As-You-Go** subscription if this is not what you have been using so far. Azure Databricks requires eight cores of computing resources. The trial Azure subscription has only four computing resource cores. If you are using an Enterprise or MSDN Azure subscription, it should contain enough resources for Azure Databricks.

How to do it...

Let's create our cluster. It will be used for all the remaining recipes in this chapter:

1. From the Databricks workspace, click on the **Clusters** icon in the leftmost toolbar as shown in the following screenshot:

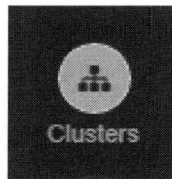

Figure 7.6 – Databricks Clusters

2. Click on the **+ Create Cluster** button at the top left as shown in the following screenshot:

Figure 7.7 – Databricks Create Cluster button

3. On the **Create Cluster** screen, fill out the properties as shown in the following screenshot. Uncheck the **Enable autoscaling** checkbox and type 1 in the **Workers** textbox. You can also change **Terminate after ... minutes of inactivity** to a smaller number than the default one. Click on **Create Cluster** once completed:

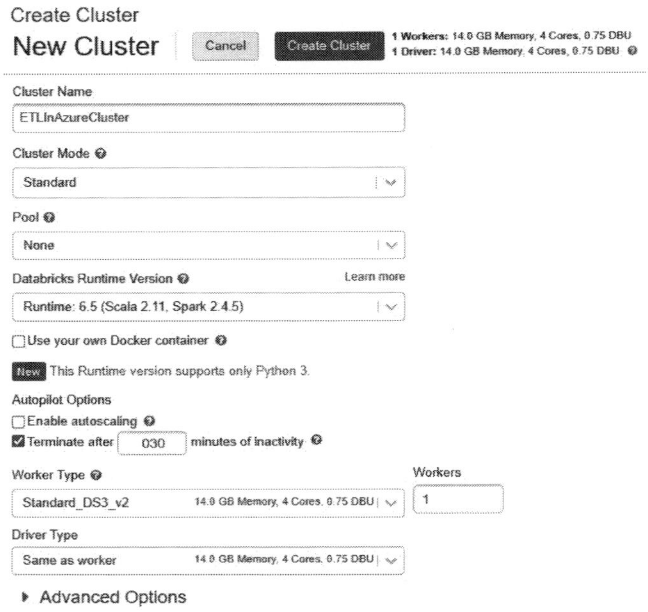

Figure 7.8 – Databricks Create Cluster screen

4. Back to the clusters screen, your cluster will appear in the **Interactive Clusters** list. It will be automatically started as shown in the following screenshot:

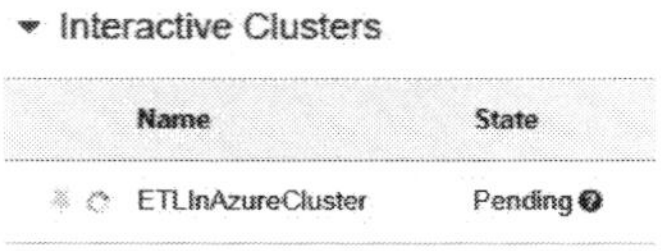

Figure 7.9 – Databricks cluster created

Voila! We have successfully created a cluster that we will use in the remaining recipes of this chapter.

How it works...

Having a cluster is required to use our Databricks workspace. In this recipe, we created the smallest possible cluster because we will not work with a large amount of data. A larger cluster size would be used in a production environment.

Connecting to an internet data source

This recipe will teach you how we can connect to a data source from a public internet URL. We're going to use demographic income (Statistics of Income - SOI) data from the **Internal Revenue Service (IRS)**. We will explore and transform this data with our Databricks workspace environment.

We will get data from the following links:

- `https://www.irs.gov/pub/irs-soi/17zpallnoagi.csv`: This is a CSV file that contains the year 2017 incomes per state per zip code.

- `https://worldpopulationreview.com/static/states/abbr-name.csv`: This CSV file contains state abbreviations (codes) and state names.

The first file contains income data and state codes. We will use the second file to augment the first one with state names. We will also aggregate the state income file to get one state income per state instead of zip code.

Getting ready

As with every recipe in this chapter, you will need to upgrade your trial Azure subscription to a **Pay-As-You-Go** subscription if this is what you have been using so far. Azure Databricks requires eight cores of computing resources. The trial Azure subscription has only four computing resources cores. If you are using an Enterprise or MSDN Azure subscription, it should contain enough resources for Azure Databricks.

How to do it...

OK, let's dig into the recipe!

1. Open your Databricks **Workspace** as shown in the previous recipe, *Creating a Databricks workspace.*

2. Click the **Home** icon in the workspace, select **<your email address>**, click on the arrow to the right, and select **Create** > **Notebook** as shown in the following screenshot:

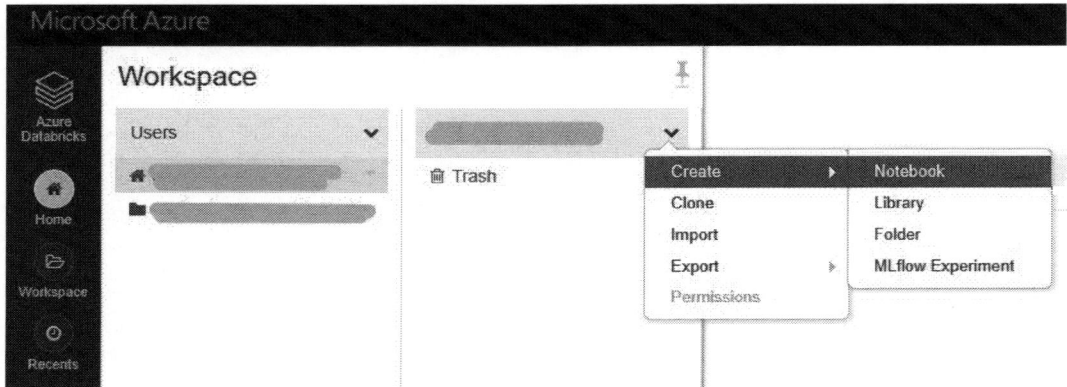

Figure 7.10 – Adding a new notebook

3. The **Create Notebook** dialog box appears. As shown in the following screenshot, enter a name for the notebook. We'll use Python as the default language. Databricks commands can be written in four languages – **Python, Scala, SQL,** and **R**:

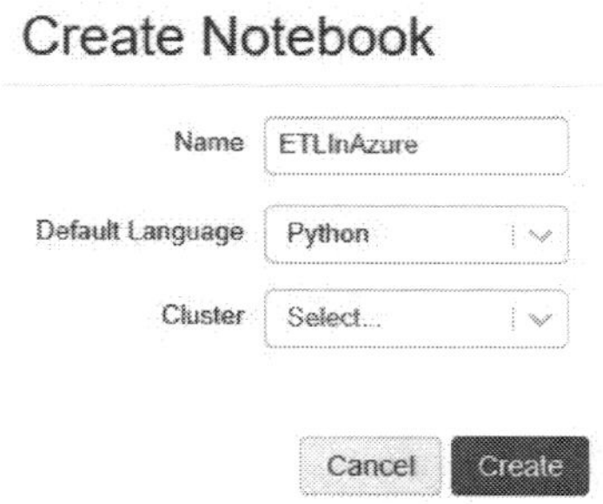

Figure 7.11 – Naming a new notebook

4. A new empty notebook appears. A notebook can contain comment cells known as "Markdown" as well as code cells. Type the following code in the first cell. The `%md` in the cell indicates that it is a Markdown cell. The hashtag # characters determine the size of the font:

```
%md
#####Add widgets (parameters)
```

5. Click outside of the cell. Your notebook should now have a cell as in the following screenshot:

Cmd 1

Add widgets (parameters)

Figure 7.12 – Adding a new Markdown cell for widgets

6. An input widget is a placeholder for a parameter in notebooks. There are various types of input widgets: **text, dropdown, combobox,** and **multiselect**. We are going to use two input widgets: one that will contain the URL for the state demographic incomes and the other one for the state names. This allows us to avoid hardcoding the URLs in our code. Hover your mouse over the bottom of the first cell and click on the + sign as shown in the following screenshot:

Figure 7.13 – Adding a new cell

7. Enter the following code in the cell. Press *Ctrl + Enter* to run the cell (make sure that each command is on one line, otherwise, the command will fail):

```
dbutils.widgets.removeAll()
dbutils.widgets.text("urlStateAbbr", "https://
worldpopulationreview.com/static/states/abbr-name.csv",
"State Abbreviations URL")
dbutils.widgets.text("urlStateData", "https://www.irs.
gov/pub/irs-soi/17zpallnoagi.csv", "State Income Data
URL")
```

288Azure Databricks

8. The first line of code removes any existing widgets, while the two other lines add textbox widgets. Run the cell and you should find two input widgets at the top of the notebook as shown in the following screenshot:

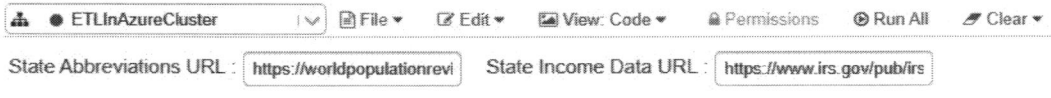

| ETLInAzureCluster | File ▾ | Edit ▾ | View: Code ▾ | Permissions | Run All | Clear ▾ |

State Abbreviations URL : `https://worldpopulationrevi`   State Income Data URL : `https://www.irs.gov/pub/irs`

Figure 7.14 – Databricks input widgets added

9. An input widget is created by calling the `dbutils.widgets.text()` function. It takes three arguments:

   a) The name of the input widget: a unique name for the widget.

   b) The default value: it is useful to have a default value as it gives a hint to the notebook's users of what kind of value can be used.

   c) The label: this is the text at the left of the widget that describes what value can be entered in the widget.

10. Add a new cell and enter the following code in it. This is a Markdown cell that documents what we will do next:

```
%md
####Variables assignment
```

11. Next, we will initialize some variables with the widget's content. Add another cell and enter the following code. We are using the `dbutils.widgets.get()` function to initialize the two variables: `urlStateAbbr` and `urlStateData`. The last line will display the content of the `urlStateData` variable under the cell:

```
urlStateAbbr = dbutils.widgets.get('urlStateAbbr')
urlStateData = dbutils.widgets.get('urlStateData')
urlStateData
Out[<a number>]: 'https://www.irs.gov/pub/
irs-soi/17zpallnoagi.csv'
```

12. Now, we are going to import the CSV abbreviations file into a DataFrame. Add one cell with the following code and run it:

```
%md
#####Read states abbreviations into a dataframe
```

13. To read the URL, we're using a Python pandas method. So, we hav that library first. Also, we are applying a schema to the DataFram would get *0* and *1* as column names. The next code creates the s composed of `StructTypes` that define columns and we are assig. to these columns, in our case, `StringType`. Running the cell will creatᴇ called `abbrSchema`:

```
import pandas as pd
from pyspark.sql.types import StructType, StringType
abbrSchema= (StructType()
    .add("abbr", StringType())
    .add("stateName", StringType())
    )
```

14. Next, we're going to import the abbreviations and names into a DataFrame called `abbrDF`:

```
abbrDF = (spark
        .createDataFrame(pd.read_csv(urlStateAbbr,
                                    header=None),
                    abbrSchema))
# Display the  dataframe
display(abbrDF)
```

The last line displays the DataFrame as shown in the following screenshot:

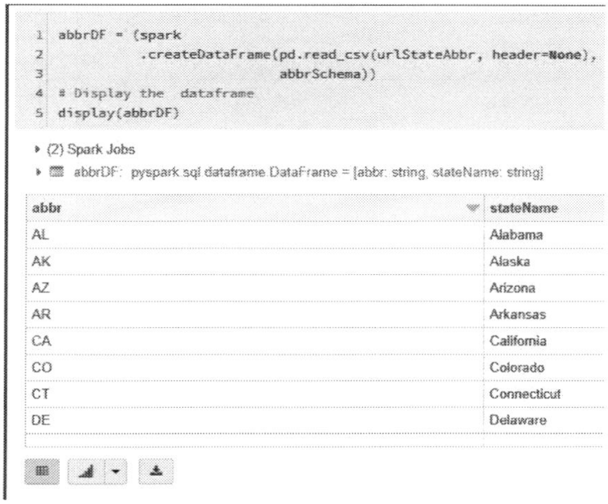

Figure 7.15 – Databricks abbrDF DataFrame created

15. We will now add more Markdown to document what we are doing next – reading the content of the state's income data:

```
%md
#####Read state income data into a dataframe
```

16. We are interested in only two columns in the state income CSV file: STATE – a string value and A02650, a long value. In the following code, we are reading those two columns; cast A02650 as a long value to be able to aggregate it. We then group the result by STATE, and we sum the cast totalIncomeAmount (originally named A02650 before the cast) and rename it summedTotalIncomeAmount. Add a new cell and enter the following code and run it:

```
from pyspark.sql.functions import col
from pyspark.sql.types import LongType
stateDataDF = (spark.createDataFrame(pd.read_
             csv(urlStateData
             .select(col("STATE").alias("state"),
             col("A02650").cast(LongType()).
             alias("totalIncomeAmount"))
             .groupBy("state")
             .sum("totalIncomeAmount")
             .select(col("state"),
             col("sum(totalIncomeAmount)").
             alias("summedTotalIncomeAmount"))
             )
# Display the dataframe
display(stateDataDF)
```

The cell and its result should look like the following screenshot (some comments have been removed in the previous step for better readability in the book). What were **27760** lines in the state income file have been aggregated to **51** lines. Make sure the layout of the code is the same as in the following screenshot:

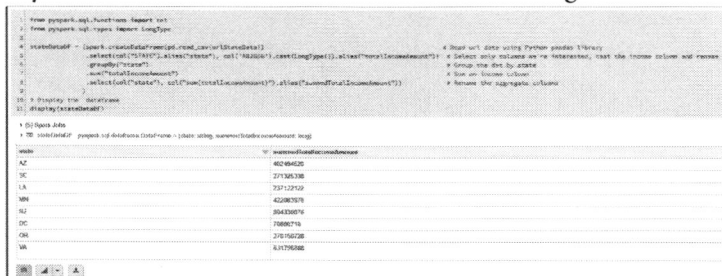

Figure 7.16 – Databricks stateIncomeDF DataFrame created

17. Now that we have read the two CSVs and transformed them, we a
them to get our result. We want to get a final DataFrame with th
code (abbr), state name (stateName), and the summed tot
(summedTotalIncomeAmount). The next code does exact
stateDataDF DataFrame to the abbrDF DataFrame using
state and abbr columns. We then select only the three columns ..
in using the select command:

```
stateIncomeDF = (stateDataDF.join(abbrDF, [stateDataDF.
                 state == abbrDF.abbr], how = "inner")
                 .select(col("abbr"), col("stateName"),
                 col("summedTotalIncomeAmount"))
                 .orderBy(col("abbr"))
                 )
# Display the dataframe
display(stateIncomeDF)
```

The cell code and its result are shown in the following screenshot:

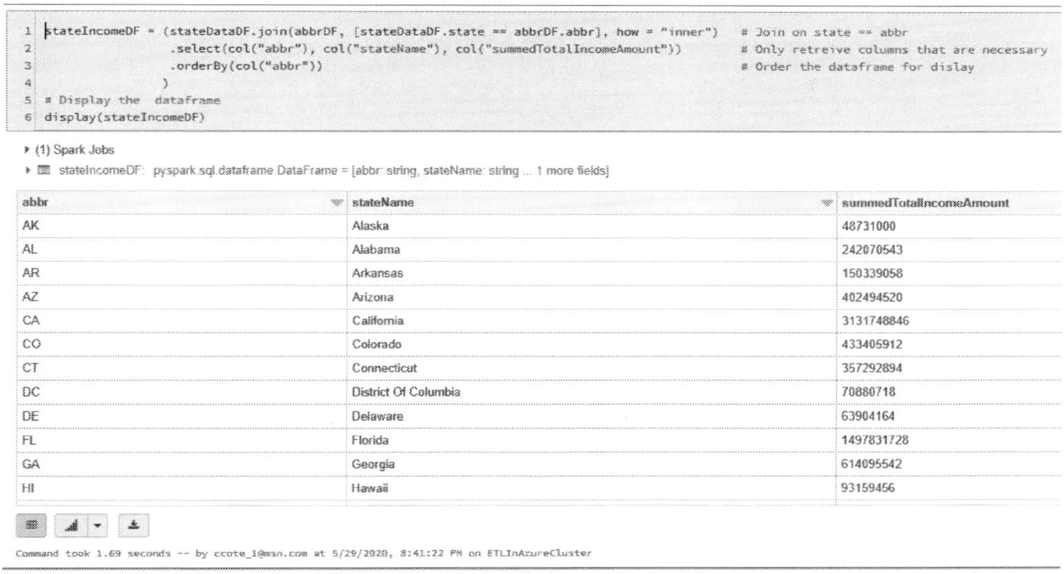

```
1  stateIncomeDF = (stateDataDF.join(abbrDF, [stateDataDF.state == abbrDF.abbr], how = "inner")   # Join on state == abbr
2                   .select(col("abbr"), col("stateName"), col("summedTotalIncomeAmount"))          # Only retreive columns that are necessary
3                   .orderBy(col("abbr"))                                                            # Order the dataframe for dislay
4                   )
5  # Display the dataframe
6  display(stateIncomeDF)
```

▶ (1) Spark Jobs

▶ ▦ stateIncomeDF: pyspark.sql.dataframe.DataFrame = [abbr: string, stateName: string ... 1 more fields]

abbr	stateName	summedTotalIncomeAmount
AK	Alaska	48731000
AL	Alabama	242070543
AR	Arkansas	150339058
AZ	Arizona	402494520
CA	California	3131748846
CO	Colorado	433405912
CT	Connecticut	357292894
DC	District Of Columbia	70880718
DE	Delaware	63904164
FL	Florida	1497831728
GA	Georgia	614095542
HI	Hawaii	93159456

Command took 1.69 seconds -- by ccote_1@msn.com at 5/29/2020, 8:41:22 PM on ETLInAzureCluster

Figure 7.17 – Databricks – the two DataFrames joined together

8. Now, let's change the list to a graph. Click on the graph icon at the bottom of the list and select **Bar chart** as shown in the following screenshot:

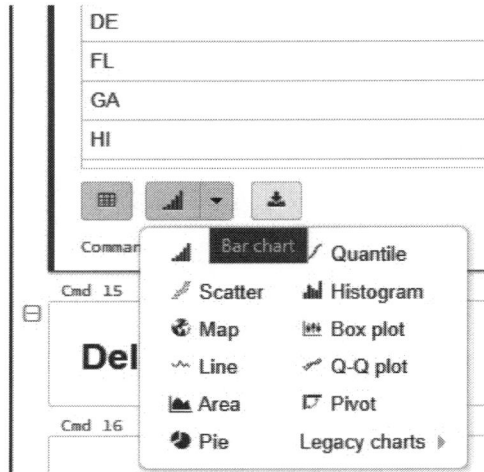

Figure 7.18 – Databricks bar chart selection

You get a bar graph as shown in the following screenshot:

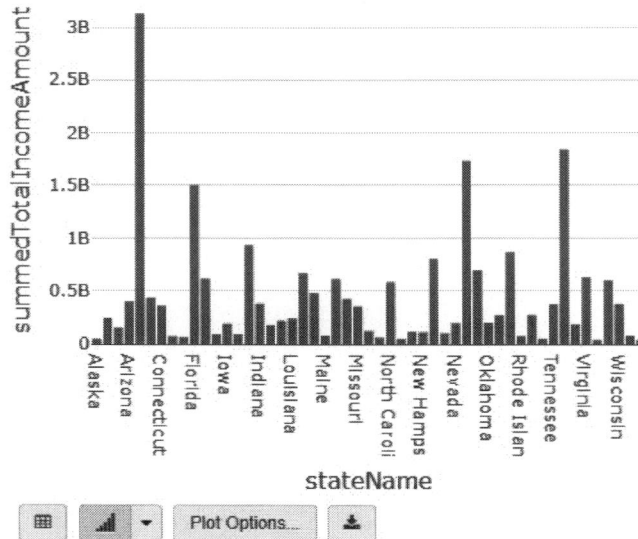

Figure 7.19 – Databricks bar chart result

That's it! We read two files from the internet and transformed them to get the total state income per state in a single result set. We'll use the dataset created here in the next recipes of this chapter.

How it works...

Databricks notebooks are great to explore and experiment with many sources of data. They can also serve as an ETL code repository and can be part of a cloud big data or data warehouse toolset.

In this recipe, we connected to a public internet data source to retrieve two **comma-separated values (CSV)** files: one for the incomes by state per zip code and another one that contains the state names. We merged them together to attach the complete state name to the income data. We then aggregated the result by removing the zip codes to get the total income per state.

This recipe used pandas, a Python library to read and import data from a URL. We used it because it would have been more complex to use Spark to directly read from the internet and the volume of data was quite small.

Python libraries are not necessarily optimized for Spark environments and should be used sparingly. When a native PySpark library or method is available and relatively simple to use, we should prefer it instead of a potentially unoptimized Python library.

Using Delta Lake

When using Databricks, we can also use its open source storage layer, Delta Lake. It is a database engine that brings lots of benefits to data lake storage. Here are a few of them:

- **Acid transactions**: It adds serializability and an isolation level to concurrent reads and writes of data.

- **Time Travel and Audit of History**: Adds snapshots that enable reversion to a previous version of the data. This is useful when we want to see what happened to our data. With the Delta Lake engine, we can see the state of the data at any time in its history.

- **Updates and Deletes**: Usually, these **data manipulation languages (DMLs)** are impossible with other big data technologies. The Delta Lake engine supports them and even adds the **Merge** command on top of them.

- **Compatible with the Apache Spark API**: Can be used in existing Spark data code without many changes.

For a complete list of features, go to the following URL:

```
https://delta.io/
```

The Delta Lake engine has the following components:

- **Databases**: A collection of tables.
- **A log folder**: Contains the history of changes made to the table's data.
- **Managed Tables**: Managed tables mean that they are stored on the cluster inside Databricks. The underlying files are not accessible unless the cluster is up and running.
- **Unmanaged tables**: The tables are stored on storage outside the cluster. The underlying files are available but cannot be read so easily since we have not applied the changes from the log folder files.
- **Storage**: Open source storage that sits on top of data lake storage such as Azure Data Lake Storage, Amazon S3, or a local HDFS storage.

In this recipe, we will save our `stateIncomeDF` created in the previous recipe, *Connecting to an internet data source,* into a Delta table. We will create a database, add the DataFrame data to a table, and show how audit history can be used.

Getting ready

If you are using a trial Azure subscription, you will need to upgrade it to a **Pay-As-You-Go** subscription. Azure Databricks requires eight cores of computing resources. The trial Azure subscription has only four computing resource cores. If you are using an Enterprise or MSDN Azure subscription, it should contain enough resources for Azure Databricks.

How to do it...

Alright, let's play with Delta Lake!

1. Add a new cell to our notebook and type the following code. This creates a Markdown cell documenting that we're going to play with the Delta Lake components:

    ```
    %md
    ###Delta Lake
    ```

2. In another cell, we are going to create a database called `ETLInAzure`. We use the SQL language for it, hence the `%sql` in the first line of the following code.

   The `SHOW DATABASES` command is used to confirm that the database has been created:

```
%sql
CREATE DATABASE ETLInAzure;
SHOW DATABASES;
```

3. The following screenshot shows that the `ETLInAzure` database has been created:

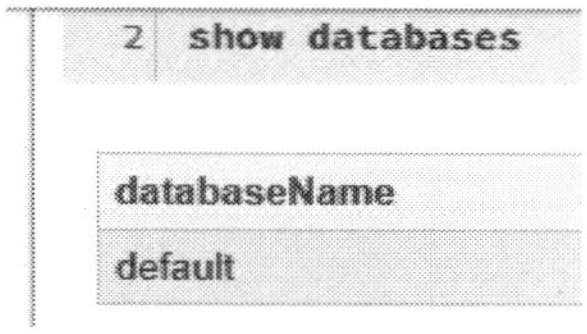

Figure 7.20 – Databricks creating database ETLInAzure

4. Next, we save our DataFrame in storage in the cluster storage. Type the following code in a new cell to save the DataFrame. We first drop the files in case there was a previous attempt to create a table in that location:

```
dbutils.fs.rm("mnt/tables/stateIncome", True)
stateIncomeDF.write.format("delta").save("/mnt/tables/
stateIncome")
```

5. Add a new cell and paste the following command. It will list files stored on the disk when we saved the DataFrame:

```
#List all the files created
display(dbutils.fs.ls("/mnt/tables/stateIncome"))
```

You should get a result like the one in the following screenshot. We can see that there is a directory called `_delta_log`. We'll have a look at it later:

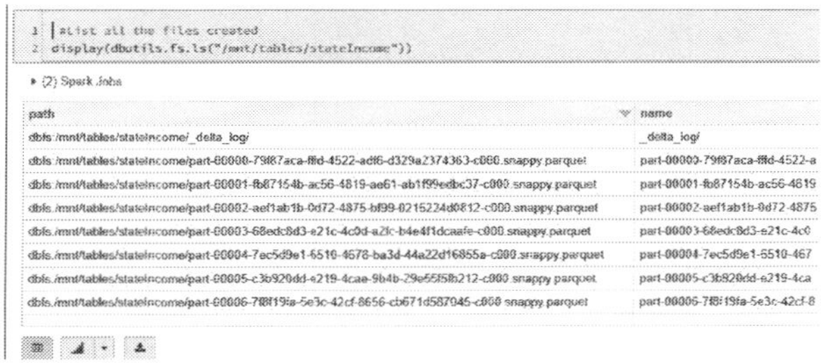

Figure 7.21 – Databricks list of files created when the DataFrame was saved

6. We have now saved our DataFrame's content into storage in the cluster. We haven't created a table on top of it yet. To create a Delta table using a specific location, we are going to use the following commands. The table will be an unmanaged table because we explicitly specify storage:

```
# Create a SQL table
# Ensure that the table is droppped or do not exists
before
spark.sql("DROP TABLE IF EXISTS ETLInAzure.StateIncome")
# Create the table
spark.sql("CREATE TABLE ETLInAzure.StateIncome USING
DELTA LOCATION '/mnt/tables/stateIncome'")
```

7. Let's now read the table. In a new cell, type the following SQL command and run it:

```
%sql
SELECT abbr
     , stateName
     , summedTotalIncomeAmount
FROM ETLInAzure.StateIncome
```

You should get a list like the following screenshot:

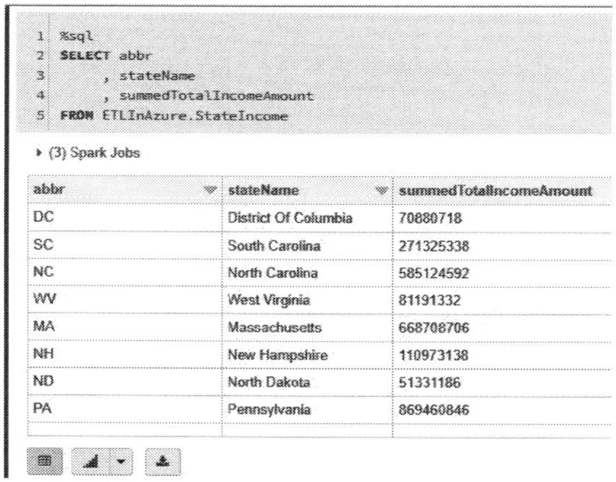

Figure 7.22 – Databricks SELECT statement result

8. Now, we will insert some data into our table. Type and run the following SQL command in a new notebook cell:

```
%sql
INSERT INTO ETLInAzure.StateIncome
SELECT "ALL" AS abbr, "AllStates" AS StateName, 999999999
AS summedTotalIncomeAmount
```

9. To see if the row has been inserted, let's type and run the following Python code in a new cell:

```
latestVersionDF = (spark .table("ETLInAzure.stateIncome")
                         .orderBy("abbr")
                  )
display(latestVersionDF)
```

10. A new DataFrame is created from the table and we display it ordered by the **abbr** column. The following screenshot shows the result set. We can see that the **ALL** state code (**abbr**) row is created:

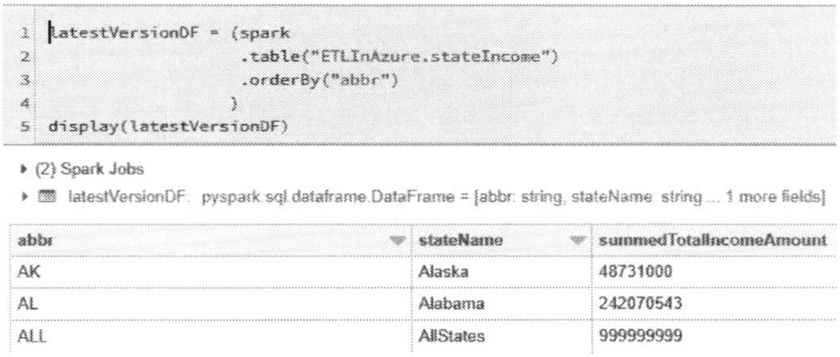

Figure 7.23 – Databricks DataFrame with row appended to it

11. We have now issued two inserts: one implicit at the table creation and the `ALL` insert statement. Let's look at our table history. We're using the `DeltaTable.forPath()` function for it. The first parameter is a constant spark, the second is the path of our table. Next, two DataFrames are created – `fullHistoryDF` and `createOperationDF`:

```
# Get Table changes
from delta.tables import *
deltaTable = DeltaTable.forPath(spark, '/mnt/tables/
stateIncome')
fullHistoryDF = deltaTable.history()    # get the full
history of the table
createOperationDF = deltaTable.history(0) # get the first
operation
display(fullHistoryDF)
```

12. The `fullHistoryDF` DataFrame contains all the history, as shown in the following screenshot:

version ▼	operationMetrics
1	▶ {"numFiles":"1","numOutputBytes":"991","numOutputRows":"1","numParts":"0"}
0	▶ {"numFiles":"51","numOutputBytes":"49873","numOutputRows":"51","numParts":"0"}

Figure 7.24 – Databricks list of changes in the table

13. To query the table before we inserted the **ALL** row, type the following code in a new cell and run it:

```
tableCreatedDF = (spark.read
                    .format("delta")
                    .option("versionAsOf", 0)
                    .load("/mnt/tables/stateIncome").
                    orderBy("abbr")
                  )
display(tableCreatedDF)
```

The result displayed should be like the following screenshot:

```
1  tableCreatedDF = (spark.read
2                      .format("delta")
3                      .option("versionAsOf", 0)
4                      .load("/mnt/tables/stateIncome").orderBy("abbr")
5                    )
6  display(tableCreatedDF)
```

▶ (4) Spark Jobs

▶ ▦ tableCreatedDF: pyspark.sql.dataframe.DataFrame = [abbr: string, stateName: string ... 1 more fields]

abbr	▼	stateName	▼	summedTotalIncomeAmount
AK		Alaska		48731000
AL		Alabama		242070543
AR		Arkansas		150339058
AZ		Arizona		402494520
CA		California		3131748846
CO		Colorado		433405912
CT		Connecticut		357292894
DC		District Of Columbia		70880718

Figure 7.25 – List of rows in the storage

14. To prove the difference, we will use a SQL command. In order to use our `tableCreatedDF` in SQL, we need to use the following operation: `createOrReplaceTempView`. Add a new cell and type and run the following command:

```
tableCreatedDF.createOrReplaceTempView("OriginalTable")
```

A new temporary view is created. It is visible by the notebook's session only. It will not be persisted if we shut down or restart the cluster; it will have to be recreated if that happens.

15. We will now test the difference between the two sets, one with the ALL abbr and the other one without. In a new cell, type and run the following SQL command:

```
%sql
SELECT abbr, stateName, summedTotalIncomeAmount FROM
ETLInAzure.StateIncome
EXCEPT
SELECT abbr, stateName, summedTotalIncomeAmount    FROM
OriginalTable
```

The result set shows that the only difference is the **ALL abbr** row as shown in the following screenshot:

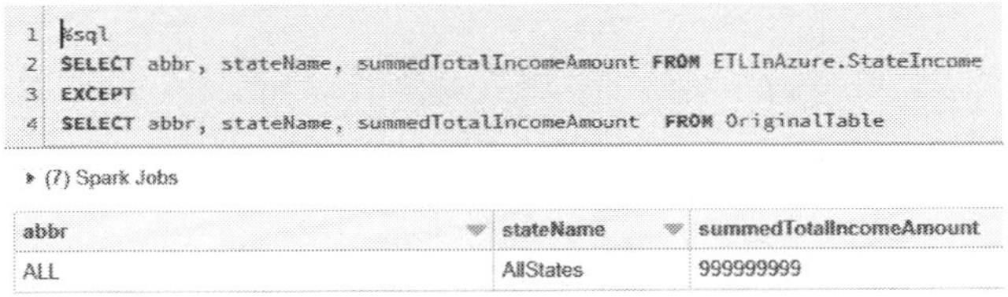

Figure 7.26 – Databricks row comparison

16. Now, let's see what we got in our directory. In a new cell, type and run the following command:

```
#List all the files created
display(dbutils.fs.ls("/mnt/tables/stateIncome/_delta_
log"))
```

17. We can now see that we have two versions (. json files). The first one,
(00000000000000000000 . json), is around 24772 bytes while the second
one, (00000000000000000001 . json), is smaller: around 897 bytes. Let's look
at the content of the second . json file. In a new cell, type and run the following
command:

```
dbutils.fs.head('/mnt/tables/stateIncome/_delta_
log/00000000000000000001.json')
```

18. The result shows the file's content. By the end of the content, we see that we
have added one record (numRecords) with the values ALL, AllStates, and
999999999:

```
{\\"numRecords\\":1,\\"minValues\\":{\\"abbr\\":\\"ALL
\\",\\"stateName\\":\\"AllStates\\",\\"summedTotal
IncomeAmount\\":999999999},\\"maxValues\\":{\\"abbr\\
":\\"ALL\\",\\"stateName\\":\\"AllStates\\",\\
"summedTotalIncomeAmount\\":999999999},\\"
nullCount\\":{\\"abbr\\":0,\\"stateName\\":0,\\
"summedTotalIncomeAmount\\":0}}"}
```

That's it! We have successfully used the Delta Lake engine to create a table out of
our URLs!

How it works...

In this recipe, we created a database using Delta Engine. We then saved our
StateIncomeDF DataFrame as a table in it. We inserted a supplemental line by creating
an artificial ALL state code. We then used the **Delta Lake Time Travel** functionality to
query the before and after insertion of the ALL state row. We were also able to see the
changes in the **log folder** of the **Delta** table.

Delta Lake keeps a version of every change made to a table. A table is represented by
a directory in storage. This directory contains a subdirectory called _delta_log/ that
contains all the change history. It would be very tedious to query a file history without
Delta Lake.

There's more...

Delta Lake is also available as a fully open source offering. We can use it without using a Databricks workspace. The latest version is available for download at `https://delta.io/`. We can use it with a local Spark installation on our machine. The following link shows how to get started with it: `https://docs.delta.io/latest/quick-start.html`. The following website shows how to accomplish this on a Windows 10 PC: `https://kontext.tech/column/spark/311/apache-spark-243-installation-on-windows-10-using-windows-subsystem-for-linux`.

Writing in Azure SQL Server

So far, we have read data from the internet and stored it in a Delta Lake table. Delta tables are fine as a consumption layer, but they have some caveats:

- We need to have a cluster running to query the data. This can be costly at times.

- Queries take longer than a regular database to get back because the cluster uses a distributed process: driver to workers – especially for small volumes.

- There's no native row-level security or dynamic data masking as we have in SQL Server.

- There are no schemas, only databases and tables. This might be an issue for certain applications.

Our `ETLInAzure.StateIncome` table holds only 52 rows. We have used Databricks to import the data from the internet and stored it in Delta Lake. To use it in our applicative database – `AdventureWorksLT` – we will copy the transformed data back to SQL Server.

In this recipe, we will save our `ETLInAzure.StateIncome` table created in the previous recipe, *Using Delta Lake*. Make sure you have created it before you do this recipe. We're also using the `AdventureWorks` Azure SQL database. We created it in *Chapter 2, Introducing ETL*.

Getting ready

If you are using a trial Azure subscription, you will need to upgrade it to a **Pay-As-You-Go** subscription. Azure Databricks requires eight cores of computing resources. The trial Azure subscription has only four computing resource cores. If you are using an Enterprise or MSDN Azure subscription, it should contain enough resources for Azure Databricks.

How to do it...

We're now ready to write data to our Azure SQL server!

1. Let's use another notebook. Create a new notebook and call it ETLInAzureSQLServer as shown in the following screenshot:

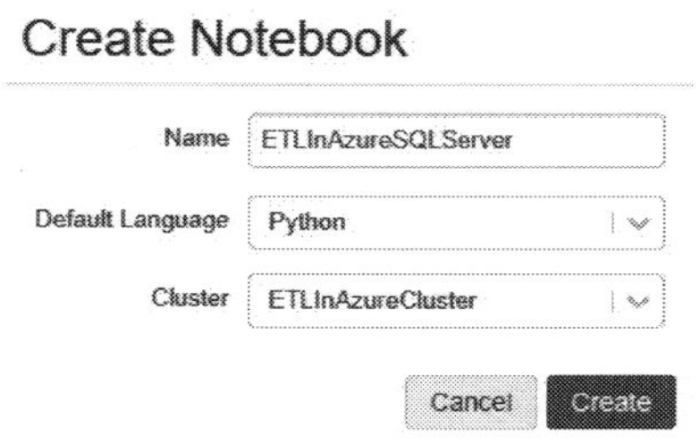

Figure 7.27 – Databricks new notebook for SQL Server

2. Now, add a Markdown cell using the following command. Leave the blank lines between the numbered list:

```
%md
### Insert data into SQL Server

1- Create a JDBC connection string

2- Connect to the database and overwrite it
3- Insert stateIncomeDF data
```

3. Then, we'll check whether the driver for our database is present on the cluster. We're using Scala syntax this time since the functionality has not been ported to other languages. Add a new cell to the notebook and type and run the following code in it:

```
%scala
//Check if the driver exists
Class.forName("com.microsoft.sqlserver.jdbc.
SQLServerDriver")

//You should get
res0: Class[_] = class com.microsoft.sqlserver.jdbc.
SQLServerDriver
```

4. We will now add some widgets to the notebook. We will use three widgets: `ServerName`, `DatabaseName`, and `ServerPort`. This way, if any of these parameters change when we call the code from, for example, Data Factory, we will not need to open the code to change one of these properties (make sure that all commands are on a single line):

```
dbutils.widgets.removeAll()
dbutils.widgets.text("ServerName", "etlinazurecookbook.
database.windows.net", "Azure SQL Server")
dbutils.widgets.text("DatabaseName", "AdventureWorksLT",
"Azure SQL Database")
dbutils.widgets.text("ServerPort", "1433", "Azure SQL
Server Port")
```

We now see the three widgets added at the top of the notebook as shown in the following screenshot:

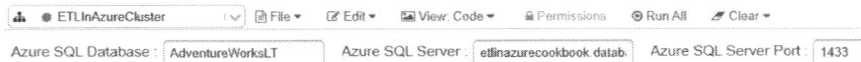

Figure 7.28 – Databricks SQL Server widgets added

5. Next, we create the JDBC connection string or URL. In a new cell, type the following code and run it. Change `jdcbUserName` and `jdbcDBPassword` to your own. Again, the commands are split across multiple lines here to fit on the book's page. It is best practice to not type the password in cleartext in the notebooks. In a real production environment, we would use Azure Key Vault as discussed in the following article: `https://docs.microsoft.com/en-us/azure/databricks/security/secrets/secret-scopes#akv-ss`:

```
jdbcHostname = dbutils.widgets.get("ServerName")
jdbcDatabase = dbutils.widgets.get("DatabaseName")
jdbcPort = dbutils.widgets.get("ServerPort")
jdbcUserName= "<Your UserName>"
jdbcDBPassword = "<Your Password>"
jdbcUrl = "jdbc:sqlserver://
{0}:{1};database={2};user={3};password={4}".
format(jdbcHostname, jdbcPort, jdbcDatabase,
jdbcUserName, jdbcDBPassword)
```

6. Now, we're going to retrieve our `ETLInAzure.StateIncome` Delta table in a DataFrame. In a new cell, type and run the following command:

```
# Load the ETLInAzure.StateIncome table in a dataframe
stateIncomeJDBCDF = spark.table("ETLInAzure.StateIncome")
display(stateIncomeJDBCDF)
```

You should get the following result on your screen:

```
1  # Load the ETLInAzure.StateIncome table in a dataframe
2  stateIncomeJDBCDF = spark.table("ETLInAzure.StateIncome")
3  display(stateIncomeJDBCDF)
```

▶ (3) Spark Jobs
▶ ▦ stateIncomeJDBCDF: pyspark.sql.dataframe.DataFrame = [abbr: string, stateName: string ... 1 more fields]

abbr	stateName	summedTotalIncomeAmount
DC	District Of Columbia	70880718
NC	North Carolina	585124592
SC	South Carolina	271325338
NH	New Hampshire	110973138
MA	Massachusetts	668708706
WV	West Virginia	81191332
RI	Rhode Island	73652196
PA	Pennsylvania	869460846

Figure 7.29 – Databricks Delta table data retrieval in a DataFrame

7. In *Chapter 6*, *Azure Data Factory*, we created a table called `SalesLT.IncomePerStates` with the following structure. If you did not create it, do it now as we will need it in this recipe:

```
CREATE Table SalesLT.IncomesPerState(
    StateAbbreviation NVARCHAR(2) NOT NULL,
    StateName NVARCHAR(100) NOT NULL,
    StateIncome BIGINT NOT NULL,
    BatchID NVARCHAR(100)
)
```

8. The target table has a field for all our Delta table fields: `delta table abbr > SQL Server StateAbbreviation`, `delta table stateName > SQL Server StateName`, and `delta table summedTotalIncomeAmount > SQL Server StateIncome`. We're only missing `BatchID`. This column is useful to know what process ID loaded the data. In SSIS, we would use `ServerExecutionID`. In *Chapter 6*, *Azure Data Factory*, we used `pipelineRunID`. In this recipe, we'll be using the notebook run ID. Enter and run the following code in a new cell.

Again, make sure that all commands are on one line as the following code might be split across multiple lines to accommodate the book's format:

```
import json , time
notebook_info = json.loads(dbutils.notebook.entry_point.
getDbutils().notebook().getContext().toJson())
runid = notebook_info["currentRunId"]

if runid is None:
  runid = "InteractiveMode - " + str(round(time.
monotonic() * 1000))

print(runid)
```

The result should be similar to `InteractiveMode - 5829221`.

The code uses the notebook context to retrieve the run ID. This run ID is only populated when the notebook is called from an external process like Data Factory or another notebook. When we are running the code interactively, a `None` value is returned. In that case, we still want a unique ID. That's why we prefix it with `InteractiveMode -` and we assign the current time in milliseconds.

9. Now, we're ready to add a new column to our `stateIncomeJDBCDF` DataFrame. Add a new cell, type, and run the following code. We use the `lit` function to add a column to the DataFrame by using a variable:

```
from pyspark.sql.functions import lit
stateIncomeJDBCDF = stateIncomeJDBCDF.
withColumn("batchId", lit(str(runid)))
```

10. To save our `stateIncomeJDBCDF` to the server, we need to align its column names to the SQL Server table. Type and run the following code in a new cell. We're using `withColumnRenamed("old name", "new name")` to rename our DataFrame columns:

```
stateIncomeJDBCDF  = (stateIncomeJDBCDF
  .withColumnRenamed("abbr","StateAbbreviation")
  .withColumnRenamed("stateName","StateName")
  .withColumnRenamed("summedTotalIncomeAmount","StateIncome
")
  .withColumnRenamed("batchId", "BatchID")
)
display(stateIncomeJDBCDF)
```

We get the following list after the code finishes running:

```
1  stateIncomeJDBCDF  = (stateIncomeJDBCDF
2    .withColumnRenamed("abbr","StateAbbreviation")
3    .withColumnRenamed("stateName","StateName")
4    .withColumnRenamed("summedTotalIncomeAmount","StateIncome")
5    .withColumnRenamed("batchId", "BatchID")
6  )
7  display(stateIncomeJDBCDF)
```

▶ (2) Spark Jobs

▶ 🔲 stateIncomeJDBCDF: pyspark.sql.dataframe.DataFrame = [StateAbbreviation: string, StateName: string ... 2 more fields]

StateAbbreviation	StateName	StateIncome	BatchID
DC	District Of Columbia	70880718	InteractiveMode - 582922
NC	North Carolina	585124592	InteractiveMode - 582922
SC	South Carolina	271325338	InteractiveMode - 582922
NH	New Hampshire	110973138	InteractiveMode - 582922
MA	Massachusetts	668708706	InteractiveMode - 582922
WV	West Virginia	81191332	InteractiveMode - 582922
RI	Rhode Island	73652196	InteractiveMode - 582922
PA	Pennsylvania	869460846	InteractiveMode - 582922

Figure 7.30 – Databricks Delta table data retrieved, column renamed, and BatchID added

11. Now, we're going to write the DataFrame to our SQL Server table. Type and run the following code in a new cell:

```
(stateIncomeJDBCDF.write.format("jdbc")
    .options(url=jdbcUrl,
            dbtable="[SalesLT].[IncomesPerState]")
    .mode("overwrite")
    .save()
)
```

12. The table is now loaded in SQL Server. To verify, we fill a new DataFrame with the SQL Server content. Type and run the following code in a new cell:

```
queryDF = "(SELECT StateAbbreviation, StateName,
StateIncome, BatchID \
 FROM [SalesLT].[IncomesPerState] ) prd"

sqlServerDF = spark.read.jdbc(url=jdbcUrl,
table=queryDF).orderBy("StateAbbreviation")
display(sqlServerDF)
```

We get a list as shown in the following screenshot:

```
1  queryDF = "(SELECT StateAbbreviation, StateName, StateIncome, BatchID \
2   FROM [SalesLT].[IncomesPerStates] ) prd"
3
4  sqlServerDF = spark.read.jdbc(url=jdbcUrl, table=queryDF).orderBy("StateAbbreviation")
5  display(sqlServerDF)
```

▶ (1) Spark Jobs
▶ 🔲 sqlServerDF: pyspark.sql.dataframe.DataFrame = [StateAbbreviation: string, StateName: string ... 2 more fields]

StateAbbreviation ▽	StateName ▽	StateIncome ▽	BatchID
AK	Alaska	48731000	InteractiveMode - 5829221
AL	Alabama	242070543	InteractiveMode - 5829221
ALL	AllStates	999999999	InteractiveMode - 5829221
AR	Arkansas	150339058	InteractiveMode - 5829221
AZ	Arizona	402494520	InteractiveMode - 5829221
CA	California	3131748846	InteractiveMode - 5829221
CO	Colorado	433405912	InteractiveMode - 5829221
CT	Connecticut	357292894	InteractiveMode - 5829221

Figure 7.31 – Databricks data retrieved from SQL Server

13. Now, let's count the number of rows. In a new cell, type and run the following code:

```
sqlServerDF.count()
```

We should get 52.

That's it! We wrote our Delta table to SQL Server.

How it works...

In this recipe, we used our Delta table created in the previous recipe, *Using Delta Lake*, and inserted its content into an Azure SQL Server table. We were able to retrieve a notebook current run ID to link the data inserted with the specific run ID of the notebook.

Java Database Connectivity (JDBC) is the key here. Almost all databases have a JDBC driver available. With it, we can read to and write from almost any database. Coupled with the fact that Databricks can read almost any storage, that makes it a tool of choice when it comes to using ETL in the cloud.

8
SSIS Migration Strategies

Many enterprises are in the process of migrating some of their on-premises **SQL Server Integration Services (SSIS)** solutions to the Azure cloud these days. There are lots of **Extract, Transform, Load (ETL)** to migrate and the cloud can represent a challenge on that front.

There are two basic strategies to migrate SSIS packages to Azure: run them as they are or re-write them. We'll explore both options in this chapter.

In this chapter, we will cover the following recipes:

- Running SSIS packages in ADF
- Rewriting an SSIS package using ADF

By the end of this chapter, you will have an understanding of how to handle SSIS package migration to Azure.

Running SSIS packages in ADF

Data Factory provides a way to run SSIS packages: SSIS integration runtimes. This recipe will teach you how to use it. This recipe shows you the steps to download the **Data Migration Assistant** (`https://www.microsoft.com/en-us/download/details.aspx?id=53595#:~:text=Data%20Migration%20Assistant%20%28DMA%29%20enables%20you%20to%20upgrade,performance%20and%20reliability%20improvements%20for%20your%20target%20environment`). At the time of writing, the Data Migration Assistant does not support SSIS 2019. Even if we could use it, it's always good to know how to do those steps manually.

To run the SSIS package in Azure, we need to set up a few things:

- Create an SSIS catalog in Azure SQL Database.
- Deploy SSIS packages to it.
- Run SSIS packages.

Getting ready

This recipe assumes that you have a valid Azure subscription and have knowledge of **ADF** (**ADF**). It also assumes that you have read and completed the recipes of *Chapter 4, Azure Data Integration*, as we'll use the packages developed in that chapter.

How to do it...

Let's dive into our SSIS migration journey!

1. We will first create an SSIS integration runtime in our factory. Open your browser and navigate to the Azure portal.

2. Go to the factory we created in *Chapter 6, ADF*. Open it by clicking on **Author & Monitor**.

3. Go to the **Management** tab and select **Integration Runtimes**. This SSIS integration runtime will set up an SSIS catalog and start **Virtual Machines (VMs)** that will run our SSIS packages. Click on **+ New**. A blade should appear on the right side of your browser. As shown in the following screenshot, select an **Azure-SSIS** integration runtime and click on **Continue**:

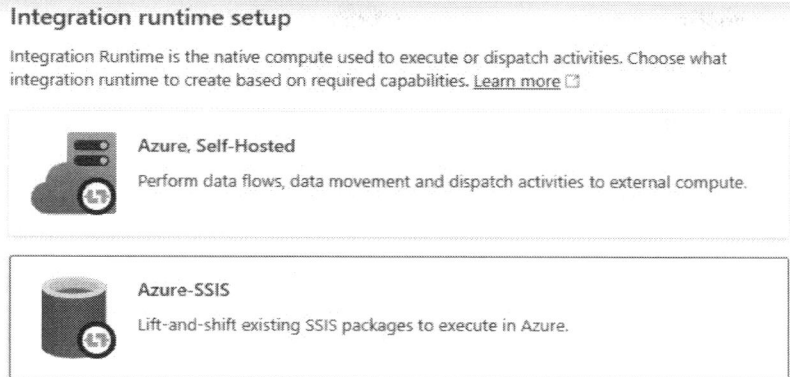

Figure 8.1 – Select an Azure-SSIS integration runtime

4. Set **Name** to **SSIS-IR**, and **Location** to your desired location. Set **Node size** to the smallest value and **Node number** to **1**. We'll use the standard SSIS license. If you have a valid SQL Server license, set the **Save money** option to **Yes** as shown in the following screenshot. Click **Continue**:

Figure 8.2 – Azure-SSIS integration runtime General settings blade

5. The **Deployment settings** blade allows us to select the Azure database where we want to deploy our SSIS catalog: `AdventureWorksLT`, the one we created in *Chapter 2, Introducing ETL*. Fill out the information and test your connection. Click on **Continue** when done:

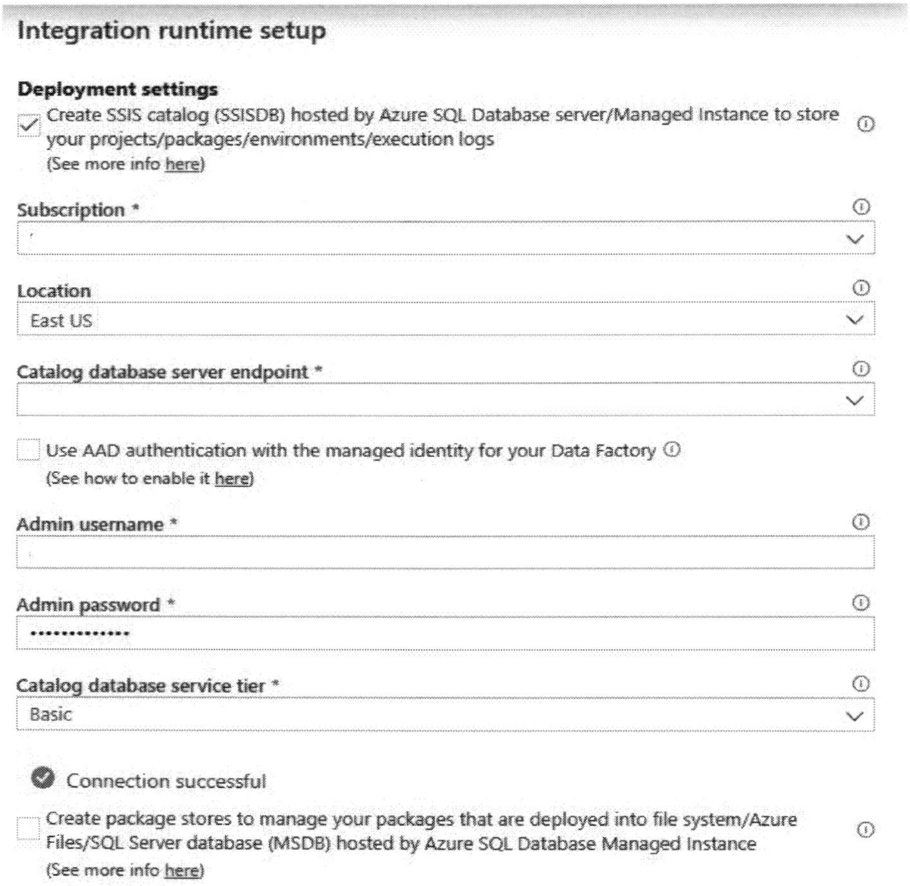

Integration runtime setup

Deployment settings
☑ Create SSIS catalog (SSISDB) hosted by Azure SQL Database server/Managed Instance to store ⓘ your projects/packages/environments/execution logs
(See more info here)

Subscription *   ⓘ

Location   ⓘ
East US

Catalog database server endpoint *   ⓘ

☐ Use AAD authentication with the managed identity for your Data Factory ⓘ
(See how to enable it here)

Admin username *   ⓘ

Admin password *   ⓘ
•••••••••••••

Catalog database service tier *   ⓘ
Basic

✓ Connection successful

☐ Create package stores to manage your packages that are deployed into file system/Azure ⓘ Files/SQL Server database (MSDB) hosted by Azure SQL Database Managed Instance
(See more info here)

Figure 8.3 – Azure-SSIS integration runtime Deployment settings blade

6. In the **Advanced settings** blade, leave the default values as shown in the following screenshot. We will not run too many packages at a time, so having **Maximum parallel executions per node** as **2** is OK, especially since we are choosing to use only one node in the general settings. The three other options refer to the installation of a third-party component, integrating into an enterprise network (**VNet**), and using a proxy to scale and secure the SSIS integrated runtime. We're not using any of these options. Click on **Continue**:

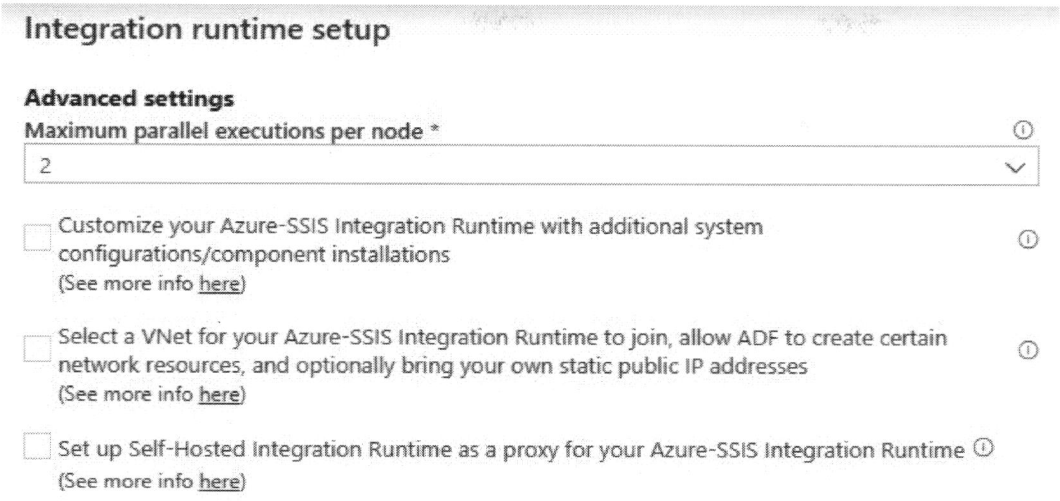

Integration runtime setup

Advanced settings

Maximum parallel executions per node *   ⓘ

> 2   ⌄

Customize your Azure-SSIS Integration Runtime with additional system   ⓘ
configurations/component installations
(See more info here)

Select a VNet for your Azure-SSIS Integration Runtime to join, allow ADF to create certain   ⓘ
network resources, and optionally bring your own static public IP addresses
(See more info here)

Set up Self-Hosted Integration Runtime as a proxy for your Azure-SSIS Integration Runtime ⓘ
(See more info here)

Figure 8.4 – Azure-SSIS integration runtime Advanced settings blade

7. Finally, the **Summary** blade shows us the various settings we have set. As
    highlighted in the following screenshot, we can review the most important settings
    and click on **Create** to create the Azure SSIS integration runtime:

Integration runtime setup

Summary
Your Azure-SSIS Integration Runtime (IR) is created with the following settings:

Azure Data Factory Settings
* **Subscription:** .
* **Resource group:** ETLInAzure
* **Name:**
* **Location:** eastus

General settings
* **Name:** SSIS-IR
* **Location:** East US
* **Node size:** Standard_D2_v3
* **Node number:** 1
* **Edition:** Standard
* **Azure Hybrid Benefit:** BasePrice

Deployment settings
* **Catalog database server endpoint:**
* **Catalog database server location:** East US
* **Catalog database service tier:** Basic

Advanced settings
* **Maximum parallel executions per node:** 2
* If you need to access data on premises, click **Previous** to do any of the followings:
    o Join your Azure-SSIS IR to a VNet connected to your on-premises network OR
    o Set up Self-Hosted Integration Runtime as a proxy for your Azure-SSIS Integration
      Runtime

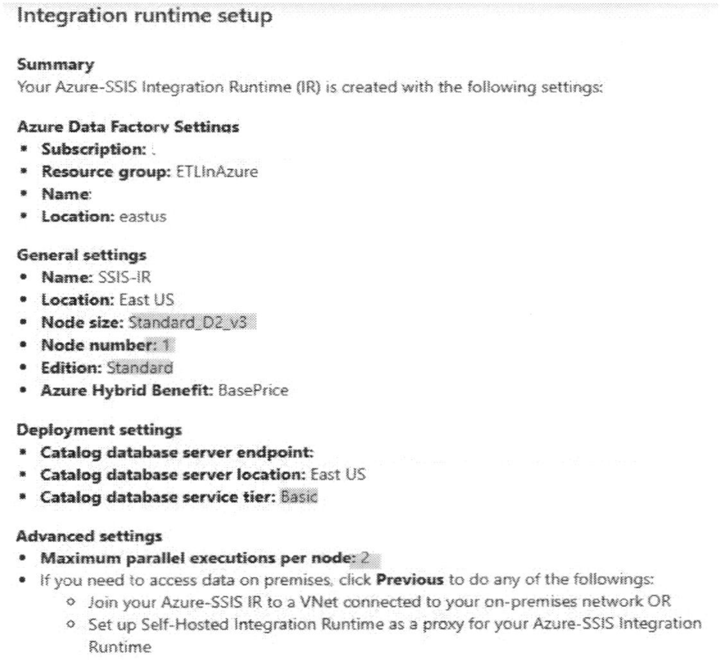

Figure 8.5 – Azure-SSIS integration runtime Summary blade

8. Creating the SSIS catalog and starting VMs can take up to 30 minutes. Once created, you should see the following information in the **Management** tab:

Figure 8.6 – Azure-SSIS integration runtime running

9. Now that our catalog is ready, let's connect to it. Start **SQL Server Management Studio (SSMS)**. Type your Azure SQL **Server name**, and enter the **Login** and **Password** information. Before connecting, click on **Options** as shown in the following screenshot:

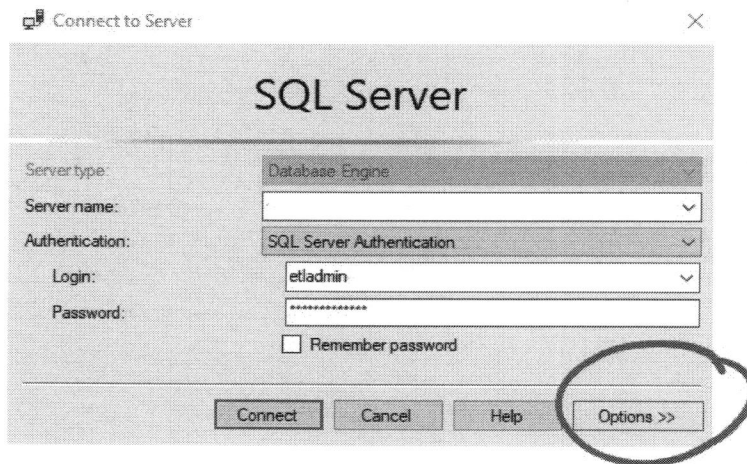

Figure 8.7 – Connect to the Azure SSIS catalog

10. As shown in the following screenshot, type **SSISDB** in the **Connect to database** property and click on **Connect**:

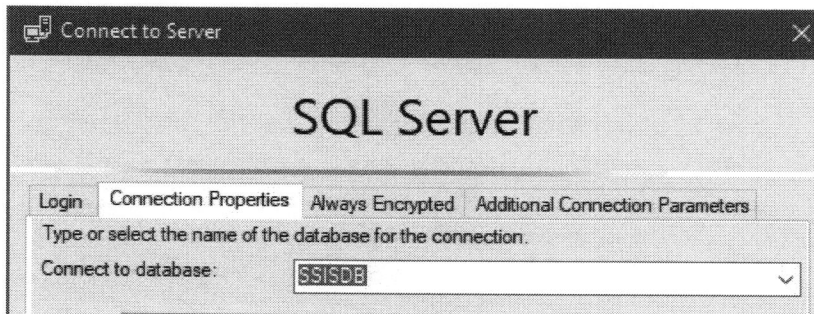

Figure 8.8 – Connect to the Azure SSIS catalog

11. In SSMS Object Explorer, right-click on **SSISDB** under **Integration Services Catalogs** and select **Create Folder...** from the submenu that appears, as shown in the following screenshot. Type **ETLInAzure** as the folder name:

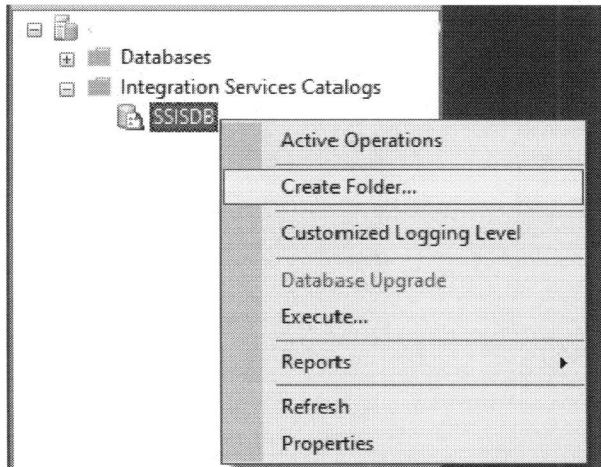

Figure 8.9 – Azure SSIS catalog – Create Folder

12. Once the folder is created, we can see it created as well as two subfolders, as shown in the following screenshot:

Figure 8.10 – Azure SSIS catalog – folder created

13. It's now time to deploy the SSIS project we created in *Chapter 4, Azure Data Integration*. Start Visual Studio and select the Chapter 4 project. In Solution Explorer, right-click on the project and select **Deploy**.

14. On the **Select Deployment Target** page, we have two options. Since we already created our SSIS integration runtime, we can either choose **SSIS in SQL Server** or **SSIS in ADF**. The latter allows you to create a factory and an Azure-SSIS integration runtime on the go. The only issue with it is that you cannot specify a specific resource group/factory combination. SSIS creates random resource groups and factories for you. Since we know what data factory to use and we've created an Azure SSIS integration runtime, we will use the first option. Click **Next**:

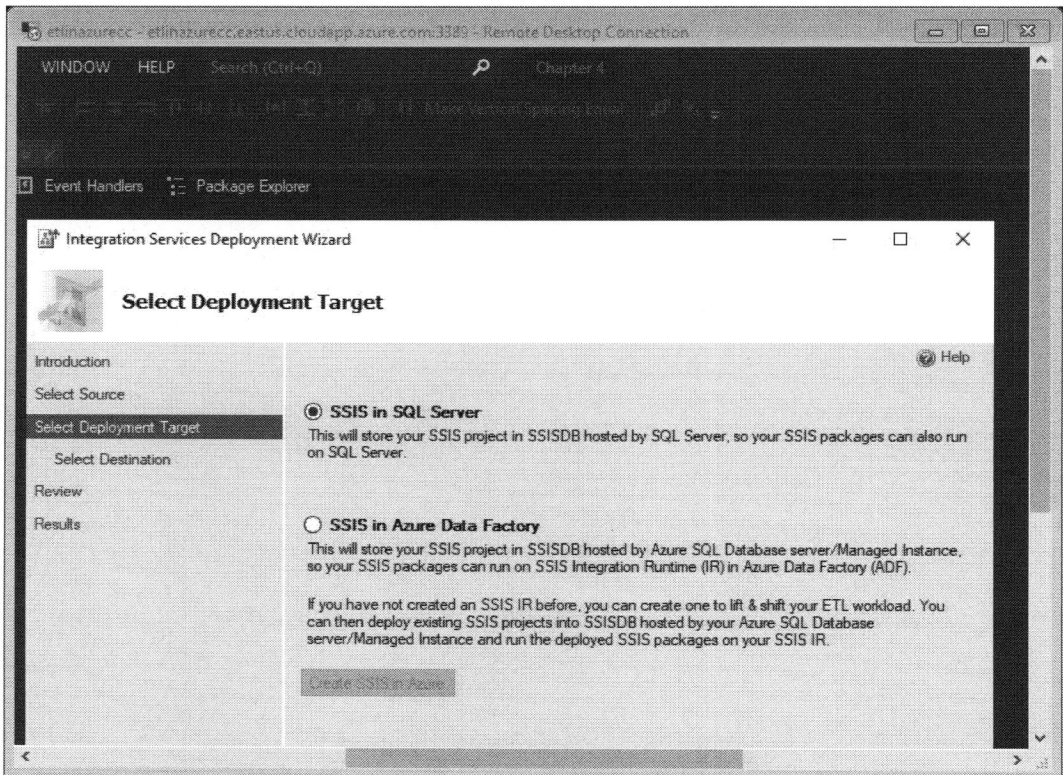

Figure 8.11 – Deploy an SSIS project

15. On the **Select Destination** page, type your Azure SSIS catalog **Server name**, **Login**, and **Password** details and click on **Connect** to connect to the catalog. Once connected, select a **path** to deploy the packages as shown in the following screenshot. Click **Next**:

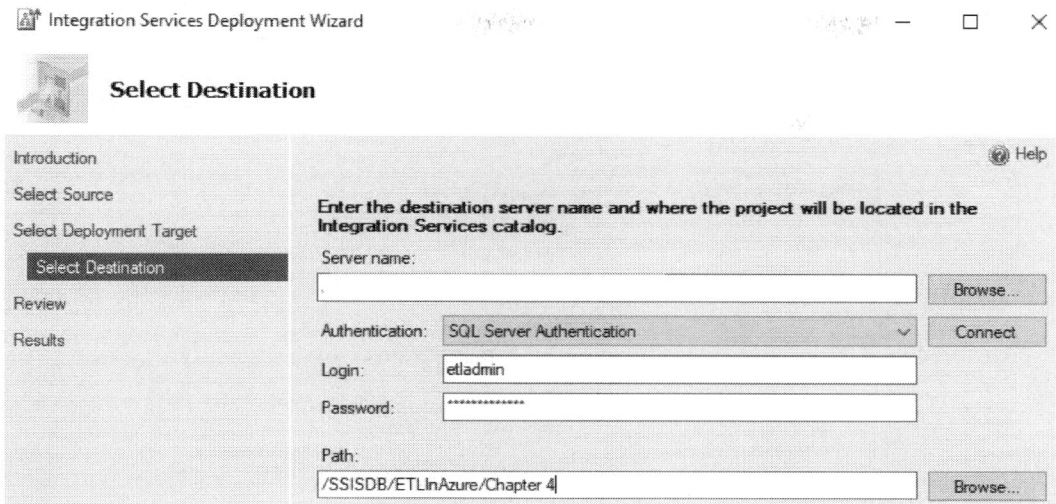

Figure 8.12 – Deploy an SSIS project – Select Destination

16. Review the summary and click on **Deploy** to deploy the project to the SSIS catalog on Azure SQL Server.

17. Once deployed, go back to SSMS. Refresh the **Integration Services Catalog** nodes and expand it up to the package levels. You should see that we have two packages deployed: **HiveSSIS.dstx** and **PigSSIS.dtsx**.

18. As shown in the following screenshot, right-click on the project and select **Configure...** from the contextual menu that appears:

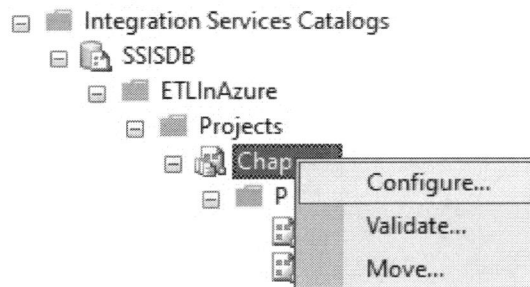

Figure 8.13 – Configure option

19. We want to configure the connection string of the on-premises connection manager **cmgr_ContonsoRetailDW** to use a fully qualified server name. In our case, the database sits on an Azure VM server, so we will add **<region>.cloudapp.database. net**. This information can be found in SSMS when you connect to your database: it's the server name. If you are using an on-premises database server, you do not need to alter the connection string. The connection string should look like the one shown in the following screenshot:

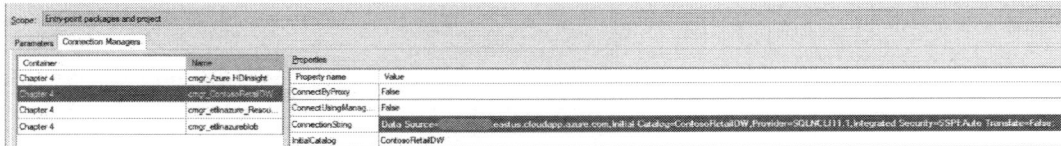

Figure 8.14 – Configure the cmgr_ContonsoRetailDW connection string

20. By default, when we install SQL Server on a development machine, the **TCP/IP** protocol is disabled. We are going to enable it. Open SQL Server 2019 Configuration Manager. As shown in the following screenshot, make sure that the **TCIP/IP** protocol is enabled. If not, right-click on it and select **Enable**:

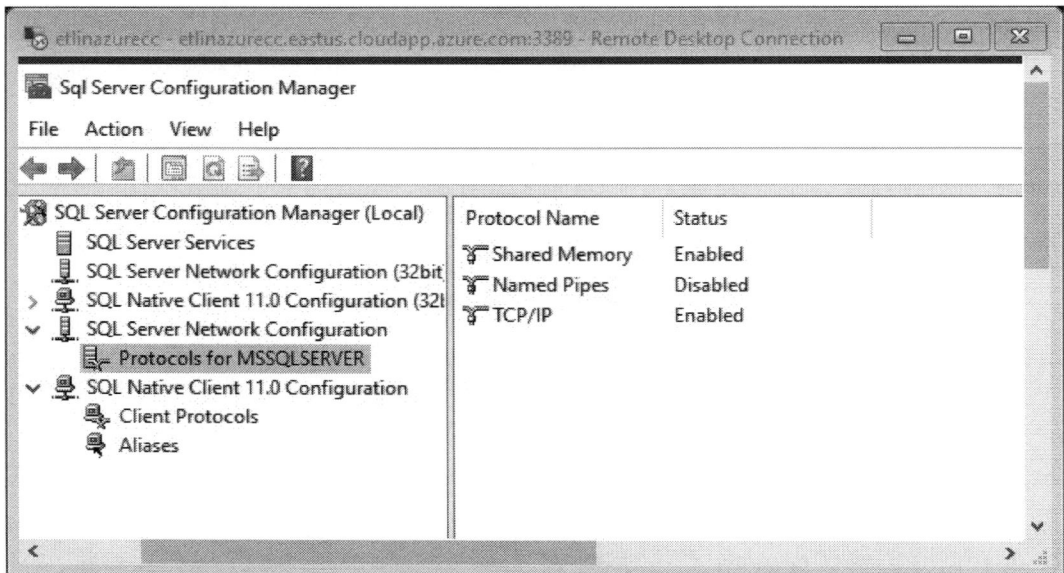

Figure 8.15 – Configure the TCP/IP network protocol

21. Restart **SQL Server Services** to enable the TCP/IP protocol.

Next, make sure that there's an inbound rule in your Windows firewall that allows SQL Server to be available to the outside world. In a production scenario, we would join our Azure-SSIS integration runtime to the network by specifying a VNet in the advanced settings at its creation. The following link shows you how to use on-premises SQL Server with the ADF Azure-SSIS integration runtime: `https://` `docs.microsoft.com/en-us/azure/data-factory/ssis-azure-` `connect-with-windows-auth#provide-domain-credentials-for-` `windows-authentication`.

22. Now, let's execute our packages from Azure SQL Server. We will try it from there because our data factory will call the same execution. Testing it from Azure SQL is faster, and we will not have to wait for the ADF status to change if a package execution fails. We're going to try the Hive package first. In SSMS, right-click on the **HiveSSIS.dtsx** package and select **Execute**. Click on **OK** to execute the package and open the execution report when asked.

23. The package fails to execute because the Azure-SSIS integration runtimes are missing the Java JRE that allows us to use the parquet format. Let's leave it like that for now and execute the `PigSSIS` package. Right-click on the **PigSSIS.dtsx** package and execute it.

24. As shown in the following screenshot, the package executes successfully:

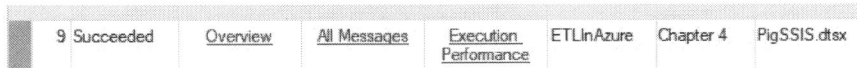

Figure 8.16 – PigSSIS execution success

25. Now that we know that the `PigSSIS` package executes correctly, let's call it from our data factory. Go back into it and add a new pipeline. Call it **PipelineSSISPIG**. Add an **Execute SSIS package** activity to it and name it **PIG**. Set the **Settings** tab's properties as shown in the following screenshot:

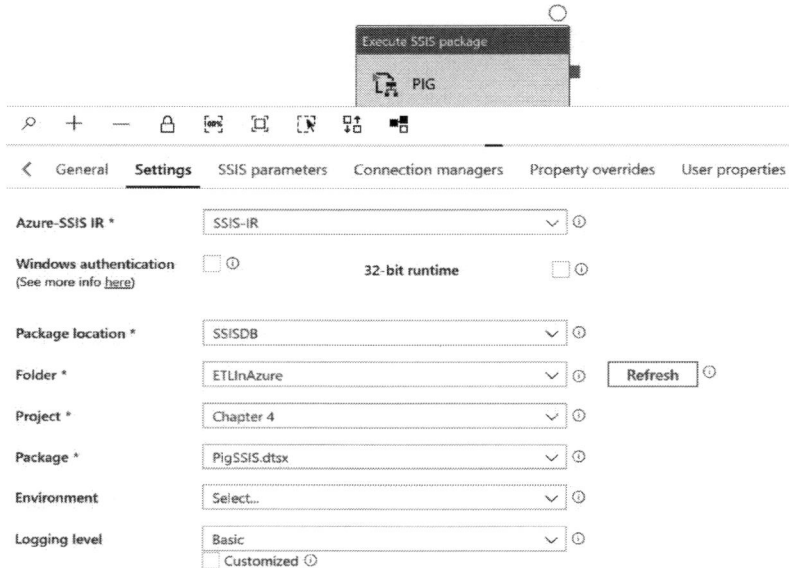

Figure 8.17 – Executing the SSIS PIG package

26. Most of these properties are selected via a drop-down list. Now, click on **Debug** at the top of the pipeline to execute the pipeline in the debug environment. After a while, the pipeline will be executed with success, as shown in the following screenshot:

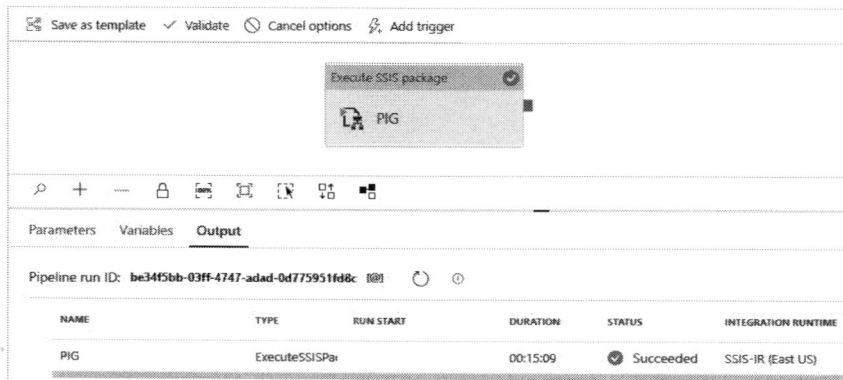

Figure 8.18 – Execute SSIS package success

27. Since the Azure-SSIS integration runtime is costly, we will now stop it as we're finished with it. Go to the **Management** tab of the factory and click on **Integration runtimes** to open its blade. As shown in the following screenshot, stop the **SSIS-IR** integration runtime to **Stop** the VMs (nodes) that execute our packages:

Figure 8.19 – Stop the SSIS-IR integration runtime

28. In a production scenario, we would start the Azure-SSIS integration runtime, execute the SSIS packages, and stop the integration runtime when not used. There is a template just for that scenario. Click on the **Data Factory** tab on the left of your browser window. As shown in the following screenshot, select **Create pipeline from template**:

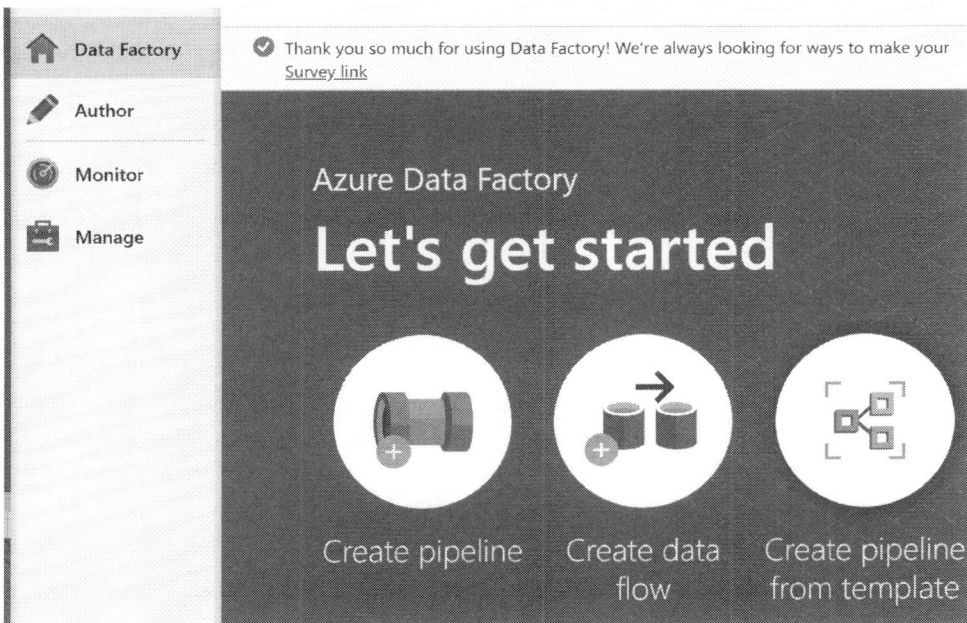

Figure 8.20 – Create pipeline from template

29. From the blade that opens, select **SSIS** in the **Filter** pane. A template called **Schedule ADF pipeline to start and stop Azure-SSIS IR...** is displayed as shown in the following screenshot. Click on it:

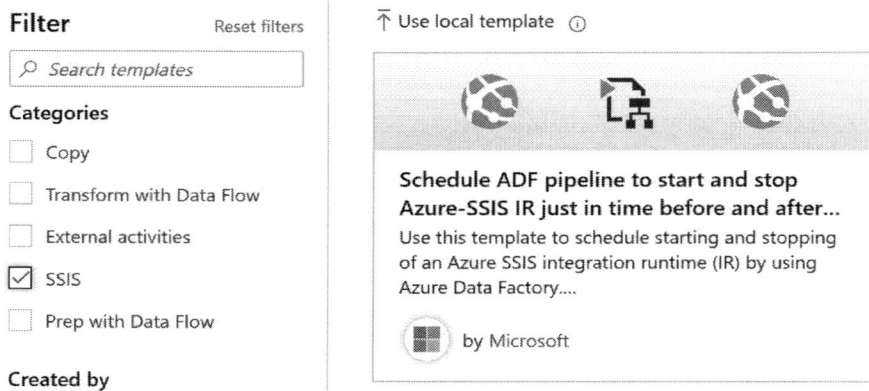

Figure 8.21 – Select template

30. Another blade opens and asks us to select the **Azure-SSIS integration runtime**. As shown in the following screenshot, select **SSIS-IR** and click on **Use this template**:

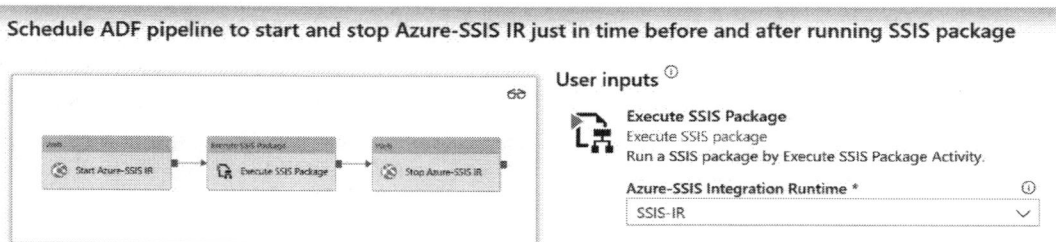

Figure 8.22 – SSIS-IR template preparation

31. Once the pipeline is created, rename it **Pipeline Start-Stop-Azure-SSIS IR SSIS PIG**. Set the **Execute SSIS package** activity name to **PIG** and its properties as we did before, as shown in the following screenshot:

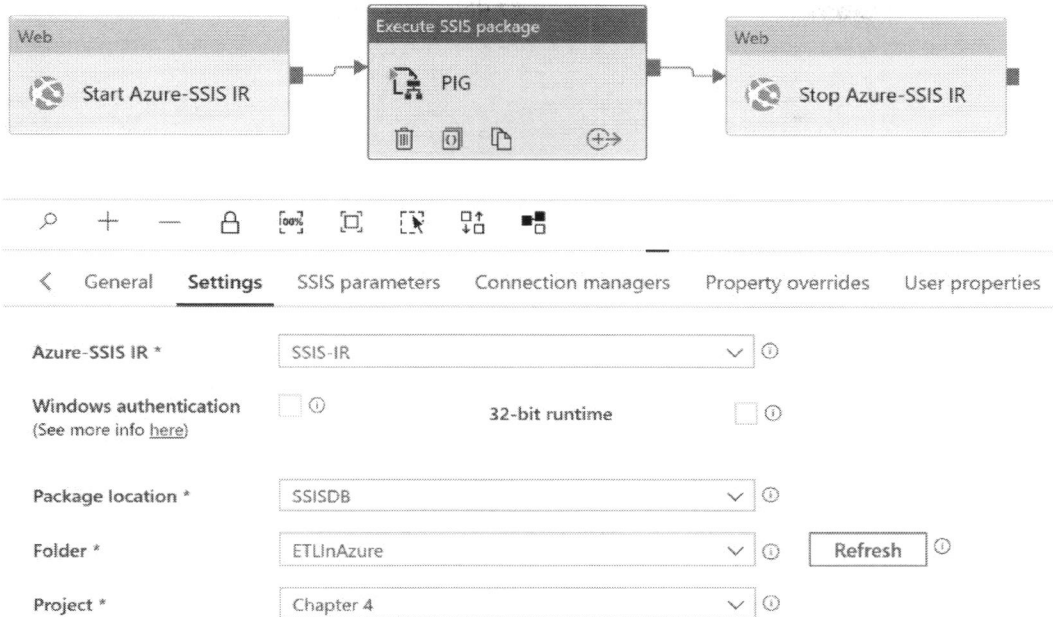

Figure 8.23 – SSIS-IR from the template

32. Now, for the web activity to be able to start and stop **SSIS-IR**, we need to assign our factory as a contributor to itself. In the Azure portal, go to the factory and select the **Access Control (IAM)** tab. Add a new role and assign the factory as a contributor, as shown in the following screenshot. Click on **Save**:

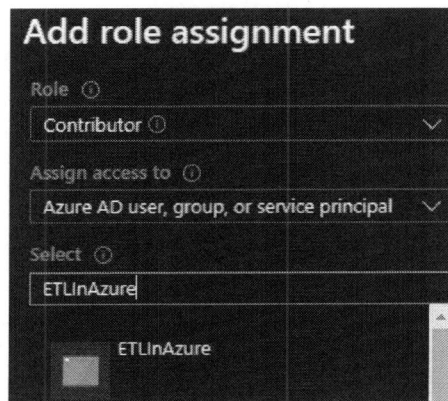

Figure 8.24 – Add a Contributor role to the factory

33. Now, we can run our pipeline. Click on **Debug** at the top of the pipeline. **SSIS-IR** will be started and the **PigSSIS** package starts as shown in the following screenshot. After the package execution has completed, **SSIS-IR** will be stopped:

NAME	TYPE	RUN START	DURATION	STATUS	INTEGRATION RUNTIME	RUN ID
Stop Azure-SSIS IR	WebActivity		00:08:09	Succeeded	DefaultIntegrationRuntime (East US)	58bbbd6b-0da8-41f9-946
PIG	ExecuteSSISPac		00:14:53	Succeeded	SSIS-IR (East US)	9dc265a0-5a0e-4b5b-b9c
Start Azure-SSIS IR	WebActivity		00:01:20	Succeeded	DefaultIntegrationRuntime (East US)	f18b9969-9f76-4993-8d90

Figure 8.25 – Pipeline executing

34. Now that we have made a few new objects, it's a good time to publish them. Click on the **Publish** button at the top of the pipeline to deploy all our changes.

We've just executed an SSIS package in the cloud!

How it works...

Running SSIS packages in Azure requires a data factory with an Azure-SSIS integration runtime. This gives us an **Integration Services** catalog in an Azure database and provides us with scalable VMs to execute our packages. Because those VMs are scalable, we can use up to 10 nodes in parallel and they can have 432 GB of RAM. This gives us lots of flexibility when it comes to executing SSIS packages in Azure. The costs can be mitigated by starting and stopping our Azure-SSIS integration runtime only when needed, that is, when we must execute our SSIS packages.

Once we've created this integration runtime, it is possible to deploy packages to it. We first connected to it in SSMS and created a folder for our project. We then deployed the packages in it and executed them from ADF.

SSIS will still be around for a few years. There are numerous third parties that have developed useful components over the past two decades that are not available in Azure yet. Having the possibility to use SSIS in an Azure pipeline gives us more flexibility when it comes to designing cloud ETL or **Extract, Load, Transform (ELT)** solutions.

Rewriting an SSIS package using ADF

From the last recipe, there was one package that did not run – `HiveSSIS.dtsx`. This was due to the fact that a component was missing in the basic SSIS integration runtime setup: the **Java Runtime Environment** (**JRE**). We could have tried to install it but since the package is quite simple, we will re-write it in the data factory.

We have several options:

- We can still use Hive in HDInsight to transform the data. This would be fast and would be the right choice if the transformation logic was complex, and we had a tight deadline. ADF has a Hive activity as well as an HDInsight cluster compute connector. So, this solution could be a valid choice. But there are cons to it as it requires Hadoop technology that can be much slower than the new kid on the block: Spark. It also makes it harder to debug as HDInsight error messages can sometimes be complex to analyze.

- Since the Hive logic is simple, we can re-write it using an ADF mapping data flow. This will allow us to expose the transformation logic using specific transformations and therefore ease the maintenance as it would be as if we were using a single technology, ADF. Also, we would leverage Spark clusters, which can be faster complex transformations, compared to Hadoop.

Both choices have one common obstacle; we insert rows into on-premises databases. From an Azure point of view, it's not automatic. But Data Factory has something for that: self-hosted integration runtimes. They allow Data Factory to access on-premises resources by using a special gateway that will allow ADF to interact with on-premises resources in a secure manner.

This recipe will teach you how to do the following:

- Create and set up a self-hosted integration runtime to access an on-premises database from the data factory.

- Refactor our HDInsight Hive package to use ADF capabilities such as a mapping data flow.

Getting ready

This recipe assumes that you have a valid Azure subscription and have knowledge of ADF. It also assumes that you have read and completed the previous recipe in this chapter, *Running SSIS packages in ADF*, and that you also created the data factory in *Chapter 6, ADF*.

How to do it...

Let's now re-write our `HiveSSIS` package using ADF!

1. Open the **ETLInADF** and go to the **Management** tab. Select **Integration Runtimes** and click on **+ New** to open the **Integration runtime setup** blade. As shown in the following screenshot, select **Azure, Self-Hosted** and click on **Continue**:

Integration runtime setup

Integration Runtime is the native compute used to execute or dispatch activities. Choose what integration runtime to create based on required capabilities. Learn more

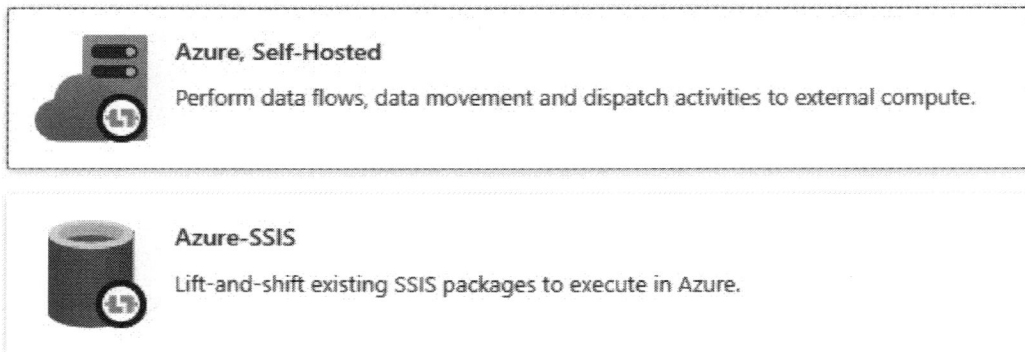

Azure, Self-Hosted

Perform data flows, data movement and dispatch activities to external compute.

Azure-SSIS

Lift-and-shift existing SSIS packages to execute in Azure.

Figure 8.26 – Azure, Self-Hosted selection pane

2. The next blade asks us whether we want to create an Azure or on-premises **Self-Hosted Integration Runtime (SHIR)**. Notice that there is also an option to use an existing SHIR. Since we have not created an SHIR so far, let's select the **Self-Hosted** option as shown in the following screenshot. Click on **Continue**:

Integration runtime setup

Network environment:

Choose the network environment of the data source / destination or external compute to which the integration runtime will connect to for data flows, data movement or dispatch activities:

Azure

Use this for running data flows, data movement, external and pipeline activities in a fully managed, serverless compute in Azure.

Self-Hosted

Use this for running activities in an on-premise / private network
View more ⌄

External Resources:

You can use an existing self-hosted integration runtime that exists in another resource. This way you can reuse your existing infrastructure where self-hosted integration runtime is setup.

Linked Self-Hosted

Learn more 🗗

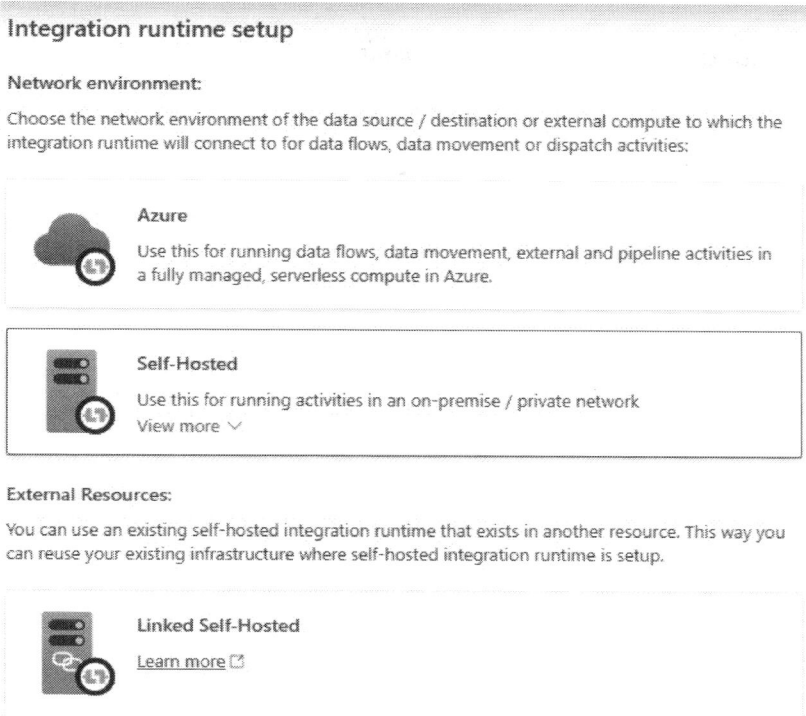

Figure 8.27 – Azure, Self-Hosted selection

3.   The name of the SHIR is not that important. In our case, we'll name it using the name of the data we want to work with: Contonso Data Warehouse. As shown in the following screenshot, we'll use **ContonsoDW** for the name. Click on **Create**:

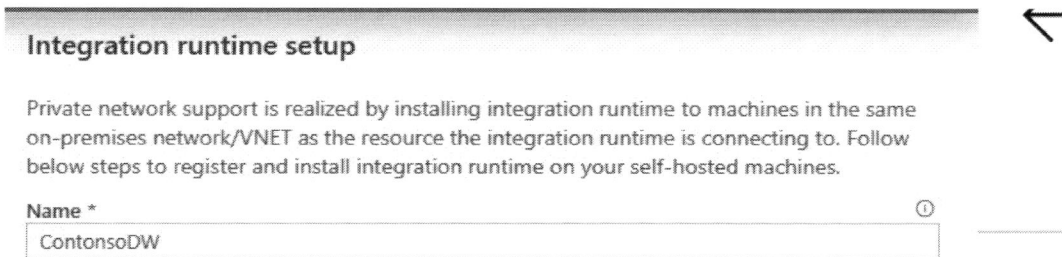

Integration runtime setup

Private network support is realized by installing integration runtime to machines in the same on-premises network/VNET as the resource the integration runtime is connecting to. Follow below steps to register and install integration runtime on your self-hosted machines.

Name *   ⓘ

| ContonsoDW |

Figure 8.28 – Naming the SHIR

4. The SHIR is now created. We will now install the Windows software that will act as a gateway between ADF and our on-premises network. We usually use a Windows VM that has access to our on-premises resource – in our case, the database. It can be on-premises or in Azure. In our case, we're installing the SHIR software on the same machine we installed the on-premises database on. As shown in the following screenshot, we're using **Option 1: Express setup**. **Option 2** would be used to download the SHIR software and install it on another machine. Click on the highlighted link to start the SHIR setup on your PC:

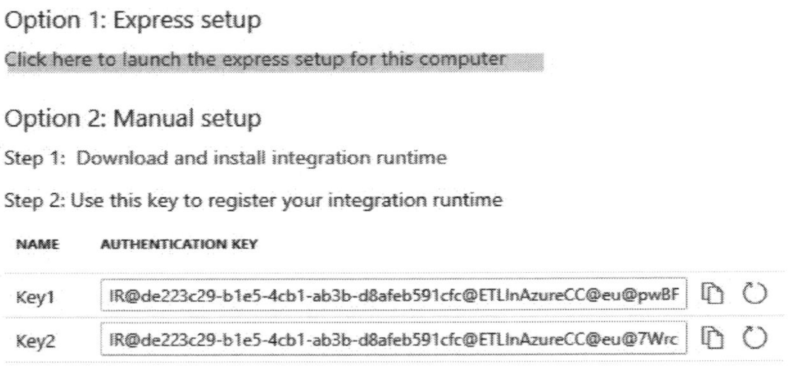

Option 1: Express setup

Click here to launch the express setup for this computer

Option 2: Manual setup

Step 1: Download and install integration runtime

Step 2: Use this key to register your integration runtime

NAME	AUTHENTICATION KEY		
Key1	IR@de223c29-b1e5-4cb1-ab3b-d8afeb591cfc@ETLInAzureCC@eu@pwBF	⧉	↻
Key2	IR@de223c29-b1e5-4cb1-ab3b-d8afeb591cfc@ETLInAzureCC@eu@7Wrc	⧉	↻

Figure 8.29 – Express SHIR setup

5. The SHIR will download and install as shown in the following screenshot. Click on **Close** once completed:

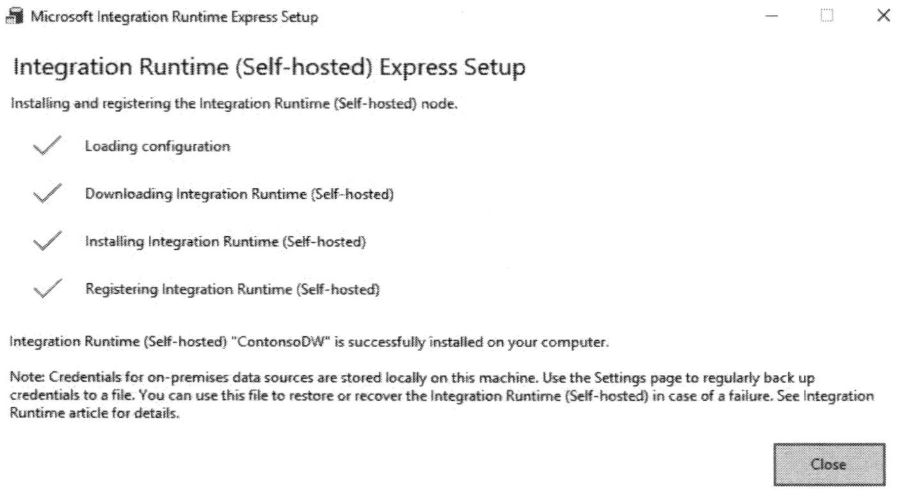

Microsoft Integration Runtime Express Setup   — □ ✕

Integration Runtime (Self-hosted) Express Setup

Installing and registering the Integration Runtime (Self-hosted) node.

✓ Loading configuration

✓ Downloading Integration Runtime (Self-hosted)

✓ Installing Integration Runtime (Self-hosted)

✓ Registering Integration Runtime (Self-hosted)

Integration Runtime (Self-hosted) "ContonsoDW" is successfully installed on your computer.

Note: Credentials for on-premises data sources are stored locally on this machine. Use the Settings page to regularly back up credentials to a file. You can use this file to restore or recover the Integration Runtime (Self-hosted) in case of a failure. See Integration Runtime article for details.

Close

Figure 8.30 – Express SHIR setup completed

6. We click on **Close** on the SHIR setup screen as we will not configure any other options for this recipe.

7. Make sure that the SHIR is up and running as shown in the following screenshot:

Figure 8.31 – ADF SHIR up and running

8. We will now use this SHIR to create a linked service to our on-premises SQL Server database. From the **Management** tab, click on **Linked Services** and then **+ New** to create a **New linked service**.

9. From the **New linked service** blade, type **sql** in the search textbox and select **SQL Server** as shown in the following screenshot. Click on **Continue**:

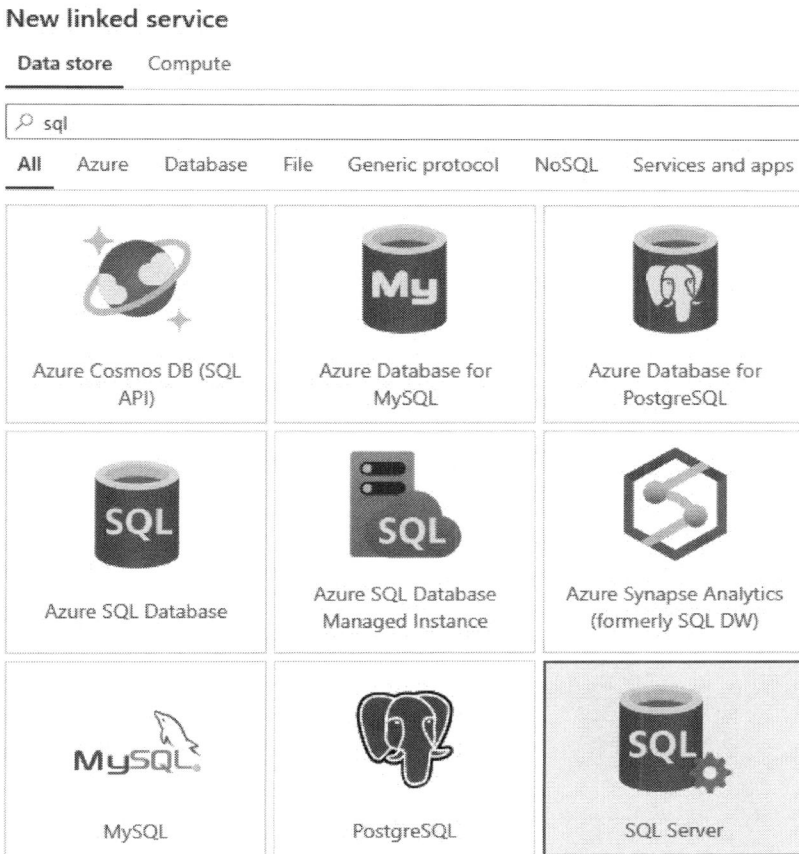

Figure 8.32 – ADF linked service SQL Server on-premises

10. On the next blade, use **LNK_ContonsoDW** for **Name** and select the **ContonsoDW** linked service. Fill in the other properties as shown in the following screenshot. Click on **Test connection** to ensure that the connection is working and then **Create** to create the linked service:

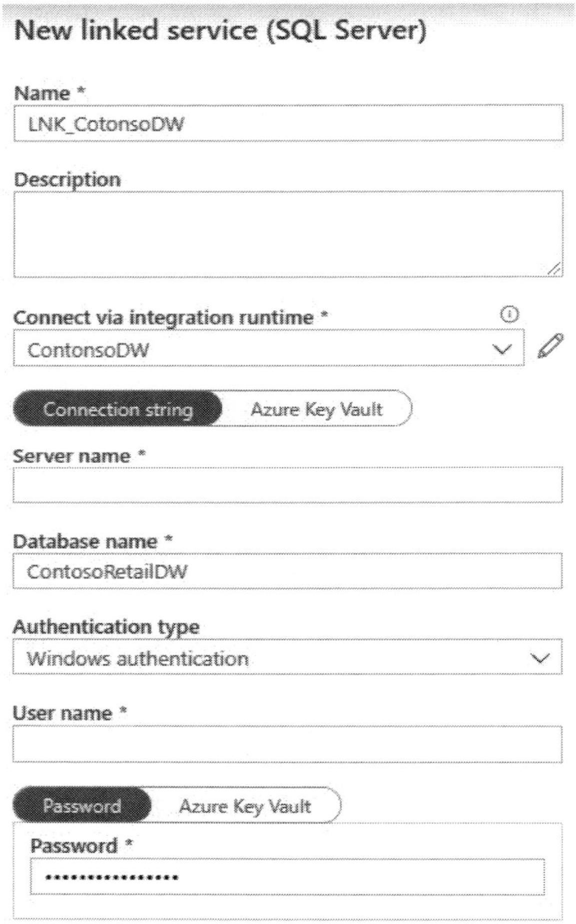

Figure 8.33 – ADF linked service SQL Server on-premises creation

11. Confirm that the **LNK_ContonsoDW** linked service is created as shown in the following screenshot:

Figure 8.34 – ADF linked service SQL Server on-premises created

12. We will now add a pipeline that will copy data from the on-premises SQL Server to our Azure storage account, transform the data, and copy it back to the on-premises SQL Server databases. Basically, the same steps we used for the `HiveSSIS` package, except that we have fewer steps involved since ADF will take care of the compute resource as we're leveraging the **Mapping** data flow to transform the data instead of HDInsight, as done in the SSIS package.

13. Go to the **Pipeline** tab and add a new pipeline to the factory. Name it **PipelineAggregateContonsoRetailDW**. Drag a **copy activity** onto it and name it **Copy_FactSalesData**. Go to the **Source** tab and click on + **New** at the right of the **Source dataset** property to create a new dataset. As shown in the following screenshot, select **SQL Server** as the dataset type. Click **Continue**:

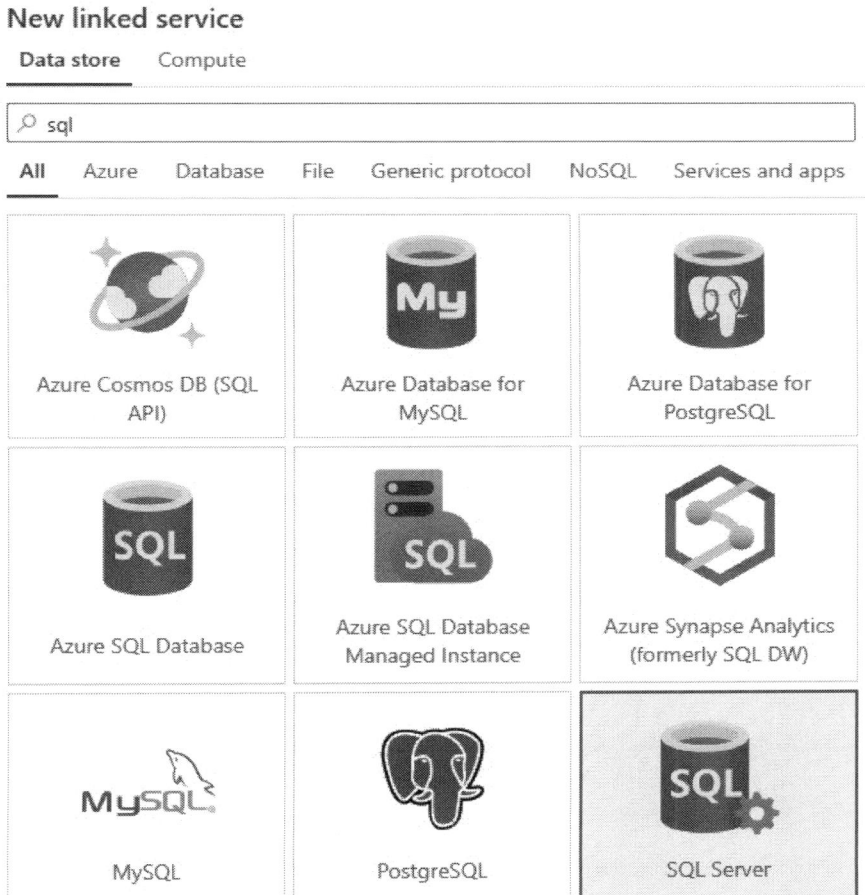

Figure 8.35 – ADF dataset SQL Server on-premises selection

14. Name the dataset **FactSales** and select the **LNK_ContonsoDW** linked service. Leave both the **Table name** and **Import schema** properties as **None** as shown in the following screenshot. Click on **Create**:

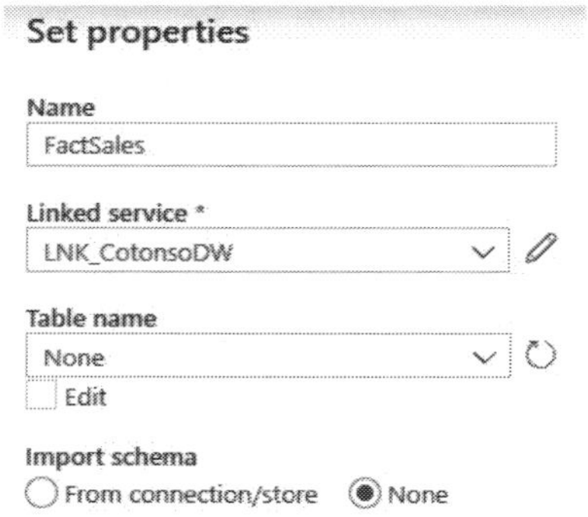

Figure 8.36 – ADF dataset SQL Server on-premises creation

15. Back to the **Copy_FactSales** activity in the pipeline, select **Query** as **Use query**, and type the following SQL statement in the **Query** textbox:

```
SELECT    s.StoreName, s.ZipCode, d.FullDateLabel,
f.UnitCost, f.UnitPrice, f.SalesAmount, f.SalesQuantity,
d.CalendarMonth
FROM      FactSales AS f INNER JOIN
          DimDate AS d ON f.DateKey = d.Datekey INNER JOIN
          DimStore AS s ON f.StoreKey = s.StoreKey
WHERE     (d.CalendarYear = 2009) AND (CAST(RIGHT(d.
CalendarMonth, 2) AS int) < 6)
```

16. Your screen should look like the following screenshot. You can click on **Preview data** to see a sample of the data returned by the query and test whether the connections are working properly:

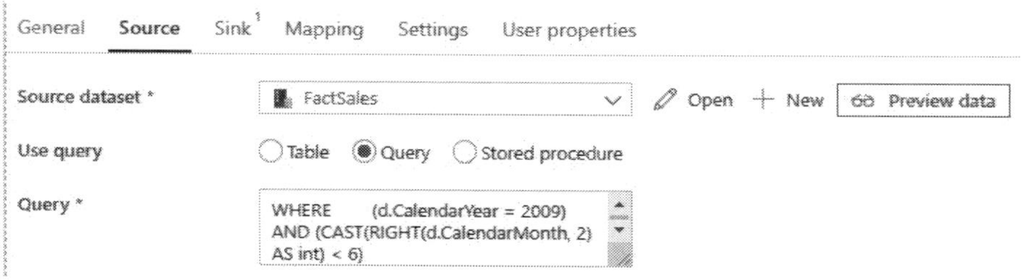

Figure 8.37 – ADF copy activity Source preview

17. Go to the **Sink** tab. Create a new dataset to copy source data to our storage account. Name it **FactSalesParquet**, and use the **LNK_ETLInAzure** link service we created in *Chapter 6*, *ADF*. The format of the file is parquet. Make sure that you set the path as shown in the following screenshot:

Figure 8.38 – ADF copy activity Sink dataset

18. Back to the **Copy_FactSales** activity, click on the **Mapping** tab and import the schemas. You should now see the schema imported as shown in the following screenshot:

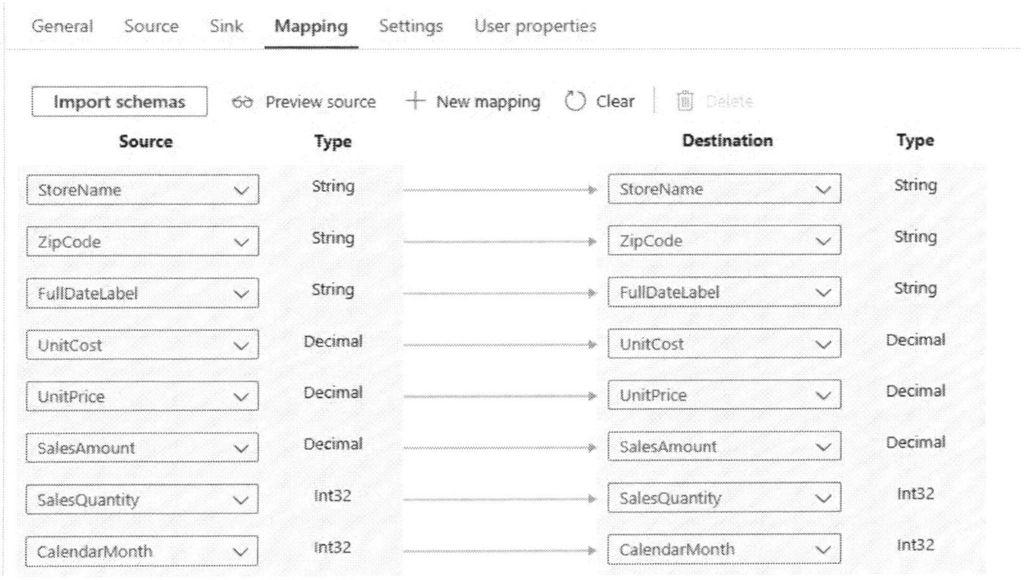

Figure 8.39 – ADF copy activity mappings imported

19. Now, let's copy the data. Click on **Debug** to test our copy activity. After a few seconds, the data should be copied into the storage account as shown in the following screenshot:

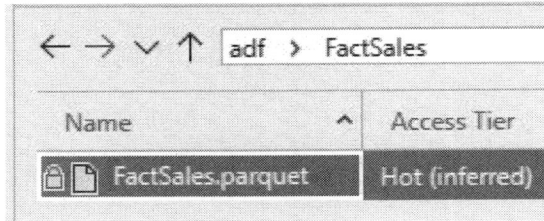

Figure 8.40 – ADF copy activity success run

20. Now, let's add a **Data Flow** activity to the pipeline. Select **Mapping Data Flow** and name it **DFT_SalesAgg**. Click on **Add Source**, name it **FactSalesParquet,** and select **FactSalesParquet** as the dataset. You should have a screen like the following screenshot:

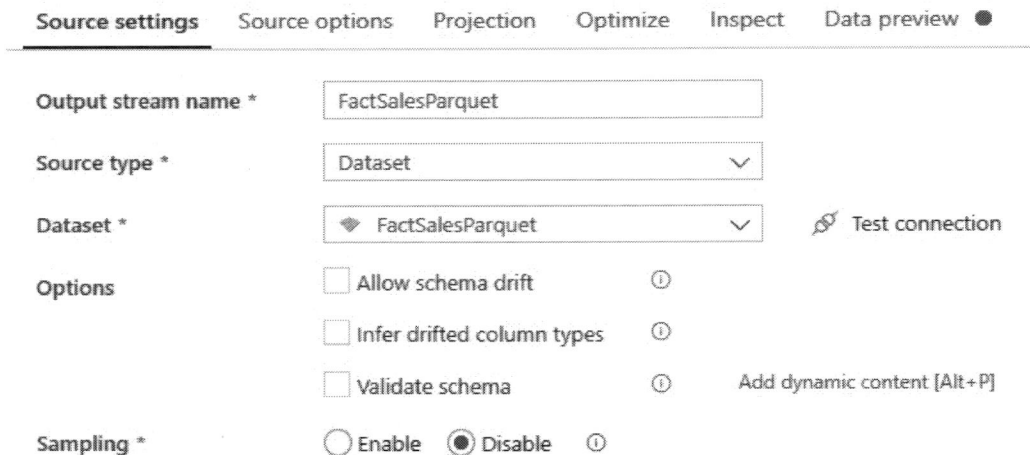

Figure 8.41 – ADF DFT Source settings

21. Make sure the **Data flow debug** option is running at the top of the factory as shown in the following screenshot. If the debugger is not running, start it. It might take several minutes to start:

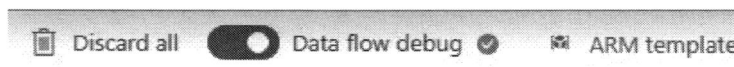

Figure 8.42 – ADF DFT Data flow debug running

22. Go to the **Projection** tab and click on **Import projection** as shown in the following screenshot:

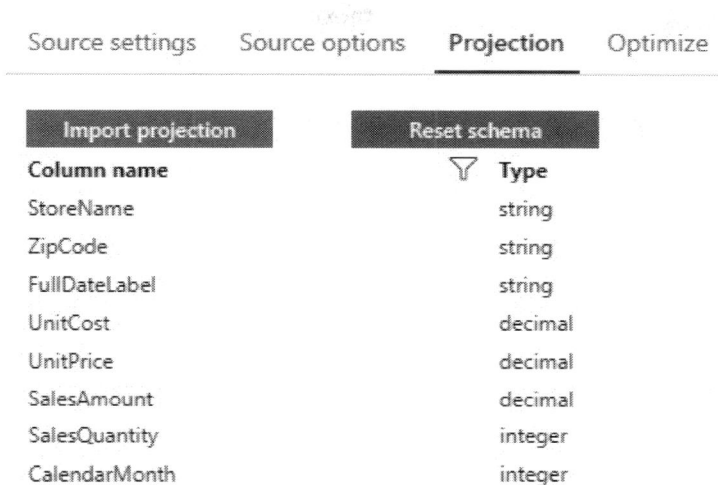

Figure 8.43 – ADF DFT source projection columns

23. Now, clicking on the + sign at the bottom right of **FactSalesParquet**, add an **Aggregate** transformation. Name it **AGGFactSales**. Add the following columns in the **Group by** section – **StoreName**, **ZipCode**, and **CalendarMonth** – as shown in the following screenshot:

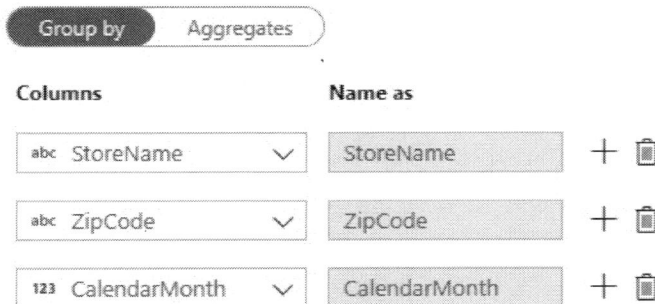

Figure 8.44 – ADF DFT aggregate Group by columns

24. Click the **Aggregates** button. We're going to aggregate some columns here. Select **UnitCost** in the first cell on the left. Click on the cell on the right to open the **Visual expression builder**. As shown in the following screenshot, type `avg(UnitCost)` under **EXPRESSION FOR FIELD "UNITCOST"**. Click on **Save and finish** to save the expression:

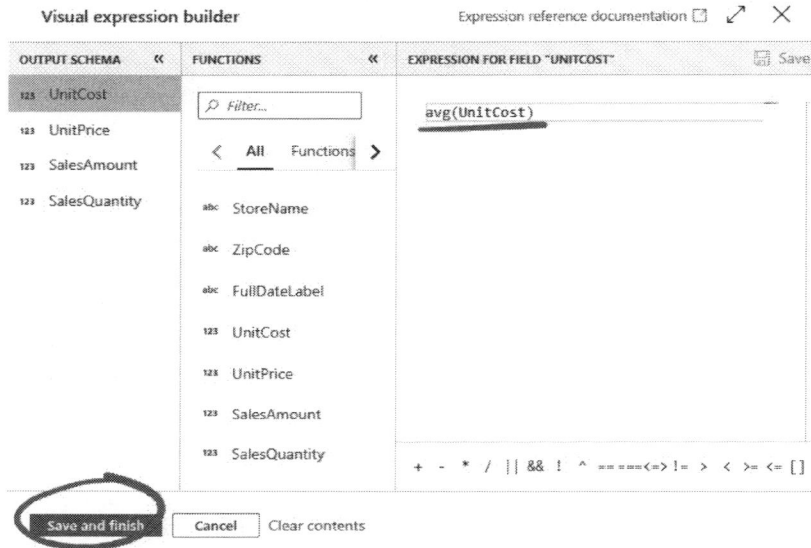

Figure 8.45 – ADF DFT aggregate, the Visual expression builder

25. Use the average function for the **UnitCost** and **UnitPrice** columns. Use the **sum** function for the **SalesAmount** and **SalesQuantity** columns as shown in the following screenshot:

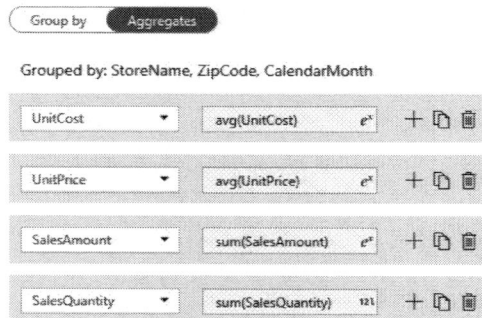

Figure 8.45a – ADF DFT aggregate columns

26. Click anywhere in the data flow background. Click on **Parameters** at the bottom of the screen. Add a parameter named **pipeLineRunID** and set its default value to **"000"** as shown in the following screenshot:

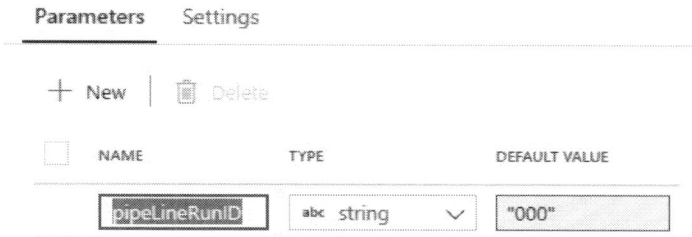

	NAME	TYPE	DEFAULT VALUE
	pipeLineRunID	abc string ⌄	"000"

Parameters   Settings

+ New   🗑 Delete

Figure 8.46 – ADF DFT pipeLineRunID parameter

27. Add a **Derived** column after the **AGGFactSales** transformation. Add a column called **pipeLineRunID** and use the parameter we just added in *Step 26* – as shown in the following screenshot. Call the derived column transform **DERpipeLineRunID**:

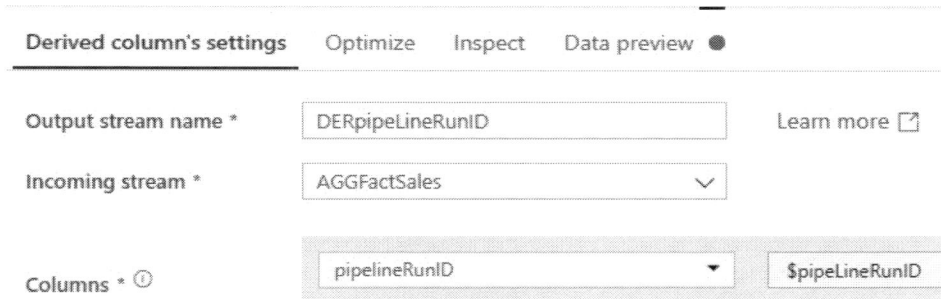

Derived column's settings   Optimize   Inspect   Data preview ●

Output stream name *   DERpipeLineRunID   Learn more ↗

Incoming stream *   AGGFactSales   ⌄

Columns * ⓘ   pipelineRunID   ▼ $pipeLineRunID

Figure 8.47 – ADF DFT derived column for the pipeLineRunID parameter

28. Next, add a sink and name it **SalesPerMonth**. Add a new **dataset** based on the Azure storage account and use the Parquet file format. Name it **SalesPerMonth** and set **File path** to **adf/salesPerMonth**. Do not input any filename as shown in the following screenshot:

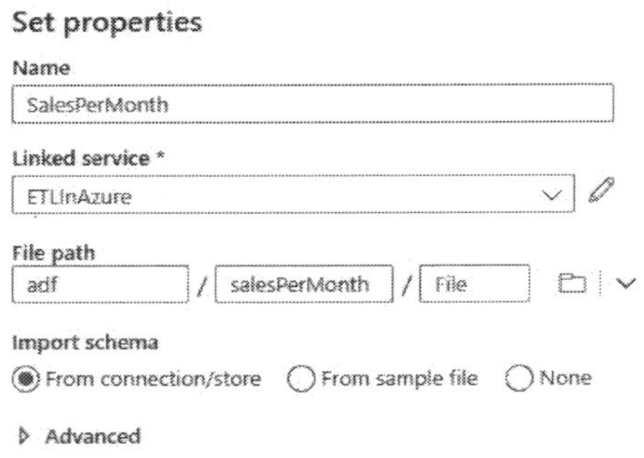

Figure 8.48 – ADF DFT Sink dataset

29. Leave the **Allow schema drift** property checked as we do not have an imported schema yet. Your **Sink** should look like the following screenshot:

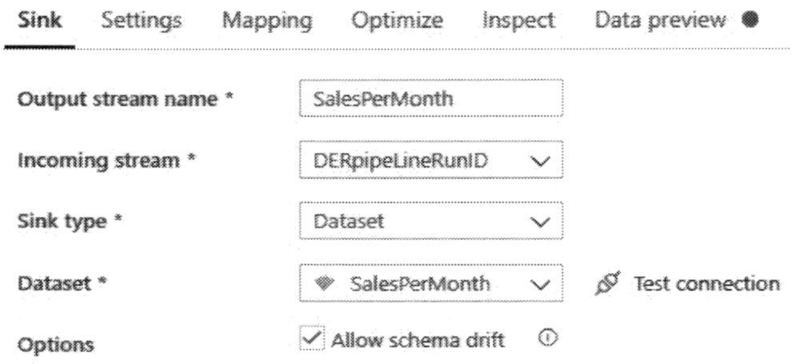

Figure 8.49 – ADF DFT Sink

30. Click on the **Settings** tab. Set the properties as shown in the following screenshot. Select **Output to single file** and set the filename to **SalesPerMonth.parquet**. You will get a warning that we need to change the output partition setting:

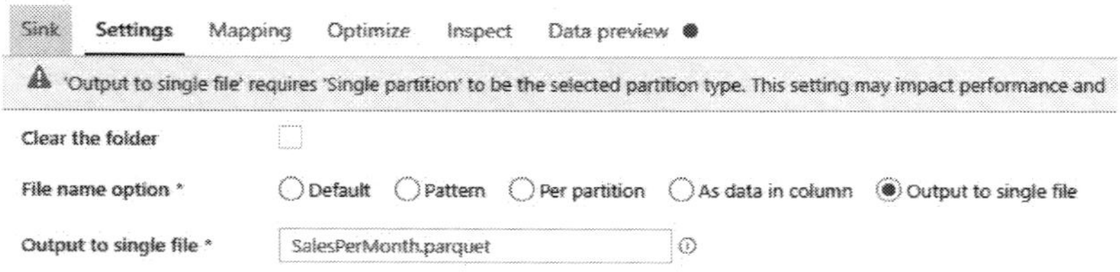

Figure 8.50 – ADF DFT Sink settings

31. Click on the **Optimize** tab and select **Single partition**. That will get rid of the error we had with the **Settings** tab.

32. Go back to the pipeline. Link the **DFT_SalesAgg** data flow activity to the **Copy_FactSales** activity. Click on **Parameters**, choose **Pipeline expression**, and add the **pipeline().RunId** pipeline parameter from the system variables as shown in the following screenshot:

Data flow parameters ⓘ

NAME	VALUE	TYPE	EXPRESSION ⓘ
pipeLineRunID	@pipeline().RunId	string	☐

Figure 8.51 – ADF DFT add the parameter

33. Now, run the pipeline by clicking the **Debug** button at the top of the data factory. The pipeline will run successfully. Go to your storage account to validate that the file has been produced as shown in the following screenshot:

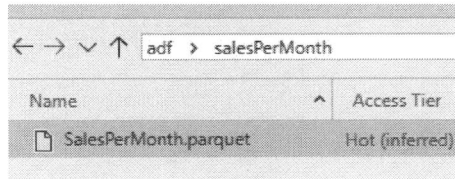

← → ⌄ ↑   adf > salesPerMonth

Name	^	Access Tier
🗋 SalesPerMonth.parquet		Hot (inferred)

Figure 8.52 – ADF DFT SalesPerMonth file created

34. Viewing the data flow's detailed execution (hover over **DFT_SalesAgg** in the run output and click on the glasses icon) will show the following information. We read **358k** rows and aggregated **1505** rows in the sink:

DFT_SalesAgg ◯ Refresh   Auto refresh 🔵 On ⓘ
Data flow

FactSalesParquet   AGGFactSales   DERpipeLineRunID   SalesPerMonth ✅
Sink: ●   Sink: ●   Sink: ●

SalesPerMonth ✅

Processing time: 21s 15ms

TRANSFORM	ROWS	TIME
● FactSalesParquet	358k	1s 50ms
● SalesPerMonth	1505	
● DERpipeLineRunID	1505	
● AGGFactSales	1505	4s 748ms

Figure 8.53 – ADF DFT SalesPerMonth execution details

35. The last step is to copy the parquet file back to the **dbo.SalesAgg** table in our on-premises database. With SSIS, we use **ServerExecutionID** to get an audit of the process that inserted the table's data. This is very useful to check the ID of the process and find out when it ran. For ADF loads, we'll use the pipeline run ID, which is a string column, so it cannot be inserted into the existing table's **ServerExecutionID** column; its data type is `BIGINT`. We'll add a new column to the table called **BatchID** for that purpose. Open SSMS, connect to the on-premises SQL Server, and run the following SQL command:

```
ALTER TABLE   [ContosoRetailDW].[dbo].[SalesAgg] ADD
BatchID NVARCHAR(100) NULL
```

36. Now back to the factory. We have copied data from our on-premises database, transformed it, and stored the result in our storage account. It's now time to copy the information back to the on-premises SQL Server table. Add a **Copy** activity to the pipeline. Link it to the **DFT_SalesAgg** data flow. Name it **Copy_dbo_SalesAgg**.

37. Set the **Source** tab as shown in the following screenshot. Notice that we add a column to map to **ServerExecutionID**. If we don't add the column, the copy will fail. To add the value of the column, we need to check the **Edit** checkbox:

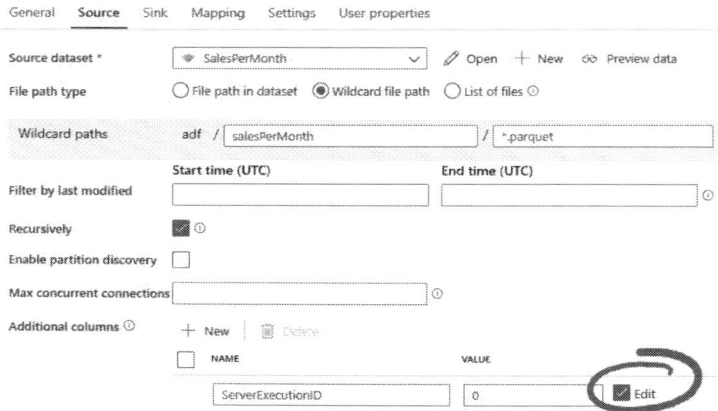

Figure 8.54 – ADF Copy_dbo_SalesAgg source tab

38. Go to the **Sink** tab. Create an SQL Server dataset named `dbo_SalesAgg`.

39. Type in the following SQL command in the **Pre-copy script** textbox:

```
TRUNCATE TABLE [dbo].[SalesAgg]
```

40. Go to the **Mapping** tab. Click on **Import schemas**. Set the column's mapping like the one in the following screenshot. Map **pipeLineRunID** to the **BatchID** column:

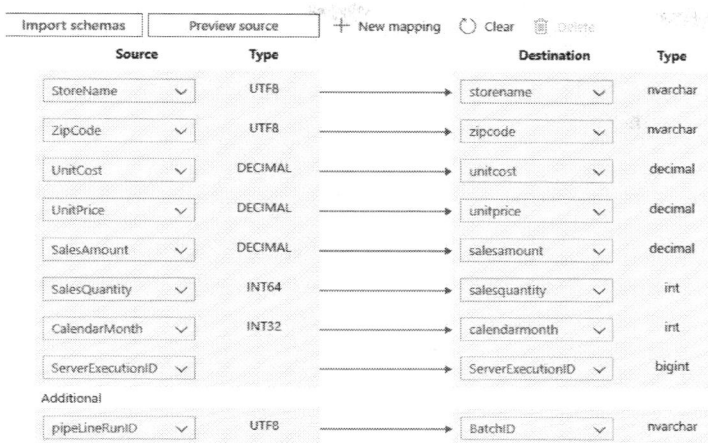

Figure 8.55 – ADF Copy_dbo_SalesAgg Mapping tab

41. Now, run the pipeline in debug mode. It should execute in a few minutes as shown in the following screenshot:

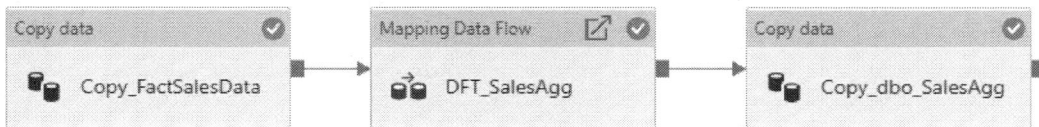

Figure 8.56 – ADF pipeline completed and run successfully

42. Now, go to SSMS and run the following query:

```
SELECT [storename]
      , [zipcode]
      , [unitcost]
      , [unitprice]
      , [salesamount]
      , [salesquantity]
      , [calendarmonth]
      , [ServerExecutionID]
      , [BatchID]
  FROM [ContosoRetailDW].[dbo].[SalesAgg]
```

43. We get a result similar to the one in the following screenshot in SSMS:

	storename	zipcode	unitcost	unitprice	salesamount	salesquantity	calendarmonth	ServerExecutionID	BatchID
1	Contoso Shanghai No.2 Store	201800	150.6010	373.5491	1170613.4190	6021	200905	0	70133f92-d8cd-4bf9-84b3-3aed8d7bcbb8
2	Contoso Norfolk Store	23504	180.3896	432.4625	569675.8500	2199	200904	0	70133f92-d8cd-4bf9-84b3-3aed8d7bcbb8
3	Contoso Plano Store	75201	154.1758	358.8195	441887.1500	1761	200905	0	70133f92-d8cd-4bf9-84b3-3aed8d7bcbb8
4	Contoso Islamabad No.2 Store	15890	160.2909	384.7990	899752.8540	4363	200903	0	70133f92-d8cd-4bf9-84b3-3aed8d7bcbb8
5	Contoso New London Store	6320	180.1943	434.7510	437068.4490	1693	200903	0	70133f92-d8cd-4bf9-84b3-3aed8d7bcbb8
6	Contoso Waukesha No.1 Store	54001	150.6531	355.0229	497895.4500	2375	200905	0	70133f92-d8cd-4bf9-84b3-3aed8d7bcbb8
7	Contoso Bishkek Store	720005	143.1737	339.7082	1047905.8740	6015	200905	0	70133f92-d8cd-4bf9-84b3-3aed8d7bcbb8
8	Contoso Milwaukee No.1 Store	54001	148.5360	355.0122	349182.8385	1556	200902	0	70133f92-d8cd-4bf9-84b3-3aed8d7bcbb8
9	Contoso Fall City Store	97001	170.8739	421.3210	586296.3000	2261	200904	0	70133f92-d8cd-4bf9-84b3-3aed8d7bcbb8

Figure 8.57 – ADF pipeline execution result

44. Now, we've made lots of changes to the factory. Save the changes by publishing them. Click on **Publish all** at the top of the factory to publish the changes outside the sandbox environment.

That's it! We have re-written our `HiveSSIS` package in ADF!

Our `HiveSSIS` package resulted in a faster pipeline in Data Factory, and now the mapping data flow is similar to SSIS data flows.

How it works...

It takes a few minutes to run the pipeline compared to the SSIS package. This is due to the fact that the compute is optimized in ADF compared to if we started and stopped an HDInsight cluster. We're using a native compute environment with ADF. Also, we have more control over the output produced by the mapping data flow. Remember that the HDInsight cluster created several output files with system names. With ADF, we have control over the output file naming. It helps a lot to maintain and understand the pipelines as it produces a cleaner output.

9
Profiling data in Azure

Data profiling is an important part of every data project. It helps the data modeler create an accurate data model and tells ETL developers what type of data we have and how clean the data is. It will also dictate the various transformations we should apply to it.

Data profiling can help us find what metrics we can derive from the source dataset and to what extent we need to change (transform) the data to meet business rules. It can also help us find data inconsistencies before starting the ETL phase and derive a valid data model based on the source dataset.

The process flow from data ingestion to reporting can be described with the following diagram:

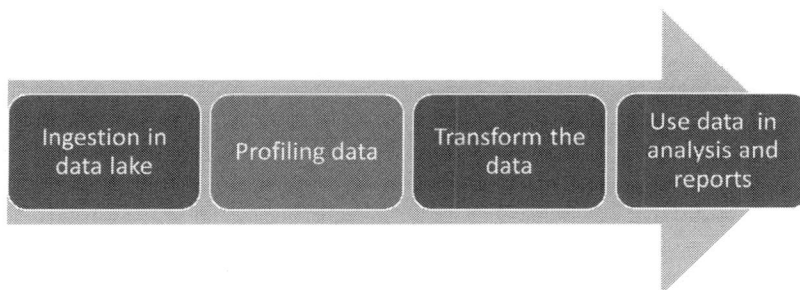

Figure 9.1 – An overview of the data profiling process

This chapter will focus on the **Profiling data** step shown in the preceding diagram. Here, you will learn common techniques to achieve data profiling.

In this chapter, we will cover the following recipes:

- Using SQL in Spark
- Using Spark built-in functions
- Using pandas profiling

Technical requirements

Recipes in this chapter require Azure Databricks, so a Databricks workspace and a Databricks cluster need to be created. Please refer to *Chapter 7, Azure Databricks*, specifically to the recipes *Creating a Databricks workspace* and *Creating a cluster on our workspace*, where it is covered in detail.

Using SQL in Spark

Using Spark SQL to profile data is useful when we want to do basic data profiling, or we want to dig into a specific aspect of our source dataset. This recipe will teach you some techniques to get some quick and dirty data profiling reports. We will use an open dataset in CSV format, load it in the DataFrame, and use SQL to run some straightforward profiling queries.

Getting ready

This recipe uses Azure Databricks. If you are using a trial Azure subscription, you will need to upgrade it to a **Pay-As-You-Go** subscription. Azure Databricks requires eight cores of computing resources. The trial Azure subscription has only four computing resource cores. If you are using an Enterprise or MSDN Azure subscription, it should contain enough resources for Azure Databricks.

Start your Databricks cluster before beginning the recipe. The cluster needs to be started for the code to run.

How to do it...

Let's start our first recipe:

1. In the web browser, go to the Azure portal at `https://portal.azure.com/`, go to the `ETLInAzureCookBook` resource group, and from there launch the Azure Databricks workspace that you created in *Chapter 7, Azure Databricks*.

2. Click on **New Notebook** on the Databricks home page. A **Create Notebook** form will appear.

   Choose the name for your new notebook; for example, `DataProfiling`. Leave all other settings as the default. If the Databricks cluster is starting, it will appear already selected in the **Cluster** drop-down list. Click **Create**, as shown in the following screenshot:

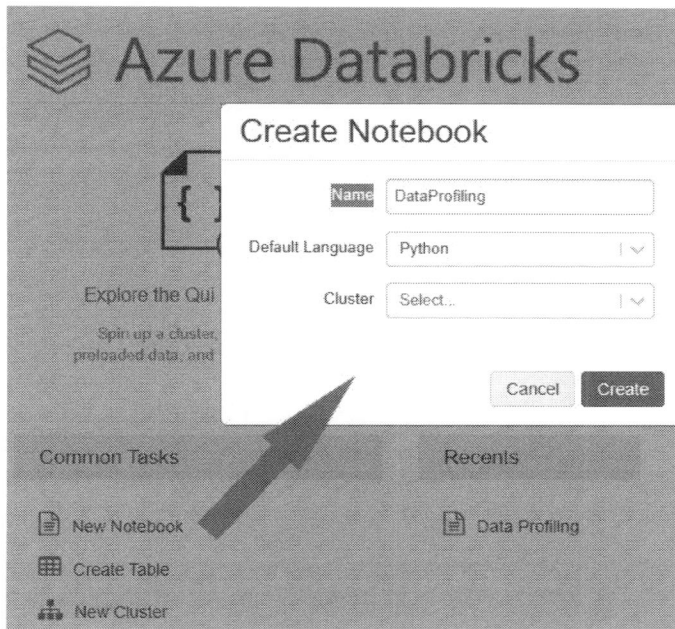

Figure 9.2 – A screenshot showing adding a new Databricks notebook

3. The `DataProfiling` notebook will open with a cell (**Cmd 1**) where we will start writing code.

4. To connect to the CSV file on the internet at `https://www.irs.gov/statistics/soi-tax-stats-individual-income-tax-statistics-2017-zip-code-data-soi`, add the following code into the **Cmd 1** command cell:

```
dbutils.widgets.text("urlStateData", "https://www.irs.
gov/pub/irs-soi/17zpallnoagi.csv", "State Income Data
URL")
urlStateData = dbutils.widgets.get('urlStateData')
```

When copying the code into the notebook, make sure the `dbutils` command is all on one line, as shown in the screenshot for *Step 5*.

5. Hover your mouse under the **Cmd 1** command cell, and a small button with a + icon will appear. Click on it to add a new cell to the notebook, as shown in the following screenshot:

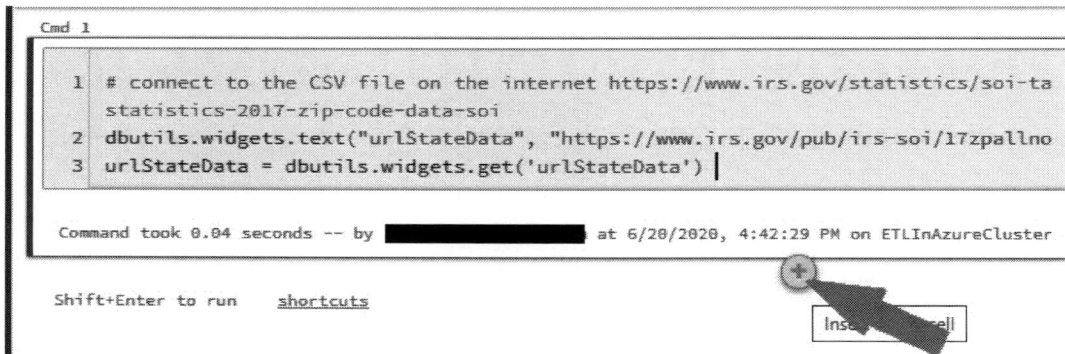

```
Cmd 1

1  # connect to the CSV file on the internet https://www.irs.gov/statistics/soi-ta
   statistics-2017-zip-code-data-soi
2  dbutils.widgets.text("urlStateData", "https://www.irs.gov/pub/irs-soi/17zpallno
3  urlStateData = dbutils.widgets.get('urlStateData')
```

Command took 0.04 seconds -- by ▓▓▓▓▓▓▓▓ at 6/20/2020, 4:42:29 PM on ETLInAzureCluster

Shift+Enter to run   shortcuts

Figure 9.3 – A screenshot showing adding a new Databricks notebook cell

6. A new cell will be added to the notebook. To create a new DataFrame from the CSV file hosted on the external website using the Python pandas library, add the following code into the cell. Note that code also contains a `display` function call to preview the data:

```
import pandas as pd
stateDataDF = (spark.createDataFrame(pd.read_
csv(urlStateData)))
# Display the dataframe
display(stateDataDF)
```

7. Before we can run the code, we need to make sure our notebook is attached to a running cluster. In the top-left corner of the notebook, ensure that a running cluster is selected, as shown in the following screenshot:

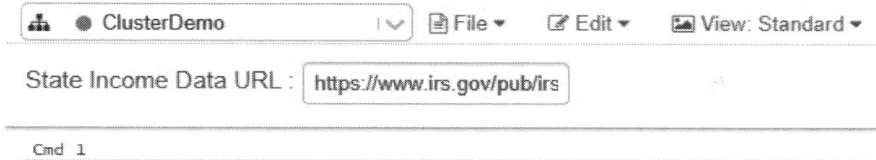

Figure 9.4 – A screenshot showing that the notebook is attached to a cluster

8. Now click on the **Run All** button on the upper menu to run both cells and preview the data in the DataFrame. The result is shown in the following screenshot:

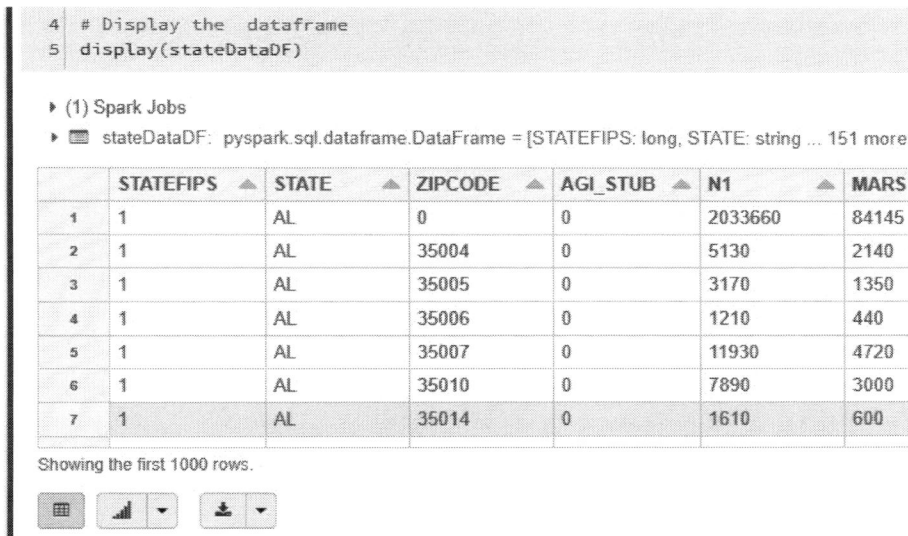

Figure 9.5 – A screenshot showing the displayed DataFrame

9. Add a new cell and add the following code into it to create a temporary view to be able to use StateDataDF in SQL:

```
stateDataDF.createOrReplaceTempView("StateData")
```

10. Add a new cell and write the following code in it. Note that %sql is a magic command that allows you to write SQL code in the cell:

```
%sql
SELECT 'COUNT DISTINCT' AS RowValue,
```

```
COUNT(DISTINCT STATE) AS State, COUNT(DISTINCT ZIPCODE)
AS ZipCode,
COUNT(DISTINCT AGI_STUB) AS AdjustedgrossIncome,
COUNT(DISTINCT MARS4) AS HeadofHouseholdReturns,
COUNT(DISTINCT A02650) AS TotalIncomeAmount
FROM StateData
UNION
SELECT 'MAXIMUM' AS RowValue,
MAX(STATE) AS State, MAX(ZIPCODE) AS ZipCode,
MAX(AGI_STUB) AS AdjustedgrossIncome,
MAX(MARS4) AS HeadofHouseholdReturns,
MAX(A02650) AS TotalIncomeAmount
FROM StateData
UNION
SELECT 'MINIMUM' AS RowValue,
MIN(STATE) AS State, MIN(ZIPCODE) AS ZipCode,
MIN(AGI_STUB) AS AdjustedgrossIncome,
MIN(MARS4) AS HeadofHouseholdReturns,
MIN(A02650) AS TotalIncomeAmount
FROM StateData
```

In this step, we are using SQL code to do basic data profiling on the dataset.

11. Run both cells by clicking the corresponding **Run Cell** icon in the top-right corner of the cell to see the results shown in the following screenshot:

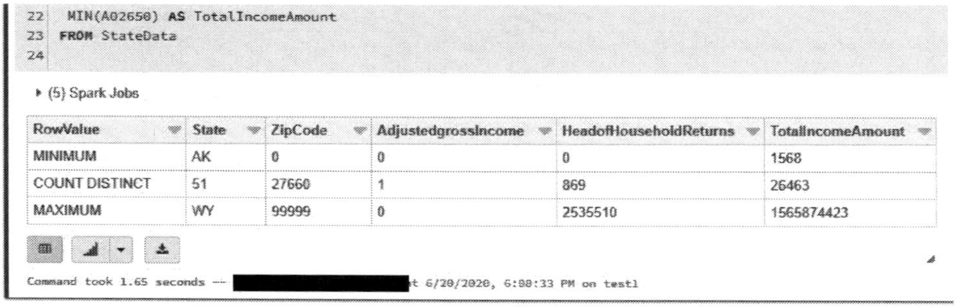

```
22   MIN(A02650) AS TotalIncomeAmount
23   FROM StateData
24
```

▸ (5) Spark Jobs

RowValue	State	ZipCode	AdjustedgrossIncome	HeadofHouseholdReturns	TotalIncomeAmount
MINIMUM	AK	0	0	0	1568
COUNT DISTINCT	51	27660	1	869	26463
MAXIMUM	WY	99999	0	2535510	1565874423

Command took 1.65 seconds — ▮▮▮▮▮▮ t 6/20/2020, 6:88:33 PM on test1

Figure 9.6 – A screenshot showing how to run a new Databricks notebook

This is the result of the SQL query on the data retrieved from the CSV file where we manually profiled data in Databricks.

12. Now, let's go a bit further. We'll check the maximum length of string columns. Add a new cell to the notebook and type the following code snippet:

```sql
%sql

SELECT 'MAX LENGTH STATE' AS RowValue,
MAX(length(STATE))
FROM StateData
UNION ALL
SELECT 'MAX LENGTH ZIPCODE' AS RowValue,
MAX(length(ZIPCODE))
FROM StateData
```

13. Running the cell by hitting *Ctrl + Enter* or by clicking the **Run Cell** icon in the top-right corner of the cell, you should see a result like the one in the following screenshot:

RowValue ▼	max(length(STATE))
MAX LENGTH STATE	2
MAX LENGTH ZIPCODE	5

Figure 9.7 – A screenshot showing the max length profiling result

14. Lastly, we're going to count whether we have NULL values in the subset of the columns. Add a new cell and type the following code snippet:

```sql
%sql

SELECT
SUM(CASE WHEN STATE IS NULL THEN 1 ELSE 0 END) AS
ZIPCodeIsNULL,
SUM(CASE WHEN ZIPCODE IS NULL THEN 1 ELSE 0 END) AS
ZIPCodeIsNULL,
SUM(CASE WHEN AGI_STUB IS NULL THEN 1 ELSE 0 END) AS
AdjustedgrossIsIncomeNULL,
SUM(CASE WHEN MARS4 IS NULL THEN 1 ELSE 0 END) AS
HeadofHouseholdReturnsIsNULL,
SUM(CASE WHEN A02650 IS NULL THEN 1 ELSE 0 END) AS
TotalIncomeAmountIsNull
FROM StateData
```

15. Running the cell by hitting *Ctrl + Enter* or by clicking the **Run Cell** icon in the top-right corner of the cell, you should get a result like the one shown in the following screenshot:

▸ (1) Spark Jobs

ZIPCodeIsNULL	ZIPCodeIsNULL	AdjustedgrossIsIncomeNULL	HeadofHouseholdReturnsIsNULL	TotalIncomeAmountIsNull
0	0	0	0	0

Figure 9.8 – A screenshot showing NULL value counts

Let's move on to the next section!

How it works...

In this recipe, we have performed basic data profiling manually. We have loaded open government statistics data from the CSV file into the DataFrame and created a temporary view that we could query using SQL. At this point, we have used SQL to get the DISTINCT, MIN, and MAX values of every column, then we displayed the MAX length of string columns and checked the nullability of every column. This is the basic profiling data that could help us in understanding the nature of the data that we are receiving.

Profiling data manually sometimes requires lots of steps and it may be time-consuming. The advantage of doing it is that you can customize the profiling you want to achieve and meet your project's goals in terms of data analysis.

Using Spark built-in functions

Spark has built-in functions that can be used to augment manual profiling. It can replace some manual data profiling queries. This recipe will teach you about two basic built-in functions that, when used in conjunction with manual profiling, provide useful information to both data modelers and data scientists. In this recipe, we will use the DataFrame created in the first recipe and call Spark built-in functions.

Getting ready

This recipe uses Azure Databricks. If you are using a trial Azure subscription, you will need to upgrade it to a **Pay-As-You-Go** subscription. Azure Databricks requires eight cores of computing resources. The trial Azure subscription has only four computing resource cores. If you are using an Enterprise or MSDN Azure subscription, it should contain enough resources for Azure Databricks.

How to do it...

Now let's see how we can profile data with Spark built-in functions. We will be adding the code for this recipe in the same notebook that we created in the previous recipe:

1. In the web browser, go to the Azure portal at `https://portal.azure.com/`, and from there launch the Azure Databricks workspace.

2. On the Databricks home page, you can open the `DataProfiling` notebook by clicking on the **DataProfiling** notebook name under **Recents**.

3. Let's look at the `describe` functionality with SQL. Add a new command cell by clicking on the + icon below the last cell. In the new cell, add the following code:

```
%sql
describe formatted StateData
```

4. Click the **Run Cell** icon in the top-right corner of the cell to execute the code and see the results, as shown in the following screenshot:

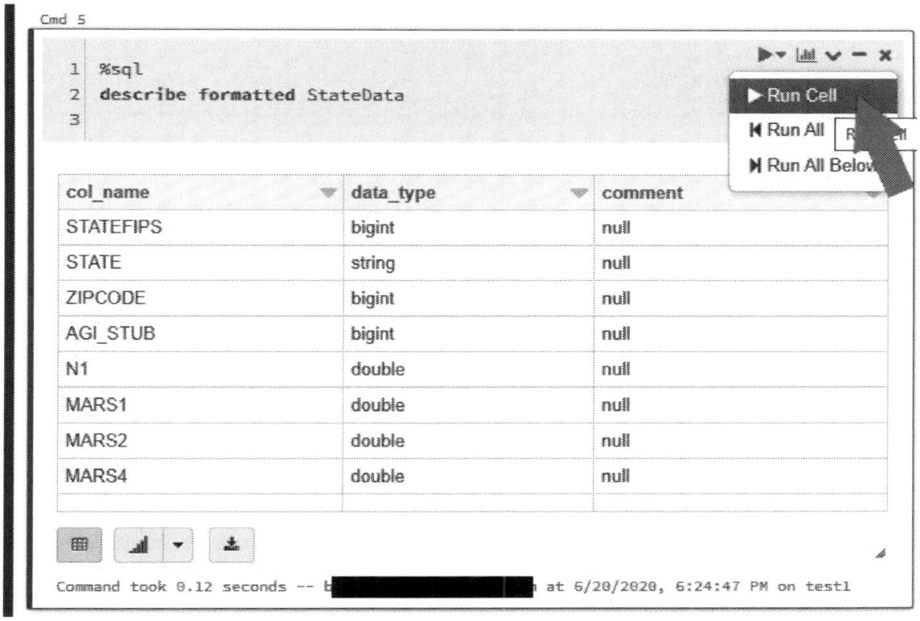

Figure 9.9 – A screenshot showing how to run a new Databricks notebook

5. Using the SQL command to get the basic schema allows us to download the data if needed. Click on the **download** icon at the bottom of the result set to download the CSV file, as shown in the following screenshot:

Figure 9.10 – A screenshot showing how to save a Databricks notebook cell result

6. Now we can try the `printSchema()` function, which could give us useful information about our data. Add a new command cell by clicking on the + icon below the last cell. In the new cell, add the following code to look at the schema derived for the CSV file:

```
stateDataDF.printSchema()
```

7. You should click on **Run Cell** to see the results. They are shown in the following screenshot for your reference:

Figure 9.11 – A screenshot showing the Databricks notebook cell printSchema() result

8. Now let's try a simpler way to gain knowledge about our data with PySpark. Add a new command cell by clicking on the + icon below the last command cell. In the new cell, add the following code to use the PySpark `describe()` functionality:

```
display(stateDataDF.describe())
```

9. Select the current command cell and press the *Shift + Enter* shortcut to execute the code in the selected cell and see the results, as shown in the following screenshot:

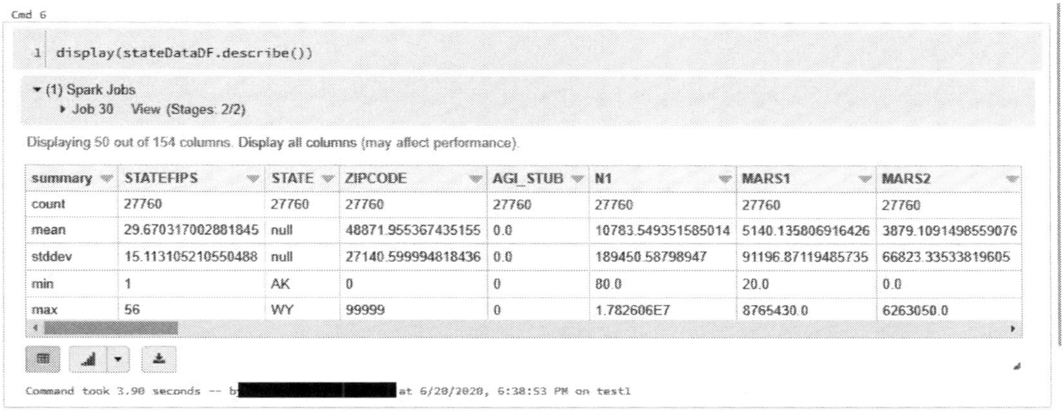

```
Cmd 6

1  display(stateDataDF.describe())

▼ (1) Spark Jobs
   ▶ Job 30   View (Stages: 2/2)

Displaying 50 out of 154 columns. Display all columns (may affect performance).
```

summary ▾	STATEFIPS ▾	STATE ▾	ZIPCODE ▾	AGI_STUB ▾	N1 ▾	MARS1 ▾	MARS2 ▾
count	27760	27760	27760	27760	27760	27760	27760
mean	29.670317002881845	null	48871.955367435155	0.0	10783.549351585014	5140.135806916426	3879.1091498559076
stddev	15.113105210550488	null	27140.599994818436	0.0	189450.58798947	91196.87119485735	66823.33533819605
min	1	AK	0	0	80.0	20.0	0.0
max	56	WY	99999	0	1.782606E7	8765430.0	6263050.0

```
Command took 3.90 seconds -- by ███████████████ at 6/28/2020, 6:38:53 PM on test1
```

Figure 9.12 – A screenshot showing the Databricks notebook PySpark describe() result

Now let's move on to the next section where we'll recap.

How it works...

This recipe covers the steps required to do profiling using Spark built-in functions. We are building on top of the first recipe, so the data from CSV is already loaded in the DataFrame. Three different functions were used to quickly gain information about data: `describe` SQL functionality, `printSchema()`, and the PySpark `describe()` function.

Using built-in Databricks functions might be sufficient for basic profiling. The built-in functions are not enough to understand the data completely, however. We usually use a mixture of simple built-in functions and fill the gaps with manual profiling.

Using pandas profiling

Pandas profiling is a common library used to profile data. It goes beyond everything we have done so far and produces an HTML report that contains valuable information for both the data scientist and data modeler. This recipe will teach you how to install and use pandas profiling. In this recipe, we will use the DataFrame initialized in the first recipe and use the pandas profiling library to show the rich visual data profiling reports that can be achieved with it.

Getting ready

This recipe uses Azure Databricks. If you are using a trial Azure subscription, you will need to upgrade it to a **Pay-As-You-Go** subscription. Azure Databricks requires eight cores of computing resources. The trial Azure subscription has only four computing resource cores. If you are using an Enterprise or MSDN Azure subscription, it should contain enough resources for Azure Databricks. It also needs you to be the administrator of the cluster as we'll install some libraries on it to achieve our data profiling.

How to do it...

Let's continue working with our `DataProfiling` notebook to learn about the benefits of pandas profiling. Before writing any code, we will need to import the pandas profiling library to our Databricks cluster:

1. Click on the **Clusters** icon on the left-hand side menu to go to the **Clusters** page.

2. In the list of interactive clusters, select `ETLInAzureCluster`, and if it is not running, start it by clicking the **Start** button.

3. If **ETLInAzureCluster** is running, go to the **Libraries** tab as shown in the following screenshot:

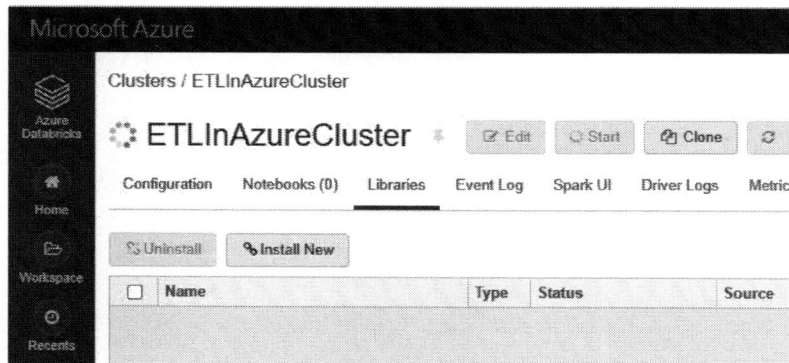

Figure 9.13 – A screenshot showing Databricks cluster library installation

4. Click the **Install New** button. Select **PyPI** as **Library Source**, and enter `pandas_profiling` into **Package**, as shown in the following screenshot. Click **Install**.

5. Upon successful installation, you should see that the **pandas_profiling** library has a status of **Installed**:

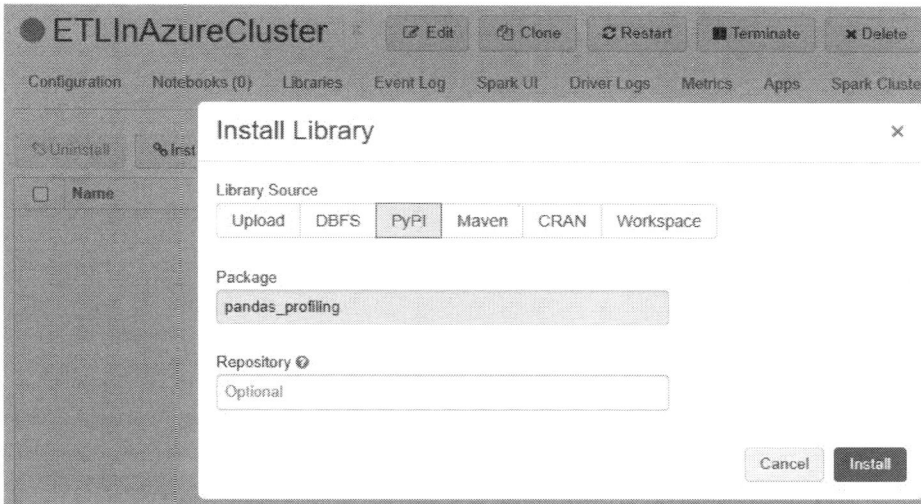

Figure 9.14 – A screenshot showing Databricks cluster library selection

6. Now we can proceed with coding. Open the `DataProfiling` notebook.

7. In this step, we will create a pandas DataFrame from the Spark DataFrame and select our five columns for profiling.

   Add the following code in the new command cell to do so:

```
from pyspark.sql.functions import col
import pandas_profiling
# Choose 5 columns
pdf = stateDataDF.select(col("STATE"), col("ZIPCODE"),
col("AGI_STUB"), col("MARS4"), col("A02650")).toPandas()
# Create a profiling IPython.core.display variable
prof = pandas_profiling.ProfileReport(pdf,title='State
Income for 2017 Profiling Report')
```

   When copying the code into the notebook, make sure the last line of the command is all on one line.

8. Click on **Run Cell** to execute the code in the command cell.

9. Let's convert our profiling data to HTML format now. You can do this by adding the following code in the new command cell:

```
displayProfile = prof.to_html()
```

10. Click on **Run Cell** to execute the conversion.

11. Now add a new command cell with the following code:

```
displayHTML(displayProfile)
```

12. Click on **Run Cell** to produce the report. Take a look at the following screenshot to see the **Overview** section of the result:

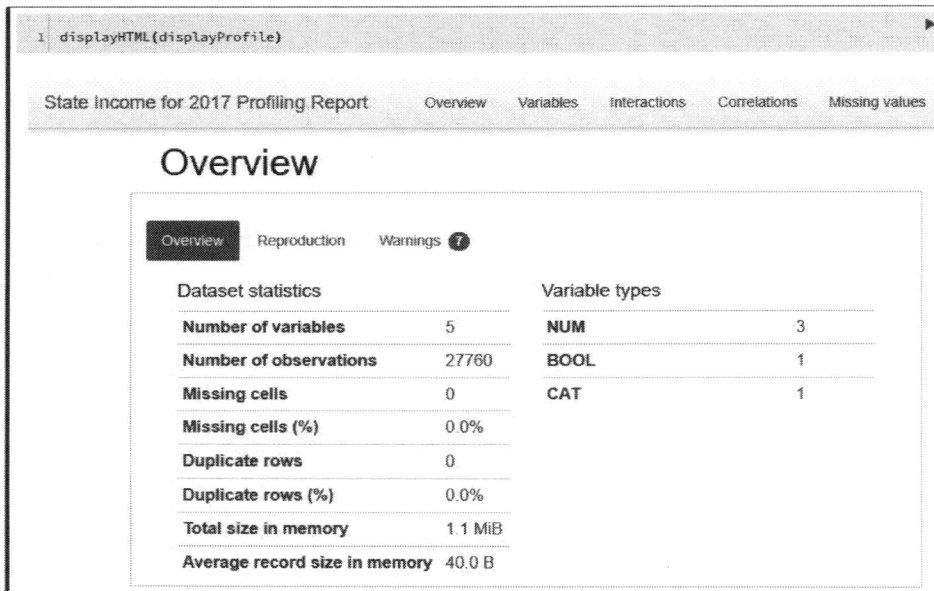

Figure 9.15 – A screenshot showing the pandas profiling report overview

Each column is detailed in the **Variables** section, as shown in the following screenshot:

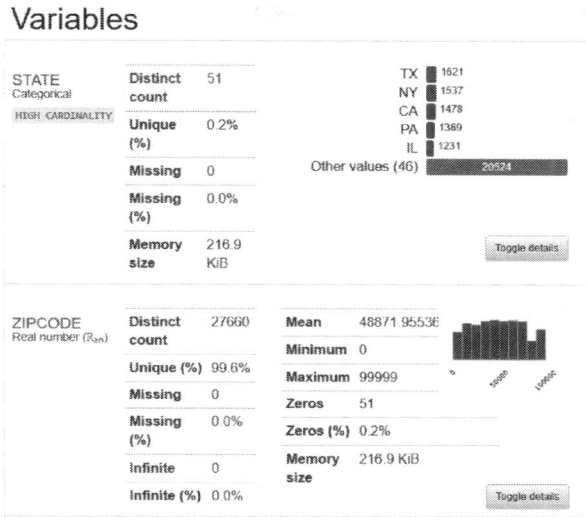

Figure 9.16 – A screenshot showing the pandas profiling variables overview

See how we clearly see a problem with the **AGI_STUB** column, shown in the following screenshot:

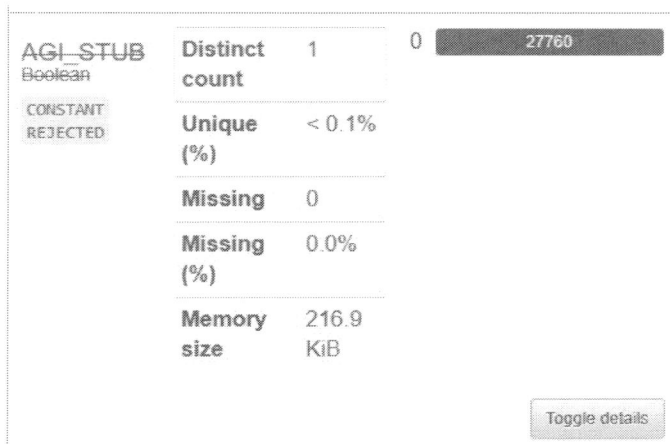

Figure 9.17 – A screenshot showing a pandas profiling variable warning

Take a look at the following screenshot to see how much useful information was derived for numeric columns by pandas profiling:

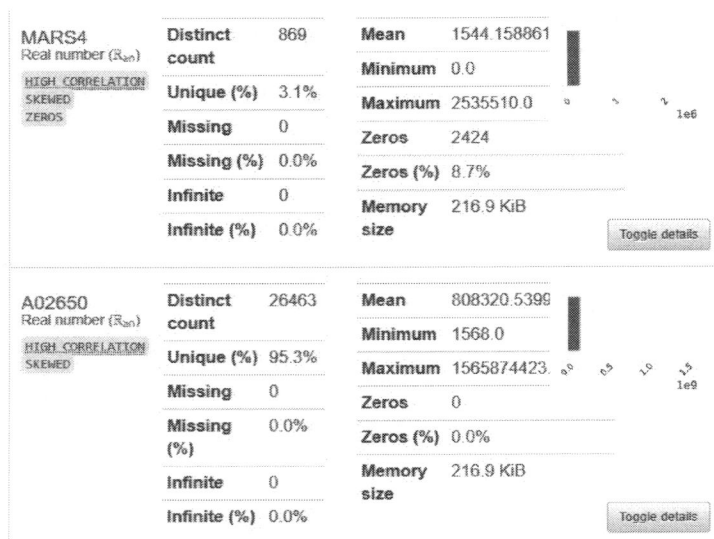

MARS4	Distinct	869	Mean	1544.158861
Real number (ℝ≥0)	count		Minimum	0.0
HIGH CORRELATION				
SKEWED	Unique (%)	3.1%	Maximum	2535510.0
ZEROS	Missing	0	Zeros	2424
	Missing (%)	0.0%	Zeros (%)	8.7%
	Infinite	0	Memory	216.9 KiB
	Infinite (%)	0.0%	size	

A02650	Distinct	26463	Mean	808320.5399
Real number (ℝ≥0)	count		Minimum	1568.0
HIGH CORRELATION				
SKEWED	Unique (%)	95.3%	Maximum	1565874423.
	Missing	0	Zeros	0
	Missing (%)	0.0%	Zeros (%)	0.0%
	Infinite	0	Memory	216.9 KiB
	Infinite (%)	0.0%	size	

Figure 9.18 – A screenshot showing pandas profiling numeric variable details

The following screenshot shows the **Interactions** section of the profiling report:

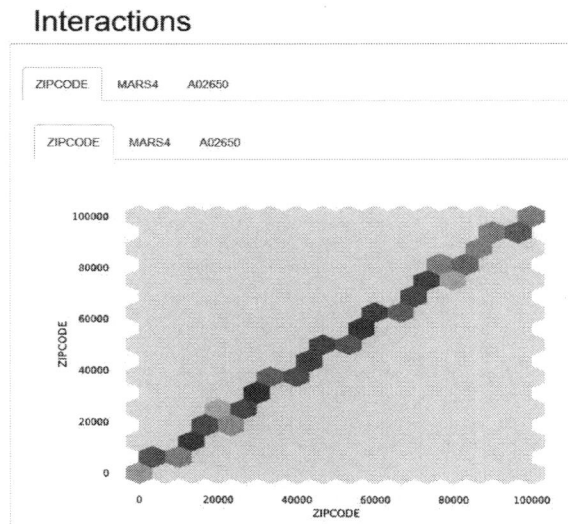

Figure 9.19 – A screenshot showing pandas profiling ZIPCODE interaction

There is also a **Missing values** section in the report, shown in the following screenshot:

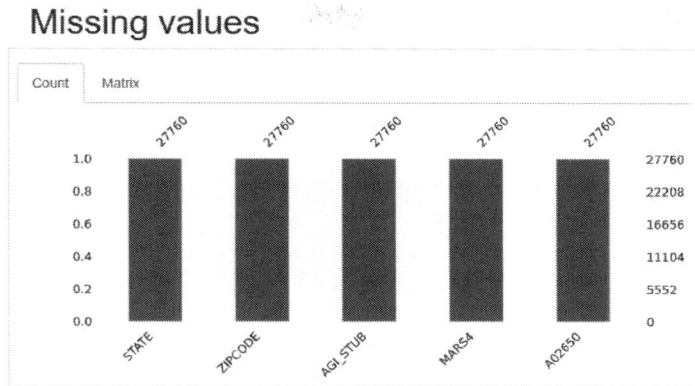

Figure 9.20 – A screenshot showing pandas profiling variables missing values

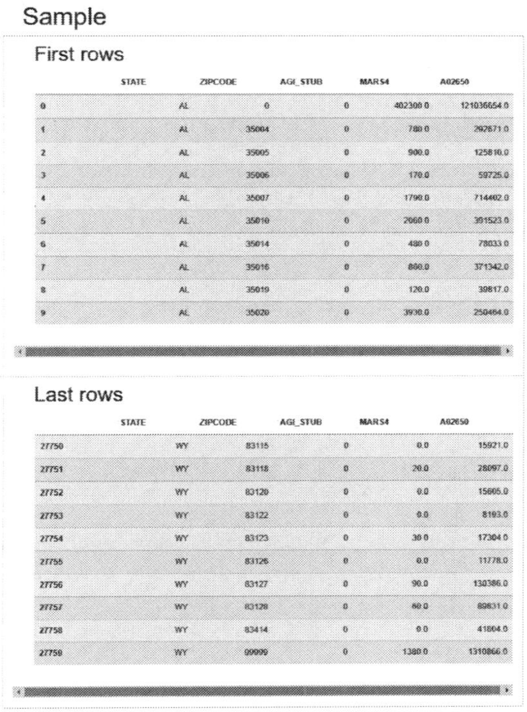

And lastly, we can get a taste of the data itself from the **Sample** section of the report, shown in the following screenshot:

Sample

First rows

	STATE	ZIPCODE	AGI_STUB	MARS4	A02650
0	AL	0	0	402300.0	121036654.0
1	AL	35004	0	780.0	292671.0
2	AL	35005	0	900.0	125810.0
3	AL	35006	0	170.0	59725.0
4	AL	35007	0	1790.0	714402.0
5	AL	35010	0	2060.0	391523.0
6	AL	35014	0	480.0	78033.0
7	AL	35016	0	880.0	371342.0
8	AL	35019	0	120.0	39817.0
9	AL	35020	0	3930.0	250464.0

Last rows

	STATE	ZIPCODE	AGI_STUB	MARS4	A02650
27750	WY	83115	0	0.0	15921.0
27751	WY	83118	0	20.0	28097.0
27752	WY	83120	0	0.0	15605.0
27753	WY	83122	0	0.0	8193.0
27754	WY	83123	0	30.0	17304.0
27755	WY	83126	0	0.0	11778.0
27756	WY	83127	0	90.0	130386.0
27757	WY	83128	0	60.0	89831.0
27758	WY	83414	0	0.0	41804.0
27759	WY	99999	0	1380.0	1310866.0

Figure 9.21 – A screenshot showing pandas profiling sample values

13. Let's save the data profiling results to our storage. Copy the unique **Access Key** of the storage account. To get the **Access Key**, go to the **Storage account** page in the Azure portal, go to the **Access keys** tab, and copy the **Key** from there, as shown in the following screenshot:

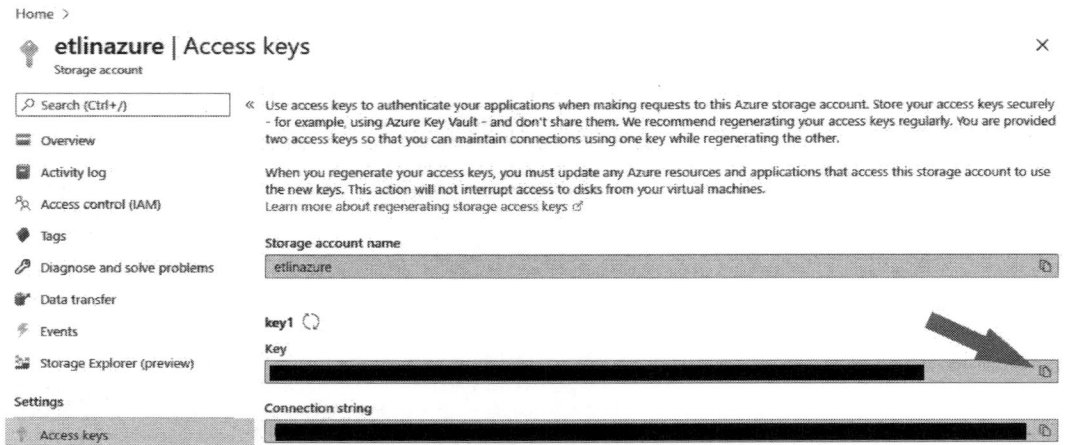

Figure 9.22 – A screenshot showing Azure storage account key access

14. While we are still on the **Storage account** page, go to **Containers** and create a new **profiling** container by clicking the + **Container** link. You should see your **profiling** container after you have created it, as shown in the following screenshot:

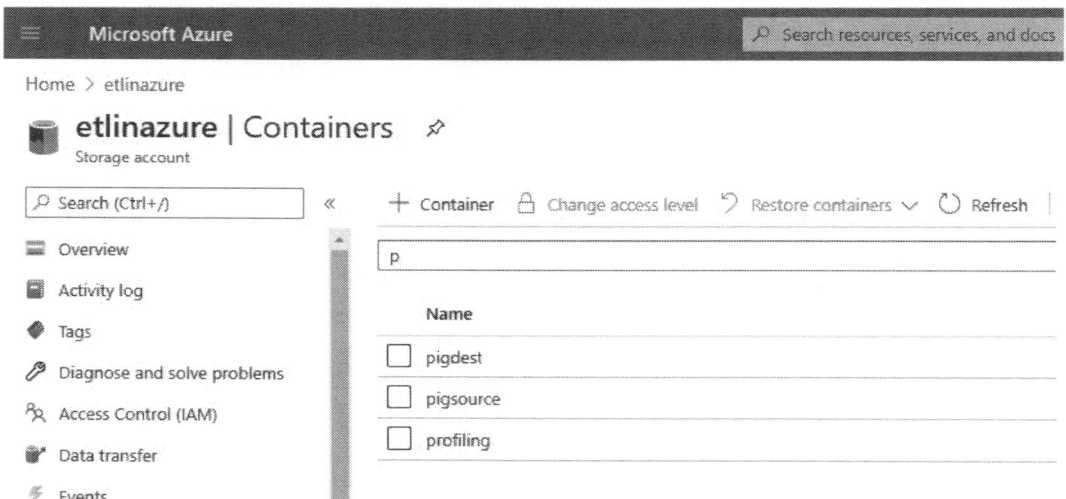

Figure 9.23 – A screenshot showing the profiling container in the storage account

15. Add the following code to the new command cell. Put the copied access key into the `storage_account_access_key` variable, replacing the xxx placeholder between double quotation marks in the following code:

```
storage_account_name = "etlinazure"
storage_account_access_key = "xxx"
spark.conf.set(    "fs.azure.account.key."+storage_account_
name+".blob.core.windows.net",
    storage_account_access_key)
```

Please note that you should use your own storage account name in the code since storage account names must be unique. You should also make sure that " .blob. core.windows.net " is all on one line.

16. Click **Run Cell** to execute the command. Now, add a new command cell and put the following code inside to prepare the output location for the report:

```
outputFilePath = "wasbs://profiling@etlinazure.blob.core.
windows.net/ProfileReport.html"
dbutils.fs.put(outputFilePath, prof.to_html(),
overwrite=True)
```

Please ensure that the path is all on one line – there should not be any line breaks in it. Also, the path should be a path to your storage account, and you should already have the `profiling` container created.

17. Click **Run Cell** to execute the command. Now we will use the `display()` function to see whether the file was copied into the storage. Add a new command cell with the following code to do so:

```
display(
dbutils.fs.ls(
"wasbs://profiling@etlinazure.blob.core.windows.net"))
```

18. Click **Run Cell** to execute the command. You will see in the output the information about the new file with the profile report that was created. You should see a result that looks like the following screenshot:

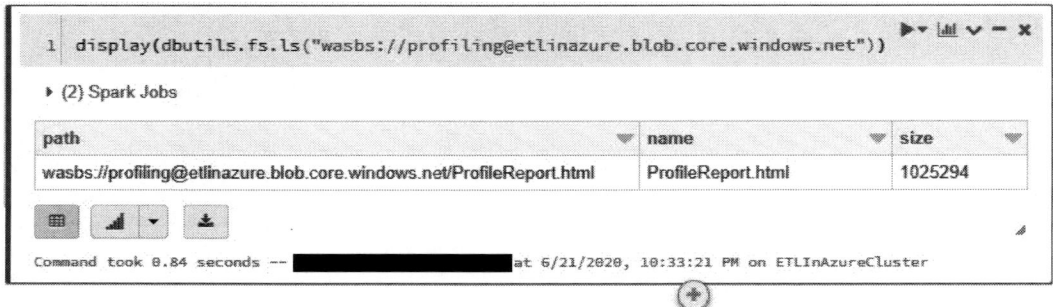

Figure 9.24 – A screenshot showing the Azure storage content

19. If you go to the storage account, you will be able to download and open the HTML file containing the data profiling report, as shown in the following screenshot:

Figure 9.25 – A screenshot showing the profiling report saved to the Azure storage account

The report can now be shared and used to better understand the source dataset and help in making decisions on how business rules can be applied to it.

How it works...

This recipe uses pandas profiling to gain more insights into the data. This recipe is built upon previous recipes, so the data is already loaded in the DataFrame.

We installed the `pandas_profiling` library on the Databricks cluster and generated profiling data on the DataFrame. After this, we converted profiling data into HTML format to visualize the reports. HTML reports produced by pandas profiling show different aspects of the data in a visual format. We also showed how to save data profiling reports in a storage account, so that they can be shared with others or archived.

Using pandas profiling does lots of work for us. It goes beyond the Databricks built-in functions and brings us useful visualizations that help us have a better view of the data quality. The report can be uploaded to blob storage using a command such as `dbutils.fs.put(<output file name and path, prof.to_html(), overwrite=True)`. The report can be shared with data modelers and scientists to help them define various analyses with the source dataset.

As good as pandas profiling is, it has some limitations. For example, it requires us to use `pandas DataFrames`, which do not scale as much as their Sparks counterparts when we analyze multiple dataset attributes. That's why we limited the analysis to only a few columns in this recipe; using all columns would have required a much bigger cluster and would have taken longer to execute.

This recipe concludes our chapter on data profiling with Databricks. Let's reiterate why we need to pay attention to data profiling.

Transforming data is basically a column mapping between source and target datasets and aggregations with values. This takes lots of time as the data is never accurate enough to be used as is. It also cannot be imported unless we know what data types we're dealing with.

Years ago, we would import the source dataset into a database and profile from there. We always faced some challenges finding the right data type, so we usually ended up using character data types most of the time. We also could not analyze the entire dataset as it was oftentimes a tedious effort for the database engine to query very large datasets with column casting from character to other data types.

Nowadays, we have tools such as Databricks to come to our rescue. With it, we do not need to define a schema in advance; we simply bring the data into a DataFrame and go from there. Also, it's worth mentioning that we can analyze a lot more data since Azure storage accounts can store almost an unlimited amount of data and Databricks clusters can be scaled to do computation on a very large amount of data too.

10

Manage SSIS and Azure Data Factory with Biml

Many developers will agree, I think, that one of the hardest things to bear at work is not solving complex problems or rushing to meet a deadline, but the boredom. The boredom of uninspiring tasks, the lack of an intellectual challenge, and repeating the same code, the same logic, and the same field names over and over. Let's take developing SSIS packages as an example: many SSIS development tasks may seem repetitive and boring because the same patterns apply to multiple packages, and we just change table names and the set of columns from package to package.

This is why I am thrilled to introduce **Biml** in this book! Biml stands for **Business Intelligence Markup Language**, and it does what I've always wished for – it generates SSIS packages based on the pattern that you design.

What's more, Biml can generate anything based on a given pattern: T-SQL, text, JSON, tabular models, Azure Data Factory, PowerShell scripts, and more. The only difference between these formats when it comes to Biml is that some things are easier to generate than others because they are supported natively by Biml.

I want to introduce the power of Biml in this chapter and show through the recipes how it can make coding more fun and efficient.

Here is the list of recipes that this chapter will cover. We will start with the most basic one and progress to more advanced recipes:

- Installing prerequisites
- Generating T-SQL select statements for all tables
- Generating T-SQL to drop and create all indexes
- Generating a basic SSIS package
- Generating an SSIS package with Execute SQL tasks
- Using Convert SSIS package to Biml
- Generating a mass change to stored procedures
- Generating an SSIS package containing a Data Flow Task
- Generating your first Azure Data Factory
- Loading multiple files using Data Factory

Technical requirements

Visual Studio 2019 and a Microsoft SQL Server instance should already be installed on the machine. Visual Studio 2019 Community is a free version and can be downloaded from `https://tinyurl.com/y5tuzs2y`. The installation of Visual Studio 2019 and Microsoft SQL Server was covered in *Chapter 1, Getting Started with SSIS 2019*. BimlExpress 2019, which is free, has to be installed using this link: `https://www.varigence.com/bimlexpress`. What we need to prepare for this chapter are two sample databases – `WideWorldImporters` and `WideWorldImportersDW` – and an imported SSIS project: `Daily.ETL.ispac`. We will go over the installation of the sample SSIS project in our first recipe.

Installing prerequisites

In order to complete the recipes in this chapter, we first need to install the following prerequisites.

How to do it...

Install the sample SSIS project with the `DailyETLMain.dtsx` SSIS package that comes with the `WideWorldImporters` sample database by following these steps:

1. Go to GitHub at `https://github.com/Microsoft/sql-server-samples/releases/tag/wide-world-importers-v1.0`, and download `Daily.ETL.ispac`, which is located under the **SQL Server Integration Services** header.

2. Open Visual Studio 2019 and click on **Create a new project**, then select **Integration Services Import Project Wizard**. On the **Configure your new project** form, specify **ETLInAzure** as the name of the SSIS project, choose the location `C:\Projects\` and click **Create**.

3. The **Integration Services Import Project Wizard** screen will appear. Just click **Next**.

4. On the **Select Source** screen, keep the **Project deployment file** option selected, then click **Browse** to select the `Daily.ETL.ispac` file that was downloaded from GitHub, as shown in the following screenshot:

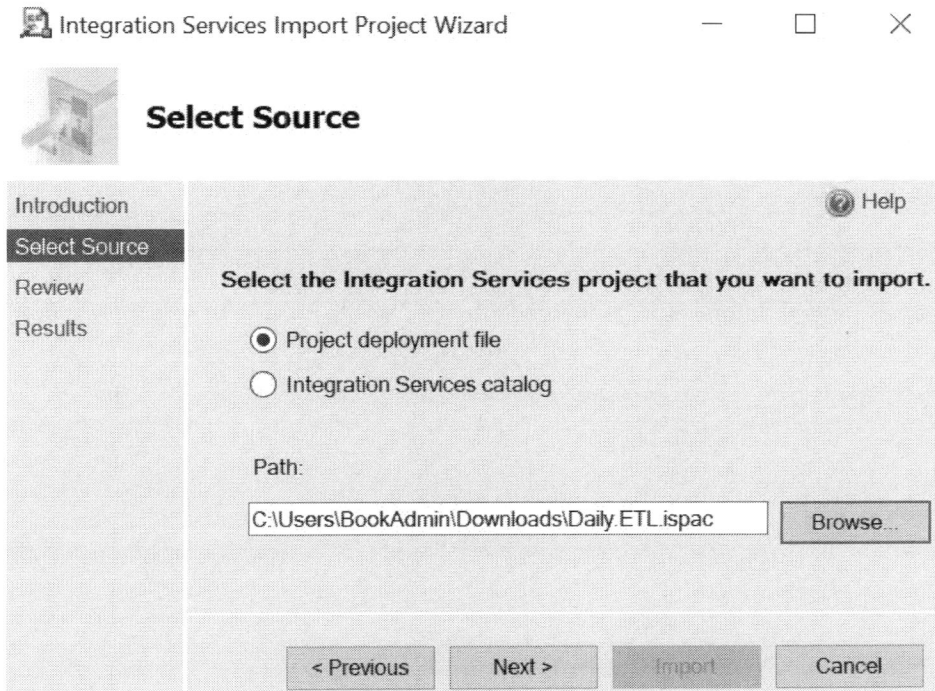

Figure 10.1 – A screenshot showing the Integration Services Import Project Wizard

5. Click **Next**. Then click **Import**. After a successful import, all import actions will have green success icons and you can click on the **Close** button.

6. The **ETLInAzure** SSIS project will open, as shown in the following screenshot:

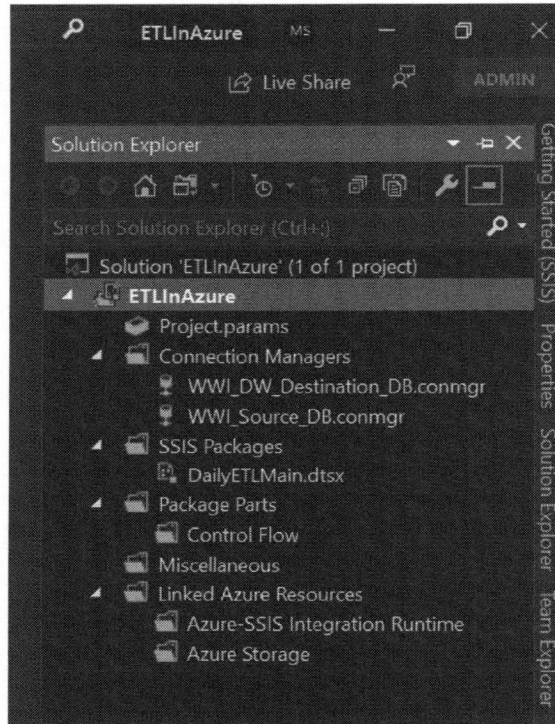

Figure 10.2 – A screenshot showing the ETLInAzure SSIS project

The opened project will contain a single SSIS package called `DailyETLMain.dtsx`.

How it works...

Now that the SSIS project is imported, we can begin the main recipes. In the SSIS recipes of this chapter, we will learn how to write Biml code that can generate the `DailyETLMain.dtsx` sample package from scratch. We'll approach this task incrementally in subsequent recipes, going step by step from the simplest concepts to a complete solution.

Generating T-SQL select statements for all tables

Let's start with the most straightforward and demonstrative example – generating a T-SQL statement. Biml has access to a treasure trove of metadata, or database information, such as table names, schema names, column names, foreign keys, indexes, and more. Having this valuable data, we can do lots and lots of useful things! We will see how we can generate a list of select statements for every table in a database that counts the number of rows of each table.

Getting ready

Open Visual Studio 2019, and then open the **ETLInAzure** SSIS project that was created in the *Installing prerequisites* section.

How to do it...

Add a new `BimlScript` file and, using the power of Biml native objects, generate your T-SQL code:

1. To add a new `BimlScript` file to your solution, right-click on the SSIS project name and choose **Add New Biml File** as shown in the following screenshot:

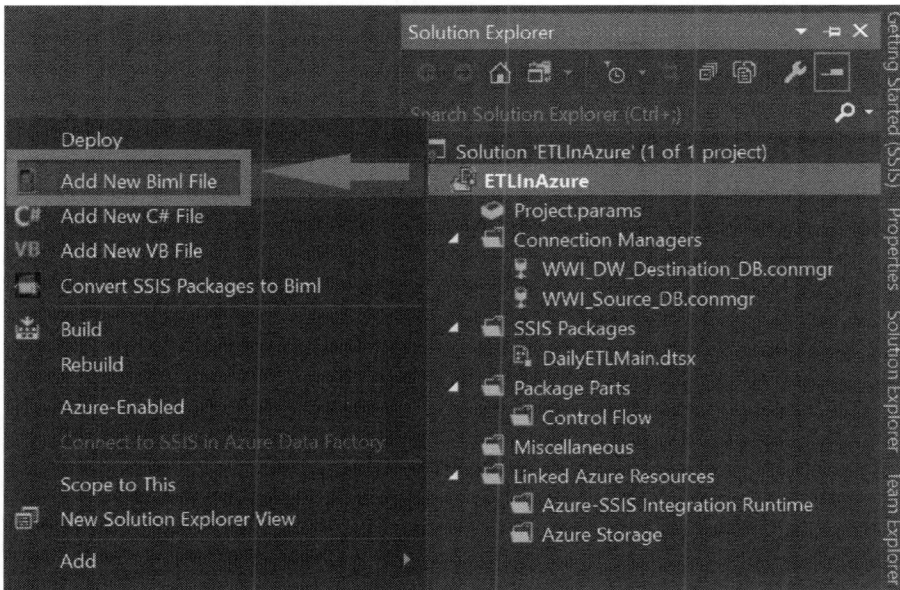

Figure 10.3 – A screenshot showing adding the new Biml file

This will add a new file called `BimlScript.biml` in the `Miscellaneous` folder of the project. Rename it to `Recipe1.biml` and reopen it. Initially, it will only contain the opening and closing tags of the Biml root element.

2. Open the `Recipe1.biml` file and add the following code between Biml tags to configure a database connection and get the metadata of the database using the `GetDatabaseSchema()` method:

```
<# var sourceConnection = SchemaManager.
CreateConnectionNode("Destination", @"Data
Source=ETLInAzureBook\MSSQL2019;Initial
Catalog=WideWorldImportersDW;Provider=
SQLNCLI11.1;Integrated Security=SSPI;Auto
Translate=False;");

var sourceMetadata = sourceConnection.
GetDatabaseSchema();
```

3. In a `foreach` loop, go through every table and generate the T-SQL statement for counting every row in the table. Add the following code to the control block:

```
foreach (var table in sourceMetadata.TableNodes) {#>
SELECT COUNT(1) FROM [<#=table.Schema#>].[<#=table.
Name#>]
<#}#>
```

4. Click **Save**. At the bottom right of the **preview pane**, click **Update**. You should see the generated T-SQL code in the **preview pane** as shown in the following screenshot:

```
1 <Biml xmlns="http://schemas.varigence.com/biml.xsd">
2    <# var sourceConnection = SchemaManager.CreateConnectionNode("Destination",
3       var sourceMetadata = sourceConnection.GetDatabaseSchema();
4
5       foreach(var table in sourceMetadata.TableNodes) {#>
6 SELECT COUNT(1) FROM [<#=table.Schema#>].[<#=table.Name#>]
7    <#}#>
8
```

```
1 <Biml xmlns="http://schemas.varigence.com/biml.xsd">
2 SELECT COUNT(1) FROM [Dimension].[City]
3 SELECT COUNT(1) FROM [Dimension].[Customer]
4 SELECT COUNT(1) FROM [Dimension].[Date]
5 SELECT COUNT(1) FROM [Dimension].[Employee]
6 SELECT COUNT(1) FROM [Dimension].[Payment Method]
7 SELECT COUNT(1) FROM [Dimension].[Stock Item]
8 SELECT COUNT(1) FROM [Dimension].[Supplier]
9 SELECT COUNT(1) FROM [Dimension].[Transaction Type]
10 SELECT COUNT(1) FROM [Fact].[Movement]
11 SELECT COUNT(1) FROM [Fact].[Order]
12 SELECT COUNT(1) FROM [Fact].[Purchase]
13 SELECT COUNT(1) FROM [Fact].[Sale]
14 SELECT COUNT(1) FROM [Fact].[Stock Holding]
15 SELECT COUNT(1) FROM [Fact].[Transaction]
16 SELECT COUNT(1) FROM [Integration].[City_Staging]
17 SELECT COUNT(1) FROM [Integration].[Customer_Staging]
```

Figure 10.4 – A screenshot showing the generated T-SQL code

The `BimlScript` file view in Visual Studio is usually split into two parts. The upper part is the Biml code part, and the bottom part is the preview part where you can have a look at what the script is producing after it has been compiled.

How it works...

In this recipe, we have harnessed the database structure that the Biml engine has acquired from connecting to Microsoft SQL Server and used it to generate a T-SQL statement based on our select statement template for each table.

Let's look closely at what's going on in this recipe. The Biml script connects to the SQL server specified in the connection string, loads the database schema, and in the `foreach` loop over a collection of table elements, generates a SELECT statement using `<#=table.Schema#>.<#=table.Name#>`, where the `table` object is a row representing SQL table.

The `BimlScript` file that we have created in this recipe consists of two parts: a **text block** and a **control block**. The text block here contains the `SELECT * FROM` T-SQL statement and the Control block is a BimlScript code nugget that contains logic telling the Biml engine how to put all of the building blocks together to produce a complete **business intelligence (BI)** asset.

In *step 2* of this recipe, we used `<#` to signal the beginning of the control block. Control blocks can be written in either VB or C#; we will use only C# in our recipes.

In *step 3*, we used `#>` after the curly bracket of the `foreach loop` to signal the end of the control block.

`<#=` and `#>` are used to indicate an **expression block** that provides access to a compiled value, and in our example, it is providing the values of the table schema and table name that are needed for the select statement.

There's more...

In a similar fashion, you can generate view statements for each table. You could use the `GetColumnList()` method of the Biml `TableNode` class to produce the list of all table column names. It is also possible to generate `drop` and `create` Data Definition Language (DDL) statements for each object in the database, as we will see in the next recipe. I would encourage you to play with built-in methods that are available from the live Biml database schema object retrieved by the `GetDatabaseSchema` function. Using the preview pane and the `<#= #>` expression block that shows you the compiled values of variables, you can learn a lot of things and use them when building your solution.

Expression blocks can also be used for debugging purposes when you want to see what exactly the code has access to.

Generating T-SQL to drop and create all indexes

In this second recipe, we will demonstrate another Biml metadata-based superpower. Sometimes you will need to drop all your table indexes and then recreate them. Instead of doing it through dynamic SQL, you can do it faster with Biml, because it gives you complete SQL statements. Let's generate SQL statements to drop and create indexes for each table.

Getting ready

Open Visual Studio 2019, and then open the **ETLInAzure** SSIS project.

Just think of a name for your second BimlScript file. Let's be original and call it `Recipe2.Biml`.

How to do it...

Let's add a new BimlScript file for this recipe.

1. Add a new BimlScript file to your solution. Rename it to `Recipe2.biml`. It should contain only opening and closing Biml tags.

2. Add the following code between Biml tags to configure a database connection and get the metadata of the database using the `GetDatabaseSchema()` method:

   ```
   <# var sourceConnection = SchemaManager.
   CreateConnectionNode("Destination", @"Data
   Source=ETLInAzureBook\MSSQL2019; Initial
   Catalog=WideWorldImportersDW; Provider=SQLNCLI11.1;
   Integrated Security=SSPI; Auto Translate=False;");
   var sourceMetadata = sourceConnection.
   GetDatabaseSchema();
   ```

3. In a `foreach` loop, go through every table and generate the T-SQL statement for dropping and creating indexes in each table. Add the code shown in the following snippet to do so:

   ```
   foreach(var table in sourceMetadata.TableNodes) {
   foreach(var key in table.Indexes) {
   #>
   <#=key.GetDropAndCreateDdl()#>
   <#}}#>
   ```

   Here, we have two loops. The outer loop goes into each table definition, and the inner loop goes through each index and retrieves a `drop` and `create` statement for it.

4. Click **Save**. In the bottom right of the preview pane, click **Update**. You should see the generated T-SQL code, as shown in the following screenshot:

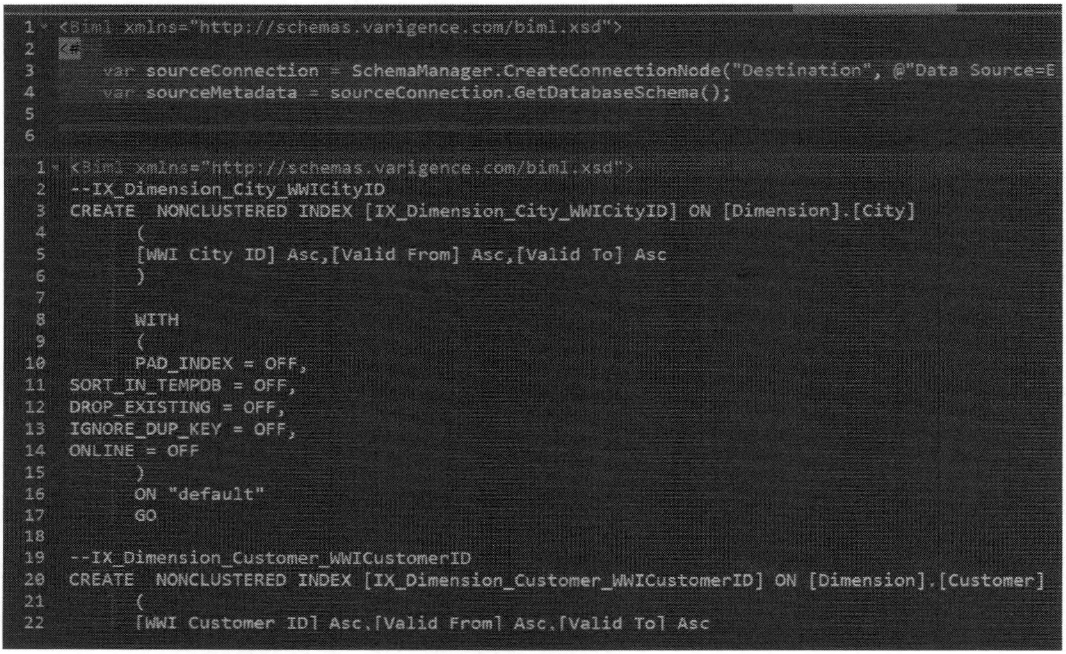

```
1  <Biml xmlns="http://schemas.varigence.com/biml.xsd">
2  <#
3      var sourceConnection = SchemaManager.CreateConnectionNode("Destination", @"Data Source=E
4      var sourceMetadata = sourceConnection.GetDatabaseSchema();
5
6
```

```
1  <Biml xmlns="http://schemas.varigence.com/biml.xsd">
2  --IX_Dimension_City_WWICityID
3  CREATE  NONCLUSTERED INDEX [IX_Dimension_City_WWICityID] ON [Dimension].[City]
4      (
5      [WWI City ID] Asc,[Valid From] Asc,[Valid To] Asc
6      )
7
8      WITH
9      (
10         PAD_INDEX = OFF,
11  SORT_IN_TEMPDB = OFF,
12  DROP_EXISTING = OFF,
13  IGNORE_DUP_KEY = OFF,
14  ONLINE = OFF
15     )
16     ON "default"
17     GO
18
19  --IX_Dimension_Customer_WWICustomerID
20  CREATE  NONCLUSTERED INDEX [IX_Dimension_Customer_WWICustomerID] ON [Dimension].[Customer]
21     (
22     [WWI Customer ID] Asc,[Valid From] Asc,[Valid To] Asc
```

Figure 10.5 – A screenshot showing the generated T-SQL code

The T-SQL generated in the preview pane can now be copied and pasted in **Microsoft SQL Server Management Studio** (**SSMS**) and executed, after removing the very first and last lines containing opening and closing `Biml` tags.

How it works...

This simple example just loops through a collection of `Table` elements, and then through a collection of `Indexes` of each `Table` and gets the `DROP` and `CREATE` statement of that `Index`.

Generating a basic SSIS package

Now we are ready to get to SSIS packages. Let's start with an SSIS package that is similar to a master package, because that type of package is best suited to automation. Master packages are usually simple and call other packages in a linear manner. We will use a Wide World Importers sample SSIS project for this recipe. In the Wide World Importers sample project, `DailyETLMain.dtsx` is a single package, and it contains a set of `Sequences` for each destination table. Each sequence has more logic in it. All we want to do in this recipe is to generate an SSIS package with a collection of empty `Sequence Containers` for each destination table.

Getting ready

There are a couple of steps we need to take before beginning:

1. Open Visual Studio 2019 and then open the **ETLInAzure** SSIS project. First, we will need to prepare our driving force: metadata. You will need to create a new SQL Server database, `BIMLMetadata`, where the metadata and configuration for this project are going to reside.

2. Open **Microsoft SQL Server Management Studio (SSMS)** and connect to the SQL server `ETLInAzureBook\MSSQL2019`. Open the **New Query** window and run the following T-SQL statement to create the metadata database:

    ```
    CREATE DATABASE [BIMLmetadata]
    ```

3. Create a single table, `TableConfig`, in the `BIMLMetadata` database. We will store table names and other useful information in it. Open the **New Query** window and run the following `CREATE TABLE` statement:

    ```
    CREATE TABLE [dbo].[TableConfig](
        [TableType] [nvarchar](50) NULL,
        [SchemaName] [nvarchar](256) NULL,
        [TableName] [nvarchar](256) NULL,
        [StagingTableName] [nvarchar](256) NULL,
        [GetStoredProc] [nvarchar](256) NULL,
        [MigrateStoredProc] [nvarchar](256) NULL,
        [TableOrder] [int] NULL
    ) ON [PRIMARY]
    ```

4. Populate the `TableConfig` table with the metadata for each destination table. We will use only `TableType` and `TableName` in this recipe, but other columns will be useful for our upcoming recipes. Open the **New Query** window and run the following `CREATE TABLE` statement:

```
INSERT [dbo].[TableConfig] VALUES (N'Dimension',
N'Dimension', N'City', N'City_Staging',
N'GetCityUpdates', N'MigrateStagedCityData', 1),
(N'Dimension', N'Dimension', N'Customer',
N'Customer_Staging', N'GetCustomerUpdates',
N'MigrateStagedCustomerData', 2),
(N'Dimension', N'Dimension', N'Employee',
N'Employee_Staging', N'GetEmployeeUpdates',
N'MigrateStagedEmployeeData', 3)
```

This script inserts only the first three rows of the table. For the complete T-SQL script, please refer to GitHub.

How to do it...

Open Visual Studio 2019, and then open the **ETLInAzure** SSIS project.

Add a new BimlScript file to your solution. Rename the new BimlScript file to `Recipe3. biml`. We will generate a basic frame for an SSIS master package:

1. Between Biml tags, add directives that specify the two .NET namespaces needed to access the Biml metadata database and to load metadata in a collection of rows:

```
<#@ import namespace="System.Data" #>
<#@ import namespace="System.Data.SqlClient" #>
```

2. Below the directives, in a control block, declare a `connectionString` variable with a connection string to the metadata database, as shown in the following code snippet:

```
<#
string connectionString = @"Data Source=ETLInAzureBook\
MSSQL2019; Persist Security Info=true; Integrated
Security=SSPI; Initial Catalog=BIMLmetadata";
#>
```

3. Now in the text block, create a skeleton for the package by first adding a `Packages` collection element, and then adding a `Package` element. Add a `Name` attribute to the `Package` element and set it to `Recipe3`. Inside the `Package` element, we need to define a `Tasks` collection element:

```
<Packages>
<Package Name="Recipe3">
        <Tasks>
        </Tasks>
</Package>
</Packages>
```

4. Now we need to stuff our package with a collection of `Sequence` containers – one for each destination table. The information about destination tables is stored in our metadata table. We will fetch table information from our metadata database, loop through it, and create a `Sequence Container` for each data row. We will put a control block that does just that within the `Tasks` collection element. Add the following code snippet between `Tasks` tags:

```
<#
DataTable dtTables = new DataTable();
using (SqlConnection sqlConn = new SqlConnection
(connectionString))
{
    string sqlCmd = @"SELECT * from dbo.TableConfig;";
    SqlDataAdapter sqlDtAdp = new SqlDataAdapter(sqlCmd,
sqlConn);
    sqlDtAdp.Fill(dtTables);
}
foreach(DataRow drTable in dtTables.Rows) {
#>
<Container Name="Load <#=drTable["TableName"]#>
<#=drTable["TableType"]#>">
</Container>
<#}#>
```

5.   We are done! All we need to do now is to save our BimlScript file; right click on the file and choose **Generate SSIS Packages**, as shown in the following screenshot:

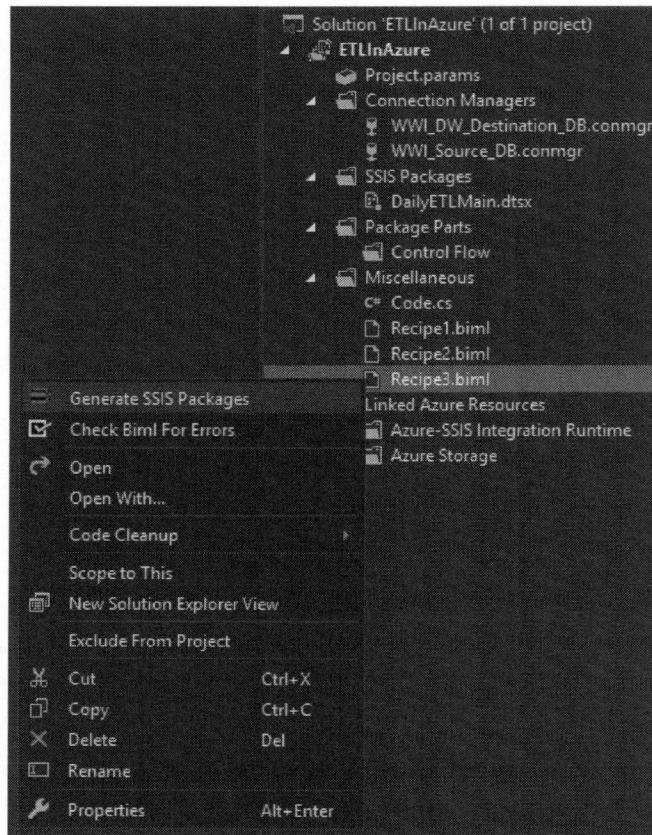

Figure 10.6 – A screenshot showing the Generate SSIS Packages menu item

This will generate a new SSIS Package called `Recipe3.dtsx` with a set of empty `Sequence Containers`, as shown in the following screenshot:

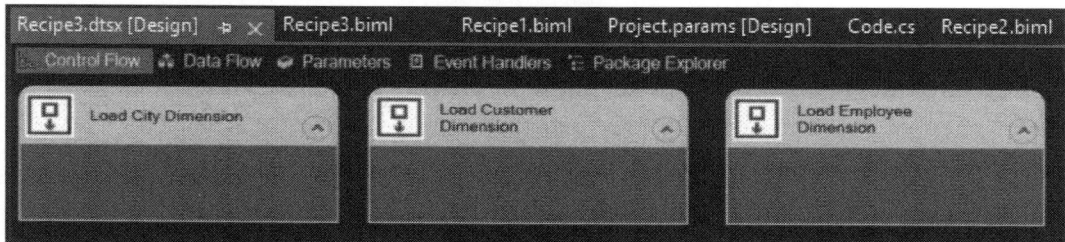

Figure 10.7 – A screenshot showing the generated SSIS package

The only purpose of this recipe is to demonstrate how to use Biml to generate a simple SSIS package based on a metadata table. This package will not do anything, but it shows the concept of generating SSIS tasks based on a pattern and external configuration data coming from a metadata table.

How it works...

In this recipe, Biml loops through a set of records and generates Sequence Container elements for each record. It takes TableName and TableType values from every row to generate a sequence container name. In this example, we have two types of code – one is written in XML and the other in C#. Using the combination of them, we can tell Biml what SSIS elements we want to have in our SSIS package, and how we want to add them. We use C# loops here to repeat the Sequence Container element for every table that we have, and by using XML we are saying that we want to add a Sequence Container and what parameters we want to give it.

SqlDataAdapter can be used to load metadata tables and to iterate through their records, usually containing table or column information, to implement the automation.

There's more...

In the SSIS package that was generated, all the Sequence Containers are configured for parallel execution, so when the package is executed, they will all run in parallel. If we want to create a sequence and execute them one after another, we can set the ConstraintMode property of the package to make all tasks execute on success, one after another. See the following screenshot, for example:

```
<Packages>
    <Package Name="Recipe3" ConstraintMode="LinearOnSuccess">
        <Tasks>
```

Figure 10.8 – A screenshot showing the ConstraintMode property

Another option is to set ConstraintMode to LinerOnCompletion. This will string the tasks together to run in a sequence on completion, regardless of whether it was a success or failure.

What's great about BimlExpress is its **IntelliSense**, a code-completion aid that makes code writing more efficient. The developer does not have to remember all the syntax, parameters, and their allowed values. You can see an example of IntelliSense in the following screenshot:

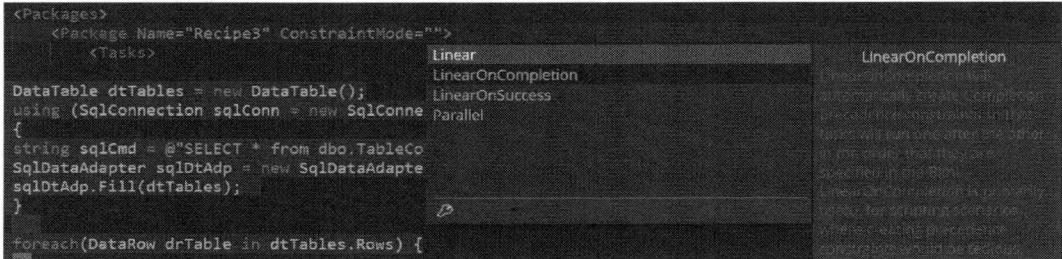

```
<Packages>
    <Package Name="Recipe3" ConstraintMode="">
        <Tasks>                              Linear                      LinearOnCompletion
                                             LinearOnCompletion
DataTable dtTables = new DataTable();        LinearOnSuccess
using (SqlConnection sqlConn = new SqlConne  Parallel
{
string sqlCmd = @"SELECT * from dbo.TableCo
SqlDataAdapter sqlDtAdp = new SqlDataAdapte
sqlDtAdp.Fill(dtTables);
}

foreach(DataRow drTable in dtTables.Rows) {
```

Figure 10.9 – A screenshot showing the use of IntelliSense

As long as the code has no errors, IntelliSense is working. When IntelliSense stops working, that's because there is a problem in the code somewhere and you need to fix it.

Generating an SSIS package with Execute SQL Tasks

Now let's create an SSIS package with some more meat on it. The original SSIS package that I want to generate automatically, `DailyETLMain.dtsx`, contains multiple tasks within each Sequence Container, such as an Expression Task and Execute SQL Tasks, as shown in the following screenshot:

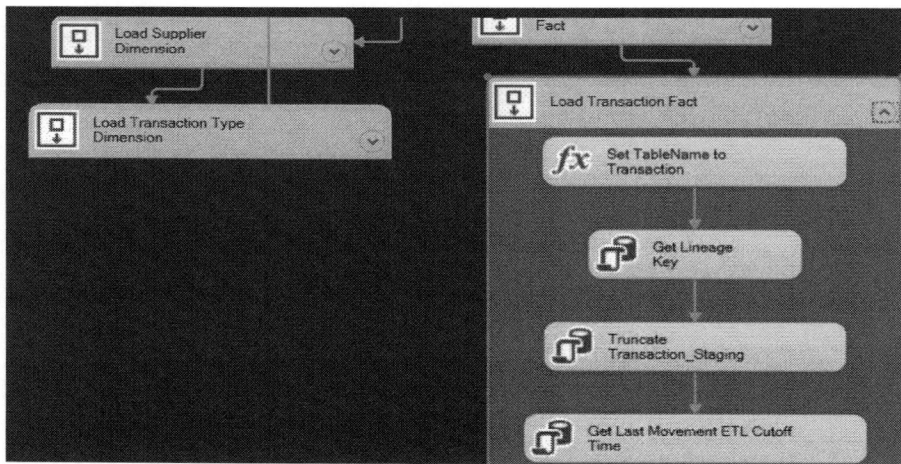

Figure 10.10 – A screenshot showing DailyETLMain.dtsx

We will begin with the Biml code that was started in the previous recipe and programmatically add precedence constraints, connections, variables, and tasks within each `Sequence Container`. What we want to accomplish in this recipe is generating an SSIS package with Sequence Containers that will run one after another on success. Each sequence container will contain four tasks: one `Expression Task` and three `Execute SQL Tasks`. The resulting package will be one more step toward using Biml to automatically generate a sample `DailyETLMain.dtsx` SSIS package from the Wide World Importers project.

Getting ready

Open Visual Studio 2019, and then open the **ETLInAzure** SSIS project.

How to do it...

Add a new BimlScript file to your solution and rename it to `Recipe4.biml`. Copy the code from `Recipe3.biml` to the new BimlScript file because it will be our starting point:

1. Change the name of the package in the `Package` element to `Recipe4`. Move the code that populates the `DataTable` object with the metadata to the top of the file, under the connection string initialization. It is better to have most of the control block bulk at the top of the file, rather than scattered everywhere, as this makes the file more readable.

    See the following screenshot for a reference on how the control block should look after the `DataTable` initialization code is moved to the top of the file:

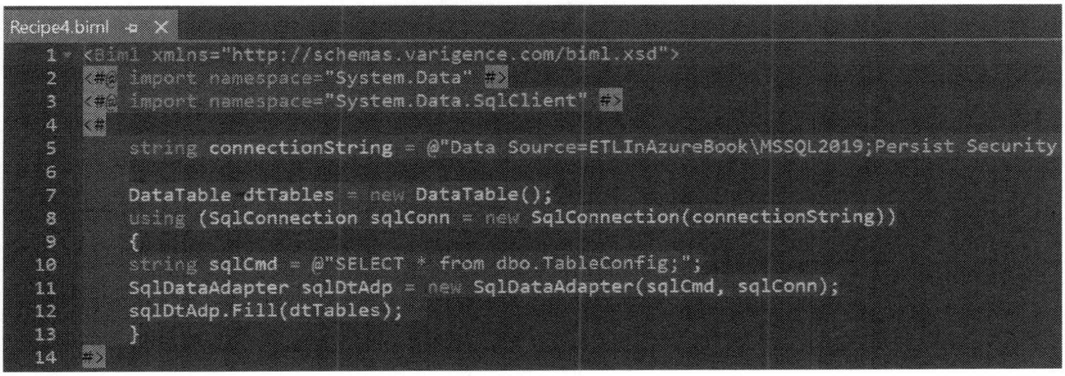

```
Recipe4.biml ⊕ ✕
     1 ▾ <Biml xmlns="http://schemas.varigence.com/biml.xsd">
     2   <#@ import namespace="System.Data" #>
     3   <#@ import namespace="System.Data.SqlClient" #>
     4   <#
     5       string connectionString = @"Data Source=ETLInAzureBook\MSSQL2019;Persist Security
     6
     7       DataTable dtTables = new DataTable();
     8       using (SqlConnection sqlConn = new SqlConnection(connectionString))
     9       {
    10           string sqlCmd = @"SELECT * from dbo.TableConfig;";
    11           SqlDataAdapter sqlDtAdp = new SqlDataAdapter(sqlCmd, sqlConn);
    12           sqlDtAdp.Fill(dtTables);
    13       }
    14   #>
```

Figure 10.11 – A screenshot showing the control block in Biml

2. Let's add **Connections** to the SSIS package, we will need them for our Execute SQL Task. In the BimlScript file, right above the **Packages** element, add the following code snippet:

```
<Connections>
        <Connection Name="WWI_
Source_DB" CreateInProject="true"
ConnectionString="Data Source=.;Initial
Catalog=WideWorldImporters;Provider=SQLNCLI11.1;
Integrated Security=SSPI;Auto Translate=False;" />
        <Connection Name="WWI_DW_
Destination_DB" CreateInProject="true"
ConnectionString="Data Source=.;Initial
Catalog=WideWorldImportersDW;Provider=SQLNCLI11.1;
Integrated Security=SSPI;Auto Translate=False;" />
</Connections>
```

We are defining two connections here – one is for the WideWorldImporters source database, and another one is for the destination database, WideWorldImportersDW. Both will be used in this recipe and in the following recipes.

3. Inside of the **Package** XML element, add a new attribute:

```
ConstraintMode="LinearOnSuccess"
```

This will create a precedence constraint between tasks in the order in which those tasks are added to the package.

4. Now we will need to add variables. There are four variables that are required for our final package. Add the following code right under the Package opening tag:

```
<Variables>
<Variable Name="LastETLCutoffTime" DataType="DateTime"
IncludeInDebugDump="Include">4/11/2016 10:39:10 AM</
Variable>
        <Variable Name="LineageKey" DataType="Int32"
IncludeInDebugDump="Include">0</Variable>
        <Variable Name="TableName" DataType="String"
IncludeInDebugDump="Exclude"></Variable>
        <Variable Name="TargetETLCutoffTime"
DataType="DateTime" IncludeInDebugDump="Include">4/13/2016
11:25:23 AM</Variable>
</Variables>
```

The `Variables` collection will be located above the `Tasks` element, as shown in the following screenshot:

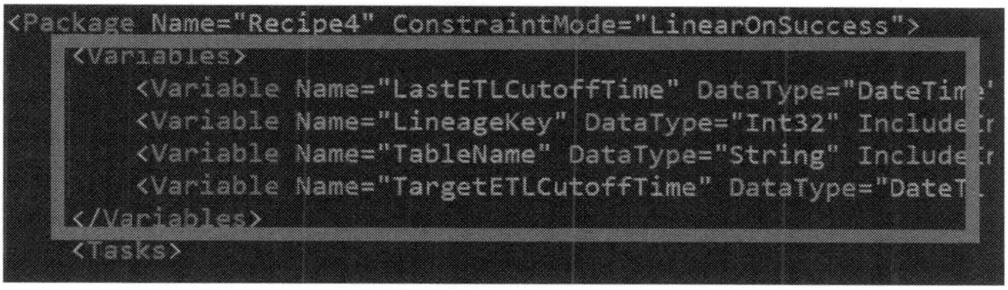

```
<Package Name="Recipe4" ConstraintMode="LinearOnSuccess">
    <Variables>
        <Variable Name="LastETLCutoffTime" DataType="DateTime"
        <Variable Name="LineageKey" DataType="Int32" Include
        <Variable Name="TableName" DataType="String" Include
        <Variable Name="TargetETLCutoffTime" DataType="DateT
    </Variables>
    <Tasks>
```

Figure 10.12 – A screenshot showing the Variable definition in Biml

5. Add a **ConstraintMode** attribute to the `Container` element and set it to **LinearOnSuccess**, because we want the tasks within to be executed one after another:

```
<Container Name="Load <#=drTable["TableName"]#>
<#=drTable["TableType"]#>"
ConstraintMode="LinearOnSuccess">
```

6. Add the `Tasks` collection element to the `Container` to start adding tasks inside the container. Then, inside of the `Tasks` collection element, the first `Task` that we will add is an **Expression Task**, which sets an SSIS user variable to the value of the destination table, as shown in the following code snippet:

```
<Expression Name="Set TableName to
<#=drTable["TableName"]#>" Expression="@[User::TableName]
= &quot;<#=drTable["TableName"]#>&quot;" />
```

We can reference a user variable in Biml using this syntax: `@ [User::<VariableName>]`. You will also notice the use of `&quot;` – it is needed to represent a quotation mark. The Biml file is an XML file and it is sensitive to special characters such as less-than, `<`; greater-than, `>`; apostrophe, `'`; double quotes, `"`; and the ampersand, `&`. Please refer to `https://support.varigence.com/hc/en-us/articles/360000975975-Protected-XML-Characters-in-Biml` for the list of special characters in Biml that need to be represented with escape sequences.

7. Next, add the XML code for `Execute SQL Task`, called `Get Lineage Key`, as
    shown in the following code snippet:

```
<ExecuteSQL Name="Get Lineage Key" ConnectionName="WWI_
DW_Destination_DB" ResultSet="SingleRow">
  <Results>
            <Result Name="LineageKey" VariableName="User.
LineageKey" />
    </Results>
    <Parameters>
            <Parameter Name="0" VariableName="User.
TableName" Length="-1" DataType="String" />
            <Parameter Name="1" VariableName="User.
TargetETLCutoffTime" Length="-1" DataType="Date" />
    </Parameters>
<DirectInput>EXEC Integration.GetLineageKey ?,?;          </
DirectInput>
</ExecuteSQL>
```

Now let's go over each XML element and attribute:

a) The `ConnectionName` attribute of `ExecuteSQL` is where we specify the name
   to the destination connection.

b) The `Results` element contains information on where to assign the returned
   value. Here, we assign it to the user variable `LineageKey`.

c) The `Parameters` collection element contains information on which input
   parameters are needed for the Execute SQL Task. Here, we need two parameters:
   `TableName` and `TargetETLCutOffTime`. We need to specify their names
   and data types within the `Parameters` collection element. Just as in SSIS, the
   names of these parameters are the order in which they will be referenced in the
   `Execute` statement.

d) And finally, in the `DirectInput` element, we can specify the T-SQL statement
   that we want to execute. We call a stored procedure, `[Integration].`
   `[GetLineageKey]`, and pass two of our parameters to it. The result will be
   returned in the `LineageKey` variable.

8. Let's add a second Execute SQL Task to truncate the destination table, as shown in the following code snippet:

```
<ExecuteSQL Name="Truncate
<#=drTable["StagingTableName"]#>" ConnectionName="WWI_DW_
Destination_DB">
<DirectInput>DELETE FROM
Integration.<#=drTable["StagingTableName"]#>;</
DirectInput>
</ExecuteSQL>
```

Here, we have a simpler Execute SQL Task that uses a connection with ConnectionName `WWI_DW_Destination_DB` and executes a single line T-SQL statement on a table. The table name for the SQL statement is provided at compile time from the value in the `StagingTableName` column of the metadata table.

9. Add the last Execute SQL Task to the BimlScript file for this recipe. Similar to the first Execute SQL Task, it has `Results`, `Parameters` and `DirectInput` elements. We also specify that the `ResultSet` is `SingleRow`. Add the following code snippet to the BimlScript file:

```
<ExecuteSQL Name="Get Last <#=drTable["TableName"]#>
ETL Cutoff Time" ConnectionName="WWI_DW_Destination_DB"
ResultSet="SingleRow">
    <Results>
        <Result Name="CutoffTime" VariableName="User.
LastETLCutoffTime" />
    </Results>
    <Parameters>
        <Parameter Name="0" VariableName="User.TableName"
Length="-1" DataType="String" />
    </Parameters>
        <DirectInput>EXEC Integration.GetLastETLCutoffTime
?;</DirectInput>
</ExecuteSQL>
```

This Execute SQL Task retrieves `LastETLCutOffTime` for a table.

10. Now we are ready to generate our bulkier SSIS package that has some real work units. Let's right-click on `Recipe4.biml` and choose **Generate SSIS Package**. This will generate a new SSIS package, `Recipe4.dtsx`. You can open it to see what we were able to build so far. I moved the `Sequence Containers` sideways so that they fit better on the screen because Biml generated the SSIS package with all the `Sequence Containers` arranged one below another. It should look like the following screenshot:

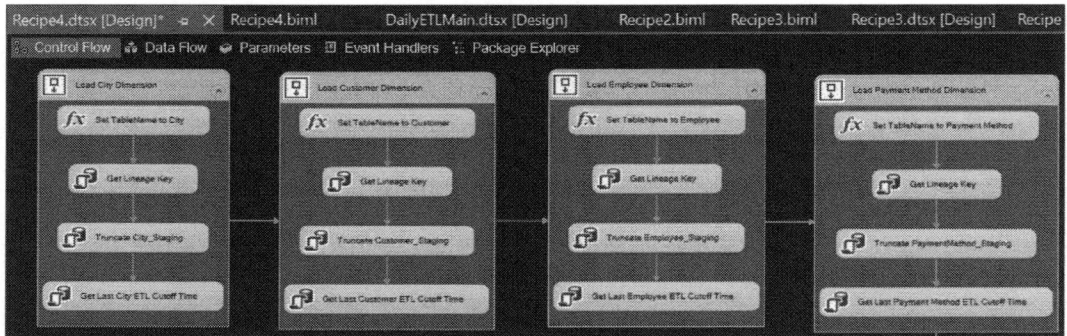

Figure 10.13 – A screenshot showing the generated SSIS package

You can even run this package in debug mode to see if everything is working as it should. As this package is not complete yet, all we really do here is truncate destination tables. The goal of this recipe was to move one step toward using Biml to automatically generate a sample `DailyETLMain.dtsx` SSIS package from the Wide World Importers project.

How it works...

Going through every row of the table with the metadata, Biml creates one `Sequence Container` with four tasks inside – one `Expression Task` and three `Execute SQL Tasks` – for each table. Since `Execute Tasks` need to have a database connection, Biml expects a `Connection` element. It is usually very simple and all that it has is a connection name and a connection string.

To better understand how it works, let's look more closely at the preview pane from this recipe. The preview pane shows the compiled Biml and this can help greatly when debugging. Looking at the preview pane here, we see how Biml went through the metadata table and produced Biml elements for every row, as shown in the following screenshot.

I highlighted every place on the screenshot where Biml puts a value from the metadata table, as it was instructed to do:

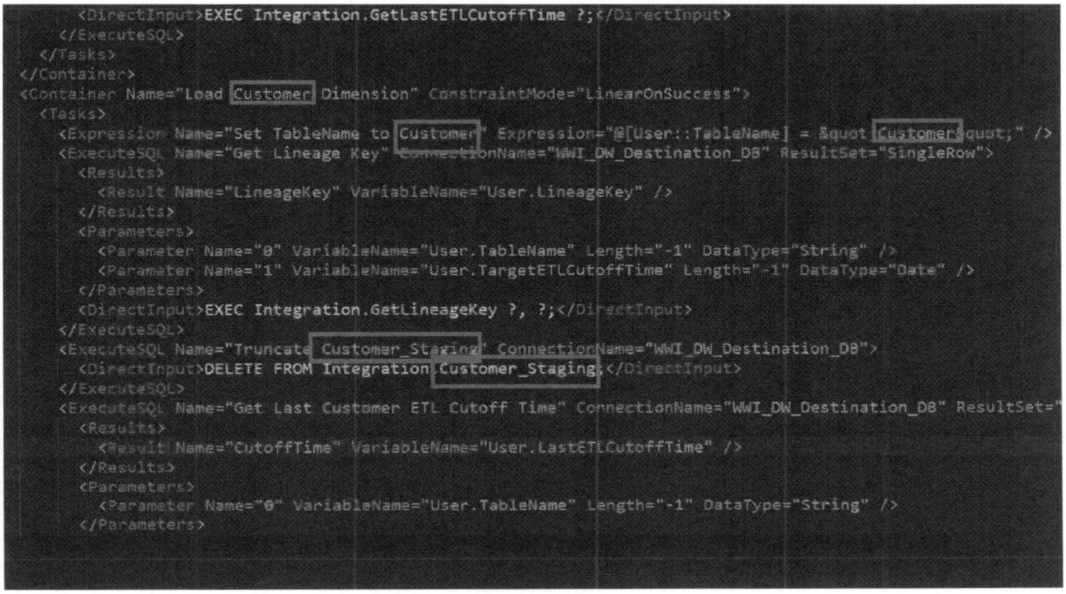

```
        <DirectInput>EXEC Integration.GetLastETLCutoffTime ?;</DirectInput>
      </ExecuteSQL>
    </Tasks>
  </Container>
  <Container Name="Load Customer Dimension" ConstraintMode="LinearOnSuccess">
    <Tasks>
      <Expression Name="Set TableName to Customer" Expression="@[User::TableName] = &quot;Customer&quot;" />
      <ExecuteSQL Name="Get Lineage Key" ConnectionName="WWI_DW_Destination_DB" ResultSet="SingleRow">
        <Results>
          <Result Name="LineageKey" VariableName="User.LineageKey" />
        </Results>
        <Parameters>
          <Parameter Name="0" VariableName="User.TableName" Length="-1" DataType="String" />
          <Parameter Name="1" VariableName="User.TargetETLCutoffTime" Length="-1" DataType="Date" />
        </Parameters>
        <DirectInput>EXEC Integration.GetLineageKey ?, ?;</DirectInput>
      </ExecuteSQL>
      <ExecuteSQL Name="Truncate Customer_Staging" ConnectionName="WWI_DW_Destination_DB">
        <DirectInput>DELETE FROM Integration.Customer_Staging;</DirectInput>
      </ExecuteSQL>
      <ExecuteSQL Name="Get Last Customer ETL Cutoff Time" ConnectionName="WWI_DW_Destination_DB" ResultSet="
        <Results>
          <Result Name="CutoffTime" VariableName="User.LastETLCutoffTime" />
        </Results>
        <Parameters>
          <Parameter Name="0" VariableName="User.TableName" Length="-1" DataType="String" />
        </Parameters>
```

Figure 10.14 – A screenshot showing the compiled Biml

The preview pane shows the intermediate code that is produced by Biml before generating an SSIS package. This is where we can see how the BimlScript of the control block is being compiled and how the original Biml XML is expanded following the instructions given in the control block. In this recipe, in the BimlScript file, we have a `foreach` loop that loops through every record in the metadata table and for each record, it instructs Biml to generate a `Sequence Container` and its tasks. In the preview pane, the `foreach` loop is already compiled and the result is multiple `Sequence Containers` listed one after another, connected by precedence constraints, and containing four tasks inside each container.

There's more...

When the Biml code becomes too big and you want to use the entire screen to see it, click **Hide Preview** on the righthand side to hide the preview pane and to see the code fully on your screen. You can always get the preview back by clicking **Show Preview**. The preview pane shows the compiled Biml and can help greatly while debugging your code.

Whenever you make changes to your Biml code and save the file, the preview pane is usually updated and refreshed with the newly compiled results. If this doesn't happen and you do not see **Preview is up-to-date** at the bottom right, use the **Update** button to update the preview.

Using Convert SSIS package to Biml

The sample `DailyETLMain.dtsx` SSIS package for the `WideWorldImporters` solution first has three tasks that precede a list of `Sequence Containers`, and they are quite basic. So, instead of going over the Biml to create them, which we have already covered in previous recipes, let's demonstrate one helpful functionality in BimlExpress that can be a great learning tool as well – it is the option to **Convert SSIS Package to Biml**.

What we want to accomplish in this recipe is to do the opposite of what we were doing in previous recipes and to generate Biml code from an existing SSIS package.

Getting ready

Open Visual Studio 2019, and then open the ETLInAzure SSIS project.

How to do it...

Add a new Biml file to your solution and rename it to `Recipe5.biml`. Copy the code from `Recipe4.biml` to the new Biml file because it will be our starting point:

1. Change the name of the package in the **Package** element to `Recipe5`.

2. Right-click on the original SSIS package for the `WideWorldImporters` solution, called `DailyETLMain.dtsx` and choose the **Convert SSIS Packages to Biml** option, as shown in the following screenshot:

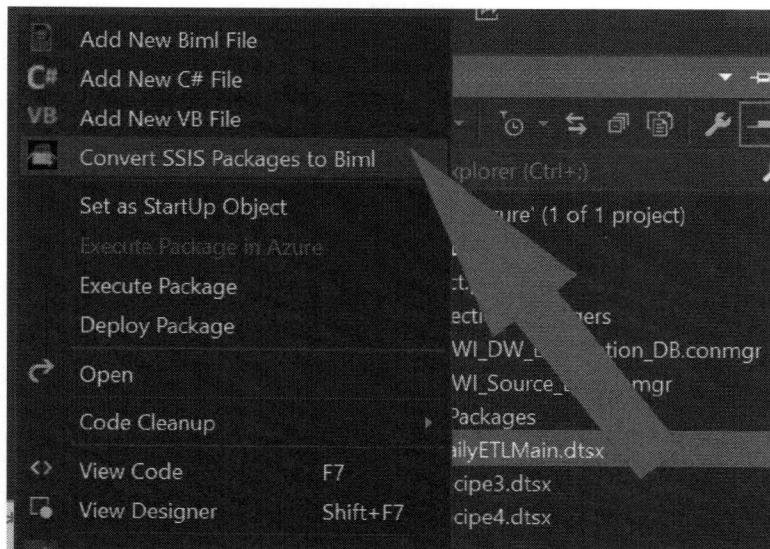

Figure 10.15 – A screenshot showing the Convert SSIS Packages to Biml menu item

3. The **Import Packages** screen will open. Leave all values as the default and click **Import**, as shown in the following screenshot:

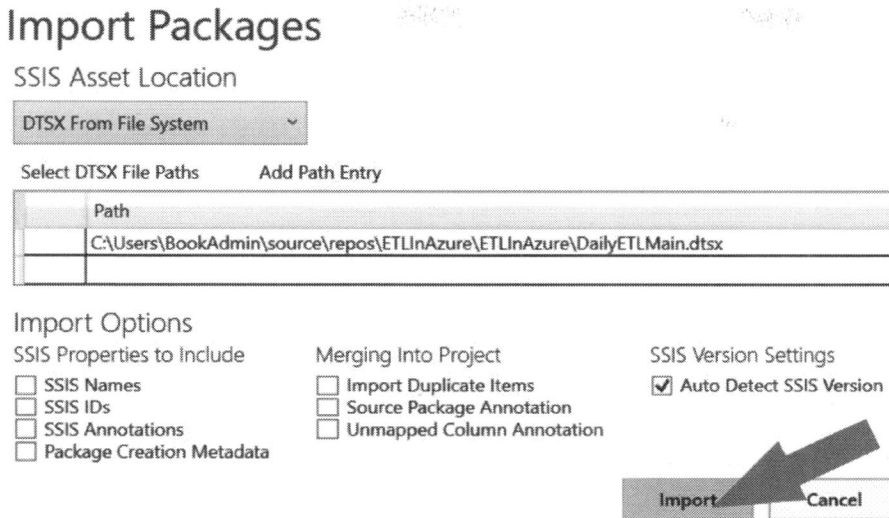

Import Packages

SSIS Asset Location

DTSX From File System

Select DTSX File Paths   Add Path Entry

Path
C:\Users\BookAdmin\source\repos\ETLInAzure\ETLInAzure\DailyETLMain.dtsx

Import Options

SSIS Properties to Include
- ☐ SSIS Names
- ☐ SSIS IDs
- ☐ SSIS Annotations
- ☐ Package Creation Metadata

Merging Into Project
- ☐ Import Duplicate Items
- ☐ Source Package Annotation
- ☐ Unmapped Column Annotation

SSIS Version Settings
- ☑ Auto Detect SSIS Version

Import   Cancel

Figure 10.16 – A screenshot showing the Import Packages wizard

4. The screen will change and an **Add To Project** button will appear. Click on it.

5. A new Biml file will be added to the project with the default name `BimlScript.biml` and opened in Visual Studio. Inside, you will see the Biml script that corresponds to the original SSIS package. You can use it as is to generate a package identical to the original SSIS package.

6. Let's select the Biml script for the three tasks that we need and copy it to our clipboard, as shown in the following screenshot:

```
</Variables>
<Tasks>
    <Expression Name="Calculate ETL Cutoff Time backup" Expression="@[User::TargetETLCutoffTi
    <Expression Name="Trim Any Milliseconds" Expression="@[User::TargetETLCutoffTime] = DATEA
    <ExecuteSQL Name="Ensure Date Dimension includes current year" ConnectionName="ImportedPr
        <DirectInput>DECLARE @YearNumber int =  YEAR(SYSDATETIME());
tegration.PopulateDateDimensionForYear @YearNumber;</DirectInput>
    </ExecuteSQL>
    <Container Name="Load City Dimension" ConstraintMode="LinearOnSuccess">
        <Tasks>
            <Expression Name="Set TableName to City" Expression="@[User::TableName] = &quot;C
```

Figure 10.17 – A screenshot showing the tasks defined in Biml

The three tasks that we need are located between the `Variables` elements and the first `Container` element.

7. Paste the copied script in `Recipe5.biml`, directly under the opening `Tasks` element and above the `foreach` control block, as shown in the following screenshot:

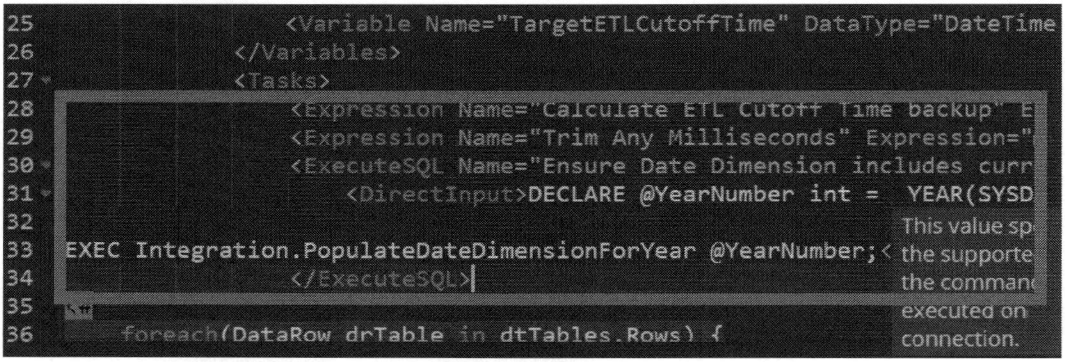

```
25              <Variable Name="TargetETLCutoffTime" DataType="DateTime
26         </Variables>
27         <Tasks>
28              <Expression Name="Calculate ETL Cutoff Time backup" E
29              <Expression Name="Trim Any Milliseconds" Expression="
30              <ExecuteSQL Name="Ensure Date Dimension includes curr
31                  <DirectInput>DECLARE @YearNumber int =   YEAR(SYSD
32                                                               This value sp
33   EXEC Integration.PopulateDateDimensionForYear @YearNumber;<  the supporte
34                  </ExecuteSQL>                                 the comman
35                                                               executed on
36         foreach(DataRow drTable in dtTables.Rows) {           connection.
```

Figure 10.18 – A screenshot showing the tasks defined in Biml

8. The generated Biml code did not use the connection names that we defined in `Recipe5.biml`, so we'll need to update the `ConnectionName` in the Execute SQL Task and set it to the name of the destination database, as shown in the following code snippet:

```
<ExecuteSQL Name="Ensure Date Dimension includes current
year" ConnectionName="WWI_DW_Destination_DB">
```

9. Save the `Recipe5.biml` file and right-click on it. Choose **Generate SSIS Packages**.

10. Open the generated `Recipe5.dtsx` and run in the debug mode, just to make sure that everything is OK.

Let's move on to the next section!

How it works...

In this recipe, we used the BimlExpress Import Packages tool to generate a Biml portion that we needed for our Biml file. Sometimes it is faster to use the Import Packages tool than writing Biml manually. Since the goal of using Biml is efficiency and time economy, I find this tool extremely useful!

There's more...

Let's say we want to Biml-ize an ETL pattern that applies to multiple tables. To do that, we can manually create an SSIS package the way we want it to be generated, then convert it to Biml using **Convert SSIS Package to Biml**. Next, we build a metadata configuration with elements that change from table to table, such as table names, columns, primary keys, or indexes. Then we write C# code nuggets around Biml XML that generates multiple SSIS packages just like the original package but for all the tables configured in the metadata. That's a meta-recipe for Biml-izing ETL solutions.

> Tip
>
> I would recommend using this Import Packages tool very often in the beginning, as it will make learning Biml quick and easy. It is much faster to learn new things in Biml by converting an SSIS functionality and then looking at the produced Biml code than by reading articles or scouring the internet in the search of an example.

We have covered only one option here to import an SSIS package with default settings, but the Import Packages tool can import entire SSIS projects as well. You can also try different **Import** options.

Generating a mass change to stored procedures

If we want to automatically generate the sample SSIS package for the `WideWorldImporters` solution, as we intended to do in the beginning, we need to work on some prerequisites. These prerequisites are so interesting and challenging that it is best to dedicate a separate recipe to them. The SSIS package from the sample `WideWorldImporters` solution uses `Get stored procedures` in the **Data Flow Task OLE DB Source** to retrieve data from the source. In the original package, the `EXECUTE` statement calling each `Get stored procedure` uses the `RESULT SET` clause to specify data types and column names for the return result set. This is necessary for SSIS to work correctly because all `Get stored procedures` use **temp** tables and since temp tables are resolved at runtime, SSIS is unable to retrieve metadata for every output column of the result dataset.

The use of temp tables is a challenge for Biml as well, and in addition to the `RESULT SET` clause, we need to do something else. The limitation in Biml is the same: Biml cannot retrieve the metadata that it needs to generate Data Flow Output columns.

Source columns, metadata information is essential to Biml to be able to generate a Data Flow Task correctly, so we must help Biml get this information.

> **Tip**
> This workaround was sourced from the community on `stackoverflow.com`; here is the link to the idea that we are exploring in this recipe: `https://stackoverflow.com/questions/1579476/using-temp-tables-in-ssis/5076757#5076757`.

What we want to do is, in the `Source Database`, go through every stored procedure used in Data Flow Tasks to get the source data and add a fake `SELECT` statement at the top of the Stored Procedure code that will provide information on what columns will be returned by this stored procedure. This `SELECT` statement will be inside a conditional statement that will always evaluate to false, as shown in the example in the following code snippet:

```
IF 1 = 0 -- This will never really execute.
BEGIN
    SELECT
        CAST (0 AS int)            AS [WWI City ID],
        CAST (NULL AS nvarchar(50)) AS City,
        CAST (NULL AS nvarchar(50)) AS [State Province] ,
        CAST (NULL AS nvarchar(50)) AS Country ,
        CAST (NULL AS nvarchar(30)) AS Continent ,
        CAST (NULL AS nvarchar(50)) AS [Sales Territory] ,
        CAST (NULL AS bigint)       AS [Latest Recorded
Population],
        CAST (NULL AS datetime2(7)) AS [Valid From],
        CAST (NULL AS datetime2(7)) AS [Valid To]
END
```

Now we can begin the recipe.

Getting ready

Open Visual Studio 2019, and then open the **ETLInAzure** SSIS project.

How to do it...

Add a new Biml file to your solution and rename it to `Recipe6.biml`:

1. Copy only the control block C# code from the previous recipe, `Recipe5.biml`, to the new Biml file. Only copy the part between the opening `<Biml>` element and the `<Connections>` element, as shown in the following screenshot:

```
<Biml xmlns="http://schemas.varigence.com/biml.xsd">
<#@ import namespace="System.Data" #>
<#@ import namespace="System.Data.SqlClient" #>
<#
    string connectionString = @"Data Source=ETLInAzureBook\MSSQL2019;Persist Security Info=true;Integr

    DataTable dtTables = new DataTable();
    using (SqlConnection sqlConn = new SqlConnection(connectionString))
    {
    string sqlCmd = @"SELECT * from dbo.TableConfig;";
    SqlDataAdapter sqlDtAdp = new SqlDataAdapter(sqlCmd, sqlConn);
    sqlDtAdp.Fill(dtTables);
    }
#>
    <Connections>
```

Figure 10.19 – A screenshot showing the Control Blocks in Biml

2. Add a new C# file by right-clicking on the SSIS project and choosing **Add New C# File**, as shown in the following screenshot:

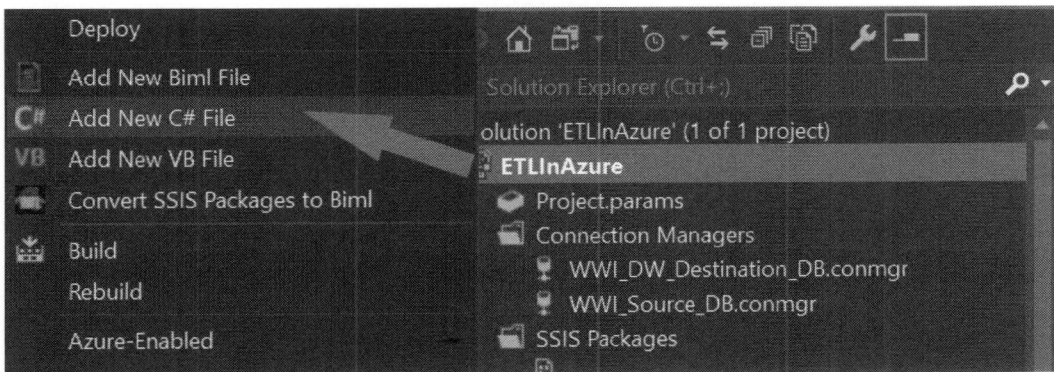

Figure 10.20 – A screenshot showing how to add a new C# file

3. Rename it to `Code.cs`. We need to create this small utility C# class to help us with generating a data type T-SQL string from SQL Server metadata. Putting this logic outside of the Biml file helps us keep the Biml file manageable and lets us reuse the logic in other Biml files.

4. Open the `Code.cs` file, and replace the default class, `MyClass`, with the following code snippet:

```
public static class BIMLHelper
{
    public static string GetDataType(string strDataType,
    string CharLength, string NumPrecision, string NumScale,
    string DatePrecision)
    {
        string strResult = strDataType;
        if (strDataType == "int" || strDataType ==
"bigint" || strDataType == "geography" || strDataType ==
"varbinary" || strDataType == "date")
            strResult += "";
        else if (!string.IsNullOrEmpty(CharLength))
            strResult += " (" + CharLength + ")";

        else if (!string.IsNullOrEmpty(NumScale) &&
NumScale != "0" && !string.IsNullOrEmpty(NumPrecision))
            strResult += " (" + NumPrecision + "," +
NumScale + ")";
        else if (!string.IsNullOrEmpty(NumPrecision))
            strResult += " (" + NumPrecision + ")";
        else if (!string.IsNullOrEmpty(DatePrecision))
            strResult += " (" + DatePrecision + ")";
        return strResult;
    }
}
```

The `BIMLHelper` class and the `GetDataType()` method have to be static because we do not need to instantiate objects; it's just a utility function that we want to use.

5. Add a reference to the new `Code.cs` file in the `Recipe6.biml` Biml file. To do so, add the following directive right under the opening `<Biml>` element, on line 2 of the file:

```
<#@ code file="Code.cs" #>
```

This directive should be at the top of the file, next to the `import` directives, and it informs Biml that we will reference `Code.cs` in our control block. This will allow the calling of the method defined in the `Code.cs` file, directly from the Biml file.

6. Add a new connection string for the destination `WideWorldImportersDW` database. To do so, add the following code snippet under the line that initializes the connection string to the `BIMLmetadata` database:

```
string connStrDest = @"Data Source=ETLInAzureBook\
MSSQL2019;Persist Security Info=true;Initial
Catalog=WideWorldImportersDW;Integrated Security=SSPI;";
```

This connection string needs to be added because we will connect to the destination database to read the metadata of the destination tables.

7. Add the following code at the end of the control block:

```
foreach(DataRow drTable in dtTables.Rows) {
string strColumnSQL = string.Format(@"SELECT * FROM
INFORMATION_SCHEMA.COLUMNS WHERE TABLE_SCHEMA =
'Integration' AND TABLE_NAME = '{0}' AND NOT (DATA_TYPE =
'int' AND COLUMN_NAME LIKE '% key') AND ORDINAL_POSITION
> 1
ORDER BY ORDINAL_POSITION",drTable["StagingTableName"]);
string strInject = @"IF 1 = 0
    BEGIN
    SELECT
    ";
using (SqlConnection sqlConnDest = new
SqlConnection(connStrDest))
    {
        SqlCommand command = new
SqlCommand(strColumnSQL,sqlConnDest);
        sqlConnDest.Open();
        SqlDataReader reader = command.ExecuteReader();
        if (reader.HasRows) {
            while (reader.Read())
        { strInject += @" CAST(NULL AS " +
BIMLHelper.GetDataType(reader["DATA_TYPE"].
ToString(),reader["CHARACTER_MAXIMUM_LENGTH"].
ToString(),reader["NUMERIC_PRECISION"].
ToString(),reader["NUMERIC_SCALE"].
```

```
ToString(),reader["DATETIME_PRECISION"].ToString()) + @")
AS [" + reader["COLUMN_NAME"] + @"],"; }
        }
        reader.Close();
        strInject = strInject.TrimEnd(',') + @" END";
    }
```

After this code, the control block should be closed by the closing tag, #>.

8. Now we'll start writing our text block, which will contain T-SQL code. Place this code right under the control block:

```
DECLARE @sp NVARCHAR(MAX)
DECLARE @marker NVARCHAR(MAX) = 'SET NOCOUNT ON;
    SET XACT_ABORT ON;'
DECLARE @inject NVARCHAR(MAX) =
'SET NOCOUNT ON;
    SET XACT_ABORT ON;
    <#=strInject#>

'
SELECT @sp = OBJECT_DEFINITION(OBJECT_ID('[Integration].
[<#=drTable["GetStoredProc"]#>]'))
SET @sp = REPLACE(@sp,' PROCEDURE ', ' OR ALTER PROCEDURE
')
SET @sp = REPLACE(@sp,@marker,@inject)
PRINT @sp
EXEC (@sp)
GO
```

This is the shell of the T-SQL statement that will be repeated for every stored procedure. The core of the statement comes from the strInject variable prepared in the control block, as was explained in the previous step.

9. Now, the last thing to do is to add a closing tag for the foreach loop:

```
<#}#>
```

This is where we close the outer foreach loop.

10. Save the Biml file and update the preview by clicking the **Update Preview** button. The code that will appear in the preview is T-SQL code. Copy the T-SQL code and paste it into a **New Query** window of **SSMS**. Remove the opening and closing <Biml> tags and execute the code on the source database – WideWorldImporters, as shown in the following screenshot:

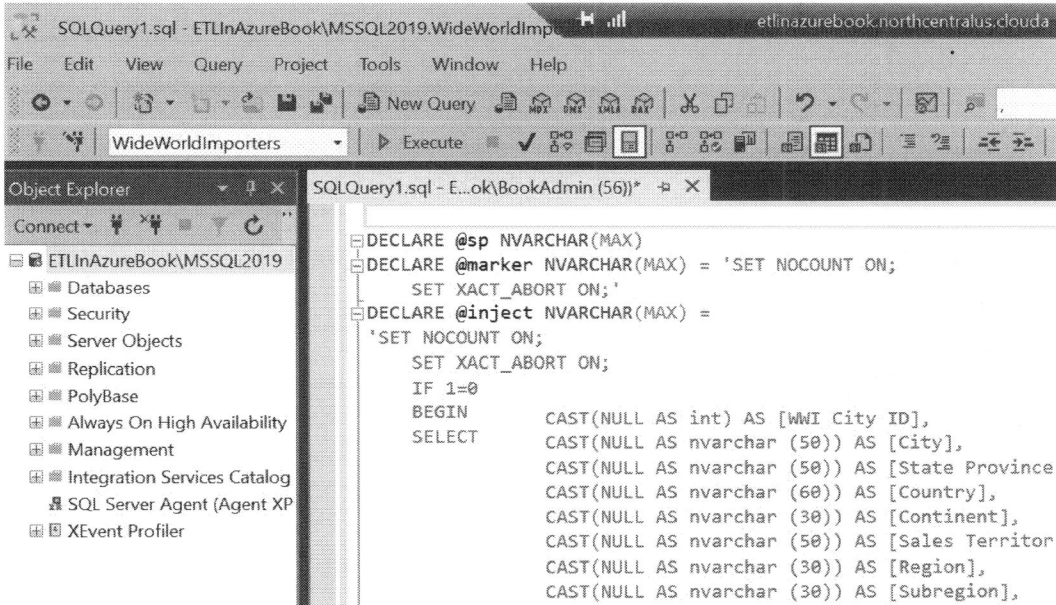

Figure 10.21 – A screenshot showing generated T-SQL code pasted into SSMS

Let's look under the hood and see how it works.

How it works...

In this example, we are doing important preparation work in the WideWorldImporters source database. We are making a change to every stored procedure that retrieves the source dataset for each Data Flow Task in the DailyETLMain.dtsx SSIS package.

Let's look closely at *Step 7* of this recipe. The code contains two loops: the first one – a foreach loop – goes over a list of tables and gets the column metadata from SQL Server for each table, and the inner while loop iterates through every column and produces a T-SQL statement for every column with a cast to a corresponding SQL Data Type.

In the outer `foreach` loop, we initialize a `strInject` variable to store a `SELECT` T-SQL statement. This `SELECT` statement is important because it shows Biml what the output columns will look like when the stored procedure is called. The inner `while` loop is responsible for producing a T-SQL statement like this:

```
CAST(NULL AS <datatype>) AS <ColumnName>
```

To help with producing a good T-SQL statement for a data type, we call a static method, `GetDataType()`, which was prepared in *Step 4* and added in a helper C# file, `Code.cs`. It converts SQL Server metadata information for a column into a data type T-SQL expression that corresponds to it. To get the column metadata, we connected to the destination database and got the column information from the **INFORMATION_SCHEMA.COLUMNS** system view.

The outer `foreach` loop bundles all the columns of a table into a `SELECT` statement like this:

```
SELECT
CAST(NULL AS <datatype>) AS <ColumnName1>
, CAST(NULL AS <datatype>) AS <ColumnName2>
, CAST(NULL AS <datatype>) AS <ColumnName3>
```

It puts it inside a conditional statement that should never run:

```
IF 1 = 0
BEGIN
...
END
```

In the last step, we construct an `ALTER DDL` T-SQL statement that takes a definition of the existing stored procedure and adds to it the conditional statement prepared above. This conditional statement is added at the very beginning of the stored procedure and doesn't affect the logic of the stored procedure in any way.

As we execute the generated `ALTER DDL`, we replace the old stored procedure code in the source database with the new one.

Now, every stored procedure that is called in the Data Flow Task is able to show Biml what column metadata it will return.

There's more...

Before proceeding to a complex SSIS package, I would like to mention here one more trick that I use quite often in C# code nuggets, and it is **Language Integrated Query (LINQ)**. LINQ is a query syntax and it lets you use SQL-like queries in C#. So if you need to join a Biml metadata dataset returned by `GetDatabaseSchema()` with custom metadata datasets from the `BIMLmetadata` database, you can do it using LINQ. This is a very useful and powerful syntax and I strongly recommend getting familiar with it if you want to implement complex logic in your Biml.

See the example of the use of LINQ in the following code snippet:

```csharp
var sourceConnection = SchemaManager.
CreateConnectionNode("Destination", @"Data Source=.;Initial
Catalog=WideWorldImportersDW;Provider=SQLNCLI11.1;Integrated
Security=SSPI;Auto Translate=False;");

var sourceMetadata = sourceConnection.GetDatabaseSchema();

DataTable dtTables = new DataTable();

using (SqlConnection sqlConn = new
SqlConnection(connectionString))

{

    string sqlCmd = @"SELECT * from dbo.TableConfig;"

    SqlDataAdapter sqlDtAdp = new SqlDataAdapter(sqlCmd,
sqlConn);

    sqlDtAdp.Fill(dtTables);

}

var tableConfig = from DataRow myRow in dtTables.Rows select
myRow;

var metadataCols = from tables in sourceMetadata.TableNodes.
ToList()

join sqltables in tableConfig on new {Table = tables.Name.
ToString()} equals new {Table = sqltables["StagingTableName"].
ToString()}

select new { Columns = tables.Columns, SqlCode
= tables.GetTableSql(), Name = tables.Name,
TableType = sqltables["TableType"], GetStoredProc
= sqltables["GetStoredProc"], StagingTableName =
sqltables["StagingTableName"] };
```

Now let's move on to the next recipe!

Generating an SSIS package containing a Data Flow Task

Here, we are finally getting to a more complicated SSIS package that will contain a Data Flow Task, and in a previous recipe, *Generating a mass change to stored procedures*, we already made some preparation changes to stored procedures in the sample `WideWorldImporters` database to overcome the limitations of the Biml related to the use of temporary tables. Now we can concentrate on the Data Flow Task itself.

Getting ready

This is our last recipe for SSIS packages, and it is the most complex one, so let's buckle up and get ready for a bumpy ride! Open Visual Studio 2019, and then open the **ETLInAzure** SSIS project.

How to do it...

Let's add a new Biml file to start our recipe:

1. Add a new Biml file to your solution. Rename it to `Recipe7.biml`. Copy all the code from `Recipe5.biml` into `Recipe7.biml`, because in this recipe we are going to continue to build upon what was done in the *Generating an SSIS package with Execute SQL Tasks recipe*.

2. Change the name of the package in the `<Package>` element to `Recipe7`.

3. As in thw *Using Convert SSIS package to Biml recipe*, add a new connection string for the `WideWorldImportersDW` destination database. Add the following code snippet under the line that initializes the connection string to the `BIMLmetadata` database:

```
string connStrDest = @"Data Source=ETLInAzureBook\
MSSQL2019;Persist Security Info=true;Initial
Catalog=WideWorldImportersDW;Integrated Security=SSPI;";
```

This connection string needs to be added because we will connect to the destination database to get the column metadata of the destination tables.

4. Just like in the previous recipe, *Generating a mass change to stored procedures*, add a reference to the `Code.cs` file. To do so, add the following directive right under the opening `<Biml>` element, on `line 2` of the file:

```
<#@ code file="Code.cs" #>
```

We will use the `BIMLHelper` class again in this recipe.

5. Find the line containing a `foreach` statement; it should be right above the `<Container>` opening element. Add the following code to the control block, right under the `foreach` statement:

```
string strColumnSQL = string.Format(@"SELECT * FROM
INFORMATION_SCHEMA.COLUMNS WHERE TABLE_SCHEMA =
'Integration' AND TABLE_NAME = '{0}' AND NOT (DATA_
TYPE = 'int' AND COLUMN_NAME LIKE '% key') AND
ORDINAL_POSITION > 1 ORDER BY ORDINAL_POSITION",
drTable["StagingTableName"]);
```

```
string strResultSet = @"WITH RESULT SETS ( (";
```

```
using (SqlConnection sqlConnDest = new
SqlConnection(connStrDest)) {
```

```
    SqlCommand command = new
SqlCommand(strColumnSQL,sqlConnDest);
```

```
    sqlConnDest.Open();
```

```
    SqlDataReader reader = command.ExecuteReader();
```

```
      if (reader.HasRows) {
```

```
          while (reader.Read()) {
```

```
              strResultSet += @"[" + reader["COLUMN_
NAME"] + "] " + BIMLHelper.GetDataType(reader["DATA_
TYPE"].ToString(),reader["CHARACTER_MAXIMUM_
LENGTH"].ToString(),reader["NUMERIC_PRECISION"].
ToString(),reader["NUMERIC_SCALE"].
ToString(),reader["DATETIME_PRECISION"].ToString()) +
@","; } }
```

```
          reader.Close();
```

```
          strResultSet = strResultSet.TrimEnd(',') +
@")); "; }
```

After this code, the control block should be closed by the closing tag, `#>`.

6. Add the following Biml code for the first part of the Data Flow Task below the last Execute SQL Task, **Get Last <Table> ETL Cutoff Time**:

```
<Dataflow Name="Extract Updated <#=drTable["TableName"]#>
Data to Staging">
```

```
  <Transformations>
```

```
    <OleDbSource Name = "Integration_
Get<#=drTable["TableName"]#>Updates" ConnectionName =
```

```
"WWI_Source_DB">
        <Parameters>
            <Parameter Name="@LastCutoff:Input"
VariableName="User.LastETLCutoffTime" />
            <Parameter Name="@NewCutoff:Input"
VariableName="User.TargetETLCutoffTime" />
        </Parameters>
        <DirectInput>EXEC
Integration.<#=drTable["GetStoredProc"]#>
<#if(!drTable["GetStoredProc"].ToString().
Equals("GetStockHoldingUpdates")){#>?, ?<#}#>

<#=strResultSet#>
        </DirectInput>
    </OleDbSource>
```

In this step, we add an opening tag of the <Dataflow> element, then we provide the details for the OLE DB source, just like we would have in a Visual Studio OLE DB source: a connection name, parameters, and the SQL command.

Note that the WITH RESULTS SET statement is in the strResultSet variable.

7. Let's work on the OLE DB destination for the Data Flow Task. Add the following code to complete the Data Flow Task definition in Biml:

```
        <OleDbDestination
Name="Integration_<#=drTable["StagingTableName"]#>"
ConnectionName="WWI_DW_Destination_DB" TableLock="false">
            <ExternalTableOutput Table="[Integration].
[<#=drTable["StagingTableName"]#>]" />
        </OleDbDestination>
    </Transformations>
</Dataflow>
```

We have specified here the connection, table name, and a table lock option for the destination. Note how a table name is retrieved using the Expression control block, <#=drTable["StagingTableName"]#>, which is reading the table name from the StagingTableName column of the metadata table.

8. Now add the last `Execute SQL Task` below the Data Flow Task, as shown in the following code snippet:

```
<ExecuteSQL Name="Migrate Staged <#=drTable["TableName"]#>
Data" ConnectionName="WWI_DW_Destination_DB">
<DirectInput>EXEC
Integration.<#=drTable["MigrateStoredProc"]#>;</
DirectInput>
</ExecuteSQL>
```

9. Save the `Recipe7.biml` file and right-click on it. Choose **Generate SSIS Packages**. Uncheck the connection manager from the list of items in the **Confirm Overwritten Items** dialog and click **Commit**.

10. Open the generated `Recipe7.dtsx` and run it in debug mode. Compare it with the original `DailyETLMain.dtsx` package. Both packages should be identical.

Now we can find out how it works.

How it works...

This recipe completes our task of rebuilding an SSIS package for a sample `WideWorldImporters` solution using Biml and a metadata configuration table. In this recipe, we add the Data Flow Task to every `Sequence Container` of the SSIS package. In the original SSIS package provided for the `WideWorldImporters` demo, the Data Flow Source SQL is calling a stored procedure that uses a temp table to produce a source dataset. SSIS cannot deal with datasets returned by temp data tables, because it cannot understand the return dataset structure in advance, so we have to use the `WITH RESULT SET` expression in SSIS and explicitly tells what metadata is returned by the stored procedure. In addition, Biml itself is not very happy with the use of the temp tables, so we had to modify every stored procedure and add a `SELECT` statement that will never execute but that will predict the return dataset structure for Biml.

Let's take a closer look at *Step 5*. The code demonstrated in that step contains logic that retrieves column metadata from the destination database for each table. It then loops through data type information for every column and constructs a `WITH RESULTS SET` statement that informs the Data Flow Task Source of the output columns, metadata. We used the `GetDataType()` method from the `Code.cs` C# file here again to help us correctly construct the `WITH RESULTS SET` statement.

This code is similar to the code that we prepared in a previous recipe because it does almost the same thing but on a different level. The *Generating a mass change to Stored Procedures* recipe was required because Biml could not understand the column metadata returned from stored procedures. In this step, we are providing column metadata to SSIS, because it is SSIS that now needs column metadata and cannot get it from stored procedures.

In *Step 6*, a stored procedure name is retrieved using the Expression control block `<#=drTable["GetStoredProc"]#>`, which reads the stored procedure name from the `GetStoredProc` column of the metadata table.

Having done all the hard work dealing with temp tables, the rest is easy – Biml for the Data Flow Task is laconic and only requires the essential information, such as Source and Destination Connection names, the Source SQL statement, the Destination table name, and a Destination table lock option. You don't have to worry about column mapping, as they map automatically because the source and destination column names match exactly. Biml takes care of all that meticulous work for you.

Generating your first Azure Data Factory

Now we will hop on the cloud and start playing with Azure Data Factory. Working in Biml with Azure Data Factory is outside the realms of a BimlExpress add-on and requires the BimlStudio standalone application to work. For the purpose of Azure Data Factory recipes, you can install a trial version of BimlStudio, which will let you try it out for free for 30 days.

What I want to show in this recipe is how to generate and deploy a simple Data Factory in BimlStudio 2019. This Data factory will have two linked services, two datasets, and one Copy Activity that copies data from the source Http dataset to the sink Azure Data Lake Storage Gen2 dataset. The Http linked service is pointing to an open data source, `https://cadatacatalog.state.gov/`. We will also write a PowerShell script that will deploy this Data Factory code to Azure.

Getting ready

Download and install a trial version of the Varigence BimlStudio 2019 from `https://varigence.com/BimlStudio`.

You will need to have Windows PowerShell 7.x, or you can install it later on your machine. Usually, Windows PowerShell comes installed by default in every Windows system, but you can always install the latest version of PowerShell available for your operating system from `https://tinyurl.com/yd5bxsy6`:

1. Install Azure PowerShell by following the instructions described on this web page: `https://docs.microsoft.com/en-us/powershell/azure/install-az-ps?view=azps-3.7.0&viewFallbackFrom=azps-3.2.0`.

2. Open Windows PowerShell and type the following command:

```
Install-Module -Name Az -AllowClobber
```

3. Press *Enter*, then choose Y when prompted to install NuGet provider.

   Enter A for **Yes to All** to proceed with installing the Az package.

   That's it, now you are ready to use Azure PowerShell for your Azure Data Factory deployments.

   You will also need to connect to your Azure subscription and account, as follows.:

4. Open the **Microsoft Windows PowerShell Integrated Scripting Environment (ISE)** as an administrator and type the following command, where <xxxx-xxxx-xxxx> is your subscription ID:

```
Connect-AzAccount -Subscription <xxxx-xxxx-xxxx>
```

To get your subscription ID, go to the Azure portal, then go to your subscription, and copy the subscription ID, as shown in the following screenshot:

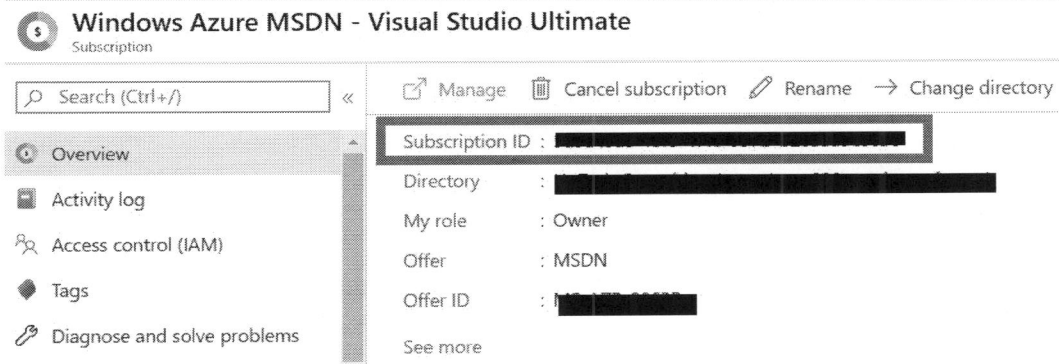

Figure 10.22 – A screenshot showing where to get Subscription ID

5. Click on the green **Run Script** button, as shown in the following screenshot:

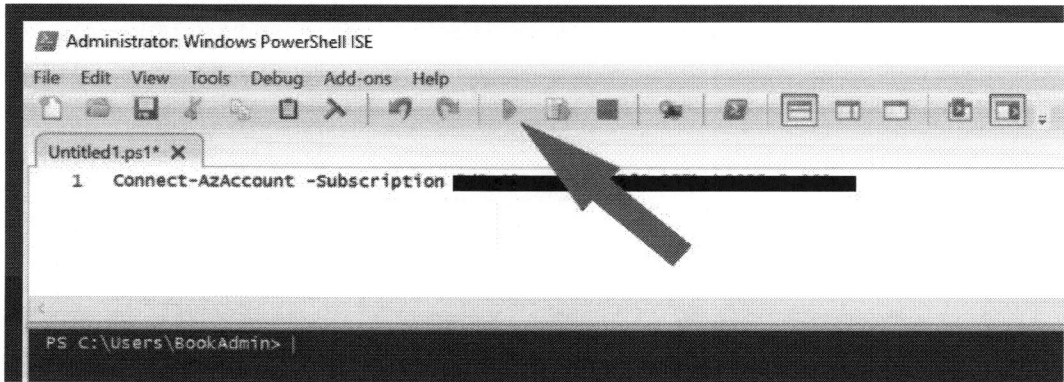

Figure 10.23 – A screenshot showing how to run scripts in the Windows PowerShell ISE

You will be prompted to enter your credentials.

6. Sign in with your Azure account. Upon successful sign-in, you should see the following output:

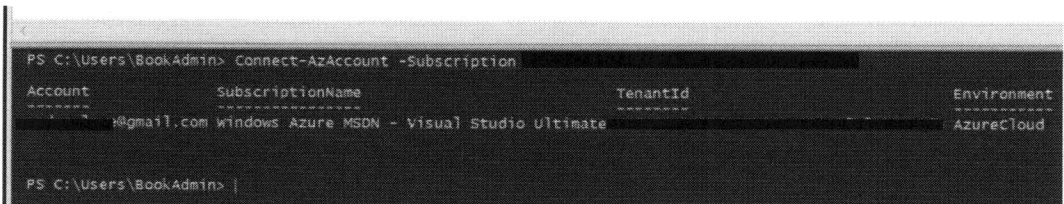

Figure 10.24 – A screenshot showing a successful sign-in to Azure PowerShell

That is it; we are signed in and are ready to start!

How to do it...

BimlStudio 2019 does not support some Azure Data Factory components or generates incorrect JSON code for them, so we will have to create a **Linked Service** for **Azure Data Lake Storage Gen2** manually in the Data Factory:

1. In the browser, go to the Azure portal and create a resource group called **ETL**. Create an empty Azure Data Factory V2 called **ETLInAzure** in the ETL resource group.

2. In the empty **ETLInAzure** Data Factory, go to **Connections**, then to **Linked Services**. Click on the **+ New** button at the top left. Select **Azure Data Lake Storage Gen2** and click **Continue**.

3. Enter **ETLInAzure** for **Name** and choose **Managed Identity** for **Authentication method**. Select **Enter manually** in **Account selection method**. In the **URL** field, enter the URL of **Azure Data Lake Storage Gen 2**, as shown in the following screenshot. This storage account creation is covered in *Chapter 4, Azure Data Integration*:

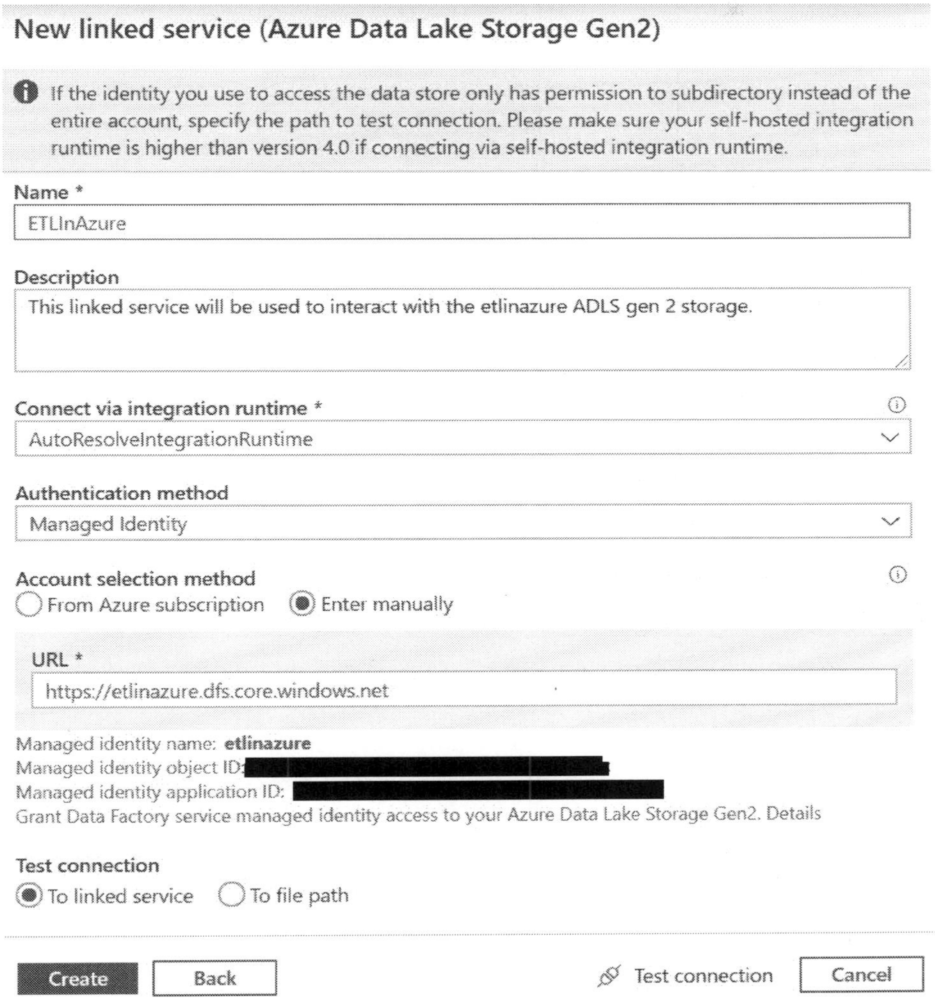

New linked service (Azure Data Lake Storage Gen2)

> ⓘ If the identity you use to access the data store only has permission to subdirectory instead of the entire account, specify the path to test connection. Please make sure your self-hosted integration runtime is higher than version 4.0 if connecting via self-hosted integration runtime.

Name *

ETLInAzure

Description

This linked service will be used to interact with the etlinazure ADLS gen 2 storage.

Connect via integration runtime *   ⓘ

AutoResolveIntegrationRuntime   ⌄

Authentication method

Managed Identity   ⌄

Account selection method   ⓘ

◯ From Azure subscription   ⦿ Enter manually

URL *

https://etlinazure.dfs.core.windows.net

Managed identity name: **etlinazure**
Managed identity object ID: ▮▮▮▮▮▮▮▮▮▮▮▮▮▮▮▮▮▮▮
Managed identity application ID: ▮▮▮▮▮▮▮▮▮▮▮▮▮▮▮▮▮
Grant Data Factory service managed identity access to your Azure Data Lake Storage Gen2. Details

Test connection

⦿ To linked service   ◯ To file path

[Create]   [Back]   ✐ Test connection   [Cancel]

Figure 10.25 – A screenshot showing the creation of the new linked service

4. Click **Test connection** at the bottom right, and if everything is OK, a **Connection successful** message should appear.

5. Click **Create** to save your changes. The first linked service is done now, and we can proceed with the BimlStudio work.

6. Open BimlStudio 2019. Create a new project using **Local Templates**.

7. Name the new project **ADFCloudETL**, choose a location in the files system where the BimlStudio project is going to be saved, and click **OK** as shown in the following screenshot:

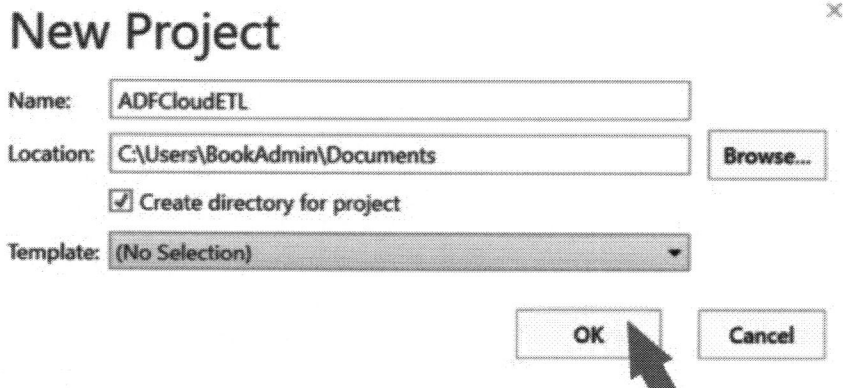

Figure 10.26 – A screenshot showing the creation of the new project in BimlStudio
BimlStudio will open a new empty project named ADFCloudETL.mst.

8. Just as in Visual Studio, you will be able to see the project structure on the right. Go to the **Azure Data Factory** section, right-click, and select **Add Data Factory**, as shown in the following screenshot:

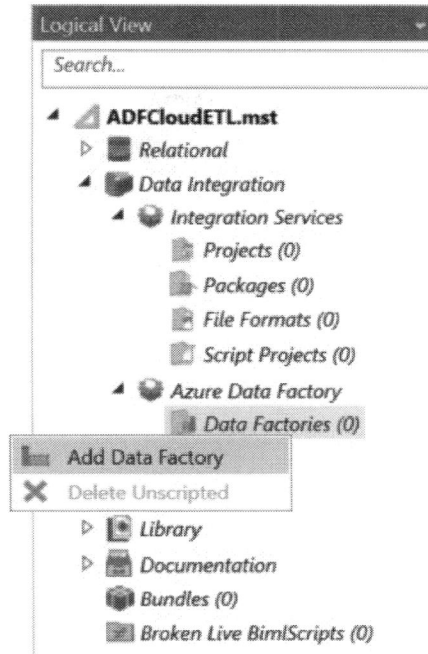

Figure 10.27 – A screenshot showing adding a new Data Factory

Right-click the new Data Factory and rename it to `ADFCloudETL`. Click **Save All**.

9. In the Biml file, replace the default `<DataFactory>` element with the following code:

```
<DataFactory Name="ADFCloudETL">
    <LinkedServices>
        <HttpServer Name="LSHTTP"
AuthenticationType="Anonymous" Url="https://
cadatacatalog.state.gov/"/>
        <AzureDataLakeStoreGen2 Name="ETLInAzure"
AccountKey="xxx" Url="https://etlinazure.dfs.core.
windows.net"/>
    </LinkedServices>
    <Datasets>
        <HttpFile Name="DSHTTP" LinkedServiceName="LSHTTP"
RelativeUrl="/dataset/dbadcbe4-3d99-4225-b0e1-
5f300f2ccb62/resource/94d1147b-03ad-431a-98ba-
71e0f6d8a879/download/geopoliticalregion.json" />
        <AzureDataLakeGen2 Name="DSDL2"
```

```
        LinkedServiceName="ETLInAzure" FolderPath="geo"
        File="geopoliticalregions.json"/>
      </Datasets>
      <Pipelines>
        <Pipeline Name="Copy Political Regions">
          <Activities>
            <Copy Name="Copy Regions">
              <HttpSource DatasetName="DSHTTP"/>
              <AzureDataLakeGen2Sink DatasetName="DSDL2"/>
            </Copy>
          </Activities>
        </Pipeline>
      </Pipelines>
    </DataFactory>
```

The preceding Biml has three sections – `<LinkedServices>`, `<Datasets>`, and `<Pipelines>`; and they correspond to Data Factory concepts that you can define manually in the Data Factory:

a) In the `<LinkedServices>/<HttpServer>` element, the `Url` attribute is pointing to an open data source at `https://cadatacatalog.state.gov/`.

b) In the `<LinkedServices>/<AzureDataLakeStoreGen2>` element, the `Url` attribute contains the URL of the Azure Data Lake Store Gen 2 that was created in *Chapter 4*, *Azure Data Integration*, and the `AccountKey` attribute should contain the unique account key of the storage account. Since at the moment, BimlStudio 2019 cannot correctly generate the linked service for Azure Data Lake Storage Gen2, we can leave it as is.

c) In the `<Datasets>/<HttpFile>` element, the `RelativeUrl` attribute contains the path to a JSON file that we want to download. This path changes from time to time, so to get the working URL, go to `https://cadatacatalog.state.gov/dataset/reference-data` and copy the path for the `geopoliticalregion` dataset by clicking **Download**, and then copying the relative path. At the time of writing, it was `/dataset/dbadcbe4-3d99-4225-b0e1-5f300f2ccb62/resource/94d1147b-03ad-431a-98ba-71e0f6d8a879/download/geopoliticalregion.json`.

In the `<Datasets>`/`<AzureDataLakeGen2>` element, `FolderPath` and `File` attributes must be set to the corresponding values where the file will be downloaded and what the file will be called.

10. Click **Save All** in the top-left corner to save `Biml` for the Azure Data Factory.

11. Build the project to have Azure JSON files generated. Right-click on the `ADFCloudETL.mst` project and select **Build**, as shown in the following screenshot:

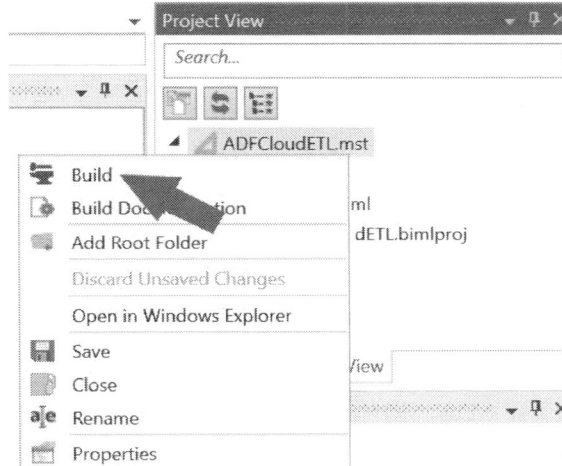

Figure 10.28 – A screenshot showing how to build the project

Upon a successful build, JSON files for the `ADFCloudETL` Data Factory will be generated in the output folder. Linked services JSON files, one for each linked service, will be created in the `output\DataFactories\ADFCloudETL\ LinkedServices` folder, the same as the `Dataset` and `Pipelines` JSON files that will be generated in their corresponding folders, as shown in the following screenshot:

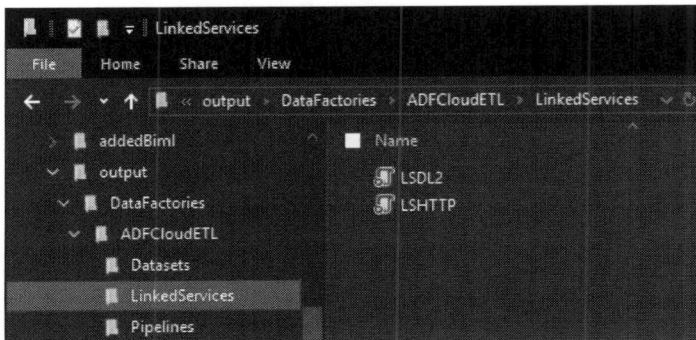

Figure 10.29 – A screenshot showing generated JSON

Now that the JSON files are created, we need to find a way to put them in Azure. We can do it manually by creating Linked Services, Datasets, and a Pipeline manually and then copying and pasting JSON code in each one, but this is not the most efficient way to do it. So, in the next step, we will use the power of PowerShell to help us deploy JSON files to Azure faster.

12. Open the Windows PowerShell ISE and create a new file, `ADFCloudETLRecipe8.ps1`, with the following script:

```
$resourceGroupName ="ETL"

$dataFactoryName = "ADFCloudETL"

$rootPath = "C:\Users\BookAdmin\Documents\ADFCloudETL\
output\DataFactories\ADFCloudETL"

Set-AzDataFactoryV2LinkedService -DataFactoryName
$dataFactoryName  -ResourceGroupName $resourceGroupName
-Name "LSHTTP" -DefinitionFile ($rootPath +"\
LinkedServices\LSHTTP.json")

Set-AzDataFactoryV2Dataset -DataFactoryName
$dataFactoryName -ResourceGroupName $resourceGroupName
-Name "DSHTTP" -DefinitionFile ($rootPath +"\Datasets\
DSHTTP.json")

Set-AzDataFactoryV2Dataset -DataFactoryName
$dataFactoryName -ResourceGroupName $resourceGroupName
-Name "DSDL2" -DefinitionFile ($rootPath +"\Datasets\
DSDL2.json")

Set-AzDataFactoryV2Pipeline -DataFactoryName
$dataFactoryName -ResourceGroupName $resourceGroupName
-Name "Copy Political Regions" -DefinitionFile
($rootPath+"\Pipelines\Copy Political Regions.json")
```

13. Replace the path of `$rootPath` with the correct value for the output folder. Run the PowerShell by clicking on the green `Run Script` button. If the deployment is successful, you will see an output like the one shown in the following screenshot:

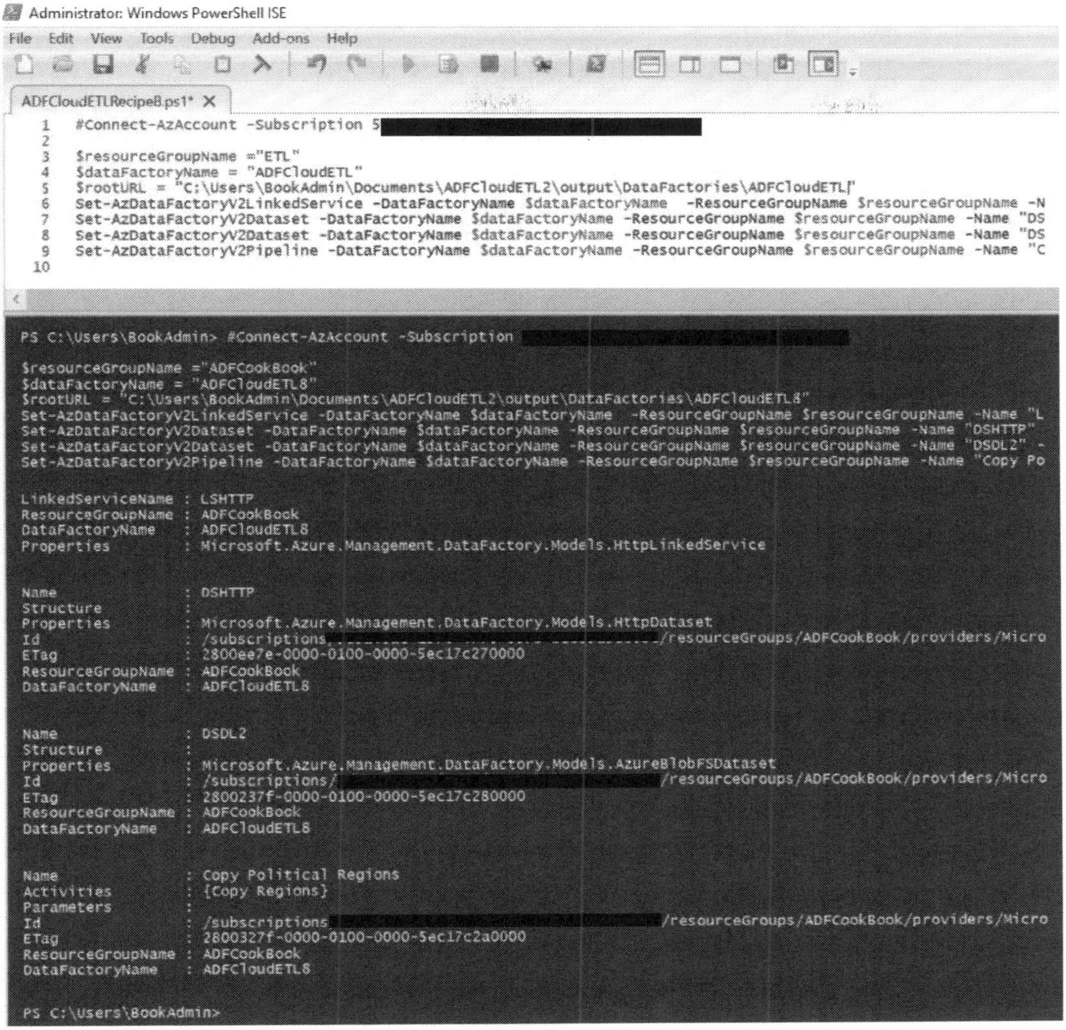

Figure 10.30 – A screenshot showing the deployment of the Data Factory

14. Go to the Azure portal to see the result. Go to the `ADFCloudETL` Data Factory. You should see two linked services, as shown in the following screenshot:

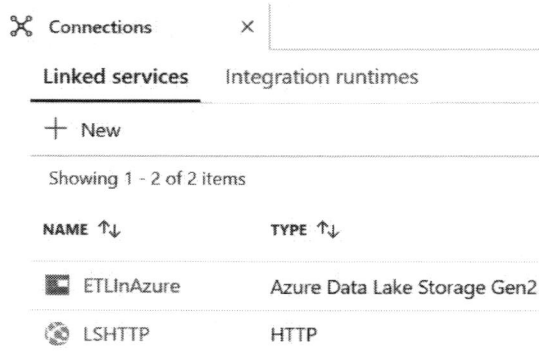

Figure 10.31 – A screenshot showing the deployment of the Data Factory

You will also see a Pipeline and two datasets deployed to your Data Factory, as shown in the following screenshot:

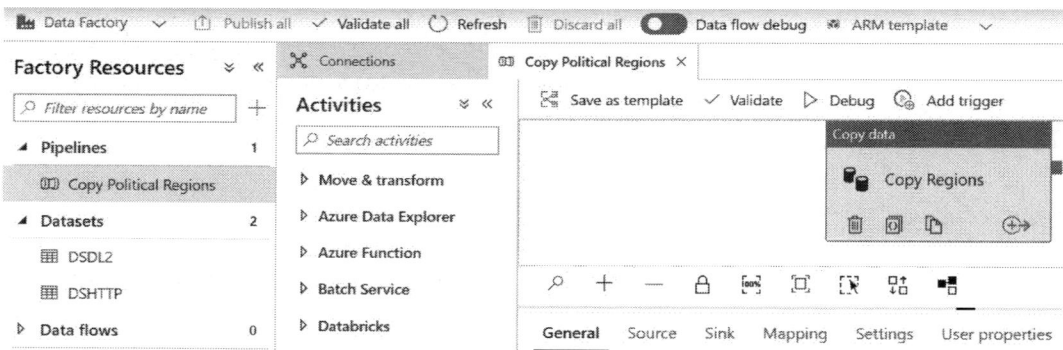

Figure 10.32 – A screenshot showing the deployment of the Data Factory

15. Run the pipeline in **Debug** mode by clicking the **Debug** button.

Upon successful execution, a new JSON file will appear in the storage container `geo/geopoliticalregions.json`.

How it works...

BimlStudio 2019 generates all JSON files that are defining Data Factory concepts, such as Linked Services, Datasets, Pipelines, Triggers, and Gateways. It generates one file per component, and to facilitate the deployment of these files to Azure Data Factory, we PowerShell script that deployed everything to Azure.

There's more...

If you cannot use BimlStudio 2019, but still want to generate Azure Data Factory data with Biml, you can do so with the free version of BimlExpress. You will be responsible, of course, for generating the entire JSON code for every component, just like we did with T-SQL in earlier recipes. It's a bit more work, but if your objects are very repetitive, it is realistic.

Loading multiple files using Data Factory

We are going to use BIMLStudio 2019 to build a more elaborate solution. Let's say we want to load a set of files available online into our on-premises SQL Server database. We want to use the data from these files to do reports by joining them with on-premises data. In this recipe, we will look at creating a Data Factory solution that loads a set of data files in parallel from the website FiveThirtyEight.com into **Azure Data Lake Storage Gen2**, and then into an on-premises SQL Server database. FiveThirtyEight.com is a data journalism organization that provides opinions and analysis on politics, economics, and sport, based on data science and analytics. The site provides access to a collection of datasets easily available for download. For our recipe, we will be downloading a set of CSV files containing statistical weather data, such as actual temperature, maximum temperature, minimum temperature, and levels of precipitation for every city, every day during a one-year period. Every CSV file contains data from a single city in the US. We will use a small metadata table with the list of filenames to drive the generation of the Data Factory solution.

Getting ready

Open **SSMS** and connect to a metadata configuration BIMLmetadata database. Run the following script to create a metadata table for CSV files:

```
CREATE TABLE [dbo].[CSVConfig](
    [CSVName] [nvarchar](50) NULL,
    [CityName] [nvarchar](256) NULL,
    [State] [nvarchar](256) NULL
) ON [PRIMARY]
```

Insert the CSV setup data into this table by running the following script:

```
INSERT INTO [dbo].[CSVConfig] ([CSVName],[CityName],[State])
VALUES
( 'KCLT.csv','Charlotte','NC'),
( 'KCQT.csv','LosAngeles','CA'),
```

```
( 'KHOU.csv','Houston','TX'),
( 'KIND.csv','Indianapolis','IN'),
( 'KJAX.csv','Jacksonville','FL'),
( 'KMDW.csv','Chicago','IL'),
( 'KNYC.csv','NewYork','NY'),
( 'KPHL.csv','Philiadelphia','PA'),
( 'KPHX.csv','Phoenix','AZ'),
( 'KSEA.csv','Seattle','WA')
```

Now let's proceed with the preparation steps for the ADFCloudETL Data Factory. We will need to do some setup in Data Factory manually, because BimlStudio 2019 doesn't support some Data Factory components, or generates incorrect JSON code for them. First, we will create a **Self-Hosted Integration Runtime** called **DWsOnPremises** in the Data Factory. It should be hosted on the same server that is used for the SQL server containing a WideWorldImportersDW database. You can follow the steps in *Chapter 8, SSIS Migration Strategies*, where the creation of the Self-Hosted Integration Runtime is explained in detail. As a result, a **DWsOnPremises** runtime should be up and running in the **Integration runtimes** section of the Data Factory, as shown in the following screenshot:

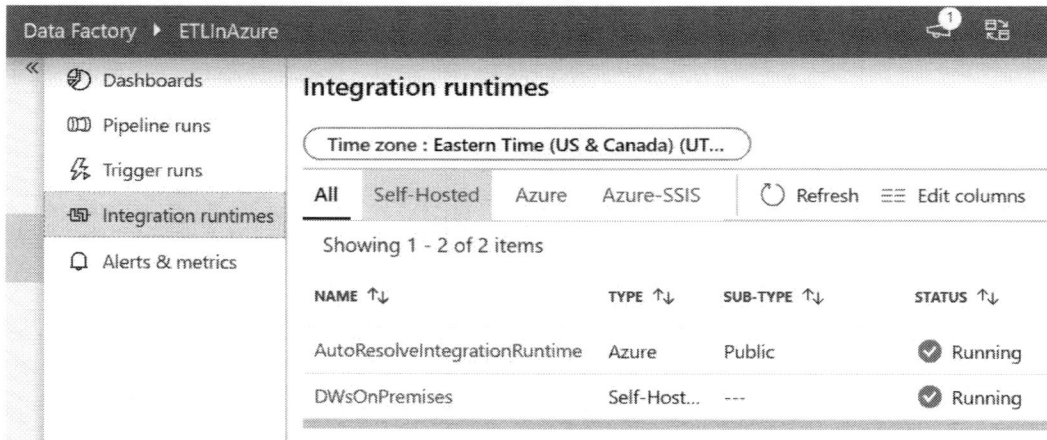

Figure 10.33 – A screenshot showing the DWsOnPremises integration runtime

Now that we have completed our preparations, let's move on to the recipe itself.

How to do it...

We need to do a preliminary step to prepare destination SQL tables for use in this recipe. Since we will load a set of CSV files into a set of corresponding destination tables, we must create these tables in the destination database.

As I mentioned earlier, BimlStudio 2019 does not support some of the Azure Data Factory components or generates incorrect JSON code for them, so we will have to create two linked services manually in the Data Factory:

1. In the browser, go to the existing **ADFCloudETL** Data Factory with the Self-Hosted Integration Runtime already configured. An Azure Data Lake Storage Gen 2 linked service should also be created as it was part of the previous recipe, *Generating your first Azure Data Factory*.

    In the Data Factory, go to **Connections**, then **Linked Services**. Click on the **+ New** button at the top left. Select **SQL Server** and click **Continue**.

2. In the **New linked service** form, enter the **Name** of WideWorldImportersDW, and select **DWsOnPremises** as **Integration runtime**. Add the SQL **Server name** and **Database name** and choose **Windows authentication** as **Authentication type**. Finally, fill in **User name** and **Password**, as shown in the following screenshot:

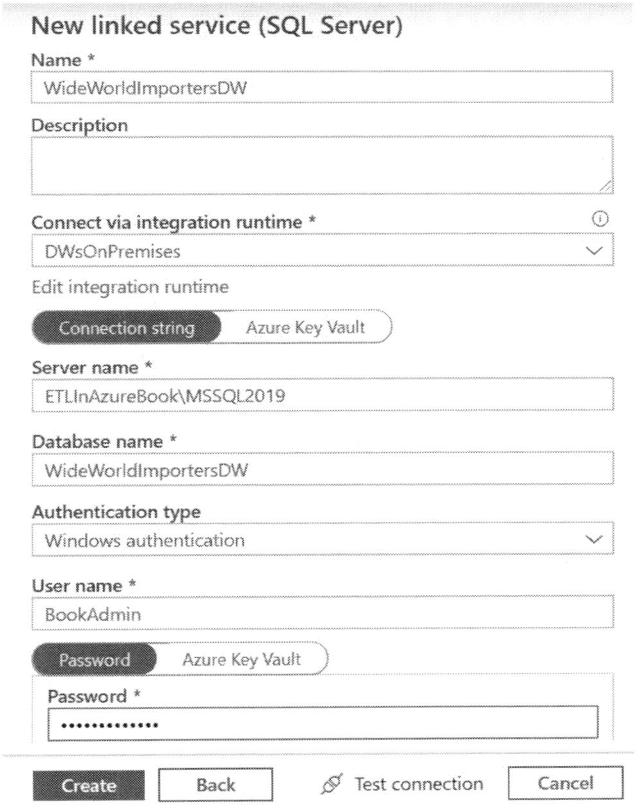

Figure 10.34 – A screenshot showing the creation of the new SQL Server linked service

Click **Test connection** at the bottom right, and if everything is OK, a **Connection successful** message should appear.

3. Click **Create** to save your changes. The SQL Server Linked Service is done now, and we can proceed with the next steps.

4. Open Visual Studio 2019, and then open the **ETLInAzure** SSIS project.

5. Add a new Biml file to your solution and rename it to `Recipe9.biml`.

6. Copy the directives and control block from `Recipe6.biml` just above the `foreach` statement into `Recipe9.biml`, replacing `dbo.TableConfig` with `dbo.CSVConfig` in the `SELECT * FROM` statement, as shown in the following code snippet:

```
<Biml xmlns="http://schemas.varigence.com/Biml.xsd">
<#@ code file="Code.cs" #>
<#@ import namespace="System.Data" #>
<#@ import namespace="System.Data.SqlClient" #>
<# string connectionString = @"Data Source=ETLInAzureBook\
MSSQL2019;Persist Security Info=true;Integrated
Security=SSPI;Initial Catalog=BIMLmetadata";
DataTable dtTables = new DataTable();
using (SqlConnection sqlConn = new
SqlConnection(connectionString))
{
    string sqlCmd = @"SELECT * from dbo.CSVConfig;";
    SqlDataAdapter sqlDtAdp = new SqlDataAdapter(sqlCmd,
sqlConn);
    sqlDtAdp.Fill(dtTables);
}
#>
```

7. In a text block below the control block write a T-SQL statement to create a separate schema for the destination tables, as shown in the following code snippet:

```
CREATE SCHEMA Data538
AUTHORIZATION dbo
```

8. Add a control block with a `foreach` statement that will loop through a list of CSV files that was loaded into a `dtTables` object:

```
<#
        foreach(DataRow drTable in dtTables.Rows) {
#>
```

9. In a text block below, write a T-SQL statement for a destination table creation. The following script will create a table for each CSV file. There is one CSV file per city, so the destination tables are named after the city and will have three default columns with default values of a city, weather station code name, and a state name in addition to a standard set of columns that are coming from the CSV files:

```
CREATE TABLE [Data538].[<#=drTable["CityName"].
ToString()#>](
[city] nvarchar(256) NULL
DEFAULT('<#=drTable["CityName"]#>'),
[weatherstationcode] nvarchar(6) NULL
DEFAULT('<#=drTable["CSVName"].ToString().Replace(".
csv","")#>'),
[state] nvarchar(2) NULL DEFAULT('<#=drTable["State"]#>'),
[date] [nvarchar](60) NULL,
[actual_mean_temp] [nvarchar](60) NULL,
[actual_min_temp] [nvarchar](60) NULL,
[actual_max_temp] [nvarchar](60) NULL,
[average_min_temp] [nvarchar](60) NULL,
[average_max_temp] [nvarchar](60) NULL,
[record_min_temp] [nvarchar](60) NULL,
[record_max_temp] [nvarchar](60) NULL,
[record_min_temp_year] [nvarchar](60) NULL,
[record_max_temp_year] [nvarchar](60) NULL,
[actual_precipitation] [nvarchar](60) NULL,
[average_precipitation] [nvarchar](60) NULL,
[record_precipitation] [nvarchar](60) NULL
) ON [PRIMARY]
```

10. Add a one-line control block to close the `foreach` loop:

```
<#}#>
```

11. Now we will add a text block with T-SQL code that will produce a single view that combines data from all the tables into a single dataset. We can use this view to query weather data from a single place with the city and state name. As you can see in the following code snippet, the text block is sprinkled with small pieces of control blocks that contain a `foreach` loop, and with Expression Blocks that provide us with table names used in the `UNIONs` statements:

```
CREATE VIEW [Data538].[weather] AS
<#
int I = 1;
foreach(DataRow drTable in dtTables.Rows) {
#>
SELECT * FROM
[Data538].[<#=drTable""CityNam""].ToString()#>]
<#
if(i < dtTables.Rows.Count){#>
UNION
<#}
i++;
}#>
```

12. Save the Biml file and update the preview by clicking the **Update Preview** button. The code that will appear in the preview is T-SQL code that should be copied and pasted into a **New Query** window of **SSMS** and executed on the `WideWorldImportersDW` database.

    Here, we complete the preparation of destination tables in the `WideWorldImportersDW` database and can proceed with the Data Factory solution.

13. Open BimlStudio 2019. Go to your existing `ADFCloudETL.mst` project in BimlStudio. Let's build this recipe on top of the previous recipe, so we'll be adding to an existing Biml Data Factory Biml file.

14. Open `ADFCloudETL.biml`.

15. At the top of the file, add directives to reference the two .NET namespaces needed to access the Biml metadata database:

```
<#@ import namespace""System.Dat"" #>
<#@ import namespace""System.Data.SqlClien"" #>
```

16. Above the `<DataFactories>` collection element, add a control block enclosed between `<#` and `#>`, which will connect to a `BIMLmetadata` database and read data from a `dbo.CSVConfig` table that contains information about the CSV files:

```
<#
string connectionString = ""Data Source=ETLInAzureBook\
MSSQL2019;Persist Security Info=true;Integrated
Security=SSPI;Initial Catalog=BIMLmetadat"";
DataTable dtTables = new DataTable();
using (SqlConnection sqlConn = new
SqlConnection(connectionString))
{
    string sqlCmd = ""SELECT * from dbo.CSVConfig"";
    SqlDataAdapter sqlDtAdp = new SqlDataAdapter(sqlCmd,
sqlConn);
    sqlDtAdp.Fill(dtTables);
}
#>
```

17. In the XML Biml block, find the existing `<LinkedServices>` collection element. From the previous recipe, it should contain two linked services. Here, we need to add two more, as shown in the following code snippet:

```
<SqlServer Name""WideWorldImportersD""
Username""BookAdmi"" Password""zz""
ConnectionString""integrated security=True;data
source=ETLInAzureBook\\MSSQL2019;initial
catalog=WideWorldImportersD"">
    <ConnectVia IntegrationRuntime""dWsOnPremise""></
ConnectVia>
</SqlServer>
<HttpServer Url""https://raw.githubusercontent.
com/fivethirtyeight/data/master/us-weather-
history"" AuthenticationType""Anonymou""
```

```
Name""FiveThirtyEightHTT"">
</HttpServer>
```

Don't worry about getting the `SqlServer` linked service correct, as we will set it manually in the Data Factory. The `HttpServer` Linked Service URL is the root link to the location of the weather CSV files, `https://raw.githubusercontent.com/fivethirtyeight/data/master/us-weather-history/`.

18. In the Biml block, find the `<Datasets>` collection element. It already has two datasets from the previous recipe. Add the following code snippet to add three more datasets for each line in the CSV configuration table:

```
<#foreach(DataRow drTable in dtTables.Rows) {#>
<HttpFile Name""DSHTTP<#=drTable""CityNam""]#""
LinkedServiceName""FiveThirtyEightHTT""
RelativeUrl""<#=drTable""CSVNam""]#"" />
    <AzureDataLakeGen2
Name""DSDL<#=drTable""CityNam""]#""
LinkedServiceName""ETLInAzur""
File""<#=drTable""CityNam""]#>.cs"" FolderPath""weathe"">
        <TextFormat FirstRowAsHeader""tru""
ColumnDelimiter""""""></TextFormat>

    </AzureDataLakeGen2>
    <SqlServer LinkedServiceName""ADFCloudETL.
WideWorldImportersD"" Name""DSSQL<#=drTable""CityNam""]#""
Table""Data538.<#=drTable""CityNam""]#"" />
<#}#>
```

It will loop through the `dbo.CSVConfig` table and add one HTTP dataset, one Azure Data Lake Storage Gen 2 dataset, and one SQL Server dataset for each CSV file.

19. Still in the Biml block, go to the `<Pipelines>` collection element. Under the existing `Copy Political Regions` pipeline, add a new pipeline: `CopyUSWeather`. There will be one activity per CSV file in this pipeline. In a `foreach` loop for every CSV file, a new `Copy` activity will be added to the pipeline, as shown in the following code snippet:

```
<Pipeline Name""CopyUSWeathe"" DependencyMode""Parallel"">
    <Activities>
```

```
<#foreach(DataRow drTable in dtTables.Rows)  {#>
    <Copy Name""Copy Weather <#=drTable""CityNam""]#"">
        <HttpSource
DatasetName""DSHTTP<#=drTable""CityNam""]#""  />
        <AzureDataLakeGen2Sink
DatasetName""DSDL<#=drTable""CityNam""]#""  />
    </Copy>
  <#}#>
    </Activities>
</Pipeline>
```

20. Under the `CopyUSWeather` pipeline, add another pipeline: `CopyUSWeatherSQL`. In this pipeline, there will be one activity per CSV file. In a `foreach` loop for every CSV file, a new `Copy` activity will be added to the pipeline:

```
<Pipeline Name="CopyUSWeatherSQL"
DependencyMode="Parallel">
<Activities>
            <#foreach(DataRow drTable in dtTables.Rows)
{#>
                <Copy Name="Copy Weather
<#=drTable["CityName"]#> to SQL" >
    <AzureDataLakeGen2Source
DatasetName="DSDL<#=drTable["CityName"]#>" />
                <SqlServerSink
DatasetName="DSSQL<#=drTable["CityName"]#>"/>
                </Copy>
            <#}#>
        </Activities>
</Pipeline>Save ADFCouldETL.biml file.
```

21. On the top-left side, click on the little anvil icon to build the project, as shown in the following screenshot:

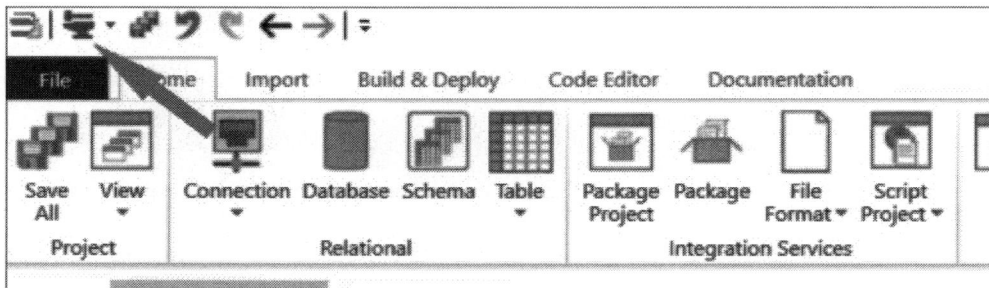

Figure 10.35 – A screenshot showing how to build a BimlStudio project

22. The successful build should update the output directory and generate JSON files in the corresponding directories.

   Deploying all these files manually to the Data Factory one by one would be very inefficient, so we should use Biml to generate a PowerShell script that will take care of deployment.

23. On the right side, in **Project View**, expand the folders to get to the **addedBiml** folder and right-click to add a new Biml file:

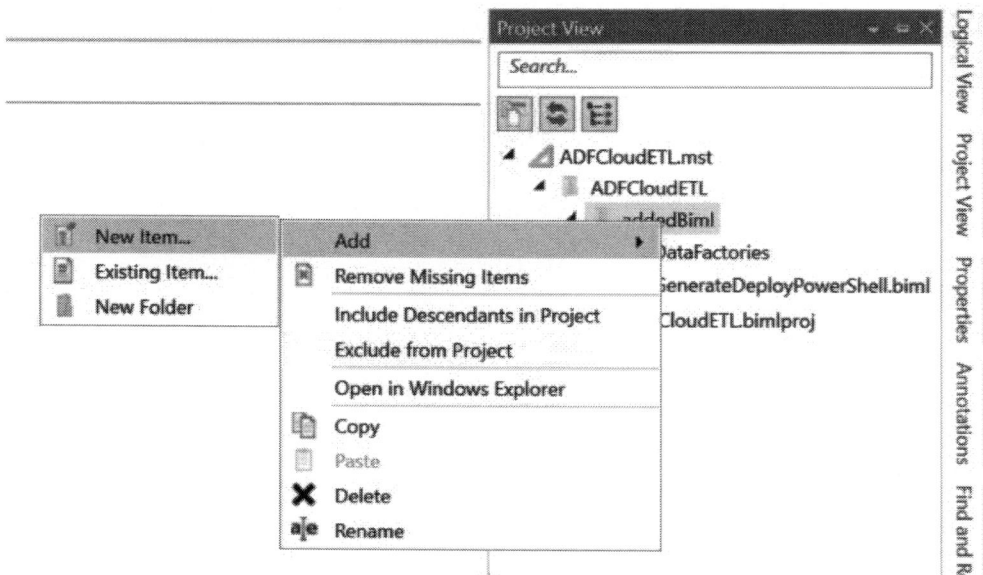

Figure 10.36 – A screenshot showing how to add a new Biml file

24. Rename the new Biml file to `GenerateDeployPowerShell.biml` and open it.

25. Insert the following code snippet into this file:

```
<#@ import namespace="System.Data" #>
<#@ import namespace="System.Data.SqlClient" #>
<Biml xmlns="http://schemas.varigence.com/Biml.xsd">
<# string connectionString = @"Data Source=ETLInAzureBook\
MSSQL2019;Persist Security Info=true;Integrated
Security=SSPI;Initial Catalog=BIMLmetadata";
DataTable dtTables = new DataTable();
using (SqlConnection sqlConn = new
SqlConnection(connectionString)){
    string sqlCmd = @"SELECT * from dbo.CSVConfig;";
    SqlDataAdapter sqlDtAdp = new SqlDataAdapter(sqlCmd,
sqlConn);
    sqlDtAdp.Fill(dtTables);   } #>
$resourceGroupName ="ETL"
$ADFName = "ADFCloudETL"
$rootPath = "C:\Users\BookAdmin\Documents\ADFCloudETL\
output\DataFactories\ADFCloudETL\"
```

26. Below the previous snippet, add the following code snippet to generate the PowerShell script:

```
Set-AzDataFactoryV2LinkedService -DataFactoryName
$ADFName  -ResourceGroupName $resourceGroupName
-Name "FileThirtyEightHTTP" -DefinitionFile
($rootPath+"LinkedServices\FileThirtyEightHTTP.json")
<#foreach(DataRow drTable in dtTables.Rows) {#>
Set-AzDataFactoryV2Dataset -DataFactoryName $ADFName
-ResourceGroupName $resourceGroupName -Name
"DSHTTP<#=drTable["CityName"]#>" -DefinitionFile
("$rootPath+"Datasets\DSHTTP<#=drTable["CityName"]#>.
json") -Force
Set-AzDataFactoryV2Dataset -DataFactoryName $ADFName
-ResourceGroupName $resourceGroupName -Name
"DSDL<#=drTable["CityName"]#>" -DefinitionFile
($rootPath+"Datasets\DSDL<#=drTable["CityName"]#>.json")
-Force
Set-AzDataFactoryV2Dataset -DataFactoryName $ADFName
-ResourceGroupName $resourceGroupName -Name
```

```
"DSSQL<#=drTable["CityName"]#>" -DefinitionFile
($rootPath+"Datasets\DSSQL<#=drTable["CityName"]#>.json")
-Force
```
```
<#}#>
```
```
Set-AzDataFactoryV2Pipeline -DataFactoryName
$ADFName -ResourceGroupName $resourceGroupName -Name
"CopyUSWeather" -DefinitionFile ($rootPath+"Pipelines\
CopyUSWeather.json")    -Force
```
```
Set-AzDataFactoryV2Pipeline -DataFactoryName
$ADFName -ResourceGroupName $resourceGroupName -Name
"CopyUSWeatherSQL" -DefinitionFile ($rootPath+"Pipelines\
CopyUSWeatherSQL.json") -Force
```
```
</Biml>
```

27. Save the file and expand the preview pane where the PowerShell script is generated, as shown in the following screenshot:

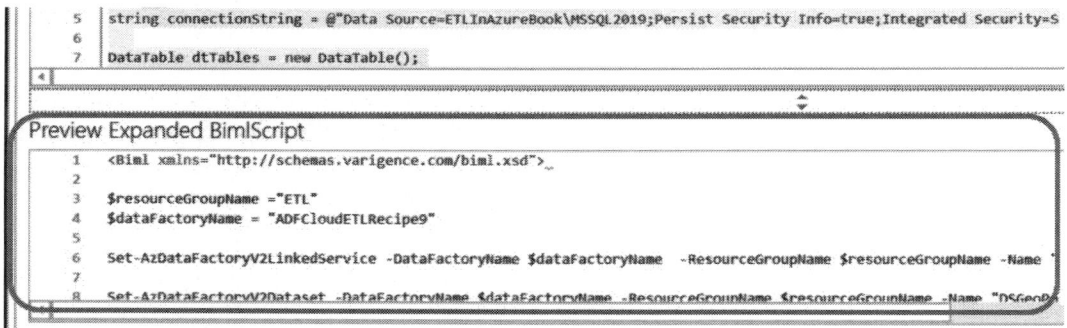

Figure 10.37 – A screenshot showing the generated PowerShell script

28. Copy and paste the generated PowerShell script into a new ps1 file – ADFCloudETLRecipe9.ps1.

29. Open the Windows PowerShell ISE and open the ps1 file. Execute the PowerShell script by clicking on the **Run Script** button. Since we use -Force in our PowerShell script, we do not have the prompt **Are you sure you want to overwrite?** for every existing component.

30. Now go to the Azure portal to see the results. You should see something like the following screenshot:

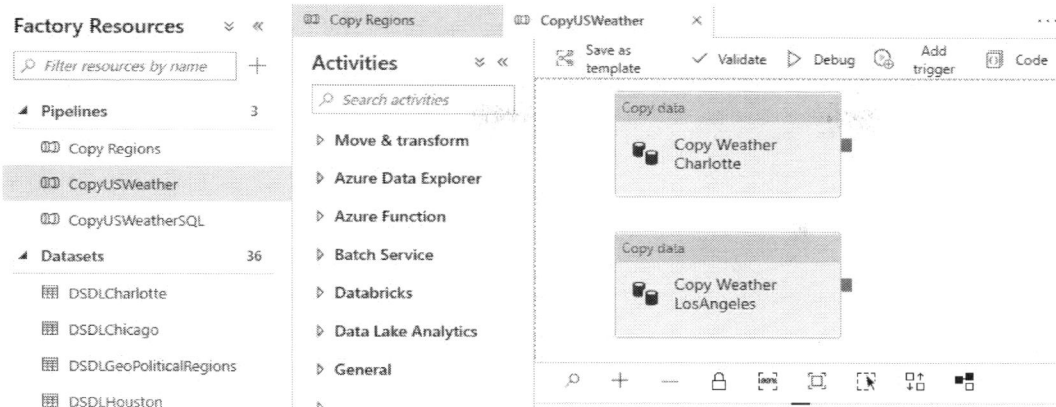

Figure 10.38 – A screenshot showing results in the Azure portal

31. Let's run the **CopyUSWeather** pipeline in debug mode, and this will load CSV data from the HTTP source to **Azure Data Lake Gen2 Storage**.

32. Second, run the **CopyUSWeatherSQL** pipeline in **Debug** mode to load data **from Azure Data Lake Gen2 Storage** to SQL Server.

33. Now the data is loaded into an on-premises SQL server and you can use it to make reports, cross-referencing your on-premises data with weather data loaded from the online source. I cross-referenced weather and sales data for the summer months (May – September) as shown in the following code snippet:

```
SELECT SUM(profit), CAST(w.actual_mean_temp AS INT),
w.state, MONTH(s.[Invoice Date Key]), YEAR([Invoice Date
Key])
FROM (
    SELECT SUM(profit) AS profit, RIGHT(c.Customer,3) as
[state], [Invoice Date Key]
    FROM [WideWorldImportersDW].[Fact].[Sale] sale
    INNER JOIN [Dimension].[Customer] c ON sale.[Customer
Key] = c.[Customer Key]
    GROUP BY RIGHT(c.Customer,3) , [Invoice Date Key]
) s
INNER JOIN [Data538].[weather] w ON s.[state] =
w.[state] + ')' AND w.[date] = s.[Invoice Date Key]
GROUP by CAST(w.actual_mean_temp  AS INT), w.state,
MONTH(s.[Invoice Date Key]), YEAR([Invoice Date Key])
ORDER BY 1
```

The report shows that sale numbers are highest when the weather is comfortable for the customer – not too hot and not too cold. This report does not consider many other important points, for example, the average temperatures in a specific region. Our focus here is not data science, but on showing how online data can be quickly integrated into our on-premises data warehouse. The following chart is the visual representation of the report:

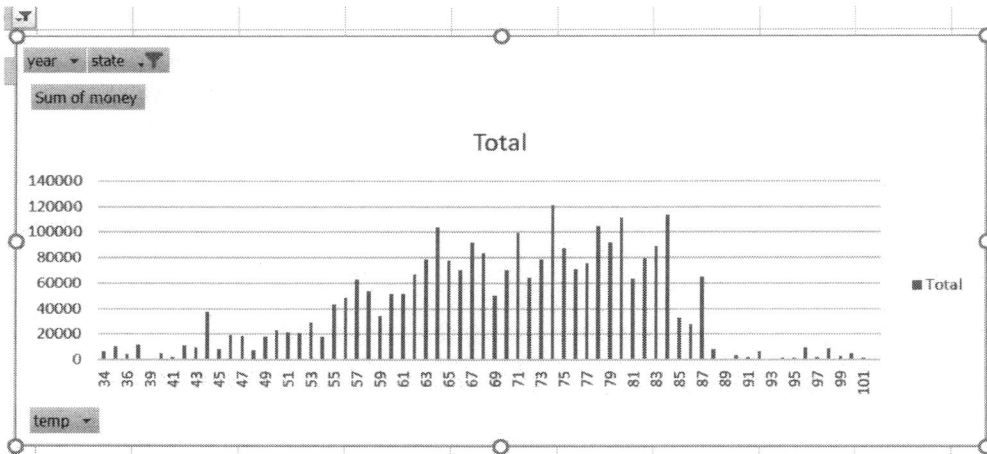

Figure 10.39 – A screenshot showing the report results

How it works...

We used Biml to generate CREATE TABLE statements for every destination table.

We can't use a single destination table here because it requires adding additional columns to the dataset to differentiate between data files, and this does not work with automatically generated Data Factory datasets. Also, using a stored procedure in SQL sink was considered, but invoking a stored procedure processes the data row by row instead of by using a bulk operation, so this option is not optimal for data processing.

BimlStudio 2019 is used here to apply a repetitive pattern to the task of loading multiple CSV files with identical schema and generating Data Factory components (datasets and copy activities) for each file. We also used Biml to generate a PowerShell script that deploys each component to Azure.

This is the last recipe in this chapter, but this topic truly deserves many more pages devoted to it. If you have started on this path, the adventure awaiting you ahead is exciting and satisfying, because the mindset that you acquire and hone using Biml will prove useful far beyond Biml and SSIS. This is the mindset of being effective and having a keen eye for patterns and abstraction.

See also

At the conclusion of this last recipe, I would like to provide a reference to an outstanding resource for Biml developers: Catherine Wilhelmsen's website, `https://www.cathrinewilhelmsen.net/biml/`, where she has training material that can help you learn Biml with zero previous experience, including best practices and useful examples.

Biml was released by **Varigence**, a company founded by Scott Currie, in 2009. It is being constantly improved and developed, and more and more material is available online for developers that use Biml. If you want to learn Biml from its creator, Scott Currie, go to `http://www.bimlscript.com/`. This website has a lot of training material that teaches Biml from beginner to advanced level and has many helpful examples.

There are many more resources available online for Biml, but the two websites that I have mentioned have the most complete and easy-to-understand material that I have seen on this topic.

Biml is a tool that accelerates development enormously. I hope that you enjoy learning it and using it as much as I did!

Other Books You May Enjoy

If you enjoyed this book, you may be interested in these other books by Packt:

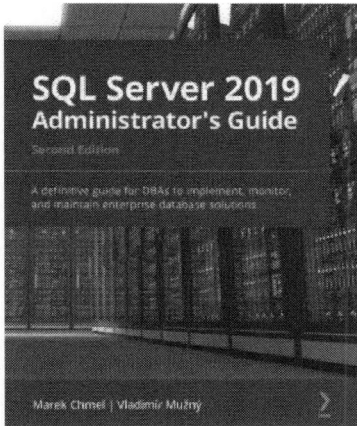

SQL Server 2019 Administrator's Guide

Marek Chmel, Vladmir Mužný

ISBN: 978-1-78995-432-6

Manage AI workflows by using AWS cloud to deploy services that feed smart data products

- Discover SQL Server 2019's new features and how to implement them
- Fix performance issues by optimizing queries and making use of indexes
- Design and use an optimal database management strategy
- Combine SQL Server 2019 with Azure and manage your solution using various automation techniques
- Implement efficient backup and recovery techniques in line with security policies
- Get to grips with migrating, upgrading, and consolidating with SQL Server
- Set up an AlwaysOn-enabled stable and fast SQL Server 2019 environment
- Understand how to work with Big Data on SQL Server environments

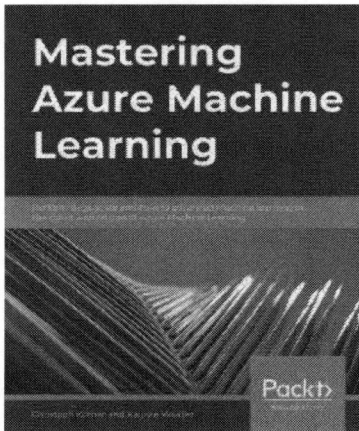

Mastering Azure Machine Learning

Christoph Körner, Kaijisse Waaijer

ISBN: 978-1-78980-755-4

- Gain useful insights into different machine and deep learning models

- Setup your Azure Machine Learning workspace for data experimentation and visualization

- Perform ETL, data preparation, and feature extraction using Azure best practices

- Implement advanced feature extraction using NLP and word embeddings

- Train gradient boosted tree-ensembles, recommendation engines and deep neural networks on Azure Machine Learning

- Use hyperparameter tuning and Azure Automated Machine Learning to optimize your ML models

- Employ distributed ML on GPU clusters using Horovod in Azure Machine Learning

- Deploy, operate, and manage your ML models at scale

- Automated your end-to-end ML process as CI/CD pipelines for MLOps

Leave a review - let other readers know what you think

Please share your thoughts on this book with others by leaving a review on the site that you bought it from. If you purchased the book from Amazon, please leave us an honest review on this book's Amazon page. This is vital so that other potential readers can see and use your unbiased opinion to make purchasing decisions, we can understand what our customers think about our products, and our authors can see your feedback on the title that they have worked with Packt to create. It will only take a few minutes of your time, but is valuable to other potential customers, our authors, and Packt. Thank you!

Index

Printed in Great Britain
by Amazon